CW00540515

The Facts
LUTHER

"Be not led away with various and strange doctrines."

—Hebrews 13:9

Martin Luther
1483-1546
The Founder of Protestantism

The Facts About LUTHER

By

Msgr. Patrick F. O'Hare, LL.D.

Revised Edition

Notes by TAN Books and Publishers, Inc.

"For there shall be a time, when they will not endure sound doctrine; but, according to their own desires, they will heap to themselves teachers, having itching ears: And will indeed turn away their hearing from the truth, but will be turned unto fables."

—2 Timothy 4:3-4

TAN BOOKS AND PUBLISHERS, INC.
Rockford, Illinois 61105

Nihil Obstat: Rev. Remy Lafort, S.T.D.
Censor

Imprimatur: ✠ John Cardinal Farley
Archbishop of New York
New York, July 4, 1916

Originally published by Frederick Pustet Co., Cincinnati, Ohio, 1916. This edition was retypeset from Pustet's revised edition.

Library of Congress Catalog Card No.: 87-50945

ISBN: 0-89555-322-8

Printed and bound in the United States of America.

TAN BOOKS AND PUBLISHERS, INC.
P.O. Box 424
Rockford, Illinois 61105

1987

"But though we, or an angel from heaven, preach a gospel to you besides that which we have preached to you, let him be anathema. As we said before, so now I say again: If any one preach to you a gospel, besides that which you have received, let him be anathema."

—Galatians 1:8-9

"Whosoever revolteth, and continueth not in the doctrine of Christ, hath not God. He that continueth in the doctrine, the same hath both the Father and the Son. If any man come to you, and bring not this doctrine, receive him not into the house, nor say to him, God speed you. For he that saith unto him, God speed you, communicateth with his wicked works."

—2 John 1:9-11

"I know that, after my departure, ravening wolves will enter in among you, not sparing the flock. And of your own selves shall arise men speaking perverse things, to draw away disciples after them."

—Acts 20:28-30

TABLE OF CONTENTS

PREFACE

IT IS an accepted conclusion nowadays among the best students of the Protestant Rebellion of the sixteenth century that there are "two Luthers—the Luther of panegyric, of romance, and fiction, and the Luther of history and fact. The former appears in the pulpit, in the Sunday school, and in partisan biographies; the latter may be discovered from a careful study of his writings and those of his contemporaries, but above all from his private letters, of which former devotees of Luther would only publish what they thought to his credit, garbling or suppressing the rest." These words, quoted from a rare little tract on Luther, written nearly thirty years ago by a prelate of the Church, who was one of the foremost Reformation scholars of that day, may well serve as the keynote of this present work with its powerful contrasts between the Luther of fact and the Luther of fiction. They also sum up the result of all the studies made in the life and works of Martin Luther since the last great international celebration of 1883—the four hundredth anniversary of his birth at Eisleben. There are many who still remember the interest and zeal evidenced by the Protestant churches throughout Christendom when that fourth centenary was given a world-wide recognition. It was a celebration with far-reaching effects—with fatal effects, indeed, for the hero worship so dear to Luther's followers. In Germany, especially, scholars and publishers vied with one another in acclaiming him as the man to whom the modern world owed most, if not all, of its present liberty. He was hailed as the restorer of the truer evangelical life, as the spiritual liberator of the human race; and from that time down to the present, no ordinary reader has been able to keep pace with the output of Lutheran literature.

Probably no man ever lived about whom so much has been written as Luther, but it is from the last notable Luther celebration of 1883 that we can date the foremost works which have appeared on the subject. Today no important source on Luther's life and works remains unpublished. The Weimar Edition of his works, the typical edition, began to appear in 1883. Most of the Protestant authors, from whose works Monsignor O'Hare takes his quotations, have written since that date: Köstlin, Kawerau, Paulsen, Kolde, Hagen, Hausrath, Beard and others, have all written under the impulse of the Luther revival of thirty odd years ago. Throughout the whole period of this activity, the Luther of fiction and the Luther of historic fact have come boldly into conflict, and scholars know with what deplorable results for the heresiarch of Protestantism. But the ordinary man-in-the-street, for whom this volume is particularly designed, is still unaware of these revelations.

Throughout the whole period of this activity, the Luther of fiction has been relegated to the realm of the unhistorical. Scholars can no longer satisfy themselves with the general platitude that the greatest achievement of the race to which he belonged and the most important event in history is the Protestant Rebellion of the sixteenth century. We can no longer hold in the face of what modern scholarship has brought to light since 1883 that Luther's rebellion was essentially the beginning of a new religious movement. The Protestant Rebellion marked no new stage in human progress; it did not close the eyes of a dying medieval Church; it marked no new dawn of the modern era. Protestant scholars of repute no longer hold out to their disciples the old misconceptions that the Rebellion in Germany secured greater purity and spirituality in religion. It did not contribute, as we have been told so often, to the elevation of the laity and to the advancement of woman. It did not fashion a separation of secular from ecclesiastical power. It gave no extraordinary impulse to literature or to science. It did not establish liberty of conscience. In a word, it had nothing in its principles or methods which was to ennoble our modern civilization.

These truths have been self-evident to scholars the past twenty-five years. Like all corporate bodies built on error, the Lutheran Church of the sixteenth century has fared badly under the piercing light of modern research, and Luther himself has become more and more remote from all those characteristics of modern civilization to which his followers lay claim as the legacy of his apostasy. Protestant scholars in America, England and Germany have made plain that Luther's idea of God is repugnant to our natural feelings. Since the publication of Denifle's works, the suite of events in Luther's apostasy has had to be changed; and we see at last that the furthermost point backwards to which his cleavage from the Church can be traced is not opposition to the Papacy, but the false idea, which seems to have haunted him into obsession—his total impotency under temptation. It was this negation of the moral value of human actions, this denial of one's ability to overcome sin, which led to his famous doctrine on the worthlessness of good works. The only hope he had was in a blind reliance on God, whose Son, Jesus Christ, had thrown around him the cloak of His own merits. From this starting point it was *facilis descensus Averni* [an easy descent to Hell].

Opposition to all good works, and in particular to monastic regulations and to indulgences, led to opposition to authority, episcopal and papal. Germany was politically ripe for revolt at that moment, and the union of the Empire and the Papacy made it impossible to distinguish the victims, once the national spirit was aroused. That Luther aided, and aided powerfully, in this opposition to the Holy Roman Empire of both Church and State is undeniable; but what Protestant scholars have denied in no uncertain terms is the long litany of triumphs accredited to the Luther of fiction. His greatest work—the translation of the Bible into German—is openly called a plagiarism. The claim that he is the father of popular education is ridiculed by leading Protestant historians. His economic views are considered retrogressive, even for his own time. The assertion that he is the founder of the modern State is denied categorically by his latest non-Catholic biographer, who tells us that he preferred despotism to democracy and that he never doubted the right and duty of the State to persecute for heresy. The Luther of fiction is being more and more obscured by the Luther of fact. But it takes time for the conclusions of scholars to reach the multitude, and with very little limitation the old shibboleths of the middle nineteenth century are being repeated today in Lutheran pulpits, Sunday schools, and partisan biographies.

We have reached another century mark in the history of the Protestant church. Four hundred years ago, on All Saints' Eve—the Hallow E'en of our days—the young Professor of Sacred Scripture in the University of Wittenberg attached ninety-five propositions, or theses, to the university bulletinboard on the portals of the old Castle Church of the town. Historians and theologians, both Catholics and Protestants, have viewed that act in many ways. To some it was a defiance hurled at the immoral conditions of Europe, a gage thrown down at last, after several centuries of spiritual confict, for Rome to pick up or to be branded as a cowardly antagonist of German aspirations, of German love and devotion for pure doctrine, for pure moral living. To others, it was only an incident—an incident, it is true, which was to set Europe ablaze within five years—but still an incident, which might have been seen and soon forgotten, had not the temporal condition of Europe been ready for the outbreak which followed it. Both sides admit that the Christian faith had then fallen upon evil days, but both sides have since torn away every vestige of hero worship from the militant figure of the man who centered Europe, political and religious, around himself at the Diet of Worms, three years afterwards. Both sides have yielded much for and against him in the discussions, the polemics, the attacks, the accusations which have swirled around him since. The Protestant religious world, although deprived of valuable auxiliaries in the *Sturm and Drang* [storm and fury], of the conflict which is now throwing the world into confusion, will not allow this fourth centenary of Luther's Theses to pass without an attempt to rehabilitate their great hero, despite the results of modern scholarship.

It is hardly an exaggeration to say that were it not for such a work as this, the general reading public—both Catholic and Protestant—might have suffered this rehabilitation without protest; but Monsignor O'Hare has thrown a bridge over the chasm which now separates the Luther of 1917 from the Luther of 1883, and the contrast is so prominent that his conclusions cannot be ignored. The reader is brought in these pages into a close, intimate relation with Luther's friends and opponents, and every statement is based on the most reliable authorities in the Protestant school of historical science. The whole gamut of the apostate's life is here described in a calm, impartial manner which permits no gainsaying. There are many hideous scenes in Martin Luther's life; there are scenes of coarseness, vulgarity, obscenity and degrading immorality which can never be forgiven because of a "rugged peasant nature." The man stands revealed as the opposite of all that Protestantism has claimed for him. But the reader may take up this work with the assurance that here there is no unfair attack upon the Founder of Protestantism. It is not with a spirit of bitterness or bigotry that Monsignor O'Hare describes the real Luther. So long as the Luther of fiction exists in popular Protestant literature, there can be no common friendly ground for the proper appraisal of the Rebellion of 1517. And no man, whether he be a Protestant or a Catholic, who has the love of Christ in his heart, can look on with indifference when there is question of an irenic state of mind on religious problems, or when there is a possibility of a union between the two leading religions of the Western world. There is no doubt that the religious problem today is still the Luther Problem, and since almost every statement of those religious doctrines which are opposed to Catholic moral teaching find their authorization in the theology of Martin Luther, every Catholic should acquaint himself with the life story of the man whose followers can never explain away the anarchy of that immoral dogma: "Be a sinner, and sin boldly; but believe more boldly still!"

Rev. Peter Guilday, Ph.D.

Catholic University of America
Washington, D.C.
September 5th, 1916

The Facts About
LUTHER

". . . there shall be among you lying teachers, who shall bring in sects of perdition, and deny the Lord who bought them: bringing upon themselves swift destruction. And many shall follow their riotousness, through whom the way of truth shall be evil spoken of."

—2 Peter 2:1-2

CHAPTER 1

LUTHER: HIS FRIENDS AND OPPONENTS

THIS modest volume is issued to present to the public at large some of the most prominent and important features in the life and career of Martin Luther, the founder of Protestantism. We wish to declare in the beginning that this little work makes no pretension to either originality or scholarship; neither does it claim to set forth in its pages anything that is not already well-known and fully authenticated in the life of Luther and the development of the new system of religion he gave to the world. Abler and more competent writers have long since covered the whole ground. Learned and distinguished historians like Janssen, Denifle, Grisar, and many others, have painted with masterly accuracy the real picture of the reformer from material supplied for the most part by his own acknowledged writings. These celebrated authors have practically pronounced the last word on the protagonist and champion of Protestantism, and there seems to be slight justification for the publication of a new work on the old subject.

Whilst we recognize all this to be true, we feel that we may be pardoned for attempting to tell anew, but in greater brevity and directness, the salient and more striking features connected with the apostate monk of Wittenberg and his religious movement, because there is a large number in the community who in the hurry and high pressure of modern life have not the time to examine the ponderous and exhaustive volumes of the authors alluded to above and who moreover have not the means to secure these works, much as they might desire to do so, on account of prohibitive prices. Taking all this into consideration, we believe we will be excused for intruding on a field that has already been well covered and for presenting to the general public a plain but well-authenticated sketch of the man who in the sixteenth century inaugurated a movement which bears the name of "Reformation" and caused a large and fearful defection from the Church of which he was a member and to which the bulk of mankind adhered all through the centuries from its establishment by Jesus Christ. In treating of this historical character whose startling influence was exercised on his own country and on the world at large, we have no intention to wound the convictions and sensibilities of any in the community who may disagree with us. Our aim is to tell the truth about the standard-bearer of the Reformation, and of this no one should be afraid, for truth and virtue triumph by their own inherent beauty and power. The poet aptly sings:

> Truth hath such a face and such a mien,
> As to be loved needs only to be seen.

In dealing with Luther it is well to remember that students of history have given him such attention as has been accorded to few men of any age, and about fewer still have they expressed such widely divergent views. His friends insist that he was a model of virtue and possessed eminent qualities which in every way made him worthy of his position as a religious reformer, while his opponents openly denounce him and insist that in his own day he was known as a "trickster and a cheat," one whose titanic pride, unrestrained temper and lack of personal dignity utterly unfitted him to reform the Church and the age.

To his followers the name and memory of Luther are objects of religious veneration. They have for the last four centuries surrounded him with such an aura of flattery and pedantry that he is looked upon as one of the glories of Germany, nay, the foremost figure in their Hall of Immortals. By dint of minatory iteration, his admirers have been brought to believe that "he is the precious gift of God to the nation." Lutheran writers from Mathesius to Köstlin have invariably filled the German mind with all that reverent love could conjure up for their hero's justification and exaltation. To call into question the powers of the Reformer or deny the divine mission of the Reformation was ever considered blasphemous and unpatriotic.

The opponents of Luther, on the contrary, stoutly maintain that his greatness was taken on trust and that the writers alluded to in the preceding paragraph have invariably, with a fatuous blindness mistaken for patriotism, fed and nourished the German mind, not on the real Luther, but on a Luther glossed over and toned down with respectful admiration and conjured under the influence of partisan-colored traditions intended to prevent him from being catalogued in his proper page in the world's history. Reverential tenderness keyed to its highest pitch cannot, however, they claim, efface the clearly etched lineaments of the man of flesh and blood, the man of moods and impulses, of angularities and idiosyncrasies which dominated his career and singled him out as a destructive genius unfitted to carry out any kind of reformation, either in Church or State.

In discussing Luther and his religious movement, we feel at liberty to say that many, both in the ranks of his friends and of his opponents, have perhaps at times indulged in too great a display of feeling and exaggeration. It would help considerably to cool down the bitterness aroused among all parties, did they honestly endeavor to discover for themselves the findings and conclusions of non-partisan writers on the delicate but interesting question. Wiser council and juster appreciation would inevitably reward the searchers after truth, the whole truth and nothing but the truth. Of these unbiased writers, many of whom are Protestants, there is no scarcity. They have been delving into the pages of history to find out the real Luther, and they have not been afraid to tell in the interest of truth what sort of a man he actually was. These scholarly and reliable authors assert that Luther unquestionably possessed certain elements of greatness. They admit that he was a tireless worker, a forceful writer, a powerful preacher and an incomparable master of the German language. They credit him with a keen knowledge of human nature and of the trend of the world of his day. They allege, moreover, that he was capable of taking advantage of everything that favored his schemes of yoking to his own chariot all the forces that were then at work to injure and oppose the ancient and time-honored religion of Catholics. But whatever else of praise these writers bestow on the man, it is equally clear and beyond question that they are all agreed in declaring that Luther possessed a violent, despotic and uncontrolled nature. Many of these writers, although Protestants and not friendly to the Catholic Church, have not been afraid to tell their co-religionists that the rights Luther assumed to himself in the matter of liberty of conscience, he unhesitatingly and imperiously denied to all who differed from him, as many specific cases overwhelmingly confirm. His will and his alone, they declare, he dogmatically set up as the only standard he wished to be recognized, followed and obeyed. In their historical investigations they discovered many other shortcomings in the character of the man, unbecoming in one who claimed to be a reformer, and in their love of truth and real scholarship, they have honestly acknowledged that there was something titanic, unnatural and diabolical in the founder of Protestantism.

One of these fearless writers was the Protestant Professor Seeberg of Berlin. He was no friend of the Catholic Church, but his deep study of the man and his movement forced him to say: "Luther strode through his century like a demon crushing under his feet what a thousand years had venerated." The same author further remarks: "In him dwelt 'The Superhuman' or, in Nietzsche's philosophy, the 'Übermensch,' who dwells 'beyond moral good and evil.'"

In November 1883 the English Protestant Bishop

Bewick applied to Luther the epithets "foul-mouthed" and "scurrilous."

In the *Century* issued in December, 1900, Augustine Birrell, a distinguished English Protestant writer, declared that "Luther was not an ideal sponsor of a new religion; he was a master of billingsgate and the least saintly of men. At times, in reading Luther, one is drawn to say to him what Herrick so frankly says of himself: 'Luther, thou art too coarse to love.'

"Had Luther been a brave soldier of fortune, his coarseness might have passed for a sign of the times; but one likes leaders of religion to be religious; and it is hard to reconcile coarseness and self-will, two leading notes of Luther's character, with even rudimentary religion. To want to be your own pope is a sign of the heresiarch, not of the Christian."

To the testimony of Professor Seeberg and Mr. Birrell we desire to add another illustration of the change which has come over the minds of men regarding the German reformer. Licentiate Braun, in a contribution written for the *Evangelische Kirchenzeitung* (March 30, 1913, p. 195), tells in all honesty and straightforwardness how, with strips from the skin of his own co-religionists, Protestant theologians have pieced together not a fictitious, but a genuinely reliable account of the life of Luther. This able Protestant theologian writes as follows:

"How small the Reformer has become according to the Luther studies of our own Protestant investigators! How his merits have shrivelled up! We believed that we owed to him the spirit of toleration and liberty of conscience. Not in the least! We recognized in his translation of the Bible a masterpiece stamped with the impress of originality—we may be happy now if it is not plainly called a 'plagiarism'! We venerated in him the father of the popular school system—a purely 'fictitious greatness' which we have no right to claim for him! We imagined that we found in Luther's words splendid suggestions for a rational treatment of poverty and that a return to him would bring us back to the true principles of charity—but the laurels do not belong to him, they must be conceded to the Catholic Church! We were delighted to be assured that this great man possessed an insight into national economics marvelous for his day—but 'unbiased' investigation forces the confession that there were many indications of retrogressive tendencies in his economic views!"

"Did we not conceive of Luther as the founder of the modern State? Yet in all that he said upon this subject there was nothing of any value which was at all new; as for the rest, by making the king an 'absolute patriarch' he did not in the least improve upon the coercive measures employed by the theocracy of the Middle Ages."

"Just think of it, then, all these conclusions come to us from the pen of Protestant theologians! Reliable historians give book and page for them. What is still more amazing, all these Protestant historians continue to speak to Luther in tones of admiration, in spite of the admissions which a 'love of truth' compels them to make. Looking upon the 'results' of their work thus gathered together, we cannot help asking the question: What, then, remains of Luther?"

The question, remember, is put not by a Catholic, but by an eminent Protestant theologian. It is an important question and deserves serious consideration. Who will answer it? The bigot and the preacher of "The Gospel of Hate" resent the question and, like all enemies of truth, they refuse to give it consideration. They hate the light and close their eyes to its illumination. Many of them hate truth as a business. Their books and their lectures bring them reputation or money. Like Judas they ask, "What will you give me?" For a price the low, the vile, the false feed the fires that burn in the hearts of certain fanatics. Unlike these are the Seebergs, the Birrells and the Brauns. They are not afraid of the truth. They sought it with unbiased minds, and once they discovered it they boldly communicated their findings to the world. Ask them the question who and what Luther really was, and their answer is straightforward, direct and unhesitating. They tell that nothing remains but an unpleasant memory of the man who divided the Church of God and who, destitute of constructive genius, depraved in manners and in speech, falsely posed as a reformer sent by God. The investigations they made in the field of reliable history convinced them that the father of Protestantism appeared to fill the world with light, but it was only the light of a passing meteor consuming and destroying itself in its fall. To the enemies of truth these scholarly researches are most embarrassing and disappointing. As a distinguished writer puts it, "They pluck jewel after jewel from Luther's crown and make the praises chanted to him by the ranters of all times sound hollow in honest ears attuned to truth."

All impartial history proclaims that Luther had very few, if any, of the qualifications that men naturally expect to find in one who poses as a religious reformer. The "Man of God," "the supernatural spirit," in which role he is represented by partisan writers, Luther was only in romance and myth. He attempted reformation and ended in deformation. Unfitted for the work he had outlined for himself, his ungovernable transports, riotous proceedings, angry conflicts and intemperate controversies frustrated his designs at every turn. His teaching, like his behavior, was full of inconsistencies, and his contempt of all the accepted forms of human right and of all authority, human and divine, could not but result in lamentable disaster. His wild pronouncements wrecked Germany, wrecked her intellectually, morally and politically. The havoc wrought directly or indirectly by him is almost without example in history. The outcome in the century following was that the nation became a mere geographical term and was thrown back two hundred years in development, in culture and in progress.

History presents no apology for the unbridled jealousy,

fierce antagonism and unremitting opposition that marked the career of this man toward the Church of his forefathers. He was a revolutionist, not a reformer. The true reformer restores society to its primitive purity; the revolutionist violently upsets the constitution of society, putting something else in its place. While pretending to reform, he wrote and preached not for but against good works, and the novel teaching was eagerly accepted by the unthinking and bore those awful fruits of which the historians of the sixteenth and seventeenth centuries have painted the sorrowful picture. He rent asunder the unity of the Church till, alongside of the one true Church, there have arisen hundreds of warring sects; nay, there are those who extol him as the founder of a religion, forgetting that this is his greatest shame—for if he founded a religion, it is not the *Christian* religion established by Christ fifteen hundred years before. No wonder he went down in ignominious defeat and that the Church he unnecessarily attacked and relentlessly endeavored to destroy remained as the central figure of all Christendom to proclaim alike to the humblest peasant and the greatest savant its divine mission and heavenly authority to teach men the ways of eternal life.

All this may sound very strange and may shock a great many non-Catholics; but they must kindly remember that they were taught that the subject under consideration had but one side, and that inherited prejudices prevented them from examining the facts and finding the truth they really love. The light they needed was kept from them and they were innocently led to believe that Luther was justified in his defection from the Church he once loved and defended, but which he afterwards disgraced by a notoriously wicked and scandalous life. They heard him praised for what ignorant men called his "robust Christianity," which was akin to Judas's betrayal of the Master, and they believed this when they lauded him as an "apostle of liberty" in spite of the fact, as history shows, that he was one of the most intolerant of men. They have heard the anti-Catholic of every shade of character rake up the muck of history, vilify the clergy, hold up nuns as the wickedest of women, exploit the Pope as "Antichrist" and the "Man of Sin"; resort, in a word, to every known means of ridicule and misrepresentation to depict the spotless Spouse of Christ as the "great harlot of the Apocalypse," "the mother of fornications and the abominations of the earth." They have heard the wild, monstrous and even impossible statements of the lying and slanderous in the community, whose only aim is to advance the nefarious and diabolical work of inflaming the passions of the rabble and to keep alive the blind, prejudiced and irrational discrimination against everything Catholic. The pity of it all is that, in this day of enlightenment, many who would be ashamed to listen to professional charlatans in any other avocation of life will think that they are doing a "service to God" by giving a willing ear and swallowing down without a qualm the silly, senseless and unwarranted reproaches which unscrupulous haranguers, paid hirelings, and vile calumniators unblushingly and without the vestige of proof urge against the religion which Christ established for all time till the consummation of the world, and which history tells has civilized the peoples and the nations.

But, whilst this is all true, we feel that the most generous allowance must be made for the Church's enemies and their deluded followers. The fact is they cannot help their antagonism and distrust, for they have been brought up from infancy to loathe the Catholic Church, whose history they were made to believe by their false teachers was distinguished for nothing save bloodshed, crime and fraud. Their anti-Catholic views and prejudices and hostilities had their origin in the so-called Reformation period, and since that time all Protestant "mankind descending by ordinary generation" have come into the world with a mentality biased, perverted and prejudiced. They and their fathers have been steeped and nurtured in opposition, and in most cases without meaning to be unjust they feel instinctively a strong and profound antipathy to everything that savors of Catholicity. Ministers and lecturers and tracts, every channel of propagating error, bigotry and misrepresentation are used to preserve, circulate and keep alive popular hatred and distrust of the one true Church of Christ which, all who have any sense should know, is indestructible. How men in the possession of their wits can engage in the useless and vain task of attempting to displace and destroy a God-founded religion, established for all time and for all peoples, surpasses all understanding. The fact nevertheless remains that many, unfortunately for themselves, are obsessed with an insane hatred of Catholicism and in the exuberance of an enthusiasm akin to that of a Celsus, a Porphyry, and a Julian, they treat the public to a campaign of abuse and vilification of the Church which is a disgrace to themselves and a violation of all Christian teaching. All these and many other influences at work in the world to destroy true Christianity tend to bind the opponents of the Church with iron bonds to their present inherited convictions, and hence they hate the Church because they do not know her in all her beauty and truthfulness. How could it be otherwise with them? Would we ourselves have been any better under the same conditions?

Catholics expect the Church, which Christ established and organized for all time, to be misunderstood, maligned, ill-treated, pursued, persecuted and hated by the world. Her founder put the mark of the Cross on her when He said: "If they have persecuted me, they will also persecute you." (*Jn.* 15:20). In every age the Catholic Church, which is the only one of the vast number of pretending claimants to divine origin of which Christ's prediction is true, has had to suffer persecution from the enemies of order and truth, who, if they could, would wipe her from the face of the earth. This, however, they have not been able to accomplish—nor will they be able at any future time, for God ordained the Church to remain forever in her integrity, clothed with all the attributes He gave her in the beginning.

Divinity stamped indestructibility upon the brow of the Church, and though destined to be assailed always she will never be overcome by her enemies. Catholics know that Christ watches over the survival of the Church, and hence, in this day when the vast army of the ignorant and the rebellious rise up to check her development and stop her progress, they fear not, happen what will, for they are confident that as the sun will rise tomorrow and the next day and so on to the end of the world, so will the Master ever fulfill His promise concerning the Church, preserving her amid storm and sunshine till time is no more. When will the enemy realize that it is too late in the day to overthrow the Church which has stood the test of centuries and which has been accepted, loved and admired by the best minds of all the ages?

Catholics naturally feel indignant at the vilification, abuse and misrepresentation to which their ancient and worldwide religion is constantly subjected, but they are charitable and lenient in their judgment towards all who wage war against them. They are considerate with their opponents and persecutors because they realize that these are victims of a long-standing and inherited prejudice, intensified by a lack of knowledge of what the Catholic Church really upholds and teaches. Even as the Church's Founder prayed the Heavenly Father to forgive those who nailed Him to the Cross because they knew not what they did, so do His followers, with malice to none but with charity to all, pray for those who oppose the spread of the Kingdom of God on earth because they do not realize to the full that, in despising the Church, they despise Him who founded her to be the light of the world. Most of the Church's enemies are to be greatly pitied, for they have never been taught the significant lesson that the man-made system of religion they hold or adhere to is false, an offense and an apostasy in the eyes of God, who despises heresy and who warned His followers to be on guard against every teacher not commissioned by Him to announce divine truth. Of all this they are unaware. They know nothing of the Church they malign, abuse and vilify. They are ignorant of her history, of her organization, of her constitution, of her teaching, of her mission and her place in the world. They know her not, and many of them, otherwise honest but nurtured in opposition, are led to hate what with divine light they would come to admire, love and embrace.

The general ignorance that prevails in regard to the Catholic Church is most regrettable. This ignorance, however, is only surpassed by the lack of knowledge manifested by the maligners of the Catholic Church regarding their own peculiar system of belief. They are ever ready to criticize the Catholic Church, of which they know little or nothing, and yet when they are asked to give an intelligent account of their own system of belief they are unable to reply in such a way as to appeal to the honest searcher after truth. Ask some of the preachers of the "Gospel of Hate" to describe their own religion, presuming, of course, that they have a religion. Ask them to give you the real story of the origin of the word and the meaning of the system embodied in the term "Protestantism." Ask them to tell you what was there in the teaching of Luther that demanded his expulsion from the Catholic Church. Ask them to tell you of the pride of intellect which caused Luther to refuse to hear and submit to the Church of Jesus Christ. Ask them by what authority did an excommunicated man like Luther establish a system of religion in opposition to the one organized by Christ and with which He said He would "remain all days even to the consummation of the world." Ask them to tell you the difference between Christ's teaching and that of Luther. Ask them to tell you what was Luther's conception of religion, why did he decry the necesssity of good works and declare it to be the right of every man to interpret the Scriptures according to his own individual conception. Ask them to tell you why did Luther one day proclaim the binding force of the

Commandments and the next declare they were not obligatory on Christian observance. Ask them to tell you by what authority did Luther approve of adultery, favor concubinage and sanction the bigamy of Philip of Hesse. Ask them to tell you why Luther advocated freedom of conscience and at the same time compelled all to submit to his will and dictation. Ask them is the Protestantism of today the same as Luther fathered and what are the changes from the original teachings it has undergone during the last four hundred years. Ask them to tell you of the varied existence and constantly shifting position of Protestantism. Ask them to give you the names of its many contending bodies which have been tossed about by every wind of religious speculation and are still subject to everlasting drifting. Ask them to point out to you the difference noticeable between the old and the new Protestantism. Ask them could they certify that the original opinions of the sect are held in respect in modern times. Ask them would they affirm that the father of Protestantism, were he in their midst today, would he set the seal of his approbation on the myriad variations and evolutions which have affected his own false and individualistic doctrinal expositions. Ask them how does all this fit in with the teaching of St. Paul, the greatest of the Church's converts, who, putting the query, Is Christ divided? replied in the ever memorable words: "One faith, one Baptism, one Lord, and one Master of all."

These questions are pertinent, and in all fairness they should be answered by those who make it a business to wage war on the Mother Church. If the enemies of the Church are honest, God-fearing men they will not shirk their bounden duty in a matter so grave and important. Until they have settled the disorders and contentions everywhere existing in their own Protestant households, we think they should in charity cease their attacks on the Church which, as the ages have testified, cannot be displaced or destroyed. In the meantime, let them honestly probe the issue to its depths and in prayer and study seek the truth that frees, vivifies and saves. Earnest and sincere investigation will make it surprisingly evident that only the shell of Protestantism remains. All honest inquiry will show that its origin is of the earth, and decline it must. The name it bears designates it as a human institution, and history proves that it is nothing more. From its thousands of deluded followers in the sixteenth, seventeenth and eighteenth centuries, we see today but a handful left to testify to its failure. The newspapers told us recently that the exodus of Prussians from the ranks of the State Church is wholesale and that a similar defection is daily going on in England and in this country. Protestantism, as a system of religion, is undeniably dying out. It has unfortunately prepared the way for the monster agnosticism or Rationalism which confronts us today in all its horrible shapes and forms.

But to return to Luther. What about him? What do the vast bulk of non-Catholics know about the man who reviled and hated and cursed the Church of his fathers more than any other mortal ever has done? Must not the great majority of our separated brethren admit they know absolutely nothing at firsthand about the man? Beyond his name and his defection from the Mother Church they are in ignorance of his false doctrinal views and depraved manner of life. This side of his work and character is carefully concealed from their vision; and with a childlike innocence that disarms wrath, they believe their leaders and guides in religion, who know the man no better than themselves, when in pulpit and on platform they hold him up to view wreathed in a halo of glory and sanctity and proclaim him a "Reformer of Christ's Church," "an apostle of liberty," "an enlightener of the people," "a destroyer of the Papacy," etc., etc. Most Protestants do not study the career and work of their hero for themselves nor determine to find out the truth from the proper sources, and as might be expected, it is easy for them to believe their false guides when they heap unmerited titles on the man who more than any before or since his day was what St. Paul designates a "lawless one" and a contemner of constituted authority. Did they read reliable historians and learn something of his perverse principles, false teaching, unscrupulous mendacity, coarse and indecent language, they would not for long hold his memory in honor and continue their connection with the false system of religion which he founded without either warrant or authority.

It is no difficult matter, as all educated Protestants know, to show that the reformation Luther contemplated was a very strange one, for according to the open avowal of its author it led to the utter demoralization of its followers. Almost from the beginning of his movement he was disgusted on account of the little change for the better his preachments wrought in the lives of his adherents, and with each succeeding year he expressed his disappointment in the bitterest terms. "Unfortunately," he says, "it is our daily experience that now under the Gospel [his] the people entertain greater and bitterer hatred and envy and are worse with their avarice and money-grabbing than before under the Papacy." (Walch XIII, 2195). "The people feel they are free from the bonds and fetters of the Pope, but now they want to get rid also of the Gospel and of all the laws of God." (Walch XIV, 195). "Everybody thinks that Christian liberty and licentiousness of the flesh are one and the same thing, as if now everybody was allowed to do what he wants." (*Tischr.* 1, 180). "Townsfolk and peasants, men and women, children and servants, princes, magistrates and subjects, are all going to the devil." (Erl. 14, 389). "If we succeed in expelling one devil, he immediately is replaced by seven others who are much worse. We can then expect that after having driven away the monks, we shall see arise a race seven times worse than the former." (Erl. XXXVI, 411). "Avarice, usury, debauchery, drunkenness, blasphemy, lying and cheating are far more prevalent now than they were under the Papacy. This state of morals brings general discredit on the Gospel and its preachers, as the people say, if this Gospel were true, the persons professing it would be more pious." (Erl. I, 192).

We could fill a large volume with Luther's words describing the frightful corruption that followed upon the announcement of his new gospel, but we have given enough for the present to show that the so-called reformer was not unaware of the practical effect on the masses in his own day of his wild pronouncements. From his own lips, then, we learn of the utter failure of his so-called reformation movement. What else might he expect? Did he not sow the wind? Why should he not reap the whirlwind? Wherein, then, lies a reason to honor this destructive genius, and why should men of sense continue to entrust the interests of their immortal souls to his self-assumed leadership?

It is, moreover, no difficult matter, as all well-informed Protestants know, to demonstrate that Luther, German as he was to the core, in speaking of his native land used the vilest and most brutal language. Many know in a general way that Luther was in the habit of using rather hard words, to put it mildly, but few know how far he was capable of going. He was reckless to the border of irresponsible rashness, blunt to the exclusion of every qualm of delicacy, audacious to the scorn of every magnanimous restraint, coarse beyond the power of reproducible Anglo-Saxon and lubricous to a degree that pales Rabelaisian foulness. His unbridled tongue did not spare even his own country and his own people. In speech and in writing he unblushingly described the Teutonic race as "brutes and pigs," and he called the nation "a bestial race," "a sow," "a debauched people," "given over to all kinds of vice." Here are some of his sayings: "We profligate Germans are abominable hogs." "You pigs, hounds, ranters, you irrational asses!" "Our German nation are a wild, savage nation, half devils, half men." (Walch XX, 1014, 1015, 1633). In many pages of his writings he complains that "the German people are seven times worse since they embraced the Reformation."

When one ponders over the description Luther gives of his native land and its people, it is difficult to believe that there existed in his soul the faintest spark of patriotism or love of country. Compare his language with that of St. Paul, who was a real reformer, and note the difference. This great convert and distinguished Apostle, speaking of those he won to Christ, calls them his "dearly beloved brethren" and then proclaims them "my joy and my crown." (*Phil.* 4:1). On another occasion, referring to the fruits of his apostolic labors, he says to the Catholics of Thessalonica: "You became followers of us and of the Lord... so that you were made a pattern to all that believe in Macedonia and in Achaja." (*1 Thess.* 1:6-7). Which of these, think you, was the true patriot and the true reformer?

When our non-Catholic brethren thoroughly consider the vile, intemperate and disgusting language which was habitual with Luther and weigh well the opprobrious names he hurled at the race of his forefathers, how in all honesty can they give a willing ear to the praise of one so coarse and brutal and continue their association with a sect which its own founder, consumed with pride and hate and despair, pronounced a lamentable failure?

There are many strict non-Catholics today, who are, as a rule, honest and moral people. God forbid that we should offend or cause the slightest pain to them, but in the interest of truth we beg leave to remind them that it is high time for them to know that they have lived too long on legends as regards Luther and do not realize what sort of man he was. Luther when living spared not Catholicity or the Papacy. Today many of his adherents are close imitators of his violence and opposition. We must be pardoned for mildly but fearlessly resenting the vilification and misrepresentation to which the Mother Church has for four hundred years been unnecessarily subjected. Luther was the cause of it all, and ignorance among the rank and file of his sympathizers has played a most important part in perpetuating opposition to the one true Church of Christ.

To promote charity and bring about a better understanding among all, it behooves every serious man to know this charlatan for what he was and to learn that he has absolutely no claim to any consideration as a Heaven-commissioned agent, as even an ordinary "reformer" or "spiritual leader," or as in any respect a man above and ahead of the frailties of his age. Non-Catholics should in all fairness read carefully for themselves the teachings of Luther, when their eyes will be opened to the true state of things and they will cease their opposition to the Church against which as yet the gates of Hell have not been able to prevail. When the minds of men are opened to the truth, we assure them that if there be any indignation to be vented, it will not be spent on the Catholic Church, but upon the man who contemned the authoritative guidance of the religion of their forefathers.

To help to clear the way for a better understanding of differences we intend in this little work fairly and honestly to disclose some of the more important facts in the religious schism which, begun by Luther, has proved the most baneful event yet known in man's history. We will then write about Luther, not against him. We will quote his own words. If the result is not favorable to him, the fault will not be ours. We wish to assure our readers that we will not allude to half the disparaging things of the so-called Reformation and the German people that were uttered and written by the apostate Saxon monk himself. We hope none of our readers will shut their eyes to the truth and that we may be of service to the sincere and earnest to help them to discover before it is too late the Church wherein their forefathers found rest, peace and salvation. That Church is in our midst today and may easily be discovered. She stands as of old on the certainty of divine veracity and can no more be shaken than the Throne of God itself. Men like Luther, Zwingli, Calvin and others appeared upon the field of battle to wage war against this Church, but where are they now; where are their congregations; where are their sanctuaries? Who believes their doctrines? Like the fragments of a thousand barks richly laden with intellect and learning, all man-made religions are now scattered on the shores of error and delusion, while the Church of Truth still rides the waves in hope, in strength and in security. God is with her and she cannot perish. Her enemies then might reflect with profit on what St. John says in his second general Epistle: "Whosoever revolteth and hath not the doctrine of Christ, hath not God."

The Catholic Church alone has that doctrine which unites men with God. She was organized for the express purpose of teaching and preserving all things whatsoever Christ, her Founder, had commanded for the instruction and salvation of mankind to the end of the world. She is not man's work. She is Christ's work. She is His spouse, His Mystical Body, as St. Paul tells us. It is through her that He continues to communicate His doctrine to men, that He causes them to live a life of grace and leads them to their eternal happiness. He founded her that through her He may apply to mankind the fruits of His Redemption to the end of time. Hence it follows that no one who through his own fault dies out of the Church will obtain salvation. "No one," says St. Augustine, "can be saved who has not Christ for his head, and no one can have Christ for his head who does not belong to His body, the Church." These words were spoken long before Luther and his companions in revolt appeared on the scene, and they are as true today as when they were first uttered. The command of Christ to hear the Church, which is the chief work of His power, His wisdom and His love for mankind, is imperative and cannot be ignored without suffering exclusion from the inheritance of the children of God. The voice of the Good Shepherd and not that of the hireling must be heard if salvation is to be secured. Those who refuse to receive the true Christian doctrine and to enter the Church, which preaches that doctrine in its entirety, should ponder well the words of St. Paul when he says, "And though we, or an angel from heaven, preach a Gospel to you, besides that which we have preached to you, let him be anathema. If anyone preach to you a Gospel besides that which you have received, let him be anathema." (*Gal.* 1: 8-9). And again in his Epistle to Titus he says: "A man that is a heretic, after the first and second admonition, avoid. Knowing that he, that is such a one, is subverted, and sinneth, being condemned by his own judgment." (*Titus* 3:10-11).

Few men nowadays hate the Church as fiercely and intensely as St. Paul did before the grace of God touched his heart and led him into her bosom. That same grace is ever ready to be imparted to the humble, sincere, earnest inquirer after divine truth. No pretext, however specious, should deter men from acquiring a full and connected knowledge of God's revelation and enjoying that profound peace which springs from the conscious possession of the whole, complete and fixed truth as it is in Christ Jesus and in His Church. The distorted, ever-varying and changeable man-made religions of Luther, Calvin, Henry VIII, Knox, Fox, Wesley, Smith, Dowie, Eddy and innumerable others can never take the place of the Catholic Church established by God Incarnate in Christ. In it alone is infallible truth, true life and certain salvation. In asking men who are "tossed to and fro by every wind of doctrine" (*Ephes.* 4:14) to exchange their opinions for certitude, their dissensions for unity and their errors for truth, the Church is only fulfilling her divine mission and endeavoring to realize the prayer of her Founder that there may be but one Faith, one Baptism and one shepherd of souls. Fail not, then, we beseech you, to listen to her voice, investigate her teachings and accept her authority here and now, so that you may enjoy "the peace that passeth all understanding" and partake of the Bread of Life.

It is certainly high time to discern the tactics of the wolves in sheep's clothing and have sense and intellect enough to see the sham and the fraud of men-made brands of religion with their multitudinous divisions, their contradictions and their lies. The slime-vending, mud-slinging, vile detractors may try to hide the sham and the fraud of their unstable beliefs by well-planned and shameless schemes of attack on the Spouse of Christ, but the intelligent in the community, exercising sound judgment and viewing the contradictions and divisions of the enemy from the standpoint of truth, which they realize can never contradict itself, consider their efforts as a huge joke in presence of the divinely established, Heaven-united Church of all ages and of all people. Bigots come and go; they make a great splurge and bluster temporarily with their campaigns of calumny and vilification, but the Catholic Church, because she is the one established by Jesus Christ, continues on in her heavenly mission in spite of the puny weaklings who endeavor to stop her progress. The Mother Church counts not her numbers by men, but by time alone. She has seen centuries and will see more, not changing one jot in the future, but still standing and teaching as she does today. She will live to bury all her misguided enemies. She is of God and cannot be downed or displaced by men, no matter what may be their numbers, their influence or their power. "Against her, " Christ declared, "the gates of Hell shall never prevail."

CHAPTER 2

Luther Before His Defection

THE subject of these papers was born at Eisleben, in Germany, on the night of the 10th of November, 1483, about forty-five years after Gutenberg invented the printing press and nine years before Columbus discovered America. At one end of a narrow street in this little town noted for its high-roofed, red-tiled houses, or as Barbour described it, "at a meeting of three streets, with a little garden beside it, as became the place they say it was—an inn—stands the house where Luther was born. Over the door there is a head of him in stone with a commemorative inscription carved round it. You enter the first room to the left and stand where he was born. It is a largish room, day and night room it was, one would think, in the inn time." The old house was partly destroyed by fire and rebuilt in the seventeeth century. Here in Eisleben Luther first saw the light of day and here he came to close his earthly career, his demise occurring February 18, 1546. Visitors to the little town are shown both house of birth and house of death.

On the day following the birth of the little stranger, he was brought to St. Peter's Church, where he was baptized and given the name of Martin in honor of the saint whose feast it was. The font at which the waters of Baptism were poured on his head to make him a Christian is still preserved and may be inspected by the visitor. His father was named John Lüder, which was later on changed to Luther, and his mother Margaret Ziegler. The father came of peasant stock, and the mother was of the burgher class from the neighboring town of Eisenach, and as such held a higher rank in the community than her husband. Some writers have endeavored to give the parents a noble origin, but the claim cannot be sustained. Luther said to Melanchthon in after years: "I am a peasant's son. My father, my grandfather, all my ancestors were genuine peasants. My father was a poor miner." At times, when he referred to his humble origin, he declared with much force that "there is as little sense in boasting of one's ancestry as in the devil priding himself on his angelic lineage." Both parents were, according to the Swiss Kessler, "spare, short and dark complexioned." The father was a rugged, stern, irascible character and the mother, according to Melanchthon, was conspicuous for "modesty, the fear of God and prayerfulness." They were a sturdy couple, ambitious for their own and their children's advancement, and lived to a ripe old age.

The original home of the Luther family was in Mörha, a little township situated on the northwest corner of the Thuringian Forest and a few miles to the south of Eisenach. In this district a large number of the inhabitants bore the name of Luther. As late as 1901, six families still belonged to the Luthers. Mörha is up to the present a tiny hamlet with about six hundred inhabitants. It has not changed much in the process of time. In the olden days it was so unimportant as not to merit mention on the map. Then it consisted of a small collection of seventy or eighty detached dwellings of a primitive character and mostly of adjoining farmyards. With the exception of a solitary carpenter and shoemaker, both of whom seldom had occasion to ply their trades, the few hundred inhabitants were mostly woodcutters, farmers and workers in the slate mines of the district. In this town Luther's father, like many of his neighbors, owned and cultivated a small farm. He worked and struggled against great odds to eke out a frugal livelihood. The prospects for worldly advancement were far from encouraging to his ambitious disposition, yet he loved the place because from time immemorial it was the home of his ancestors. He was not destined, however, to remain for long with his kith and kin. Shortly after his marriage with Margaret Ziegler we find him abruptly abandoning his small holding in the little peasant township and hurriedly seeking a new home and a new occupation four score miles away in another hamlet, where his first child was born. Ortmann, in a work which deals in a chronological study of the Luthers and which is not unknown to students, asks: "What could have been the cause which induced John Luther to take such a step? To suddenly decamp with his wife, too, be it remembered, far advanced in pregnancy, to quit and utterly abandon the place of his birth, the home of his childhood and the site of all his belongings?"

Luther's admirers have endeavored to answer the unpleasant question, but all the explanations made, and which did service for a time, rest on such a precarious basis as to be unworthy of scholarly acceptance. That there was a cause other than such as is ordinarily assigned for John Luther's sudden departure from Mörha is certain and substantiated by documentary evidence. Henry Mayhew, a man of distinguished literary attainments and best known as one of the Mayhew brothers who founded London *Punch,* made Luther the subject of a close, careful, critical study. In an interesting work published in London, he treats of the question under consideration and declares John Luther's departure from Mörha was a "flight," and he further adds, "Men do not fly from their homes except on occasions of the greatest urgency."

"The simple fact, then," according to Mr. Mayhew, "would appear to be that John Luther—as Martin Michaelis tells us in his description of the mines and smelting houses at Kupfersuhl, a work which was first published in the year 1702—Martin's father had, in a dispute, stricken a herdsman dead to the earth by means of a horse bridle which he happened to have in his hand at the time, and was thereupon forced to abscond from the officers of justice as hurriedly as he could."

"This misfortune of John Luther," Ortmann says, "lives still in the minds of the Mörha peasantry. The villagers there tell you not only the same tale, but they show you the very spot—the field in which the tragedy occurred."

Mr. Mayhew made a special journey to Mörha in the last century and spent two weeks there with the object of probing the correctness of Ortmann's statement. He was a staunch Protestant and an enthusiastic admirer of Luther, but withal honest, fearless and careful. With method in his design he made searching inquiries concerning the local tradition in all directions and questioned and cross-examined old and young in the locality. He found invariably every person knew the same story and all could point out the identical spot where the murder was committed. "All the Mörha folk," he says, "had had the tale told them by their grandfathers, and they had it from their grandfathers before them." The story was so commonly and unquestionably accepted that he was forced to admit its credibility. "Sum up all these matters," is his conclusion, "and a mass of evidence is cumulated upon which surely no twelve common jurymen in their common senses would hesitate to bring in a verdict of guilty."

The charge of John Luther's homicide was not a recent tradition, but a charge made in Luther's own lifetime. George Wicel, who in the estimation of the Reformer was "a very learned and capable man," first called Luther's father a homicide, and that at three several times, in 1535, 1537 and 1565, and, moreover, in public print. It is recorded that on one occasion Justus Jonas assailed the integrity of the father of Wicel. The latter resented the charge as totally irrelevant to the case under consideration and declared that if such an argument possessed any validity, "he could call the father of your Luther a homicide." Luther and his friends never denied the statement. According to Karl Seidemann, an expert on Luther, "The testimony of Wicel may be taken as settling definitely the constantly occurring dispute on the subject."

Fr. Ganss in dealing with this question concludes a learned contribution to the *American Catholic Quarterly Review* (Jan. 1910) with an observation which is vitally germane to the subject, this is "The wild passion of anger was an unextinguished and unmodified heritage transmitted congenitally to the whole Luther family, and this to such an extent that the *Luther-zorn* (Luther rage) has attained the currency of a German colloquialism. Collectively it is graphically summarized by the Saxon archivist Bruckner on the basis of archival research and the official court dockets of Salzungen, the seat of the judicial district." "Mörha," is the contention of this official, "has attained the reputation for its rough and brusque character, because in the leading groups of its relationships, especially in the Luther branch, it possessed a tough and unyielding metal, and accordingly allowed itself to be drawn to a condition of refractoriness and querulous self-defense. To the police treasury of Salzungen, Mörha, with its rough-and-ready methods, was a welcome and rich source of revenue, for as the police dockets show, the village was mulcted again and again for acts of violence which its inhabitants committed, now in political or church parties, now as individuals, and foremost among them the Luthers. The parish manifested so determined an opposition and obstinacy against the legal authorities, as well as parochial, as to culminate in the brutal act of shooting at the household of the pastor. The condition of the neighbors adjoining the town, whose ready resource to arms, knives, scythes, nightly brawls and public outbreaks is often alluded to, as also the fines imposed for their misdemeanors. In these the Luther clan is mostly involved, for it carried on its feuds with others, strikes, wounds, resists and is ever ready at self-vindication and self-defense. Out of the gnarly wood of this relationship, consisting mostly of powerful, pugnacious farmers, assertive of their rights, Luther's father grew." (*Archiv. für Sachsische Geschichte* III, 38).

"It will hardly be denied that this characterization on

the whole applied to John Luther, and that, moreover, on evidence well known and abstracting from the homicide charge."

"And if we admit the leading laws of heredity, this may account for the fact," as Mayhew states it, "that Martin was a veritable chip of the hard old block," and with reasons no doubt crudely scientific but picturesquely apposite, he goes on to say: "If a gouty father or a consumptive mother, in the usual course of nature, beget a podagric or phthisic child, surely one with a temper as fiery as a blood-horse may be expected to cast a high-mettled foal. It may account for that 'terrible temper' of the Reformer, which was a dread to his antagonists, a shock to refined ears, a mortification to his friends, a sorrow to his intimates and an indelible stain on his apologetics."

The parents of Luther in the beginning of their married life were not blessed with much of the goods of this world. They had, however, a strong sense of their obligations toward their family and the courage to discharge them. Anxious for their own and their children's advancement, they worked together and toiled incessantly to provide food and clothing and education for their rising offspring. For years their means were scant enough and the struggle to meet the support of the household was both hard and grinding. Often the mother was reduced to the dire necessity of carrying home the wood for the family fire, gathered from the neighboring pine forest, on her own shoulders. In this home, like many before and since, there was unfortunately one great deficiency more intolerable than poverty, namely, the absence of the sweet joys of family life. Childish fun and frolic which beget happiness and good cheer found no encouragement in the Luther family circle. Home life was exacting, cold, dull and cheerless. The heads of the house took their parental responsibilities too seriously and interpreted them too rigorously. The father was stern, harsh, exacting and, what is rather unusual, the mother was altogether too much given to inflict the severest corporal punishments. With them "the apple did not always lie beside the rod." They were altogether too strict and exacting. They believed in work and had no relish for innocent play and amusement. In the government of their children they exercised no discrimination or moderation. Too much severity ruled the household and as usual begot disastrous results. In this over-strenuous discipline we may find to a certain degree the explanation for the development of that temper of unbending obstinacy for which their son was so remarkable not only in his earliest years, but throughout his whole life. Though he seems to have been very fond of his parents in after life and recalled how they pinched themselves to give him support and education, it appears from his own statement that they were extremely exacting and punished him cruelly for the most trifling offenses. As examples of the harsh treatment to which he was subjected in his youth, he tells us that on one occasion his father, in a fit of uncontrollable rage, beat him so mercilessly that he became a fugitive from home and was on this account so "embittered against him that he had to win me to himself again." (*Tischreden,* Frankfort, 1567, fol. 314 a.). At another time, he says, "his mother in her inflexible rigor flogged him, until the blood flowed, on account of a worthless little nut."

In school he met with the same severity that was meted out to him at home. The rule here also was that of the rod. The schoolmaster of that day was generally a harsh disciplinarian and inspired a fear in pupils which was difficult to remove ever afterward. Speaking later of his school-day experience, Luther relates that he was beaten fifteen times in succession during one morning and, to the best of his knowledge, without much fault of his own. He probably brought the punishment on himself by insubordination and obstinacy. Whether there was exceptional provocation or not, the flogging only served to anger him and retard progress in study. Under this harsh treatment he learned, as he confesses, nothing. Even the customary religious training he received at the time does not seem to have raised his spirits or led to a free, more hopeful development of his spiritual life. In a fiery character such as his, the cruel treatment to which he was subjected both at home and in school could only lay the foundation of that stubborness which afterwards became one of the leading features of the man; naturally enough it could intimidate the violence of his disposition, but could not remove it. "This severity," he says later on, "shattered his nervous system for life."

When Martin was only six months old his parents left Eisleben and moved to Mansfeld, a thriving, busy mining town. Here they hoped to obtain a fairer share of worldly success. At an early age, Martin was sent to a school in which the Ten Commandments, Child's Belief, The Lord's Prayer and the Latin Grammar of Donatus were taught. His stay in this place was uneventful. In 1497, when he was fourteen years old, he was went to school with the Franciscans at Magdeburg, where he spent one year, and thence to another school at Eisenach, a little town above which rises the hill crowned by the Wartburg, where long before St. Elizabeth of Hungary, the holy Landgravine of Thuringen, spent the happier part of her life. Here the young student had some relatives who, his mother thought, would give him careful attention, as he was at the time recovering from a recent attack of sickness. On his arrival he got a share of a room at the scholar's hostel.

In Eisenach Martin, like many other students of the period, was obliged on account of poverty to sing in the streets and collect alms from the kindly disposed among his hearers. He had a sweet alto voice, which later became a tenor. On one of these daily rounds from door to door, a lady of gentle birth and charitable disposition was attracted to him. Filled with pity for his condition, she invited him to her home, where ever afterwards he was treated as an intimate of the family. The home of this lady is still preserved, the first story being now a *Bierstube*, while the upper rooms are used as a Luther museum. His entrance into the hospitable family of Ursula Cotta opened up another and a new world to him. Here the growing youth got the first glimpses of the summer side of life and the first taste of culture and refinement. The roughness and uncouthness brought from the peasant's home and the mining town were gradually tempered in the boy by refined association with the gentlefolk who frequented the Cotta household. Away from the hardness and severity of his early rearing, he began now to enjoy life and experience its gentler graces and pleasures. The generosity of his benefactress made a profound impression on him. In his old age he recalled her memory with great gratitude and ever referred to her as his dear "Wirthin."

At Eisenach he applied himself diligently to the cultivation of the higher studies and laid solidly and well the foundation of his subsequent learning. Home and school and teachers here were to his liking. They were the best he had known and in marked contrast to the sort he had hitherto experienced or suffered. In an atmosphere full of fine human feelings, he studied with pleasure and mastered his tasks with ease and rapidity. In those formative years he had as principal of the high school he attended an educator who knew how to stimulate the love of study in his pupils. He was a Carmelite friar named John Trebonius, one of the most distinguished pedagogues of his day. It is related of him that upon entering the classroom, he always removed his scholar's cap and insisted that his associate teachers should follow his example, because of the respect due to pupils out of whom, he used to say, "God might make rulers, chancellors, doctors and magistrates." In Eisenach, at that time, there were besides the parish church, no less than nine monasteries and nunneries. Here Luther had ample opportunities to satisfy his devotion, and the solemn services of the Church, the religious dramas and especially the German sacred hymns which were wont to be sung by the entire congregation tended to exercise a cheerful and soothing influence upon him. Of his life in this place he had the tenderest memories and often referred to it as his "beloved town."

From Eisenach, Luther went in the summer of 1501 to Erfurt, noted for its old tile-roofed houses and known in those days as "The Kitchen Garden Town." It was a prosperous, rich and populous city. It boasted some sixty thousand inhabitants and possessed not only one of the finest cathedrals in the country, but the greatest of the German universities of the period. This university was established by a Bull of Clement VII in the year 1379 and was the fifth in rank to be founded in Germany. Its fame was widespread and its renown attracted students from all parts of the country and even from abroad. It was a common saying, "Who would study rightly must go to Erfurt." This university boasted the presence of some of the greatest professors of the time. The most remarkable of these was Jodocus Trutvetter, who, in the departments of philosophy, theology and dialectics, stood without an admitted rival in educational circles. Luther spoke of this professor later as not only "the first theologian and philosopher," but also "the first of contemporary dialecticians." Another famous professor of the university was the Augustinian friar, Bartholomaeus Arnoldi Von Usigen, who was not only a profound scholar but a most versatile and prolific writer. Loyal Germans were proud of these brilliant lights, whose fame and genius, they thought, had made the University of Erfurt as well-known as that of Paris.

Luther's father entertained a high opinion of his son's talents. He wanted him to become a great scholar and a man of renown. His ambition was to see his son hold a high and influential place in the social scale. He had hopes that in time he would reach the honorable and lucrative position of legal adviser to the Counts of Mansfeld, who had befriended him in his earlier days when he had little of life's comforts. "The father," as Vedder remarks, "wished his boy to be spared the grinding toil he had known and to enjoy advantages he had missed. He saw, as many a poor man has seen since, that for a youth of talent, ability and application, the most direct avenue to influence and power is through the higher education and the scholarly advantages thereby afforded." To further his designs, he marked out a career for his boy; he was ambitious to fit him for the profession of law, which in that day was a path to the most lucrative offices both in Church and State. As the result of frugality and industry his financial condition had improved, and he was no longer dependent on the help of strangers. He, moreover, rose in the esteem of his fellow townsmen until he became Burgomaster of Mansfeld. His improved financial standing quickened the desire he had to give his son the advantages of a university training whereby he would be fitted to become a skillful and learned lawyer and thus in time reach the mighty things expected of him through association with the influential and powerful classes. The father's joy was great when he was able to take his son out of the ranks of the "poor students" and in accordance with a long-cherished project pay with his own means for the completion of his boy's education.

The growing youth was now in his eighteenth year. He was entered in the matriculation register of the Erfurt High School as *"Martinus Luder ex Mansfelt,"* and for a considerable time thereafter he continued to spell his family name as Lüder, a form which is also to be found up to the beginning of the seventeenth century in the case of others—Lüder, Luider, Leuder. From 1512 he began, however, to sign himself "Lutherus" or "Luther," by which change of name he has been designated ever since. (Köstlin-Kawerau I, p. 754, n. 2, p. 166).

When Martin entered the university he found the students divided into two groups, one known as the "Humanists" or so-called "poets" and the other as "Scholastics" or "philosophers." The former sacredly devoted themselves to the study of the Latin classics and aimed to found all branches of learning on the literature and culture of classical antiquity; the latter, whilst they favored the pagan Latin models of style and eloquence, preferred and attached more importance to the cultivation and study of logic and scholastic philosophy. The Humanists considered that a classical training alone could form a perfect man. The philosophers, never adverse to the study of the classic languages as a means of education, were unwilling that the worldly paganized concept of life advocated by the ancients should prevail against the spiritual glorification of humanity expounded and maintained in the traditional teaching of the Church.

Luther, with his vivacity of thought and feeling, soon discovered that a number of his fellow students were secretly opposed to sound scholastic studies and vigorous mental training and covertly endeavored to bring back to Christendom the ideals of the most decadent days of Greece and Rome. Their humanistic spirit then did not impress him much, and although in his private time he studied the Latin classics, more particularly Cicero, Virgil, Livy, Ovid, also Terence, Juvenal, Horace and Plautus, it seems he never qualified to enter the secret "poetic" circle composed of many of the best minds of the day. In a spirit of genuine love of culture he studied the classic authors, but whilst Latin was the language of the classroom in all the universities and became a second mother tongue to him, as to all the scholars of the day, yet he paid little attention to grammatical details and never attained to Ciceronian purity and elegance in speech or writing. He knew Latin well enough for all practical purposes, and at a later period he was able to make skillful use of quotations from the ancient authors when occasion demanded. Whilst fair progress was made in his humanistic studies, he preferred to center his attention on the more useful branches of learning, logic and scholastic philosophy. To these studies he gave his chief attention, and whilst he made great progress, he did not particularly distinguish himself in them.

Melanchthon said: "The whole university admired his genius." The praise bestowed by the colleague of his after days does not seem, however, to have been warranted by the facts. According to Vedder, a non-Catholic writer, "Luther apparently made no deep impression on the university and probably, but for his later distinction, few or none of his fellow students would have recalled that while among them he had been known as 'Musicus,' on account of his learning to play the lute, and as the 'Philosopher' owing to his frequent fits of moodiness." "In the numerous letters left to posterity by the aspiring Erfurt Humanists, his name is never mentioned. Melanchthon's statement that Luther's talents were the wonder of the university is hardly borne out by the record, for when he took his baccalaureate degree at Michaelmas, in 1502, he ranked only thirteenth in a list of fifty-seven candidates. That is respectable, to be sure, but one requires the vivid imagination of an eulogist to see anything of startling brilliancy in it. He did better in taking his Master's degree at Epiphany in 1505, when he ranked second among seventeen candidates." (Vedder, p. 5).

Of his life during his university days we have no very clear account, owing to the silence of our sources. From scattered sayings of his own in after life we learn he did not look back with any great delight to his student days at Erfurt. He coarsely described the town as a "beer house" and a "nest of immorality."

Luther finished his general education when he was about twenty-one. The time had now come when he was to take up the study of jurisprudence in accordance with his father's long-cherished project. The prospect, however, was little to his liking, as he had a decided distaste for the legal profession. "Jurists," as he thought afterwards, "made bad Christians and few of them would be saved. They take the money of the poor and with the tongue deplete both their pocket and their purse." Notwithstanding his dislike of the legal profession, however, he began the study of law in earnest, and his work was all that could be desired.

After being a law student for only a few weeks he suddenly abandoned his studies, to the great disappointment of his father, and returned home for a brief visit during which time his thoughts turned into quite a new channel. Ignoring the course mapped out by his father for his future career, he inconsiderately and precipitately determined to abandon the world and work out his salvation within the quiet of the cloister walls. He was on his way to become an excellent professor and an accomplished advocate when, unfortunately for himself, he resolved, without due consideration of his natural disposition, to become a friar.

Before finally taking the unexpected step, he resorted to a very strange and unusual preparation for the state of life he intended to embrace. He wanted to meet, for the last time, a few of his friends and some "honest, virtuous maidens and women," and accordingly he invited them to a farewell dinner, which was given on the eve of his entrance into the Augustinian Monastery at Erfurt, July 17, 1505. At the banquet Luther outwardly was in a most cheerful mood. He was full of frolic, and while the wine cup passed freely he enlivened the gathering by his lute-playing and singing. The merry guests had little inkling of the unquiet state of his mind, and they were thoroughly surprised when he announced before the parting that he was about to renounce the world and become an Augustinian friar. "You see me today," he said, "but henceforth no more."

His guests, knowng how unfitted he seemed for the monastic career and sorry to lose a jovial companion, pleaded with him to reconsider his decision and loudly protested against his action. They looked upon him as just an average youth, in no ways remarkable for piety or religious zeal, and they knew, moreover, how he enjoyed the pleasures of life, mingling with the frivolous in the merriment of the time and indulging in boar hunting and other worldly amusements. They instinctively felt he was not qualified or fitted for the sublime vocation to which he aspired, and they accordingly used all their powers to dissuade him from the course he had chosen. All their efforts were fruitless, and from the gaiety and frolic of the banquet hall he went out to the monastery, at whose gates his jolly companions bade him farewell. This unexpected step came as a terrible blow to his father. All the plans he had made for the future well-being of his son were shattered in a moment. The sacrifices he had made and the toils he had endured to advance his son in a worldly career were made valueless by the willfulness of him for whom they had been cheerfully and generously given. The disappontment was great, and his fury broke out in uncontrollable denunciation.

We naturally ask ourselves now, how was it that Luther, with his head full of worldly ambition and already fairly distinguished by his learning and honored with the degree of Doctor of Philosophy, how was it he abandoned the secular calling to embrace the religious?

The motives that prompted Luther's sudden resolve to enter the monastery "are," says Ganss, "various, conflicting and the subject of considerable debate. He himself alleges that the brutality of his home and school life drove him into the monastery." Hausrath, one of the most scholarly Luther specialists, unreservedly inclines to this belief. The "house at Mansfelt rather repelled than attracted him" (Beard, *Martin Luther and the Germ. Ref.*, London, 1889, 146), and to "the question 'Why did Luther go into the monastery?' the reply that Luther himself gives is the most satisfactory." (Hausrath, *Luther's Leben,* 1, Berlin, 1904, 2, 22).

He, himself again, in a letter to his father in explanation of his defection from the Old Church, writes, "When I was over-stricken and overwhelmed by the fear of impending death, I made an involuntary and forced vow." (De Wette, *Dr. Martin Luther's Briefe,* II Berlin, 1825, 101). Various explanations are given of this episode. Melanchthon ascribes his step to a deep melancholy, which attained a critical point "when at one time he lost one of his comrades by an accidental death." (Corp. Ref. VI, 156). Cochlaeus relates that "at one time he was so frightened in a field at a thunderbolt, as is commonly reported, or was in such anguish at the loss of a companion who was killed in the storm, that in a short time, to the amazement of many persons, he sought admission to the Order of St. Augustine." (Cochlaeus, *Historia, D. M. Luther's Dillingen,* 1571, 2). Mathesius, his first biographer, attributes it to the fatal "stabbing of a friend and a terrible storm with a thunderclap." (op. cit., fol. 46). Seckendorf, who made careful research, following Bavarus (Beyer), a pupil of Luther, goes a step further, calling this unknown friend Alexius, and ascribes his death to a thunderbolt. (Seckendorf, *Ausführliche Historie des Lutherthums,* Leipzig, 1714, 51). D'Aubigne changes this Alexius into Alexis and has him assassinated at Erfurt. (D'Aubigne, *History of the Reformation,* New York, s. d., 1, 166). Oerger (*Vom Jungen Luther,* Erfurt, 1899, 27-41) has proved the existence of this friend, his name of Alexius or Alexis, his death by lightning or assassination, a mere legend, destitute of all historical verification. Köstlin-Kawerau (1, 45) states that returning from his "Mansfeld home he was overtaken by a terrible storm, with an alarming lightning flash and thunderbolt. Terrified and overwhelmed, he cried out: 'Help, St. Anna, I will be a monk.'" "The inner history of the change is far less easy to narrate. We have no direct contemporary evidence on which to rely, while Luther's own reminiscences, on which we chiefly depend, are necessarily colored by his later experiences and feelings." (Beard, op. cit. 146). (*Cath. Encyc.,* Vol. X, p. 439).

When we consider the motives that prompted Luther to abandon the world, we fear he knew little about the ways of God and was not well informed of the gravity and responsibilities of the step he was taking. The calling he aspired to is the highest given to man on earth, and because it is a ministry of salvation, replete with solemn and sacred obligations, it should not be embraced without prayerful consideration and wise and prudent counsel. It is only when vocation is sufficiently pronounced and when one by one the different stages of the journey in which are acquired continually increasing helps towards reaching the appointed goal, are passed, that one should enter the sanctuary. "No man," says St. Paul, "takes the honor to himself, but that is called by God." That Luther was not called by God to conventual life seems evident enough from all circumstances. Every sign and mark one looks for in aspirants to the monastic life were apparently lacking in him. Parent and friend alike knew this and opposed his course, feeling it was merely the expression of a temporary attitude of mind and not a real vocation. Luther himself admits that he was driven by despair, rather than the love of higher perfection, into a religious career. He says: "I entered the monastery and renounced the world because I despaired of myself all the while." From his earliest days he was subject to fits of depression and melancholy. Emotional by temperament, he would pass suddenly from mirth and cheerfulness to a gloomy, despondent state of mind in which he was tormented by frightful searchings of conscience. The fear of God's judgments and the recollection of his own sins sorely tried him and caused unnecessary anxiety and dread as to his fate. He saw in himself nothing but sin and in God nothing but anger and revenge. He fell a victim to excessive scrupulousness, and as he was self-opinionated and stubborn-minded, he relied altogether too much on his own righteousness and disregarded the remedies most effectual for his spiritual condition. Like all those who trust in themselves, he rushed from extreme timidity to excessive rashness. Had he consulted those who were skilled in the direction of conventual religious and made known the troubled waters beneath the smooth surface of his daily life, he might have been made to understand that, owing to his abnormal state of mind and his natural disposition, he was not fitted for the carrying out of the evangelical counsels, and thus he might have been prevented from forcing himself into a mold for which he was manifestly unsuited. In the uneasy and serious state of his conscience the advice and counsel of the wise and prudent were ignored. Moved by his own feelings and relying on his own powers, he suddenly and secretly decided for himself a career in life which, as events proved, was not only a mistake as far as he was concerned, but one fraught with disaster to innumerable others, whom he afterwards influenced to join in his revolt against the Mother Church.

Without advice and without full deliberation, even in spite of the opposition of those who knew him best, he determined to become a friar. Accordingly he wended his way to the Augustinian monastery and presented himself for admission as a novice. The prior received the young Master of Arts graciously and took him in apparently without difficulty, not fearing, as the superior of a modern religious house would most certainly fear, lest a vocation thus suddenly formed should be afterwards as suddenly abandoned. However, the Superior put the usual question, "What seekest thou, my son?" and Luther replied as was customary, "I seek the mercy of God and your fellowship." These preliminaries over, he was permitted to enter. According to the Rule of the Augustinian Order, the young postulant was now given ample time to learn what lay before him as a friar previous to donning the novice's garb. An experienced member of the Order all the while explained the Rule to him and repeatedly reminded him that he should weigh well and earnestly whether, as stated in the statutes of the Order, "the spirit which was leading him was of God." Only after this preparation was he clothed with the habit of the Order, which consisted of a white woolen tunic, a scapular, also white, falling over the breast and back and a black mantle with a hood and wide sleeves.

During the time spent in preparation for the reception of the habit Luther was invisible to the world beyond the monastery gate. When he began the novitiate, which lasted a whole year, he was required to study and live under rules and usages which regulated every hour of his monastic life. He had to spend many hours of the day and night in exercises consisting in prayers, manual labor and penitential works, all of which were intended to fit him for reception into the Order.

This was the formative period of the young novice. He was supposed to reflect seriously upon the duties and obligations which at the profession he would take upon himself, and weigh earnestly the purity of his motives and the spirit which was leading him. "The Lord forbids that a blind being should be offered up to Him," and as the religious tie was never intended to bring misery in place of the happiness which it promises, he as a novice was entirely free until the hour of profession to abandon his course and return to the world. The doors of religious houses were then as now always open to those who feel they are not called to follow the evangelical counsels.

The day came at last for Luther's profession. The ceremony brought together a large congregation. The church was crowded with the townspeople and students from the university. After the usual preliminary services and when the superiors, who made the official inquiries about the novice's motives, were satisfied he would take the vows "at his own desire, freely, not influenced by force or fear," the candidate was admitted to make his profession and was robed in the black habit and hood of the Hermits of St. Augustine. This ceremony made him no longer a man in the world, but a monk in the cloister. He now bound himself by a sacred oath to God to prepare himself for Heaven by treading a path of life in which perfection is sought in carrying out the evangelical counsels of the Saviour, and engaged throughout his mortal career to combat the temptations of the world with the weapons of poverty, chastity and obedience. The habit, however, does not make the monk; much more is required. And now we ask, if all the while during his noviceship Martin was under the impression that his vow to become a religious was only a "forced" one, as he afterwards alleged, did he act honestly when he knelt down before his prior, Winand of Diedenhofen, and bound himself by the most solemn and sacred oath to persevere until death in poverty, chastity and obedience, according to the rule of the Order of St. Augustine? Did he act honestly when he first thought of becoming a friar by concealing his impetuous resolve from the Superior of the monastery, who would hardly have received him into the Order had he been made aware of his rash selection of a state of life? Did he act honestly in holding to his resolution when he knew that a vow would not have been considered as binding unless made with full deliberation, and that even if valid when originally made, it would no longer be binding if, after conscientious self-examination, he became aware that owing to his natural disposition he had no vocation for the religious life and then was dispensed by the Church? What made him pursue such an unwise and untenable course? Was he dominated by that spirit of dogged perseverance or obstinacy whereby, as we know, he was determined, at whatever cost, always to go through with anything he had once begun?

After making his profession, the young religious was directed by his superiors to study theology. He immersed himself in his tasks and took great pleasure in supplementing the teachings of the schoolmen and the Fathers of the Church by constant and frequent reading of the Sacred Scriptures which were for him, as they should be for all, a well of instruction and enlightenment. The ponderous red copy of the Bible possessed by the monastery was well thumbed. His course in theology was not, however, as long as it might have been, for we find he was raised to the priesthood in a very short time after the year of his novitiate was completed.

He celebrated his first Mass on Cantate Sunday, May 2, 1507. It was a day of great import, an occasion for the assembling of old friends. He invited his father and many other guests to be present at the ceremony which meant so much to him, his kindred and his acquaintances. Thus, in a letter of invitation to Johann Braun, Vicar in Eisenach, who befriended him in his early struggles for an education, he shows how high an estimate he had of the sacerdotal office and dignity which had been conferred upon him. In this document, the earliest we have of him, he says that God had chosen him, an unworthy sinner, for the unspeakable dignity of His service at the altar, and he begged his good benefactor to be present at his first Mass and by his prayers to assist him, so that his sacrifice might be pleasing in the sight of God. (Euders, *Luther's Briefwerlisal* I, 1). The sacred service began. He appeared to be recollected, but in reality he was awe-stricken and oppressed beyond measure. He could hardly contain himself for excitement and fear. The sense of his unworthiness to celebrate the divine mysteries tormented him. The words *"Te igitur clementissime Pater"* ["Therefore, most merciful Father, we humbly pray and beseech Thee. . ."] at the commencement of the Canon of the Mass and *"offero tibi Deo meo vivo et vero"* ["I offer, unto Thee, my God, living and true. . ."] at the oblation brought so vividly to his mind the Awful Eternal Majesty that he was hardly able to go on. He was so greatly agitated that he would have come down from the altar had not the prior of the convent hindered him. The terrifying idea he had of God spoilt even the happiness of that day. This may account in great part for his fearful hatred of the Mass in later days. Many years afterwards he says, with reference to his entrance on the priesthood: "When I said my first Mass at Erfurt, I was all but dead, for I was without faith; it was unjust and too great forbearance in God that the earth did not at the time swallow up both myself and the bishop who ordained me."

Old Hans Luther assisted at the ceremony and brought a company of friends who rode to the convent door "on twenty horses." His heart was not really in the celebration, but the old miner did not wish by his absence to shame his oldest and most promising son. His attendance was the first sign of his acquiescence in his son's vocation. The ceremonies in the church having been concluded, a modest repast was served in the monastery to the invited guests. Then Luther and his father met for the first time since the son's last visit home on the eve of his withdrawal from the world. In the course of conversation at the dinner table the young priest endeavored to justify himself for changing the career his parent had marked out for him, and he longed to receive from his father's lips some words of approval and congratulation. He spoke of the religious calling, praised the monastic life as peaceful, pleasant and godly, and went on to recall the vow, the inconsiderate and forced vow, he had made at the time of the thunderstorm, claiming that he had been impelled by "terror from Heaven." The speech was too much for the level-headed father, who did not hesitate there and then to make known the feelings that filled his heart. Glancing round the table and addressing all thereat, he remarked dryly, "I must sit here and eat and drink, when I would much rather be anywhere else. Have you never heard that a child should obey his father and his mother? Contrary to the fourth Commandment, you have left me and your mother in our old age, when we expected help and consolation from you after expending so much upon your education." Luther tried to soften the old man's heart, but all efforts in this direction were useless. When at last he insisted that he had only followed the divine call on entering the monastery, the sturdy old peasant, highly irritated, interposed with this reply: "God grant it may not prove a delusion and a diabolical specter." Luther was stung by the remark, but did not pay much attention to it at the time. He thought the saying was only an impatient exclamation in keeping with the character of the man and with the severity which he was accustomed to from his earliest days in the home circle. He, however, never forgot the remark of his father. It afterwards caused him much anguish of spirit and doubts of the wisdom and righteousness of his course. Referring to the speech of his father in later days, he tells how "it struck such deep root in his heart that he never heard anything from his mouth which he remembered so tenaciously. He thought God spoke by his lips." "However," he goes on to say, "at that time I shut my heart as much as I could against his words, as being only of man."

Luther was now a religious and a priest. There is no reason to doubt that he realized to the fullest extent the cares, duties and responsibilities of his sacred calling, and with apparent ardor, devotion and faithfulness he endeavored to pass his life in correspondence with its spirit and requirements. The few years he spent in the priesthood before his defection were strenuous, active and busy. He lectured, as best he could and as well as his previous hurried preparation permitted, on ethics in the Faculty of Philosophy and on special portions of the Holy Scriptures in the newly founded University of Wittenberg, a town accredited then as the most bibulous one of the most bibulous province (Saxony) of Germany. In addition to these labors, he preached alternately in the monastery of his Order and the collegiate church of the town. His duties were manifold, and the largest demands were made upon his energies. He had little time left after fulfilling his various offices for intellectual pursuits. The story of his all too rapid advancement shows his preparatory studies to have been anything but deep, solid, and systematic. "Comparatively considered," Fr. Johnston says, "the theological culture he received was not on a par with that required now by the average seminarian, let alone a Doctor of Divinity." He was sharp, fiery, intelligent, and possessed much fancy and originality, but his knowledge was merely elementary. He had no appreciation of the scholastic speculation and logic so much honored at the time; in fact, he hated the whole system of the schoolmen, not excepting even the great scholar and theologian, St. Thomas. Scholastic subtleties were not always to his liking, and to show his contempt thereof he frequently paid his compliments to the "rancid rules of the logicians," and to "that putrid philosopher Aristotle." A feeling of the insufficiency of his education tormented him all through his life. He expressed very strongly to Staupitz his fear to stand for the doctorate and only consented under pressure to pass the required examination to comply with the wishes of the Superior of his Order. "I was obliged," he says, "to take the degree of Doctor of Divinity and to promise under oath that I would preach the Holy Scriptures which were very dear to me, faithfully and without adulteration." To the study of the Bible he gave himself up with great ardor, so much so that he neglected the rest of his theological education, and his teacher Usingen was obliged to protest against his one-sided study of the sacred text. It cannot be denied that he was industrious, self-reliant and ambitious, but withal, he was not a methodically trained man. At bottom he was neither a philosopher nor a theologian, and at no time of his life, despite his efforts to acquire knowledge, did he show himself more than superficially equipped to grapple with serious and difficult philosophical and religious problems. His study never rose to brilliancy.

Luther's professorial duties were interrupted for a short while when in the autumn of 1510 he set out for Rome on business connected with the welfare of his Order. His absence extended over a period of four or five months, only one of which he spent in the Eternal City. After attending to the mission entrusted to him, he spent much of his time in sightseeing, visiting the holy places, and secretly taking lessons in Hebrew from a Jew called Jacob, "who gave himself out as a physician." Like the average traveller to the city today, he could not be expected in the short time he remained there to study the character of a people of whose language he was ignorant and to set himself up as a judge of the country and a censor of its citizens. Looking at things through his German spectacles it seems, if we can credit his later writings, that his observations concerning the condition of things in Rome were not to his liking. He is said to have been thunderstruck with the wickedness and impiety of the Romans and of Italians in general. Their southern freedom and lack of restraint were not such as to appeal to his phlegmatic, northern temperament. It was, therefore, easy for him to believe all the anecdotes concerning the corruption then supposed to be rampant in lay and ecclesiastical circles which he claimed were told him by his not over-trustworthy guides and acquaintances. Most of his experiences are given in the *Table Talk* and his later writings, and may be summed up in the following words he says he heard fall from the lips of one of his companions: "If there be a Hell, then Rome is built on it." In the works alluded to, the share which he himself actually took in the pious pilgrim-exercises of the time is kept very much in the background. Indeed, he tells that whilst he was in Rome he celebrated Mass "perhaps once, perhaps ten times: i.e., occasionally, not regularly." Can it be possible that there were no good people in Rome at the time of his visit, or was it that in the moroseness of his spirit he was looking only for abominations and corruption? When was there a time when there were not scandals? It must needs be on account of the depravity of human nature that they exist. But whilst we admit that there may have been and actually were many influenced by the godless spirit of the world at the time, we cannot see how any amount of corruption of morals should unduly influence anyone who consistently and thoroughly loves virtue and hates vice. If we admit that Luther was greatly scandalized at what he heard and saw, how comes it that we hear nothing from him about his experiences in Rome after he left the city and returned home? Jürgens says, "He *may* have spoken of these things to his friends." He may, yes, but did he? (Jürgens II, 349). If his visit turned his reverence for Rome into loathing, as his admirers glory in narrating, we have no proof of it in his writings and addresses immediately after his return to Erfurt. Bayne, a non-Catholic writer, alluding to this matter says: "In his letters of those years he never mentions having been in Rome. In conference with Cardinal Cajetan, in his disputations with Dr. Eck, in his epistles to Pope Leo, nay, in his tremendous broadside of invective and accusation against all things Romish, in his 'Address to the German Nation and Nobility,' there occurs not one unmistakable reference to his having been in Rome. By every rule of evidence we are bound to hold that when the most furious assailant Rome has ever known described, from a distance of ten years upwards, the incidents of a journey through Italy to Rome, the few touches of light in his picture are more trustworthy than its black breadths of shade." (Bayne, *Martin Luther,* 1, 234). Whilst we admit that there may have been by far too much wickedness and impiety in the Rome of the Popes at the heights of the Renaissance, we beg to be allowed to question its extent and especially to doubt the accuracy of the statements made by Luther ten years after his visit to Rome, when he was exceedingly spiteful, and anger against the Holy City displaced his old-time reverence. It is hardly worthwhile to go into the details of the scandals he related when he severed his connection with the Church. The intelligent reader can determine for himself whether a man who is capable of telling or believing all the absurd anecdotes about the condition of things at Rome he mentions in his later writings can be looked upon as an impartial witness; or whether the scathing arraignment which he pronounces at a distance of ten years can be considered reliable. To say the least, Luther's whole Roman experience, as described by him in his later years when he was in open rebellion against the Church, is open to question. Hausrath, a non-Catholic writer, does not hesitate to say: "We can really question the importance attached to remarks which in a great measure date from the last years of his life, when he was really a changed man. Much that he relates as personal experience is manifestly the product of an easily explained self-delusion." (Hausrath, *Luther's Romfahrt,* p. 79).

Many non-Catholic authors delight to regale their readers with all the absurd and incredible stories Luther told later on in his life about his visit to Rome. Their object is to furnish a graphic historical beginning of the change Luther's mind was undergoing towards the Church. With all due respect for what these ill-informed writers allege, we are obliged in the interest of truth to tell them that Luther's visit to Rome in nowise shook his conviction of the authority of the Holy See or affected in the least his spiritual life and theological thought. In support of this statement, we quote Vedder, the latest of the non-Catholic writers on Luther, who says: "His faith in the Church and its system was not at that time seriously affected." (Vedder, p. 12). Long before this statement was announced, we find the non-Catholic Hausrath declaring that Luther "returned from Rome as strong in the faith as he went to visit it. In a certain sense his sojourn in Rome even strengthened his religious convictions." (Hausrath, *M. Luther's Romfahrt,* p. 98).

In the spring of 1511, when he was nearing eight-and-twenty years of age, we find him back at the University of Erfurt. At the time he journeyed to Rome, his character was not yet sufficiently formed; he was, as Oldecop says, "a wild young fellow." However, for five or six years after his return we find that he lectured, preached and wrote on the Catholic means of grace, the Mass, indulgences and prayer in entire accordance with the traditional doctrine of the Church. Just to show some of the ill-informed the Catholic thoughts which engaged him in his wanderings through Rome, we give his words on the power of the Papacy and commend them to the consideration of the serious. "If," he says, "Christ had not entrusted all power to one man, the Church would not have been perfect because there would have been no order, and each one would have been able to say he was led by the Holy Spirit. This is what the heretics did, each one setting up his own principle. In this way as many Churches arose as there were heads. Christ therefore wills, in order that all may be assembled in one unity, that His power be exercised by one man to whom also He commits it. He has, however, made this Power so strong that He looses all the powers of Hell, without injury, against it. He says: 'The gates of Hell shall not prevail against it,' as though He said: 'They will fight against it but never overcome it,' so that in this way it is made manifest that this power is in reality from God and not from man. Wherefore whoever breaks away from this unity and order of the Power, let him not boast of great enlightenment and wonderful works, as our Picards and other heretics do, for much better is obedience than the victims of fools who know not 'what evil they do.' (*Eccles.* 4:17)." (*Werke,* Weim. ed. I, 1883, p. 69).

This extract teems with respect for the head of the Church and may well be recommended for consideration to all who claim without warrant that the Reformer was disturbed by what he saw and heard in Rome.

Luther, as remarked before, led a busy life whilst he was a monk. His duties were manifold and exacting. Constant demands were made upon his time and resources on account of the many offices he was called on to fulfill. He had few spare moments for intellectual pursuits, and to allow more ample time for study his religious duties were performed but irregularly and spasmodically. This course could only bode ill for his future. Infractions of the rules, breaches of discipline, distorted ascetic practices were frequent and followed ever with increasing gravity. We are told he sometimes omitted to recite the Divine Office for three or four weeks together, a duty to which, after the observance of his vows, he was bound under the penalty of grievous sin. Then in a fit of paroxysmal remorse he would lock himself into his cell and set to work to repair the omission by a continuous recitation of all that had been left unsaid. On these occasions he would abstain from all food and drink and torture himself by harrowing mortifications.

According to the account Luther gives of himself in later years he was "a religious of the strictest observance." "I was a pious monk," he says, "and so strictly followed the Rule of my Order, that I dare to say if ever any man could have been saved by monkery, I was that monk. I was a monk in earnest, and followed the Rule of my Order more strictly than I can express. If ever monk could obtain Heaven by his monkish works, I should certainly have been entitled to it. Of all this, the friars who have known me can testify. If it had continued much longer, I should have carried my mortifications even to death, by means of watchings, prayers, readings, and other labors." How far this may have been true it is difficult to say. Whatever his fellow monks may have been able to testify, there is no extant record of their confirmatory testimony on this point. One thing at least is clear from Luther's own words. His spiritual endeavors, whether earnest or not, were singularly ill-regulated and according to an old monastic proverb: "Everything beyond obedience looks suspicious in a monk."

It seems that during his religious life he was much agitated and given to gloom and despair by the sense of sin. He saw in himself nothing but sin, more sin than he felt he could atone for by any works of penance. Apparently he had strong passions which frequently asserted themselves and which he sought to subdue in his own way. In all his prayers and fastings the conception of God he placed before his mind was very much that of a God of avenging justice and very little that of a God of mercy. The fear of the divine wrath made him abnormally apprehensive and prevented him from experiencing comfort and help in the performance of religious exercises. His sorrow for sin was devoid of humble charity, and instead of trusting with childlike confidence in the pardoning mercy of God and in the merits of Christ, as the Church always exhorted the sorely tried to do, he gave himself up to black despair. His singularity brought on distress of soul, and his anxiety increased until wakefulness became a confirmed habit. His condition became so sad that at times his fellow monks feared he was on the verge of madness. In his later days, he drew this picture of his state of soul whilst he was a monk. "From misplaced reliance on my righteousness," he says, "my heart became full of distrust, doubt, fear, hatred and blasphemy of God. I was such an enemy of Christ that whenever I saw an image or a picture of Him hanging on His Cross, I loathed the sight and I shut my eyes and felt that I would rather have seen the devil. My spirit was completely broken and I was always in a state of melancholy; for, do what I would, my 'righteousness' and my 'good works' brought me no help or consolation." (Janssen, Vol. III, p. 84).

Was this the fault of the state of life he had chosen? Perhaps, inasmuch as he had entered into it without due deliberation. But passing this consideration over, we feel that had he not disregarded the monastic regulations for those of his own devising, and had he put into practice the wise directions of his spiritual guides, his troubles of soul would certainly have been much mitigated and considerably surmounted. Like most victims of scrupulosity he saw nothing in himself but wickedness and corruption. Not content with the ordinary spiritual exercises prescribed by the rule of the Order, he marked out for himself an independent path of righteousness. He wanted to have his own way, and, as is usual in the case of all stubborn minds, the arbitrary means he resorted to for relief only made his condition worse. "I prescribed," he says, "special tasks to myself and had my own ways. My superiors fought against this singularity and they did so rightly. I was an infamous persecutor and murderer of my own life, because I fasted, prayed, watched, and tried myself beyond my powers, which was nothing but suicide." (Jurgens I, 577, 585).

Luther in his struggle to overcome his passions and attain the perfection of his priestly state seemed to forget the words of Christ: "Without Me you can do nothing." Here was his great mistake. To arrive at sanctity of life by one's own justice and the power of works alone is not only impossible, but absurd. Such a course was never advanced or advocated by the Catholic Church, and when Köstlin and other non-Catholic writers say that the Catholic teaching drove Luther to the extravagances of his distorted ascetic practices, they probably have of that teaching the same wrong idea that Luther had. "I am," he said, "a most presumptuous justifier, who trusts not in God's justice, but in my own." A true Catholic is never expected to become a "presumptuous justifier," and he never can be unless he relies too much, if not entirely, on his own merits and good works.

Luther now began to think that the sad condition of his soul resulted from the teaching of the Church on good works, while all the time he was living in direct and open opposition to the Church's doctrine and disciplinary code. Misled by the caprices of his own imagination, he became more and more subject to fits of melancholy and discouragement, so that, as he says, he even "hated God and wished that he had never been born." He would have done well had he remembered the good and sensible advice which Staupitz, his superior, gave when he said to him: "Enough, my son: you speak of sin, but know not what sin is; if you desire the assistance of God, do not act like a child any longer. God is not angry with you, but you are angry with God." The advice was certainly required in his state of intense scrupulosity, but it did not seem to have left any abiding impression on his mind. His morbid interior conflict banished all peace of soul. He was unhappy, not because he was a monk, but because, though a monk exteriorly, he never entered interiorly into the spirit of his

Rule or of his Church. A reaction was inevitable and his mind, not accustomed to self-examination and self-control, went as far as possible in the opposite direction. From extreme timidity he passed to excessive rashness. Formerly he trusted too much in his own powers and willful exertions. He perceived the absurdity and weakness of his self-reliant position and receded therefrom, entirely despairing in its help. Then, going to another extreme, he threw himself too far upon God's mercy, so far, in fact, as to renounce even cooperation with God's grace and to expect salvation without any effort or action on his own part. Thus from one absurdity he passed to another with the utmost facility. He came by degrees to believe that by reason of inherited sin, man was become totally depraved and possessed no liberty of the will. He then concluded that all human action whatever, even that which is directed towards good, being an emanation from our corrupt nature, is, in the sight of God, nothing more or less than deadly sin: therefore our actions have no influence on our salvation; we are saved "by faith alone without good works." He thought that "faith in Christ makes His merits our possession, envelops us in the garb of righteousness, which our guilt and sinfulness hide, and supplies in abundance every defect of human righteousness."

It has been long considered amongst the ill-informed that Luther inaugurated his movement against the Church of his forefathers from a desire of reform. This viewpoint is not borne out by the facts in the case. External causes played little or no part in his change of religion. The impelling motive centered in his own nature, which demanded a teaching able to assure his tormented soul of pardon of sin and ultimate salvation. Troubled with doubts as to his vocation and oppressed by "violent movements of hatred, envy, quarrelsomeness and pride," his singular self-esteem and self-reliance would not suffer him to make intelligent and enlightened use of the remedies most effectual for the cure of his abnormal spiritual maladies. Wedded to his own opinions and refusing to hear the voice of God in Catholic direction, his temptations, doubts and fears increased, as might be expected, until they drove him to despair of salvation and "plagued him with the spirit of sorrow." Tortured by the melancholy thoughts of predestination, he failed to humble himself in childlike, trustful prayer to find a way out of his spiritual troubles. He spurned the use of the approved methods of mastering spiritual difficulties, and even considered these as worthless to help in acquiring sanctity and holiness of life. Instead of overcoming such sentiments, he allowed them to develop to such an extent that an apostate spirit mastered him. Dissatisfied with the ordinary means of conquering self, he vainly thought he would find the peace of conscience he sorely needed by following his own conceptions and setting up a teaching of his own as against the traditional methods and approved theology of the ancient time-honored Catholic Church.

Led on by a spirit that was not of God, he formulated and proclaimed the blasphemous pronouncement that the Catholic Church was unable by her teaching and sacramental system to reconcile souls with God and bring comfort to those thirsting after salvation. From error to error he passed in quick succession until we find him unblushingly upholding the utter corruption of human nature because of Original Sin, denying the freedom of the will, defending the rights of reason against dogmatic authority and declaring that "reason speaks nothing but madness and foolishness." These and many other erroneous teachings, as we shall see further on, bothered him until he severed his connection with the Catholic Church and without credentials inaugurated a system of religion of his own making wherein he would be free to preach his own individual conceptions, which he thought would bring peace and happiness and comfort to struggling souls, but which ended, as sad experience attests, in conflicts, misery and despair. Was this the work of God or the work of an enemy of

God? Was this obedience to the manifest will of God in the sanctification of souls, or was it rebellion in ugliest form and with the saddest consequences? Was it reformation or was it deformation?

From out of the vast number whom the enemy of man raised up to invent heresies, which St. Cyprian says "destroy faith and divide unity," not one, or all together, ever equalled or surpassed Martin Luther in the wide range of his errors, the ferocity with which he promulgated them and the harm he did in leading souls away from the Church, the fountain of everlasting truth. The heresies of Sabellius, Arius, Pelagius and other rebellious men were insignificant as compared with those Luther formulated and proclaimed four hundred years ago and which, unfortunately, have ever since done service against the Church of the living God. In Luther most, if not all, former heresies meet, and reach their climax. To enumerate fully all the wicked, false and perverse teachings of the arch-heretic would require a volume many times larger than the Bible, and every one of the lies and falsehoods that have been used against the Catholic Church may be traced back to him as to their original formulator. When the Protestant ranks were united in a solid phalanx against the Mother Church, a lie that passed current bearing Luther's mark was good coin everywhere in heretical circles.

To get some idea of the character and extent of the false and pernicious teaching advanced by Luther, it would be necessary to spend a lifetime in the perusal of his numerous works. Amongst those that have come down to us are his Forty One Propositions, which were condemned by Leo X in his bull *Exurge Domine*, published in 1520 and found in the Bullarium of Leo X (Constit. 40), in Cochlaeus' account of Luther's proceedings and in Bernini's works. Besides the errors enumerated in the Bull of Leo X, there are a vast number of others mentioned and set forth clearly by Noel, Alexander, and Gotti, who made a special study of the various writings of Luther, particularly his treatises,

De Indulgentiis, De Reformatione, Respon. ad lib. Catharini, De Captivitate Babilonica, Contra Latomum, De Missa privata, Contra Episc. Ordinem, Contra Henricum VIII Regem, Novi Testamenti Translatio, De formula Missae et Communionis, Ad Waldenses, Contra Carlostadium, De Servo Arbitrio, Contra Anabaptistas, etc. In all these works and in some others printed in Wittenberg, we find the novel and arbitrary teachings he invented to displace, if possible, the doctrines which the Church had inherited from Christ and His Apostles. There may be seen how the primitive Christian teaching underwent, under his direction, a fundamental alteration in its most essential parts, and there also may be found the principles he laid down with an arrogance as blasphemous as it was unreasonable, for the subversion and destruction of all moral and civil order. The brazen boldness which appears on almost every page of works written to ventilate his pernicious religious and moral views has never been equalled before or since by any other enemy of the Church of God.

The Catholic Church knows that heresies must needs arise, and whilst she pities their formulators and promoters, she is always patient and forbearing. She knows their work is the work of man and, like him, destined to die. They do harm for a time. They mislead, injure and persecute while they last, but triumph they never shall. Built upon the dissolving nightmares of unhappy visionaries, their false teaching courts failure and disaster. Men, gradually through prayer and study, grow wise to the tactics of "false teachers" and organizers of "sects of perdition" and learn to beware of them, as Christ directed, for they are ranked, as St. Paul tells, amongst "murderers and idolators" "who shall not possess the Kingdom of God." A vulgar man-made form of belief can never satisfy for long the aspirations, needs, and foreshadowings of those who are in real earnest in their search for the true religion, which, by divine arrangement, was made independent of the powers of the world, and destined to continue its saving mission in spite of all opposition.

The Church of Jesus Christ can never be displaced by any or all systems of human manufacture, for they always bear on their face the stamp of error and falsehood. Built on the everlasting granite of the Petrine rock, one pebble of whose power the combined ages and nations have not succeeded in knocking from its surface, the Church has triumphed everywhere and at all times over error and its abettors. Christ said in the creation of the Church that "the gates of Hell will not prevail against her," and so speaks He every hour in her preservation. She cannot, therefore, perish and go down before the work "of sects of perdition," as St. Paul calls the organizations of religious revolutionists and anarchists. The Catholic Church is God's work, and His protecting power will ever preserve her unshaken and immovable to tell men till the last moment of time what they must believe and what they must do to gain eternal happiness.

CHAPTER 3

LUTHER AND INDULGENCES

LUTHER for some little time before his breach with the Church seemed to forget the sacred obligation he was under by reason of his doctorate to preserve Catholic orthodoxy and never in the least to depart therefrom. A great change was discernible in his spiritual life. By degrees he grew indifferent to the performance of good works and failed to meet the aims to follow the rules of monastic discipline. Neglecting to spiritualize his life by the usual and approved exercises of piety, his faith naturally weakened and grew cold and, as might be expected in such a dangerous state, he came little by little to antagonize the Church's teachings. Whether he was conscious or not of the sad condition of both soul and intellect by reason of the growing omission of his spiritual duties, he began unfortunately to find fault with certain beliefs, customs and conditions of the Church which happened to meet with his displeasure. As time went on, he grew bolder in his fault-finding and became more unduly critical and contentious. Carried away by pride and stimulated by the applause his singular methods won for him among those who longed to be freed from the requirements of Christianity, he began to denounce what he called the "buffoonery" of contemporary theologians; and conceiving himself to be the mastermind of all, he imagined that he was especially fitted to bring about a reformation of the ancient discipline of the Church and effect a sweeping change in her consecrated, fixed and accepted teachings. The course he was pursuing was characteristic of the man. As Dungersheim says: "He had always been a quarrelsome man in his way and habits," and, as his pupil Oldecop declares, "He never learnt to live at peace, and being disputatious, he was always desirous of coming off victor in differences of opinion and liked to stir up strife."

His revolutionary methods and daring innovations were fast pushing him toward the path of error. To careful observers he was becoming an object of suspicion, and among the learned of the time he was gradually losing caste and acquiring a bad name for himself on account of the growing opposition of his views to those of the Church of his forefathers. "As early as 1515," Mathesius, his pupil and first biographer, tells us, "he was already called a heretic." His rector, the famous Dr. Pollich, aware of his novel and dangerous pronouncements, is said to have given his estimate of the young professor in these words: "This monk has deep eyes; he has strange fancies and will no doubt later on disturb the teachings prevalent at the universities." Was this great scholar a prophet? Whether he was or not matters little, but of one thing we are certain, events justified the estimate formed of him.

Luther, on account of a lack of a solid systematic theological training, as well as by reason of the confusion of his mind in dealing with grave questions, together with a deficiency in real Catholic feeling, was preparing himself for revolt. He needed only time and opportunity and stubborn resolve to broach openly and give wide publicity to the strange and peculiar doctrinal views which he had secretly formed and which eventually became the fundamental articles of his new system of religion. Knowingly or unknowingly, he was preparing himself to sever his connections with the Church of his forefathers. His inward falling away from the graces of his priestly state and his trifling with most serious and sacred questions of divine faith, combined with the restless condition of his mind and attachment to his own ideas, were disposing and fitting him for a great public outbreak when he would give his novel and erroneous teachings to the world.

A favorable opportunity for airing his newfangled

notions presented itself when John Tetzel, the famous Dominican friar, was actively and zealously engaged in preaching the Indulgence granted by Pope Leo X for the construction of St. Peter's Church in Rome. This distinguished preacher no doubt would have remained but little known in history were it not for the epoch-making event in which he and Luther figured so conspicuously. Many years later Luther, in referring to the struggle which created such a great stir in the world, declared that he was drawn by force into the famous controversy and called forth unwillingly from his professorial duties into the arena of public life. He says: "I was completely dead to the world till God deemed the time had come; then Squire Tetzel excited me with the Indulgence and Doctor Staupitz spurred me on against the Pope." (*Colloquia,* ed. Bindseil, 3, p. 188). This statement, with its nasty fling at his opponent, was made years after the occurrence, when the circumstances appeared to him very different from what they really were, as we shall discover later on. Let us now pass on to the occasion which led to Luther's encounter with Tetzel.

Julius II had it brought under his notice that the ancient basilica of St. Peter, which had been given to the Church by the Emperor Constantine, was now falling into decay. He determined to use the opportunity and to employ all the architectural talent of that brilliant period in order to erect a new basilica in its place, which by its magnificence should be worthy of its position as the memorial of the great Apostle and the central church of the Catholic world. Julius II commenced the work and devoted large sums to its accomplishment. These, however, were far from sufficient, and it became evident that the cost of a building of such magnitude could be defrayed only by a successful appeal to the piety of the Christian world. Accordingly, Leo X, the successor of Julius, who died in 1513, proclaimed an Indulgence; that is to say, he granted an Indulgence of a most simple kind to all, wherever they might be, who would contribute according to their means towards the expenses of the rising edifice.

This is not the place for a detailed exposition of the Catholic doctrine of Indulgence, but it is necessary that the reader should bear in mind the official meaning of the term and what it represents. The word Indulgence in the mind of the Church signifies favor, remission or commutation. This meaning has been gradually changed by non-Catholics to convey the sense of unlawful gratification and of free scope to the passions. On this account, it happens that when some ignorant or prejudiced persons hear of the Church granting an Indulgence, the idea of license to commit sin is at once presented to their minds. This is far from the truth, for an Indulgence, as may be seen by a glance at any Catholic handbook of theology, is a total or partial remission of the temporal punishments which remain due to sin, after the guilt and eternal punishment have been forgiven. There are three things to be considered in every deadly sin: first, its guilt; second, its eternal punishment; and third, its temporal punishment. The first and second are forgiven by the Sacraments of Baptism and Penance, as the ordinary channels of pardon; the third is expiated by our sufferings and our penances, or by remission or commutation through an Indulgence.

An Indulgence, therefore, has, properly speaking, nothing to do with the guilt of, and the eternal punishment due to, mortal sin, nor does an Indulgence forgive venial sin. Much less is it a permission for the commission of future sins, as the adversaries of the Church have calumniously asserted. An Indulgence regards temporal punishment only. Many non-Catholics do not sufficiently understand the nature of an Indulgence and hence arises their misrepresentation of the doctrine. Many imagine that it forgives sin, and many more, that it is a permission to sin. They represent a man who gains a full or plenary Indulgence as one who for a certain sum of money, to be given to the pope, bishop, or priest, obtains absolution from all his crimes, without any sorrow or repentance of heart, and, at the same time, a kind of permit to sin as much as he pleases in the future. Once more, therefore, an Indulgence has nothing whatever to do with the guilt of past sins, nor their eternal punishment, much less with sins to come. And if some of the bulls or briefs regarding the grant of Indulgences speak in that strain, they are either falsified by our enemies, or else must be understood in the only Catholic sense, namely, the remission of the temporal punishments which sin deserves. Indeed, how could any honest and sensible man think the Church so silly as to contradict herself on this score? She teaches most positively that in order to obtain the pardon of sins committed after Baptism, the *only ordinary* means instituted by Jesus Christ is the Sacrament of Penance; and now, she is made to say, by the mouth and pen of our adversaries, that the Sacrament of Penance is by no means the only ordinary means, but that Indulgences, without any repentance whatsoever, will answer just as well. She says in her doctrine on confession that sorrow for sin, including a firm purpose of amendment, so firm that one should be resolved to die rather than offend Almighty God by any deadly [mortal] sin, is an absolutely necessary condition of pardon for sin; and yet in her doctrine on Indulgences she is made to say, by our adversaries, that anyone can, on paying a certain sum of money, purchase not only pardon for sins already committed, but also for such as he has a mind to commit in the future. It is important to keep in mind this explanation of an Indulgence as given by the Church in order to be guarded against those who maliciously construe her teaching to convey the sense of unlawful gratification and of free scope to the passions.

To say that an Indulgence gives a license to commit sin for money is a falsehood cut out of whole cloth. Non-Catholics who offer objections to the Church's idea of Indulgences should be careful as to how they express themselves on the question, for they profess to believe that all that the greatest sinners have to do to receive full pardon and plenary Indulgence for all their sins, past, present, and future, is to have faith. Such is the omnipotence attributed to an act by those who believe in "justification by faith alone." What hypocrisy to roll up the whites of one's eyes in a pretence of holy horror at the Catholic doctrine of Indulgences, which is severity itself compared with their sweeping act of faith which alone suffices to wash all a man's sins away, and put him at once, without penance or Purgatory, into the company of the angels in Heaven.

Now what we have to consider is whether it be true that the system of Indulgences into contact with which Luther was brought, differed in any essential particulars from our modern system. This is necessary, because the charge brought against the Catholic Church as justifying Luther's revolt from her obedience was, in its original and ancient form, that Indulgences were permissions to commit sin, or at least pretended remissions of the guilt of sin, sold in the most barefaced way, over the counter, so to speak, for sums of money, amidst degrading accompaniments. We have partially succeeded in convincing modern and more enlightened non-Catholics that this is by no means a true account of our teaching and have caused them to remodel the charge, which, as it nowadays mostly runs, is that we have altered our system from what it was in the days of Luther; that then it certainly pretended to be a sale of forgiveness for money, but that now, in deference to the outcry against such an enormity, we have revised it and cast it into a more suitable form. This, however, is not the fact. Any enlightened inquirer after truth can easily discover that in offering an Indulgence in return for alms to a good work, Leo X was acting in no way differently from the practice of the Church before or since his time. It has always been the right and the privilege of the Pope not only to grant and proclaim Indulgences, but also in dispensing these spiritual favors to stimulate and reward charitable contributions, to designate, if he so pleases, some particular object to which they may be applied, as Leo X did to carry on the sacred and splendid work of completing the erection of St. Peter's Basilica which "of temples old or altars new" now stands alone in "majesty and beauty with nothing like to it, worthiest of God, the holy and true." So far, then, we have discovered no impropriety in the Pope's action.

The bull which Leo X issued, granting a plenary Indulgence to all Christendom, reached Germany in 1515. For the preaching of this Indulgence in Germany that country was divided into three parts, with only one of which we need to concern ourselves. For the district comprising the whole of Saxony and Brandenburg this commission was divided between the guardian of the Franciscans of Mentz and Albert of Brandenburg, the newly installed archbishop of the diocese. But the guardian of the Franciscans declining to act, the entire commission passed into the hands of the Archbishop, whose office it was to see that the Indulgence was effectually made known in his district and to collect the alms of the pious donors. Albert was a young man of distinguished family, only twenty-four at the time of his appointment. He was under the usual obligation of paying the fees for his pallium, which amounted to no less a sum than thirty thousand gold florins. That there should have been such fees is quite intelligible, for the Holy See with its vast staff of officials for the conduct of a world-wide business must be supported, and it is right that those for whose benefit they are established should contribute to their upkeep. As it was not customary for the archbishops to pay the fees for the pallium out of their private sources they had to be levied on the faithful of the diocese. But this had been done twice within ten years for the immediate predecessors of Albert of Brandenburg, Archbishops Berthold and Uriel. To raise the sum a third time without a short interval seemed impossible without assistance. Wherefore, in order to afford relief to his flock, Archbishop Albert, by representing to the Pope the greatness of the crushing burdens on the revenues of the See, obtained leave to retain a portion of the proceeds of the papal indulgence to his province toward the payment of his debt. This fact suffices, in Dr. Gröne's opinion, to clear the Archbishop from the reproach of avarice cast at him by Protestant writers, who have also not failed to impute all sorts of unworthy motives to him for making choice of the Dominican, John Tetzel, as his chief sub-commissioner, or quaestor, in preaching the Indulgence.

Archbishop Albert proceeded with the greatest caution in promulgating the Indulgence. He issued a long document on the occasion, and in it he first prescribes to the preachers and their assistants the mode in which they are to conduct themselves and explains very lucidly the character and provisions of the Indulgence. In the second place he points out the nature of the grace, that is, the spiritual benefits offered. Of these the first is a "Plenary Indulgence," or plenary remission of all temporal punishment due to sin by which the pains of Purgatory are fully forgiven and blotted out. The term "plenary remission of sin" should be remarked, as it is on such a phrase that those fix who strive to make out that an Indulgence is a forgiveness of the guilt of sin. But the phrase is usual in grants of Indulgence even to this day, and means, as the expository clause just given distinctly declares, a remission of the sin as regards all its temporal punishment. In such a remission a sacramental absolution is presupposed as having taken away the guilt and eternal punishment, and it is because, by supervening on this, the Indulgence takes away likewise all the temporal punishment, that it is called a "plenary remission of sins." In the third place the Instruction of the Archbishop lays down the conditions for gaining the Plenary Indulgence. "Although," it says, "nothing can be given in exchange which will be a worthy equivalent for so great a favor, the gift and grace of God being priceless, still that the faithful may be the more readily invited to receive it, let them, *after having first made a contrite confession,* or at least having the intention of so doing at the proper time, visit at least seven churches assigned for this purpose and in each say devoutly five Our Fathers and Hail Marys in honor of the Five Wounds of Jesus Christ, by which our redemption was wrought; or else one *Miserere,* to obtain pardon for sins." The italicized clause is to be specially noticed, as proving conclusively that there was no thought of granting absolution of guilt otherwise than through the Sacrament of Penance. Another condition for the Indulgence was the contribution towards the building expenses of St. Peter's, and the Archbishop proceeds to prescribe a suitable amount according to the rank and means of the contributors. Of the poor he added specially that "those who have no money must supply by their prayers and fasts, since the Kingdom of Heaven should be made open to the poor as much as to the rich." The scale of offerings or donations laid down in the Instruction disproves the buying and selling theory. If it were true that Indulgences were offered as goods in the market, to be bought and sold, the assessments should have been uniform for all. The code of prices disappears, and that of contributions comes in, when such a scale of assignments made out according to the rank and means of the donors is borne in mind. Besides, as we have seen, the notion of price is expressly repudiated in the Archbishop's instructions.

There are some points covered in the Instruction, such as permissions to choose a confessor and grants to the priest selected of ample faculties to absolve from censures, etc., but it is not necessary to detail these as they have little bearing on the Indulgence controversy. A careful examination of Albert's Instruction to the preachers of the Indulgence will show that there is not a thought in it to which the Church at the present day would hesitate to subscribe.

"We can see now," as Fr. Smith says, "that this historical Indulgence, at all events in the form in which it was conceived by Leo X, and by his commissioner, Albert of Brandenberg, did not differ in kind, and hardly in its circumstances, from those to which we are accustomed at present. We can see, too, that the intention was to make the preaching of the Indulgence a sort of 'mission,' as we should now term it, the people being stirred up by special sermons, prayers and devotions during the period of one or two weeks, to take seriously to heart the affair of their souls, and to make a good confession and Communion. Evidently the aim was to associate the erection of a church, which was to be the head of all churches, with a grand religious awakening throughout the world. The Pope, therefore, and his commissioners must be acquitted of the blame which the attacks of Luther have heaped upon them—and this is the point of principal importance which we have desired to prove." (Smith, *Luther and Tetzel,* 18, 19).

Archbishop Albert was anxious to promote, as much as possible, the success of the pious undertaking. To help him to effect this great end, he selected John Tetzel, a Dominican friar, to whom he entrusted the actual preaching of the Indulgence, because he considered him the likeliest person he knew of on account of his eminent learning, piety and zeal in the cause of the Church and the welfare of the Holy See to stir up the religious fervor and devotion of the people. He knew that Tetzel had much experience and an uninterruptedly successful career as an Indulgence preacher during the two previous decades. He knew, moreover, that he enjoyed the renown of being one of the most popular and eloquent preachers then in Germany. His character, temperament and ability eminently fitted him to attract large congregations to hear the word of God, and to move them to contribute generously to the object advocated. The Archbishop's appointment of Tetzel as his subcommissioner is tantamount to a refutation of all the calumnies heaped upon him by his enemies, who without foundation alleged that he disregarded utterly the injunctions given him and perverted the good purpose of the Indulgence into a downright scandal.

Tetzel, on the confirmation of his appointment, entered

on his duties with his accustomed energy, activity and zeal. What he announced everywhere throughout his district and on all occasions to his hearers was in the main, be it remembered, the same doctrine as Luther quite clearly and correctly set forth regarding Indulgences in a sermon on the subject which he preached in 1516. He, like all theologians before and since his day, was careful to point out, as Grisar remarks, "that an Indulgence was to be considered merely as a remission of the temporal punishment due to sin, but not of the actual guilt of sin. He declared, quite rightly, that the erection of the Church of St. Peter was a matter of common interest to the whole Christian world, and that the donations toward it were to be looked upon as part of the pious undertakings and good works which were always required by the Church as one of the conditions for gaining an Indulgence. At the same time, in accordance with the teaching and practice of the Church, he demanded of all, as an essential preparation for the Indulgence, conversion and change of heart together with a good confession." (Grisar I, p. 328 and 328).

Towards the end of 1517, Tetzel, after having preached the Indulgence with signal success at Leipsic, Magdeburg, Halberstadt, Berlin and other places, arrived at Juterbock, a small town, only a few miles distant from Wittenberg. Into Wittenberg itself Tetzel did not enter, but the inhabitants, having heard of the reputation of the popular preacher, went off in great numbers to listen to his wonderful sermons. The very students in the new university, where Luther was one of the professors, deserted the lecture halls to hear the celebrated friar. The enthusiastic reception accorded to Tetzel augured well for the success of his mission.

Some of those who used to frequent Luther's confessional were among the crowds who went to Juterbock and they came back, it was said, refusing to give up their sins. When Luther exhorted and rebuked them, they showed him the Indulgences they had received from Tetzel and told him they had bought permission to continue in their sins, whilst nevertheless being assured of immunity from guilt and punishment. This is the traditional story that has for long done service against the Church, but as Fr. Smith aptly remarks, "a very decisive argument entitles us to dismiss it at once. Luther, as we are about to see, presently framed his indictment against Tetzel and it does not, remember, contain a word of suggestion that the latter undertook to forgive future sins. Presumedly what happened was much more simple. Those who were wont to attend Luther's confessional at Wittenberg, on this occasion went to the neighboring town to gain the Indulgence. If Luther were already set against the doctrine of Indulgences, the natural effect of such an incident would have been to stir the bile of so excitable a person, and that this was in reality his doctrinal position at the time is clear from a sermon which he forthwith delivered at the Castle Church. For in it he denounced not only Tetzel, but the formalism into which the system of Indulgences had degenerated, as well as the very doctrine itself which the Catholic Church holds still as she ever has held. It cannot be proved from Scripture, he says, that Divine Justice demands of the sinner any other penance or satisfaction save reformation of heart. He denied that satisfaction was part of the Sacrament of Penance. He denied that anything beyond contrition was needed for the remission of sin. This denial of temporal punishment for sin and the necessity of it as satisfaction for sin of course left no place for any Indulgence or commutation of it. As he denied the Indulgence to be of any avail to the living, he also declared it to be fruitless when applied to the dead. He maintained that even after receiving the Sacrament of Penance, the gaining of the Indulgence plunged the Christian back into the filth of his sin. With tirades against the schoolmen, he urged his hearers to disregard Indulgences, and give any alms they had to spare, not to the building of St. Peter's, but to the poor." The famous sermon that opened the war on the Church is a specimen of Luther's style. There is no accurate reasoning, no grasp of the subject, but plenty of violent declamation. Tetzel's reply was the plain, distinct utterance of a theologian. (Smith, *Luther and Tetzel,* 20, 26). Luther's retort was characteristic: "I laugh at your words as I do at the braying of an ass; instead of water I recommend to you the juice of the grape; and instead of fire, inhale, my friend, the smell of a roast goose. I am at Wittenberg. I, Doctor Martin Luther, make it known to all inquisitors of the faith, bullies and rocksplitters, that I enjoy here abundant hospitality, an open house, a well-supplied table, and marked attention; thanks to the liberality of our duke and prince, the Elector of Saxony." (Löscher's *Reformations-Akten,* vol. II, p. 537).

Mark the language of the Reformer, and then see how difficult it is to believe that such a one could have been raised up by God to guide men in the way of salvation.

This attack on the Indulgence-preacher and the doctrine of Indulgences was in a short time afterwards followed up by a document in which Luther formulated his new creed and embodied his notably changed views and singular opinions. Although he had promised his bishop, who was aware of his peculiar views, that he would not publish for general notice his new-fangled notions on Indulgences, Luther, with an hypocrisy and instability that does not generally rank as a mark of sanctity or divine mission, nevertheless did publish them, for forthwith he prevailed on the porter of his monastery to affix on the doors of the Castle Church his famous Theses, ninety-five in number, mostly bearing on Indulgences, but scarcely one raising a solid objection. This occurred on the eve of All Saints 1517, when the Castle Church began the celebration of its titular feast. The yearly commemorative services naturally drew a vast concourse of devout worshippers. Time and place lent themselves to a wide publication of the Saxon monk's novel doctrines. Beyond this challenge to all opposers to meet him in the arena of theological disputation, there was nothing extraordinary in the incident. When we consider that the custom of publicly challenging scholars to learned disputations was in accordance with the custom of the times, we fail to find in the nailing of his Theses to the church notice boards that act of "exceptional" and "heroic courage" over which many of his friends are still wont to go into ecstasy, nor do we think that the man himself was in the least conscious at the time how far the ball he set a rolling would develop into an avalanche. He was simply availing himself of a custom among scholars of those days to play a crafty game. Relying on his skill in debate, he looked forward to a victory over Tetzel and to an opening for commencing the war against some abuses he had heard of connected with the preaching of the Indulgence. He was much disappointed that no one came forward to dispute the questions he had raised, and he was much hurt to find his friends and intimates very silent about the matter. "The ninety-five sledge-hammer strokes delivered at the grossest ecclesiastical abuse of the age," as Lindsay, the non-Catholic writer, calls Luther's Theses, terrified nobody. They only emphasized the boldness and rashness of their author in abandoning teachings he once firmly held and in attacking the doctrines of a world-wide institution like the Catholic Church.

The well-instructed Catholic who examines Luther's theses will discover at once some erroneous, some inconsistent with others, some merely satirical cuts at the Holy See; some are merely puerile. For the most part they are full of contradictions and obscurities, and lack precision in expression to such an extent as to show lamentable deficiency in theological training. Lindsay, a non-Catholic and an admirer of Luther, declares rightly: "The Theses are not a reasoned treatise"; and Beard, another non-Catholic, says: "They impress the reader as thrown together somewhat in haste rather than showing carefully digested thought and deliberate theological intention; they bear him out one moment into the audacity of rebellion and then carry him back to the obedience of conformity." (Beard 218, 219).

The tone in which the Theses were written indicates that they were not, as he declared, advanced as tentative propositions, but that they were considered by their author as settled beforehand and irrefutable. In a letter he wrote at this time to the Bishop of Brandenburg he declared his absolute submission and his readiness to follow the Catholic Church in everything, but, at the same time, he wanted it to be known quite clearly that "in his opinion nothing could be advanced against his Theses neither from Holy Scripture, Catholic doctrine or Canon Law, with the exception of the utterances of some few canonists, who spoke without proofs, and of some of the scholastic Doctors who cherished similar views, but who also were unable to demonstrate anything." Though his language in some of the theses is comparatively guarded, he nevertheless puts forward certain opinions which show plainly enough that he means to go straight into combat with the Catholic Church. Many of the Theses, says Fr. Grisar (Vol. I, p. 331), "from the theological point of view go far beyond a mere opposition to the abuse of Indulgences. Luther, stimulated by contradiction, had, to some extent, altered his previous views on the nature of Indulgences and brought them more into touch with the fundamental principles of his erroneous theology."

"A practical renunciation of Indulgences, as it had been held up to that time, is to be found in the Theses, where Luther states that Indulgences have no value in God's sight, but are merely to be regarded as the remission by the Church of the canonical punishment. (Theses 5, 20, 21, etc.) This destroys the theological meaning of Indulgences, for they had always been considered as a remission of the temporal punishment of sin, but as a remission which held good before the Divine Judgment seat. (Cp. Nos. 19, 20 and 21 of the 41 propositions of Luther condemned in 1520). In some of the Theses (58-60) Luther likewise attacks the generally accepted teaching with regard to the Church's treasury of grace, on which Indulgences are based. Erroneous views concerning the state of purgation of the departed occur in some of the propositions. (18, 19, 29). Others appear to contain what is theologically incorrect and connected with his opinion regarding grace and justification; this opinion is not, however, clearly set forth in the list of theses."

"Many of the statements are irritating, insulting and cynical observations on Indulgences in general, no distinction beng made between what was good and what was perverted. Thus, for example, Thesis 66 declares "the treasures of Indulgences" to be simply nets "in which the wealth of mankind is caught." Others again scoff and mock at the authority of the Church, as, for example, Thesis 86, "Why does not the Pope, who is as rich as Croesus, build St. Peter's with his own money, rather than with that of poor Christians?" Now the Pope was not building a private chapel for himself, but a basilica for the whole Christian world. Another thesis declared: "Christians should be taught that he who gives to the poor, or assists the needy, does better than he who purchases Indulgences." It was the old argument of the traitor Judas, who asked: "Why was not this ointment sold for three hundred pence and given to the poor? Now he said this not because he cared for the poor." (*Jn.* 12:5-6).

This brief sketch of Luther's Theses gives the reader a slight conception of their nature, aim and scope. Ostensibly they were levelled against the alleged abuses of the papal Indulgences, but attacks on the doctrine itself, as well as on the authority of the Pope, were so insidiously and maliciously intermingled therein that it was evident to the discerning that they were not proposed as he claimed, "out of love and zeal for the ascertaining of the truth."

At first many of the learned of the day were inclined to regard Luther's challenge as one of the petty monastic intellectual squabbles which Germany frequently produced. Tetzel, however, did not consider the matter as a mere academic dispute, as Luther alleged, for "defining and elucidating truth." With his clear mind he saw plainly that the discussion which Luther wished to arouse involved a deep and significant attack covertly made against the whole penitential system of the Church, its teaching, its practice, and its authority. He recognized, moreover, the extremes Luther would be driven to by his false principles and the fatal results they were bound to produce on the masses. In the tone of a prophet he declared that many, on account of Luther's novel opinions, would contemn the authority and power of the Pope and the Roman See, would intermit the works of sacramental satisfaction, would no longer believe their pastors and teachers, but would explain, every one for himself, the Sacred Scriptures according to private fancy and whim and believe just what they might choose, to the great detriment of souls throughout Christendom, and the integrity of the Christian deposit of faith.

Luther's Theses were so pointedly directed against the doctrine of Indulgences and against the preachers that it was impossible for Tetzel to pass them over in silence. However, before taking action on so critical an occasion he sought the counsel of his archbishop and of his old friend and former professor, Dr. Wimpina. They directed him to reply to Luther's ninety-five Theses; and presently there appeared a set, or rather two sets of theses, Anti-theses they were called: one set of one hundred and six Theses being a counter statement of the doctrine of Indulgences, the other of fifty Theses on the Papal power to grant them. These Theses were drawn up for Tetzel by his old professor and showed a thorough understanding of the doctrine of Indulgences.

Tetzel assumed all responsibility for the propositions, which in the clearest and most lucid manner set forth the true Catholic doctrine of Indulgences and of the absolute necessity of repentance, confession and satisfaction required for the pardon of sin. These propositions are so forcible that we do not know where a theologian could go for a more satisfying defence of Indulgences against current Protestant difficulties. They affirmed that, though an Indulgence exempts the sinner from the vindicatory penalties of the Church, it leaves him just as much bound as ever to submit to her medicinal ones; that it does not derogate from the merits of Christ, since its whole efficacy is due to the merits of Christ, since its whole efficacy is due to the atoning Passion of Christ; as also that the Pope has power only by means of suffrage to apply the benefits of an Indulgence to souls in Purgatory. Moreover, to say that the Pope cannot absolve the least venial sin is erroneous; and equally so to deny that all vicars of Christ have the same power as Peter had; rather to assert that Peter, in the matter of Indulgences, had more power than they, is both heretical and blasphemous.

The descriptions of the Indulgence preacher as given by Hecht, Vögel, Hoffmann and other partisan writers are so full of obloquy founded on garbled quotations and falsified facts, that we are prepared to find in Tetzel's Theses the brutal, reckless and ignorant utterances of a buffoon. This is wide of the truth. What we do find is a calm and scientific theological statement, quite remarkable for its force and lucidity. His Theses are a luminous refutation of Luther's. They were so ably and brilliantly defended that about the end of April, 1518, the University of Frankfort-on-the-Oder, in recognition of the Dominican's learning, conferred upon him the degree of Doctor of Divinity.

Tetzel thoroughly grasped both the nature and the complexity of his duties in the confutation of Luther's errors. Sobriety pervades every line of his propositions, and dignified self-repression marks all his utterances in the defense of truth. He was made the victim of many outrageous charges, but there is no trace of irritation in his speech. Without sarcasm and without pronouncing anything personally offensive to his opponent, he takes up the doctrinal points one after another and in serious, enlightened, and dignified language, as becomes the teacher of God's truth, explains and defends them with clearness, force, and directness. It is only as he draws to the close of his marvelous confutation that he deigns to notice the charges so unjustly flung at him. Then he refers to them in the fewest and most becoming words. He says: "For one who has never heard them, to declare in public Theses that the Indulgence-preachers employ scandalous language before the people, and take up more time in explaining Indulgences than in expounding the Gospel, is to scatter lies picked up from others, to spread fictions in place of truths, and to show oneself light-minded and credulous, and is to fall into mischievous error." Here we think we have a true account of what happened. There were plenty of mischief-makers to concoct scandalous stories if they were likely to be listened to, and Luther had shown a readiness to welcome this kind of slander, if not to add to it from his own imagination, and the poor Indulgence-preacher was the sufferer.

Luther would not be silenced. The overweaning opinions he entertained of himself and of his own abilities made him set at naught every correct and accepted exposition of the authority of tradition and the binding force of the teaching of the Church. The defenders of truth, no matter how learned or approved they might be, were all despised when they were not in agreement with his newly formulated viewpoints on the question of Indulgences. He scoffed at all defense of the right and the true, and, as he said in his usual uncouth way, he cared as little for it as for "the braying of an ass." Such was the way in which he always endeavored to expose his adversaries, however exalted they might be in station or venerable for character and learning, to the low merriment of the people; and it was a very important element in attracting the rabble to his side. The mob is ever ready to hail with delight anyone who champions freedom from the requirements of Christianity. Some of his friends, among whom were learned theologians, saw with sorrow the downward course he was pursuing and begged him to discontinue his antagonism to the Church's teachings and practices. All their kindly admonitions were disregarded, and he continued even more than before to reprobate, denounce and misrepresent the Church's doctrines and usages.

It is interesting to note that later on, in looking back over the days that were gone, Luther had the audacity to state that he "hardly knew what an Indulgence was." In two different places in his pamphlet entitled *Hans Worst,* written about 1541, when he was blinded by rage against the Church, he solemnly declared that, "As truly as Our Lord Jesus Christ has redeemed me I did not know what an Indulgence was." (Erlanger, 26, 50, 51). This statement, notwithstanding the sacred affirmation with which he introduces it, is to say the least, of very doubtful veracity. To express himself in this way is, however, rather a poor compliment for a professor and a Doctor of Theology to pay to himself, nor can it be considered as very prudent that a man should talk about and inveigh against things of which he confesses his ignorance. Indeed, he could hardly have meant what he said had he recalled at the moment the teachings and sermons of his earlier days, when he held and asserted with absolute conviction the mind of the Church on the doctrine of Indulgences. If Luther, however, was really ignorant of the matter, he had plenty of opportunities of learning the unadulterated teaching of the Church. He could have been accommodated within the walls of his own university. The nature of Indulgences was clearly defined in ordinary manuals for the use of the clergy, then in print, such as the *Discipulus de Eruditione Christi Fidelium* issued at Cologne in 1504, and many other learned theological works. Luther, however, needed no enlightenment on the subject. He knew what an Indulgence was, its nature, its authority, its place in the spiritual order, and was quite familiar with its practice in the Church. He knew that an Indulgence was simply a remission in whole or in part, through the superabundant merits of Jesus Christ and His saints, of the temporal punishment due to God on account of sin after the guilt and eternal punishment have been remitted in the Sacrament of Penance. He knew that it gave no license to commit sin of any kind or in any form. He knew that no abuse could affect an Indulgence in itself, that an Indulgence is legitimate apart from an abuse, and that it would be a sacrilegious crime in anyone whomsoever, from the Pope down to the most humble layman, to be concerned in buying or selling Indulgences. He knew that Indulgences were never bartered for money in Germany or elsewhere for sins yet to be committed. He knew they were not marketable commodities and that no traffic or sale of Indulgences was ever authorized or countenanced by the authorities of the Church. He knew all this as well as any enlightened member of the Church in his day, for he studied the whole ins-and-outs of the matter in his earlier career. His onslaught on Indulgences was not made from any lack of knowledge of their meaning and value.

Luther had a purpose in view, and all his attacks on Indulgences were intended only as a cloak to conceal the real scheme he nursed in his rebellious heart. He might, if he would, help to correct whatever wrong was noticeable at the time, but instead of aiding the cause of right, he willfully and maliciously preferred to profit by the blunders of some imprudent underlings to advance his nefarious designs, which aimed at nothing less than the weakening and eventual destruction of the power and authority of the Holy See. He now began adroitly enough to throw the blame of whatever irregularities existed on the doctrine itself, not only to make Indulgences odious, but indirectly to discredit the Pope who granted them. By a process of false reasoning he persuaded himself to think that "Indulgences are not of faith, because not taught in the Bible, not taught by Christ and His Apostles; they emanate," he said, "only from the Pope." He thought that this pronouncement, which included the exclusive value of the Bible as the rule of faith, was incontrovertible. He little dreamt, however, that in advancing this erroneous doctrine he was passing sentence on himself as an apostate and a heretic. He must now be compelled to come out more in the open and declare himself more explicitly. To do this it was necessary to prove that besides the truths explicitly declared in Holy Writ there are other truths in the Church which its members are equally bound to believe and that they comprise all those doctrines relating to faith which are defined as such by the Apostolic See.

Much of the greater part of the guffaws Luther, at this time, received from princes, nobles, robber knights, debauched scholars and the mob, was due to the insidious attacks he made on the authority of the Holy See and its legitimate head. Tetzel was keen enough to notice this, and he determined in the interests of truth and respect for legitimate ecclesiastical authority to meet the situation. Accordingly, as noted before, he issued about the end of April, 1518, fifty Theses on the power of the Pope to show "that he alone possesses the right to decide the true sense and meaning of Scripture; that what is true and of faith about Indulgences, only the Pope can decide; that the Church has many Catholic truths which are neither expressly declared in the canon of Scripture, nor explicitly stated by the Church Fathers; that all doctrines relating to faith and defined as such by the Apostolic See are to be reckoned among Catholic truths, whether or not they are contained explicitly in the Bible." These propositions were strictly in the spirit of the scholastic theology in vogue at the time, and served to raise the contention to the plane of principle.

Luther was now challenged to come out in the open and declare himself clearly on the Pope's authority in matters of faith and practice. He at once perceived what a stumbling block Tetzel had thrown in his way. He did not attempt to dispute or contradict Tetzel's Fifty Theses. Had he done so he must have plainly acknowledged himself a heretic, cut himself off from all escape and had no other choice left than that of either being punished as a heretic or making a recantation. As matters stood this would have been premature, would have spoiled all, would have ruined him and his cause. He was not prepared as yet to enter finally on the terrible tragedy of open rebellion against the Church of God.

Tetzel, as the *Dublin Review* further remarks, had not designated Luther personally as a heretic. But Luther chose to assume that he had done so and forthwith let loose a storm against Tetzel of such brutal and malignant invective as Luther alone was capable of. Adopting the tone of an injured man, a man shamefully misunderstood, he filled Germany with hypocritical asseverations of his orthodoxy and his devotion to the See of Peter. All his party followed in the pseudo-Liberator's wake. The heathen-minded humanists, with Ulrich Von Hutten, the notoriously unprincipled libertine, at their head, were especially active in denouncing and maligning Tetzel. They singled him out as a butt of their ribald satire, holding him up to scorn and execration as the very impersonation of every imaginable monastic abuse and scandal. (Vol. V, 844). They used every conceivable means known to the abandoned and ignoble to besmirch the character, reputation and influence of Tetzel. They proclaimed everywhere to ignorant and unthinking crowds that "the avaricious monk," as they designated him, "sold grace for money at the highest price he could," that he used offensive statements respecting the Blessed Virgin, and that he magnified the effects of the Indulgence by the use of unseemly comparisons, all to "ring the money into the papal coffer in the hope of freeing souls from Purgatory's sufferings." They put the most horrid blasphemies into his mouth, so horrid that we would be ashamed to reproduce them here. Plenty of mud was flung at Tetzel, and unfortunately much of it at the time stuck and has done service ever since. The story of Tetzel and his chest, along with many others of a still more profane description, are still told to the incredulous although they have been time and again refuted. Scholars of repute nowadays dare not repeat or reassert the absurd infamies. The testimony against such a course is too overwhelming to risk exposure and defeat.

The campaign of lies, slander and calumny inaugurated and carried on unceasingly by Luther and his quarrelsome allies preyed upon the sensitive spirit of the gifted preacher, and gradually his health gave away. Wounded by the rude and unchristian treatment he received at the hands of unscrupulous enemies, and deeply affected by the sight of the mischief which had been wrought by the religious revolution he was the first to foresee, he retired to the pious seclusion of his monastery, where after a short while he died, not in disgrace, as his malefactors allege, but from a broken heart due to the persecution he had suffered. His death occurred on August 11, 1519, and he was buried before the High Altar of the Dominican Church at Leipzic.

"Tetzel could not have set up a better monument to his own character," writes Dr. Gröne, "than he did in the grief and affliction which hastened his end. The ruin of the Church, the wild infidelity and unspeakable disorders which the triumph of Luther must needs entail on Germany—this was the worm that gnawed his vital thread. It broke his heart to be forced to see how the sincere champions of the old Church truths were left alone, were slandered, despised and misunderstood by their own party, while the mockers and revilers of the immutable doctrine won applause on all sides."

"History," says the *Catholic Encyclopedia,* "presents few characters more unfortunate and pathetic than Tetzel. Among his contemporaries the victim of the most corrosive ridicule, every foul charge laid at his door, every blasphemous utterance placed in his mouth, a veritable literature of fiction and fable built about his personality, in modern history held up as a proverbial mountebank and oily harlequin, denied even the support and sympathy of his own allies—Tetzel had to await the light of modern critical scrutiny, not only for a moral rehabilitation, but also for vindication as a soundly trained theologian and a monk of irreproachable deportment." (Paulus, *Johann Tetzel,* Mainz, 1899; Hermann, *Johann Tetzel,* Frankfort, 1882; Gröne, *Tetzel und Luther,* Soest, 1860).

To describe the Dominican friar as the cause of the whole movement which began in 1517 is, in view of the facts, the merest legend. "Notwithstanding the efforts," as Grisar says, "which Luther made to represent the matter in this or a similar light, it has been clearly proved that his own spiritual development was the cause, or at least the principal cause. Other factors cooperated more or less. His false ideas on grace and justification and good works, and his determination to put a stop to the abuses connected with Indulgences, led him in 1517 to make a general attack, even though partly veiled, on the whole ecclesiastical system of Indulgences."

If we keep this in view we can easily understand what Luther wrote to his dying antagonist in the hope of affording him some consolation when he was suffering keenly from the reproaches the Reformer heaped upon him. In this letter Luther says: "You need not trouble and distress yourself, for the matter did not begin with you. This child, indeed, had quite another father." (De Wette, Seidemann, 6, 18). He himself was that father. He started the controversy, being, says his pupil Oldecop, "by nature proud and audacious." At the outset of the trouble, it was stated that as soon as Luther heard from Staupitz at Grimma of Tetzel's behavior, he exclaimed: "Please God, I will knock a hole in his drum." This saying has done service for the longest time, but no scholar today rehearses it because it lacks all basis of veritable data. Luther's rebellion against the Church would have taken place if no Indulgence had been promulgated or if Tetzel had never been born.

In due time Archbishop Albert submitted Luther's Theses

to his board of consultors at Aschaffenburg and to the professors of the University of Mayence. All the examiners gave the Theses long and careful study. After due deliberation they concluded, as a result of their findings, that the Theses were of an heretical character and that proceedings against their author should be taken. A report of their examination and the conclusions arrived at, together with a copy of the Theses, were then regularly forwarded to the Holy See. It will thus be seen that the first judicial proceeding against Luther did not emanate from Tetzel, as some authors falsely allege.

This action on the part of the authorities did not please Luther, as he was anxious to continue as long as possible in good favor with the Pope. Shortly after he learned of the official proceeding he wrote to his friend Langus and styled the Archbishop and the others who examined and condemned his propositions, "Buffoons and Earthworms." The calling of names, as we see, was no trouble to this disappointed man. Rome was slow and lenient in her action. Perhaps the Pope was right in favoring delay. Under date of Trinity Sunday, May 30, 1518, Luther wrote to Leo X a letter professing the utmost respect for His Holiness and declaring that he submitted himself in the grave circumstances unreservedly to his decision. With his wonted disingenuousness he said of his Theses and strange doctrines: "They are disputations, not doctrines, not dogmas, set out as usual in an enigmatical form; yet could I have foreseen it, I should certainly have taken part on my side, that they should be more easy to understand. Were I such a man as they wish me to appear, and all things had not been rightly handled by me in the course of disputation, it could not be that the most illustrious Prince Frederick, Duke of Saxony, Elector of the Empire, would permit such a pest in his university, pre-eminent as he is for his attachment to the Catholic apostolic truth. Wherefore, most blessed Father, I offer myself prostrate at the feet of your Holiness and give myself up to you with all that I am or have: quicken, slay, call, recall, approve, reprove, as shall please thee. It rests with your Holiness to promote or prevent my undertaking, to declare it right or wrong. Whatever happens, I recognize the voice of your Holiness as that of Christ abiding and speaking in thee. If I deserve death, I do not refuse to die." (Consult Knaake, in *Werke,* Weim. ed., I, p. 522). A more complete expression of submission to the judgment of the Apostolic See could hardly be formulated, but Luther's actions thereafter did not correspond with his language. The insincerity manifested in his letter to Leo X can be explained only by the uncommon duplicity of his character.

Very shortly after this letter to Leo X, owing to a variety of circumstances, especially the troubles which menaced Germany on account of the religious dissensions then existing, Emperor Maximilian formally denounced the agitator to the Holy See. Luther was immediately cited to appear at Rome within sixty days to answer before judges appointed by His Holiness in regard to the doctrines he had put forth. The Elector of Saxony, the ruling sovereign of the country to which Luther belonged, in the meantime requested the Pope to dispense with his personal appearance in answer to the citation and asked that instead of going to Rome he might be allowed to answer for himself before a Cardinal Legate in Germany. Rome consented and Cardinal [St.] Cajetan, a man remarkable for his erudition and greatly beloved by the workingmen of Rome because he had espoused their cause against the usurers, was detailed to give Luther a hearing and to endeavor to call him back from his errors. The Cardinal met Luther at Augsburg on October 11, 1518. All patient and condescending, he exhorted Luther to renounce his errors and to return like a repenting child to his mother, the Church. Luther professed a willingness to disavow any expressions if the legate convinced him that they were erroneous, but the Nuncio was not to be led into any dispute. He told the willful man that he was there to receive the renunciation of his errors, not to argue. "What error have I taught?" asked Luther. Cardinal Cajetan presented two errors. First, "That the merits of Christ are not the treasures of Indulgences." Second, "That faith alone is sufficient for salvation." He showed decisions of the Holy See covering the ground and again called on Luther to renounce his errors. The kind offices of the Cardinal were useless, and the meeting terminated without beneficial results. Luther, however, asked for a delay of three days, which was granted. On the morning following the conversation with the Cardinal, he sent a protest to his Eminence, declaring that he "had never intended to teach anything offensive to Catholic doctrine, to the Holy Scriptures, to the authority of the Fathers or to the decrees of the Pope." Luther did not wait for the expiration of the time he requested. He departed from Augsburg in secrecy, and in a few days afterward he gave the world another proof of his duplicity, having affixed to the gate of the Carmelite monastery where he had lodged, an appeal to the effect that if he had attacked Indulgences, it was because they were not enjoined by God. His judges, he averred, were not to be trusted; he had not gone to Rome, because there, where justice once abided, homicide now dwelt. Finally, he "appealed from the Pope ill-informed to the Pope better-instructed."

One more attempt was made by Rome later on to settle the matter without coming to extremes. A second legate was sent to Germany. Charles Miltiz, a young Saxon nobleman in minor orders who had spent some years in Rome, was chosen for the office. The appointment was unfortunate and abortive. Miltiz lacked the prudence, tact, energy and straightforwardness his difficult mission demanded. He, however, drew from Luther an act which if it "is no recantation, is at least remarkably like one." (Beard 274). "In it he promised to observe silence if his assailants did the same; complete submission to the Pope; to publish a plain statement to the public advocating loyalty to the Church; and to place the whole vexatious cause in the hands of a delegated bishop." The meeting closed with a banquet and embraces, tears of joy and a kiss of peace, only to be disregarded and ridiculed afterwards by Luther. This interview took place at Altenburg in the beginning of the year 1519.

Shortly after this meeting on March 3, 1519, Luther addressed another letter to the Pope, overflowing as usual with expressions of the greatest loyalty and most perfect submission. In it, amongst other things, he calls God and man to witness that he has never wished and does not now desire to touch the Roman Church or the Pope's sacred authority; and that he acknowledges most explicitly that this Church rules over all and that nothing in Heaven or in earth is superior to it, save only Jesus Christ Our Lord." (De Wette, I, 233, ff.). Only two weeks before he made this pronouncement calling God and man to witness his words, he wrote to his friend Scheurl: "I have often said that hitherto I have only been playing. Now at last we shall have to act seriously against Roman authority and against Roman arrogance." (De Wette I, 230). This detestable hypocrisy is further confirmed when ten days after sending to the Pope the letter of March 3rd, he declared to his friend Spalatinus: "I do not mind telling you, between ourselves, that I am not sure whether the Pope is Antichrist himself or only his apostle." (De Wette I, 239).

A terrible struggle was now going on in Luther. His mind was divided between his still remaining respect for ecclesiastical authority on the one hand, and his personal pride and attachment to his own opinions on the other. At a later period of his life he said of himself that he was "in such a state of mind at this time as to be almost out of his senses; that he was scarcely conscious whether he were awake or asleep; and that it was not without a severe struggle and great difficulty that he finally conquered his conviction that he ought to 'hear the Church.'" As late as the 15th of January, 1520, a copy of his *Protestatio* was sent to the newly elected Emperor, in which he declared that he would die a true and obedient son of the Catholic Church and expressed his willingness to submit to the decision of all the universities whose impartiality could not be suspected. (Erl. 24, 9 ff.). But in proportion as he found the authority of the Church and of learned universities ranged against him, exactly in the same proportion did his adhesion to his own opinions grow more and more obstinate.

Luther seemed not to be able to free himself from his errors. As time went on he grew bolder in his assertions and astonished his friends by advancing even more daring absurdities. In his advanced system, denying dogma after dogma, there was no longer room for Indulgences and Confession, nor for Purgatory, nor for honoring any saint, since there are no saints, but all remain corrupt for all eternity, only the corruption is covered by the cloak of Christ's merits. Man, he says, since the fall of our first parents had not possessed any liberty whatever, and that his works whether good or bad, were always offensive to God. He could not see that in denying human liberty he was expressing an opinion that is not only as false as it is repugnant to common sense, but moreover one that is offensive not only to God but also to His creatures. To secure the support of the masses, he flattered these by declaring that "all Christians are priests, all have equal authority to interpret the Bible for themselves, and there is no difference among the baptized, priest, bishop, pope, except the offices assigned to some." Nor did he forget the secular princes, who were impervious to all religious impulses and whose support he was endeavoring to secure before his final breach with the Church, for to them he announced the flattering teaching: "For as much as the temporal power is ordained of God to punish the wicked and to protect the good, therefore it must be allowed to do its work unhindered on the whole Christian body, without respect to persons, whether it strike popes, bishops, priests, monks, nuns or whom it will." "The secular power," he maintained, "should summon a free council" which "should reorganize the constitution of the Church from its foundation and must liberate Germany from the Roman robbers, from the scandalous, devilish rule of the Romans." "It is stated," he adds, "that there is no finer government in the world than that of the Turks, who have neither a spiritual nor a secular code of law, but only their Koran. And it must be acknowledged that there is no more disagreeable system of rule than ours, with our Canon Law and our Common Law, whilst no class any longer obeys either natural reason or the Holy Scripture." (Coppens, *Prot. Ref.* p. 29).

When this teaching of Luther, given in part only, is considered, it is easily seen he was no longer a Catholic, although he continued to celebrate Mass at Catholic altars and maintained that he was sound in the faith. No wonder that Duke George, astonished and provoked at the bold heretical assertions of the insolent monk, exclaimed in an angry voice, "This man's teaching is dangerous." The arbitrating universities of Cologne and Louvain, together with that of Paris, condemned his teaching and declared it heretical. Luther had shortly before looked upon these judges as "his masters in theology"; he now called them "mules and asses, epicurean swine." Rome finally discussed Luther's new doctrines with patient care and critical calmness, and was, at last, compelled to denounce them as "eccentric, radical and untenable."

There was a limit to the patience of Leo X. The gentle and learned Pope pitied the venom, hatred and indomitable stubbornness and pride of Luther, but considering the disturbed condition of religious affairs created in Germany by the agitator's misguided efforts and the religious pantheistical mysticism his system was engendering, he was compelled to act in the interest of peace and truth. He accordingly issued a Bull (1520), written in a tone rather of paternal affliction than of just severity, in which the unfortunate man's errors were denounced in forty-one propositions, some of which were qualified as evidently heretical and others as rash and scandalous. "Imitating the clemency of the Almighty," Leo says, "who wills not the death of a sinner, but that he should be converted and live, we shall forget all injuries done to us and the Apostolic See, and we shall do all we can to make him give up his errors. By the depths of God's mercy and the blood of Our Lord Jesus Christ, shed for the Redemption of man and the foundation of the Church, we expect and pray Luther and his followers to cease disturbing the peace, the unity, and the power of the Church." Thus speaks the generous heart of the Pope, who apparently suffers while he is compelled to chastise a rebellious son and declare him excommunicated unless he should retract his errors at the expiration of sixty days.

Luther's pride would not suffer him to submit. His separation from the Church, her doctrine, her public worship and her constitution was complete. Branded now as a heretic, his wrath no longer knew any bounds of moderation. He immediately issued an insolent diatribe entitled *Against the Execrable Bull of Antichrist.* (Erl. opp. Lat. var. argum. 5, 132, s. 99). "At length," he says, "thanks to the zeal of my friends, I have seen this bat in all its beauty. In truth, I know not whether the Papists are joking. This must be the work of John Eck, the man of lies and iniquities, the accursed heretic. . . I maintain that the author of this Bull is Antichrist: I curse it as a blasphemy against the Son of God. . . I trust that every Christian who accepts this Bull will suffer the torments of Hell. . . See how I retract, daughter of a Soap Bull. . . It is said that the donkey sings badly, simply because he pitches his voice on too high a key. Certainly, this Bull would sound more agreeable, were its blasphemies not directed against Heaven. Where are you, emperors, kings and princes of the earth, that you tolerate the hellish voice of Antichrist? Leo X and you, the Roman Cardinals, I tell you to your faces. . . Renounce your satanic blasphemies against Jesus Christ."

Luther followed up this imprecation and invective on

Rome by publicly burning on the 10th day of December, 1520, at the eastern gate of Wittenberg, opposite the Church of the Holy Cross, in the presence of many students, who jeered and sang ribald drinking songs, the Bull of Leo X and all his writings, together with the works of St. Thomas Aquinas and other Catholic theologians. On the day after this contemptuous exhibition, Luther preached to the people and said: "Yesterday I burned in the public square the devilish works of the Pope; and I wish that it was the Pope, that is, the Papal See, that was consumed. If you do not separate from Rome, there is no salvation for your souls."

The Gospel of Luther is now set up against the Gospel of the good and gentle Jesus. Introduced in hatred of the Pope and with the vain promise of salvation to all who abandon him whom the Master appointed to preserve the unity and well-being of His Church, it went on its course of protestation with little avail, for the Church of Christ still remains, and the offices of Peter to instruct in sound doctrine still continues and will to the end of time.

Luther, whilst he was presumably a member of the Church, denounced Indulgences in the bitterest terms, much to the delight of all his followers. But when from a reformer he becomes a revolutionist and without credentials or authority started his own church, he has nothing to say concerning the notorious scandals that disgraced its career. He was, on the contrary, most kindly disposed toward it. As every student of history knows, he tried his hand at dispensations and granted many of which the Catholic Church was never guilty. Thus, for example, he dispensed himself and Katherine Von Bora from their vows of celibacy; he dispensed every husband from his fidelity to marital vows in his shameless utterance in a public sermon, *"Si nolit domina, veniat ancilla."* ["If the mistress of the house is unwilling, let the maid come."]. (Sermon *De Matrimonio*). He gave a dispensation to Philip of Hesse to commit bigamy, and his reward was a "fuder" of wine and a protection of Protestantism. (Briefwichsel Landgraf

Philip. edit. Lenz. I, 362, f.). Bucer, who was a party to that heathenish, infamous concession, admits that "The whole Reformation was one grand indulgence for libertinism." Here are his words: "The greater part of the people seem only to have embraced the gospel in order to shake off the yoke of discipline and the obligation of fasting and penance, which rested upon them in popery, and that they may live according to their own pleasure, enjoying their lusts and lawless appetites without control. That was the reason they lent a willing ear to the teaching of justification by faith alone and not by good works, for the latter of which they had no relish." (Bucer, *De Regn.* I, c. I, 4). Bucer's words ought to bring the blush of shame to the face of all who in the hour of the blasphemy of despair attempt to vilify and misrepresent the Church of God. They ought to remember also that Luther's special brand of dispensations are not altogether out of market yet.

In the theological lectures on the Psalms, which Luther, when still a Catholic, delivered as professor in the years 1513-1516, he described from time to time the peculiarities and distinguishing features of heretics. "The principal sin of heretics is their pride," he says. "In their pride they insist on their own opinions. . . Frequently they serve God with great fervor, and they do not intend any evil; but they serve God according to their own will. . . Even when refuted, they are ashamed to retract their errors and to change their words. . .They think they are guided directly by God. . .The things that have been established for centuries and for which so many martyrs have suffered death, they begin to treat as doubtful questions. . .They interpret [the Bible] according to their own heads and their own particular views and carry their own opinions into it." (Seidemann. I, 10, 133, 250, 413. II, 101, 132, 283).

This description leaves nothing to be desired. Luther tells most accurately the traits of the false prophets and lying teachers whom the God of Truth would have His followers avoid. Think you, did the unfortunate man realize, when he described the characteristics of those who cause dissensions in the Church and among the brethren, that he was drawing his own portrait in later times? If he did, then he should have remembered the words of the great St. Paul: "I beseech you, brethren, to mark them who cause dissensions and offences contrary to the doctrine which you have learned, and to avoid them." (*Rom.* 16:17).

CHAPTER 4

LUTHER AND JUSTIFICATION

THERE are few tenets of the Catholic Church so little understood, or so grossly misrepresented by her adversaries, as her doctrine regarding justification, or sanctification.[1] Many outside the Church make the mistake of supposing that the Catholic doctrine ascribes a justifying and saving efficacy to a mere intellectual submission to Church authority, and a mere external compliance with its precepts without reference to the interior disposition of the soul toward God, or recognition of the merits of Christ as the source of all the supernatural excellence and value of good works. Most Protestants are under the impression that the Catholic substitutes the merits of the Blessed Virgin Mary, the merits of the Saints, and his own merits, as an independent ground of justification, in lieu of the merits of Christ. They believe, moreover, that merit is ascribed to mere external works, such as fasting, assisting at Mass, and performing ceremonial rites or penitential labors, on account of the mere physical nature and extent of the works done, without reference to the motive from which they proceed. These, and other calumnies or rather blasphemies of a similar nature, are frequently and confidently repeated in popular sermons and controversial tracts until non-Catholics come to reject what they suppose to be Catholic doctrine, but which is frequently only a rejection of opinions attributed by mistake to the Catholic Church.

What our adversaries allege on the question of justification is not only a misapprehension, but a travesty of genuine Catholic teaching; and the underlying purpose of the misrepresentations of the true doctrine of the Church is to prevent, if possible, all who are not of the household of faith from ascertaining with certainty the exact and complete sense of the doctrine Christ has commanded us to believe and the law He has commanded us to keep under penalty of eternal condemnation. The sooner the opinions attributed by malice or by mistake to the Catholic Church are examined carefully and candidly in relation to genuine Catholic doctrine, the better for the interests of souls who long for the truth and who earnestly desire the spread of the Kingdom of God on earth. To all who hold the views we have alluded to and who labor under a misapprehension of the Church's teaching regarding the question of man's justification, we wish to say that so far from fathering the impious and absurd doctrines our adversaries allege that we maintain, the Catholic Church rejects, condemns and anathematizes them.

It is, then, false, and notoriously false, that Catholics believe, or in any age did believe, that they could justify themselves by their own proper merits, or that they can do the least good in the order of salvation without the grace of God merited for them by Jesus Christ; or that they can deserve this grace by anything they have the natural power of doing; or that leave to commit sin, or even the pardon of any sin which has been committed, can be purchased of any person whomsoever; or that the essence of religion and our hopes of salvation consist in forms and ceremonies or in other exterior things. What the Catholic Church teaches and ever has taught her children is to trust for mercy, grace and salvation to the merits of Jesus Christ. Nevertheless, she asserts that we have free will, and that this, being assisted by divine grace, can and must cooperate to our justification, by faith, sorrow for our sins, and other corresponding acts of virtue which God will not fail to develop in us if we do not throw obstacles in the way of them.[2] Thus is all honor and merit ascribed to the Creator, and every defect and sin attributed to the creature.

The false views which have been circulated concerning man's justification, and which have for the last four hundred years done service against truth, originated in the erratic brain of Martin Luther, whose career evidenced the cold fact that he was incapable either of hard reasoning or clear thinking. We do not wish by this remark to insinuate that the "Reformer" was not endowed with talent of a high order, but, as every student of his history knows, his thought on serious topics most frequently was strikingly confused. He was not an exact thinker, and being unable to analyze an idea into its constituents, as is necessary for one who will apprehend it correctly, he failed to grasp questions which by the general mass of the people were thoroughly and correctly understood. How he missed and confounded the consecrated teaching on man's justification is a case in point. He allowed himself to cultivate an unnecessary antipathy to so-called "holiness by works," and this attitude, combined with his tendency to look at the worst side of things and his knowledge of some real abuses then prevalent in the practice of works, doubtless contributed to develop his dislike for good works in general and led him by degrees to strike at the very roots of the Catholic system of Sacraments and grace, of penance and satisfaction, in fact, at all the instruments or means instituted by God both for conferring and increasing His saving relationship with man. The extraordinary exaggerations of which Luther was guilty in this regard must be imputed, not to the Church's teaching, but to the peculiar notions he formed of it in the confusion of his own thoughts—as we shall see later on.

The Catholic Church has always insisted upon the necessity of being *"perfect even as Our Heavenly Father is perfect"* (*Matt.* 5:48) by such an entire subjugation of our passions and a conformity of our will with that of God, that *"our conversation,"* according to St. Paul, *"may be in heaven"* (*Phil.* 3:20) while we are yet living here on earth. This fundamental truth Luther knew well. Early in his career he ambitioned, as was right, to exemplify the teaching of the Church in his life. He desired to be perfect, to reach justification and to become a great saint. For a time he adopted the approved and necessary means whereby his heart's desire for perfection might be realized. In an evil moment, however, he unfortunately allowed himself to forget the indispensable necessity of humility, which is the groundwork of all the virtues, and by which, says St. Bernard, "from a thorough knowledge of ourselves we become little in our own estimation." Although this lesson was strongly enforced by Christ and His disciples, yet he seemed to entirely overlook it, and gradually he became a prey to spiritual pride, the prolific source of all evil. Dominated by this dangerous spirit, he grew careless in the use of the ordinary sane and prudent means sanctioned by all the masters of the spiritual life to acquire true peace of heart and perfect union with God. To the exclusion of all and every counsel of the experienced in the direction of souls, he, in a spirit of unbounded self-sufficiency, imagined he could acquire perfection by his own peculiar methods and exertions. As a result of his mistaken determination to reject every wise rule laid down for the acquirement of perfection, he went from one extreme to another until he exhausted himself vainly in fasts, prayers and mortifications. Moderation and common sense in his case seemed to have been unknown qualities. When at length the thought dawned on him that he had not been able in spite of all his singular, excessive, imprudent practices of piety to hide from himself the sinfulness of his nature and the continual violence of his passions, and that he had still to struggle with temptation, he was plunged more and more into sadness, desolation, and terror of God's justice. At this time he seemed to forget that if God's justice avenged sin, it also rewarded true virtue. He should have known that the Catholic Church, of which he was a member, never expected any of her subjects to propitiate God with their own works exclusively. She always taught her children that over and above the performance of legitimate and approved works of piety, they were directed to put their trust for the mastery of the flesh in the infinite merits of the Redeemer and discharge their duties in full reliance on divine grace, which is ever freely bestowed on all who earnestly strive to do good and avoid evil. Confidence in God and diffidence in self enable the humble, no matter what form passion may assume, ever to say with St. Paul, "I can do all things in him who strengtheneth me." (*Phil.* 4:13) Had Luther remembered this teaching of the Church and been obedient to the directions of his spiritual guides, he would not have been carried away by his own whims and fancies to the loss of his peace of mind and to distress and anguish of soul.

In this state of inward depression, which often prostrated him with terror, he had the pity and kindly consideration of his friends. To console and afford him relief, some of them recommended him to direct his attention in future more than he had in the past to greater confidence and reliance on God's mercy, which is infinite and ever ready to relieve sinners through the merits acquired by the death of Christ. The suggestion, which was not novel or unknown to him, inspired him for a time with new hope. It let a beam of sunlight into the darkness of his terror. This, however, was soon dispelled, for a reaction set in when he began to ponder over and put his own sense on the words of St. Paul: "The just man lives by faith." (*Rom.* 1:17; *Gal.* 3:11). By a process of reasoning peculiar to himself he construed the word "faith" to mean an assurance of personal salvation, and "justification" to mean, not an infusion of justice into the heart of the person justified, but a mere external imputation of it. Having managed to connect in his own mind, and afterwards in the minds of others, the word "faith" with this unnatural meaning, he could appeal to all the passages in St. Paul's Epistles which assert that justification is by faith and claim them as so many proofs of his newly discovered doctrine. He thinks now that self-pacification is secured and that henceforward he can dispose with all and every other virtue enjoined in Scripture and work out his salvation through "faith alone without works." How he came to hold this unwarranted position, he tells in the following words: "In such thoughts," referring to his ill will and anger against God, "I passed day and night till by God's grace, I remarked how the words hung together: to wit, 'The justice of God is revealed in the Gospel,' as it is written, 'The just man lives by his faith.' Thence have I learned to know this same justice of God, in which the just man, through God's grace and gift, lives by faith alone. . . I forthwith felt I was entirely born anew and that I found a wide and unbarred door by which to enter Paradise."

In this declaration of false security, we have the beginning of Luther's new gospel, which, needless to say, is directly and openly opposed to the Gospel of Jesus Christ. As a theologian, he should have realized that his notion of the absolute assurance of salvation imparted by faith was as false as it was unsound, and as a professor of Scripture, he should have known that faith alone is barren and lifeless apart from the meritorious works which are necessarily connected with and founded on it. To hold and declare that men are justified by faith to the entire exclusion of other divine virtues is nothing less than a perversion of the Bible, a falsificaton of the Word of God, and an injury to souls called to work out their salvation along the lines plainly designated by Jesus Christ. But Luther's self-esteem and self-conceit blinded him to the truth he once held in honor; and, instead of repelling and mastering his singular conception of salvation, as he was in duty bound to do, he held to it with unbending tenacity, developing it more and more until he finally declares in Cap. 2, ad. Gal. that "Faith alone is necessary for justification: all other things are completely optional, being no longer either commanded or forbidden." It is this doctrine which he afterwards called the *Articulus stantis vel cadentis Ecclesiae* [point on which the Church stands or falls]; and if we cannot quite accept this description of it, at least we can recognize that it is the cornerstone of the Lutheran and Calvinistic systems.

In Luther's new program of salvation the living, vital, efficacious faith that manifests itself in good works, and without which it is impossible to please God, must no longer prevail in the minds of men. All the old teachings, practices and observances of piety, so useful and helpful for man's justification and his deliverance from divine vengeance, must now be forgotten and abandoned. The priesthood, Sacraments, indulgences, intercessory prayer, fasts, pilgrimages, all spiritual works must be displaced to make way for his miserable, degrading, and colorless invention of faith without works. In his special system he wanted none of the old means for gaining eternal life. They were considered antiquated, unavailing and worthless. In his estimation it was not possible for man to perform any works which were really good and acceptable to God.[3] Man was so depraved in consequence of the Fall of Adam and Eve that he became totally corrupt, both in his intellect and his will, and was consequently incapable till regenerated of thinking, willing or doing any good thing. All his actions, therefore, even those which were most strictly accordant with the precepts of the natural and divine law, were "evil and only evil and that continually." "Corruption hung over man forever and tainted everything he did. All the works of man before justification were damnable sins; and all the works of man after justification were so sinful in the sight of God that, if He were to judge them strictly, everyone would be damned." In commenting on one of the Psalms, he makes this horrible statement: "Conceived in sorrow and corruption, the child sins even in his mother's womb, when, as yet a mere fetus, an impure mass of matter, before it becomes a human creature, it commits iniquity and incurs damnation. As he grows, the innate element of corruption develops. Man has said to sin, 'Thou art my father,' and every act he performs is an offense against God; and to the worms, 'You are my brothers,' and he crawls like them in mire and corruption. He is a bad tree and cannot produce good fruit, a dunghill and can only exhale foul odors. He is so thoroughly corrupted that it is absolutely impossible for him to produce good actions. Sin is his nature; he cannot help committing it. Man may do his best to be good, still his every action is unavoidably bad; he commits a sin as often as he draws his breath." (Consult *Wittenb.* III. 518). These were favorite sayings of Luther, and thus, if we are to believe him, every action of an unregenerate person, however just, generous or noble, is utterly perverse and corrupt. On the other hand, he maintained, "No action that was bad would bring the regenerate man under condemnation, because he was justified by faith; nor were his good actions, in even the slightest degree, meritorious, because they were done entirely through the grace given him by the Holy Ghost." He further states that "The nature of man is so corrupted that it can never be regenerated, and sin will remain in the soul, even of the just, forever. God's all-powerful grace does not cleanse from sin. The Almighty does not regard the sins of men. He covers them over with the merits of Christ and does not impute them to the sinner whose faith in the sufferings of the Redeemer is made manifest." This is the effect of faith, which, he says, "tends to prevent our filth from stinking before God." (*Walch* XIII. 1480).

Over and over again Luther asserted that man could not be just, but, in his desire of novelty, he thought there must be some way never known before whereby man could be made just, and so after a display of loose thinking, his wonderful ingenuity for mischief invented the theory of justification by the *imputation* of the righteousness of Christ, and not, as heretofore, by the *communication* of His justice. "Christ," he says, "has suffered for our sins and has fulfilled the law for us. We have only to believe in Him, and by believing in Him, take hold, as it were, of His merits and put them on like a cloak. If we do that, although imperfect and unholy, we shall be saved and considered just, not for anything that God made us, not for regeneration, or transformation, or sanctification, but for the righteousness of Christ, who in Himself was infinitely holy. All that man has to do is to remain passive; he must not attempt to do anything himself for his salvation. This would be presumption." He must remain with regard to all things which pertain to the salvation of the soul, as he states in his comment on *Genesis* 19:26, "like the statue of salt into which the wife of Lot was changed; to the trunk of a tree or a stone, like a statue, lifeless and having no use of either eyes, mouth or other senses or of a heart." "To be a Christian means to have the Evangelium [Gospel] and to believe in Christ. This faith brings forgiveness of sins and divine grace; it comes solely through the Holy Ghost, who works it through the word without any cooperation on our part. . . . Man remains passive and is acted upon by the Holy Ghost just as clay is shaped by the potter." (*Tischr.* II. C. 15. § 1).

This view of justification was forthwith made the fundamental dogma of the new religion Luther formulated for the world's acceptance. From the time this false doctrine was first announced, his followers in heresy have been taught to believe that men are saved by faith alone and that good works are altogether unnecessary. "The Gospel," Luther falsely declares, "teaches nothing of the merits of works; he that says the Gospel requires works for salvation, I say, flat and plain, is a liar." (*Table Talk,* p. 137, Hazlitt). If men believe in Christ, they are told, and accept Him as their personal Saviour, His justice will be imputed to them and they will go straight to Heaven. It does not matter what evil they have done during their lives; it does not matter whether or not they repent of their sins; it does not matter whether or not, at the moment of death, they have compunction, contrition or attrition, or are in a state of grace—if they have faith they will be saved.

Luther was the first in Christendom to proclaim to the world that man was "justified by faith alone." The doctrine was novel and admirably suited to lull and tranquilize the misgivings of conscience. Although it opened the way to carelessness of behavior, as events proved, yet he felt sure of the correctness of his teaching and wanted no discussion thereon. Anyone who would dare contradict him on the point and declare the Gospel required works for salvation was to be branded as a "liar." This appellation is not a pleasant one, but, as a matter of fact, its author deserved it better than he knew, for his singular teaching was as false as it was pernicious, and being without warrant in the divine plan of salvation, it was utterly powerless to lead souls to everlasting life.

If this teaching of Luther's were true, it is apparent that Christ, instead of declaring that the first and great Commandment was love, should have said that it was faith. But the Master did not believe that we were saved by faith alone, because when the rich young man went to Him and asked what he must do to gain Heaven, Our Lord answered: "If thou wilt enter into life, keep the Commandments." (*Matt.* 19:17). He did not say, "Believe in Me. Accept Me for your personal Saviour. Have faith in Me." No, but He did say: "If thou wilt enter into life, keep the Commandments." It is evident from this solemn declaration of Christ that He required in His followers the faith that manifests itself in such voluntary works and actions as are pleasing to Him and are performed out of love for Him. That living faith, which the Master enjoins, is inseparable from charity or the love of God, and charity is not real unless it induces us to keep the Commandments and conform our lives not to some special injunction or virtue, but to all the requirements and truths of Divine Revelation. This is the teaching which Christ constantly insisted upon, and this, and no other, was and is still the teaching which He communicated to His Church for the enlightenment and sanctification of the world until the end of time.

When Luther advanced his fanciful and mischievous conception of justification, the Church, true to her mission of safeguarding the truths of her Divine Founder, had no difficulty in showing that fiduciary faith—a confidence or hope founded only on [external imputation of] the merits of Jesus Christ—was an absolutely new invention and was not only worthless, but powerless to justify men. In her Council of Trent (1545-1563) she condemned, as was her right, the new-fangled teaching of Luther and warned her subjects against its entanglements and dangers. Then she proclaimed anew, for the enlightenment of all, the heavenly teaching committed to her keeping from the beginning and insisted that whilst faith is necessary to dispose the sinner to receive grace, it alone is not sufficient for justification. A living faith that embraces righteousness is what is required, and this manifests itself in acts of hope, of love, of sorrow and a purpose of amendment of life. It is only when God finds the sinner disposed to believe all revealed truths, observe all the Commandments and receive the Sacraments He instituted that He gives him gratuitously His grace or intrinsic justice which remits to him his sins and sanctifies him.

Faith alone has not the power of saving man, for two reasons: first, that infants are capable of justification, which we suppose no one will deny, but are not capable of an act of faith; second, that faith is a temporary virtue ceasing in the beatified state, whereas the principle of justification is permanent and eternal.

In the process of justification, the first and foremost important place is taken by faith. More, however, is required for its development, completion and perfection. It should be remembered that when God created man, He placed him in a state of probation. He constituted him a rational being and imposed certain precepts which he was free to keep or violate as he may choose, unto eternal happiness or eternal misery. Although God required the particular exercise of love which consists in a voluntary obedience of His precepts, yet He cannot dispense with love itself, which is the great and necessary requisite to a state of perfect justification. The attributes of God require Him to carry out the terms of probation to which He has subjected man. The acts which proceed from the principle of love, in order to bring the soul to God as its ultimate term, must, therefore, cover not a part, but the whole ground of the divine law and include not one but all the Commandments.

Love then is the dominating principle in the union of the soul with God and the fashioning of it for an eternity of reward.

Faith alone, whether fiduciary or dogmatic,[4] cannot then justify man. Since our divine adoption and friendship with God is based on charity or perfect love of God, dead faith, faith devoid of charity, cannot possess any justifying power. Only such faith as is active in charity and good works can justify man,[5] and this is possible even before the actual reception of Baptism or Penance—although not without the desire of the Sacrament. The essence of active justification comprises not only forgiveness of sins, but also "Sanctification and renovation of the interior man by means of the voluntary acceptation of Sanctifying Grace and other supernatural gifts."

Thus, we are justified by God's justice, not that justice whereby He Himself is just, but that justice whereby He makes us just, insofar as He bestows upon us the gift of His grace, which renovates the soul interiorly and adheres to it as the soul's own holiness.

"Love," as Möhler says, "must already vivify faith before the Catholic Church will say that through it man is truly pleasing to God. Faith in love and love in faith justify; they form here an indispensable unity. This justifying faith is not merely negative, but positive with all; not merely a confidence that for Christ's sake forgiveness of sins will be obtained, but a sanctified state, in itself agreeable to God. Charity is undoubtedly, according to Catholic doctrine, a fruit of faith. But faith justifies only when it has already brought forth this fruit."

This teaching of the Church on justification was most distasteful to Luther, and as might be expected from a man of his rebellious nature, he opposed it with all the forces at his command. In the Altenburg edition of his works we have a sample of his characteristic raving on the point at issue. "The Papists," he says, "contend that faith which is informed by charity, justifies. On this point we must contend and oppose with all our strength; here we must yield not a nail's breadth to any; neither to the angels of Heaven, nor to the gates of Hell, *nor to St. Paul,* nor to an hundred Emperors, nor to a thousand Popes, nor to the whole world; and 'this be my watchword and sign': '*tessera et symbolum* [watchword and sign].'" (Audin's Luther, II, p. 112). The consummate boldness of this call to incite rebellion against the express teaching of God regarding the salvation of man is most astonishing and scandalous.

In all the bitterness of his antagonism and opposition, he, after all, was something of a reasoner when he had an object to attain and when he wanted to make things square with his strange and novel views. He knew as well as any man of his day that the Church, to which he belonged from his youth to his excommunication, demanded from time immemorial faith and good works as essential requisites in the lives of all who were anxious to attain salvation. This time-honored doctrine, however, stood in the way and was in opposition to his heretofore unheard-of system of salvation, and, as it could not be made to agree with his fanciful and eccentric speculations, he labored in season and out of season to dethrone the Church's teaching in the minds and in the hearts of the faithful. In the execution of his mischievous work, he began to laugh and jeer at the idea of good works as necessary for justification. He denounced in unmeasured terms the works of supererogation or the counsels of perfection, and the vows by which priests, monks, and nuns consecrated themselves to the service of God. In his estimation, it was an idle thing, fondly invented, that man or woman should separate himself or herself from the world and be consecrated unreservedly to the service of the living God. And all following Our Lord in the way of self-abnegation, in the way of self-denial, in the way of the crucifixion of self and of the flesh with all its unholy desires, he completely and totally denied, and not only denied but even derided. The needlessness of all these and other consecrated means of attaining perfection hitherto in use proclaimed by Luther proved a new charter of liberty from bondage of every kind for himself, and in the end for multitudes of others. The experience of later years records the sad fact that the so-called message of emancipation left men, not better, but worse than it found them. The soothing but disastrous doctrine of faith without works could only lead to carelessness of life and open up the way to every species of unbridled lewdness and immorality. It did not bring, as was fondly contemplated, the peace and confidence and spiritual freedom expected. The very contrary results were everywhere noticeable; for all, from Luther down to the last of his misguided followers who denied the necessity of supernatural helps and earnest striving in the ways of perfection, were universally notable for such indecencies and horrible violations of God's law as shock and scandalize every impartial reader of the history of the Reformation period.

The denial of the necessity of good works for justification was, however, only a part of Luther's plan for the ruin and deception of the unwary. In order to give color to his "new experience of salvation," as Leimbech calls it, he maintained in his Commentary on the Epistle of St. Paul to the Galatians that "There is an irreconcilable opposition existing between the Law[6] and the Gospel." "The Law and the Gospel," he says, "are two contrary things which cannot be in harmony with each other," and "No man on earth can properly distinguish between the Law and the Gospel." To lend weight to this bold and untenable claim, nothing daunted, he went so far as to say that "Even the man Jesus Christ, when in the Garden of Gethsemane, suffered from such ignorance." (*Tischr.* I. C. 12. § 19). The imputation implied in this utterance is shocking, but we must pass it over for the moment. We feel, however, that Luther's ignorance was more feigned than real, because his earlier theological studies dealt exhaustively with the question of the Law and the Gospel, their nature, order and position in the divine scheme of salvation. If he declared, as he did later, that he could not sufficiently realize the question, he should not, however, have brazenly stated that "No man on earth understood it," for he confessed that his own pupils boasted they comprehended the doctrine thoroughly and had it "at their fingers' ends." He knew, too, that besides his own pupils there were thousands and thousands of the faithful in his day who realized that there was no contradiction between the Law and the Gospel and that the New or Evangelical Law was no other than the old moral law renewed, approved and perfected by Jesus Christ according to His own declaration: *"Do not think that I am come to destroy the law or the prophets. I am not come to destroy, but to fulfill."* (*Matt.* 5: 17).

Luther, however, cared little about misrepresenting the belief of the neighbor when he wanted to gain a hearing for his own false conceptions. His viewpoint was in the circumstances paramount to all else; and to advance it, he used all his energies, regardless of consequences. In his scheme for the destruction of everything hitherto held as holy and sacred, it hardly suited him to acknowledge the harmony which existed between the Law and the Gospel, for he was gradually preparing the way for the violation, destruction and abandonment of the Decalogue. Having fallen away from his original fervor and having become a breaker and not an observer of the Commandments, he wanted to strike a blow at the source of all morality, and remove, if possible, the very foundation of all moral obligation. Despite all the teaching of Christ to the effect that the Law was for all men, for all time, and for all circumstances, he imagined that a declaration of freedom from the bondage thereof would make his position more tenable and his teaching more savory and acceptable to the crowd he desired to win to his cause.

Luther, of course, wanted the Law announced. He preached and taught it; he inserted it in his catechism and he exhorted his followers to recite it daily. Nevertheless, he, at the same time, warned against allowing the Law to have any influence on the conscience, for then it would become, as he said, "a sink of heresies and blasphemies." (*Wittenb.* V. 272 b.). He considered the advocacy of the Law merely useful "to show to man that he is a sinner, to terrify him in that way and make him throw himself upon Christ." (*Ibid.* 307). To crush the "horrible monster and stiff-necked brute" of pride in man, who is ever inclined to think much of himself and of his works, "God wants," he says, "a great and strong hammer, that is, the Law, for it reveals to man his absolute inability to keep it. The laws have been given only that man should see in them the impossibility of doing good and that he should learn to despair of himself. . . . As soon as man begins to learn and to feel, from the laws of God, his own incapacity. . . he becomes thoroughly humbled and annihilated in his own eyes." (*Walch,* XIX, 1212).

Although Luther advocated the Law and wished it known by all, he, at the same time, declared that "the moral duties it enjoined were impossible of fulfillment and incited not love, but hatred of God." *"Lex summum odium Dei affert."* ["The Law brings forth the greatest hatred of God."] In this favorite declaration he gives a new proof of the contradictory character of his mind and advances a teaching which is directly opposed to that of faith and experience.

To claim that the fulfillment of the Law is impossible is as impious as it is blasphemous, inasmuch as it imputes to God the injustice of commanding us to do something above our strength. How could God, who is infinitely wise and good, command His creatures to do anything impossible to them? If the accomplishment of the Law seems to be above the powers of nature, do we not know, and have we not been assured that God is careful to offer all His divine helps to enable the will of man not only to fulfill all the duties imposed by the Law, but also to make him experience pleasure and happiness in their observance? Does not the Holy Ghost declare by the mouth of the Psalmist, "Blessed is the man that feareth the Lord. He shall delight exceedingly in his Commandments"? (*Ps.* 111:1). The example of the Saints of all ages, conditions and climes furnish unanswerable proof of this truth. God's grace is ever ready to help men of good will. He will no more fail us than He failed the saints. The same faith, the same hope, the same love, the same Sacraments, the same Gospel they had will assuredly help us, as they helped them, to subdue passion and attain to holiness of behavior. With all the divine helps God has placed at man's disposal, is it not easier to fulfill the Law than to break it? Besides, is it not more honorable to obey God than passion? Is it not sweeter to have the soul filled with peace by repressing passion than gnawed with remorse through the gratification of irregular inclinations?

The impiety and blasphemy of Luther is all the more remarkable when, after stating the impossibility of fulfilling the Law, he unblushingly declares that "the Law incites not love but hatred of God." Every reader of the Scripture knows how false and unfounded this statement is. The Law of God is the law of love. It can never inspire hatred in the mind or heart of men of good will towards its Framer. Christ's words prove this to a certainty. He says: "If any one love me, he will keep my word, and my Father will love him, and we will come to him, and will make our abode with him. He that loveth me not, keepeth not my words." (*Jn.* 14:23-24). St. Paul expresses the same teaching when he says that "Love therefore is the fulfilling of the law." (*Rom.* 13:10). St. John confirms this truth in the memorable words: "We have known and have believed the charity which God hath to us. God is charity, and he that abideth in charity, abideth in God and God in him." (*1 Jn.* 4:16). Thus faith and experience unite in proclaiming that not only is the observance of the Commandments possible, but their fulfillment incites not hatred, but love of God.

Luther at one time knew all this, but later on his anxiety to place opposition between the Law and the Gospel, and to define the place the Law occupies in the religion of Christ and the purpose for which it exists, warped his judgment and blinded his intellect regarding the true state of the question. All his efforts to explain the necessity of the Decalogue, inasmuch as he admits it at all, are not too clear, and the line he draws between the Law and the Gospel is not only unsatisfactory, but most disappointing. Here are his own words. "The Law," he says, "points out what man has to do, whereas the Gospel unfolds the gifts God is willing to confer on man. The former we cannot observe; the latter we receive and apprehend by faith." (*Tischr.* I. C. 12 § 7). "The Gospel," he would have us believe, "does not announce what we must do or omit. . . but bids us open our hands to receive gifts, and say, Behold, dear man, this is what God has done for you: for your sake He made His Son assume human nature. This believe and accept, and you shall be saved. The Gospel only shows us the gifts of God, not what we have to give to God or to do for Him as is the wont of the Law." (*Walch,* III, 4).

Luther was right in saying that the Gospel unfolds the gifts of God to mankind, but he erred grievously in declaring that it did not announce "what we must do or omit." Every reader of the Gospel knows that Christ, who was sent by His Father to instruct and guide us to perfection, not only promulgated the Law anew, but ever and always insisted on its observance. When the young man asked Christ the question, "What shall I do to be saved?" He clearly answered: "If thou wilt enter into life keep the Commandments." (*Matt.* 19:17). Now, the Decalogue, which is the application of the great precept of the love of God and one's neighbor,[7] enjoins two kinds of precepts: some positive, commanding certain things to be done; others negative, forbidding certain things to be done; all having for their end to teach us the acts by which we should exercise our charity and protect this virtue from injury and even destruction. The law of God is the law of Charity, and Charity is active in doing good and avoiding evil. It manifests itself not merely by words, but by works; the works prescribed in the Commandments. To produce the works or Charity is a duty not to be shirked. It binds at all times and under all circumstances if we would secure happiness in this world and in the next. Moreover, the observance of the Commandments shows God that He is always Our Lord and Master, having the power and the right to rule over and command His servants and children. It is from this point of view that we must contemplate the Decalogue if we would understand the profound meaning of the Saviour's numerous words regarding the sweetness of the Divine Law. To select one out of many we find Him saying: "Take up my yoke upon you and learn of me, because I am meek and humble of heart; and you shall find rest to your souls. For my yoke is sweet and my burden light," which is the same as to say, "My yoke is love," the only end of all My precepts is to preserve love; preserve it *"and you shall find rest to your souls."* It is in Charity, then, that all the Christian religion consists. It is that which distinguishes the true Christian; it is that which makes him really a child of God, a member of the Mystical Body of Christ, the living temple of the Holy Ghost, an heir and citizen of the Kingdom of Heaven.

Without Charity all is useless and profits nothing to salvation. Neither faith nor miracles, nor the most exalted gifts, nor the most generous alms, nor even martyrdom in the midst of flames, can profit us anything toward salvation without Charity or the love of God. "If I have not charity," St. Paul says, "I am nothing and it profiteth one nothing." (*1 Cor.* 13:1).

Luther endeavored with all his power to draw a distinction between Christ and His promulgation of the Law. He wanted to have it appear that the Saviour of men should be recognized for His quality of mercy and not for His justice. The thought of Christ as a judge angered by sin was abhorrent to him. All his special pleading in this direction could not, however, still the behests of conscience, which ever and always bears witness to the Law and testifies to its binding force. The precepts of the Decalogue are so fixedly impressed on the heart of man that it is impossible to violate these without feeling that the Almighty, who is set at defiance by the sinner, will surely avenge all and every transgression not atoned for. Man, Luther admitted, bears within his heart this voice, which reproaches him with a badly spent life and which threatens him with God's judgment; but, he calls this voice "the voice of the devil," "who tries to cheat man," and "who comes under the appearance of Christ and transforms himself into an angel of light," "to frighten us with the Law." (*Wittenb.* V. 321, 321B. Cfr. 382). This fanciful notion, confounding the voice of conscience with the voice of man's enemy, brought neither peace nor consolation to his hearers. The better informed realized, in spite of all his strange advice, that the voice of conscience still asserted itself and bore indubitable witness to sin and the fear of its punishment. Conscience can never be dethroned, and man cannot help realizing the presence of sin and being terrified at the thought of Hell and eternal death. Luther knew all this, but he persisted in his dogged opposition until we find him in the agony of despair, declaring with the uttermost boldness that "Man must persuade himself that he has nothing to do with the Law and that no sins can condemn him; nay, let him, so to say, boast of his sinfulness and thus take the weapon out of the devil's hand. When the devil rushes at you and tries to drown you in the flood and the deluge of your sins. . . say to him, 'Why do you wish to make a saint of me, why do you expect to find justice in me, who has nothing but sins, and most grievous ones?'" (*Wittenb.* V. 281 B.). "In fact, what would be the use of Christ, if the Law and our transgressions of the Law could still annoy and terrify us?" Therefore, he says, "When the conscience is terror-stricken on account of the Law and struggles with the thought of God's judgment, do not consult reason or the Law. . . act exactly as if you had never heard of the Law of God." (*Wittenb.* V. 303 B.). "Answer: There is a time to live and a time to die; there is a time to hear the Law and a time to despise the Law. . . Let the Law be off and let the Gospel reign." (*Wittenb.* V. 304 B.). "The body with its members," he says, "has to be subject to the Law, it has to carry its burden like a donkey, but leave the donkey with its burden in the valley when you ascend the mountain. For the conscience has nothing to do with the Law, works, earthly justice. We want indeed 'the light of the Evangelium' [Gospel] to understand this, and in this light the meaning is: 'Keep the Law, by all means; but if you do not, you need not be troubled in your conscience, for the transgression of the law cannot possibly condemn you.'" (*Witenb.* V. 304).

Some of Luther's admirers imagine that under the Church's teaching the people did not understand the Ten Commandments, and they claim forthwith that their hero came and brought back the true consciousness of them and that whatever he said about them is to be understood as an antithesis between grace and Law in the life of the Christian. If this be so, then it behooves his admirers to tell us in what possible connection it is permissible for a Christian gentleman to say, "If we allow them [the Ten

Commandments] any influence in our conscience, they become the cloak of all evil, heresies, and blasphemies." Is this the "antithesis between grace and Law"? Does not Luther make it plain enough when he says, "The Catholic theologians are asses who do not know what they maintain, when they say that Christ has only abrogated the ceremonial law of the Old Testament, and not also the Ten Commandments"? (*Epistle to the Galatians.*) Is the abrogation of the Ten Commandments an "antithesis"? "That shall serve you as a true rule, that wherever the Scriptures order and command to do good works, you must so understand it that the Scriptures forbid good works." (*Wittenb. ed.* 2, 171. 6). "If you should not sin against the Gospel, then be on your guard against good works; avoid them as one avoids a pest." (*Jena. ed.* 1. 318 b.). In what connection is it compatible with a Christian character to counsel against good works as against a "pest" and make it an "antithesis to grace"? Or, under what circumstances is it allowable for a "man of God" and a "Reformer" to say of Moses, God's chosen servant, that he should be looked upon "with suspicion as the worst heretic, as a damned and excommunicated person; yea, worse than the Pope and the devil"? (*Jena.* 4, 98. 6). "A pure heart enlightened by God must not dirty, soil itself with the Law. Thus let the Christian understand that it matters not whether he keeps it or not; yea, he may do what is forbidden and leave undone what is commanded, for neither is a sin." (*W.* XI. 447). Does this indicate a very reverential spirit towards the Law of God, and was this intended to mean that the Law was to be a guide for the life of regenerates? Is it thus that "Luther came and brought back the true consciousness of them [the Ten Commandments] to the people"? If this be so, then the "moral life and progress" his friends claim for his doctrine has its roots in the worst days of paganism, and not in the teachings of Jesus Christ and of His Church.

As might be expected from one who strove to minimize

the importance and influence of the Law in the lives of men, Luther had scant respect for him whom God selected to proclaim His will to the peoples and the nations from Sion's Mount. This mouthpiece of God became the special subject of his untiring and ceaseless abuse and vituperation. He not only acknowledges his opposition to Moses, but he urges it with all the vehemence he is master of. He went so far in his antagonism that he proclaimed the Lawgiver a most dangerous man and the embodiment of everything that can torment the soul. His hatred of the Prophet was so deep-rooted that on one occasion he cried out: "To the gallows with Moses." He disliked him because he thought that he insisted too strongly on the Law and its observance. In order to minimize his mission and destroy his influence, he boldly and untruthfully asserted that Moses "was sent to the Jewish people only and had nothing whatever to do with Gentiles and Christians." His advice to all who bothered themselves with the Lawgiver was to "chase that stammering and stuttering Moses," as he called him, "with his Law to the Jews and not allow his terrible threats to intimidate them." "Moses must ever be looked upon," he says, "with suspicion, even as upon a heretic, excommunicated, damned, worse than the Pope and the devil." (*Comment. in Gal.*). The scurrilous language applied to God's messenger reaches its depths of infamy when he says further: "I will not have Moses with his Law, for he is the enemy of the Lord Christ. . .we must put away thoughts and disputes about the Law, whenever the conscience becomes terrified and feels God's anger against sin. Instead of that, it will be better to sing, to eat, to drink, to sleep, to be merry in spite of the devil." (*Tischr.* L. C. 12. §. 17). "No greater insult can be offered to Christ than to suppose that He has come to give Commandments, to make a sort of Moses of Him." (*Tischr.* S. 66). "Only the mad and blind Papists do such a thing." (*Wittenb.* V. 292 B.). "Christ's work consists in this: to fulfill the Law for us, not to give laws to us, and to redeem us." (*Ibid.*). "The devil makes of Christ a mere Moses." (*Walch,* VIII: 58).

Luther evidently was not any more an admirer of Moses than he was, at times, of the Decalogue. His personal hatred for the great advocate of the Law was roused because of his zeal in enforcing the obligation of keeping the Commandments. The ridicule he heaped on Moses passed to the masses, and not a criminal from that time on that has not wished that the Lawgiver and the Commandments he proclaimed had never existed. To displace in men's minds and hearts the wise and beneficent code of morality God gave to mankind is nothing less than criminal. There is not one of our interests that the Decalogue does not surround with the most sacred barriers. Upon its observance depend the glory, tranquillity and prosperity of mankind in this world and their felicity in the next. To trifle with Heaven-given Law and weaken its importance is a scandal and can only result in complete disrespect and disregard for all legitimate authority, a curse which is unfortunately not unknown in the world of today. In the presence of the general depravity of the hour, it is high time to proclaim from the housetops that the sweet and gentle Gospel of the Saviour of men still exists in all its pristine beauty and force, that it tells plainly and clearly what all must do or omit, and that it is only by following its sublime injunctions that men can be freed from the error, impiety, libertinism, hatred, discord and all the other evils which make life in the world today a long and bitter torment.

Luther, as we learn from the evidence presented, held very singular views regarding sin and its commission. We do not wish to insinuate that he actually taught and approved sin, for we know that he did as a rule instruct men to avoid violations of the Law and repress the concupiscence leading thereto. But we do hold that his whole theory of justification by faith alone and his denial of moral freedom, making God "the author of what is evil in us," necessarily broke down the usual barriers against sin, and that his moral recommendations very often in the plainest of language did actually and openly encourage sin. His consuming thought is to "believe." "No other sin," he says, "exists in the world save unbelief. All others are mere trifles. . . . All sins shall be forgiven if we only believe in Christ." This thought of the all-forgiving nature of faith so dominated his mind that it excluded the notion of contrition, penance, good works or effort on the part of the believer; and thus his teaching destroyed, root and branch, the whole idea of human culpability and responsibility for the breaking of the Commandments.

Now, let us see the teaching of Luther in its practical working. He was frequently asked for advice on moral questions by his friends who were grievously troubled on account of certain temptations and who desired to know the best means to be used to overcome the affliction of their souls. One of these was Jerome Weller, a former pupil of Luther's and one of the table companions who took notes for the *Table Talk*. This young man was long and grievously tormented with anxiety of mind and was unable to quiet, by means of the new Evangel, the scruples of conscience which were driving him to despair. When he asked for advice in his sad state of soul, Luther sent him the following strange reply: "Poor Jerome Weller, you have temptations; they must be overcome. When the devil comes to tempt and harass you with thoughts of the kind you allude to, have recourse at once to conversation, drink more freely, be jocose and playful and even indulge some sin in hatred of the evil spirit and to torment him, to leave him no room to make us over-zealous about the merest trifles; otherwise we are beaten if we are too nervously sensitive about guarding against sin. If the devil says to you, 'Will you not stop drinking, answer him: I will drink all the more because you forbid it; I will drink great draughts in the name and to the honor of Jesus Christ.' Imitate me. I never drink so well, I never eat so much, I never enjoy myself so well at table as when I am vexing the devil who is prepared to mock and harass me. Oh, that I could paint sin in a fair light, so as to mock at the devil and make him see that I acknowledge no sin and am not conscious of having committed any! I tell you, we must put all the Ten Commandments, with which the devil tempts and plagues us so greatly, out of sight and out of mind. If the devil upbraids us with our sins and declares us to be deserving of death and Hell, then we must say: 'I confess that I have merited death and Hell,' but what then? Are you for that reason to be damned eternally? By no means. 'I know One who suffered and made satisfaction for me, viz., Jesus Christ, the Son of God. Where He is, there also I shall be.'" (*De Wette,* I V. 188).

Here we have a characteristic sample of Luther's strange asceticism and astounding liberalism. How different all this is from what Christ and His Church propound for the expiation of sin committed and the prevention of its recurrence. According to these, we are under the obligation to resist the irregular tendencies of the heart and to crucify it with its immoderate desires. (*Gal.* 5:24). If Luther had been a real friend of Weller's and a true master of the spiritual life, why did he not counsel him to avoid sin and cultivate a more intimate union with God through prayer, penance, and the reception of the Sacraments? Surely he must have known that there is a certain demon, according to the words of Jesus Christ, which can be conquered only by fasting and prayer. (*Mark* 9:28). But the salutary remedies of the Master did not appeal to this strange man who thought that faith in Christ alone washes all sin away. He preferred, as he said, "to leave these fine recipes to the stupid Papists." Abhorring the thought of penance and mortification and denying the necessity of good works, nothing more efficacious might be expected than the vile and pernicious prescription he gave to Weller. The true spiritual director was never known to advise more "liberal potations," "to seek company," and "to indulge in jest and play" in order to foil the devil. Like the blind leader of the blind, he wanted something unheard of before, something novel, something startling to put the devil to flight, and that, in his estimation, was always when troubled with scruples of conscience to be heedless of sin and indulge even in more frivolity than Satan suggested. Thus with a boldness that was never equalled, he unblushingly recommended remedies which, to say the least, were most dangerous to weak and afflicted souls and calculated to undermine the binding force of the Decalogue in the eyes and thoughts of men. Only one mentally unbalanced and spiritually deranged could advance such a rule of conduct in defiance of all the proprieties prescribed and sanctioned by law and order.

The unholy counsels which Luther gave to Weller, to despise sin and to meet temptation by frivolity, are explained in greater fullness in the *Table Talk*, a work which was compiled by his pupils and in which his teaching is recorded in most disgusting detail. "How often," he says, "have I taken with my wife those liberties which nature permits, merely in order to get rid of Satan's temptations. Yet all to no purpose, for he refused to depart: for Satan, as the author of death, has depraved our nature to such an extent that we will not admit any consolation. Hence I advise everyone who is able to drive away these Satanic thoughts by diverting his mind, to do so, for instance, by thinking of a pretty girl, of money-making, or of drink, or, in fine, by means of some other vivid emotion." (*Colloq. ed. Bindsell,* 2 p. 299). "Let us fix our minds on other thoughts," he had also said to Schlaginhaufen, "on thoughts of dancing, or of a pretty girl, that also is good." Such, according to his own confession, were the means he employed himself and advised others to use to get rid of the disquieting twinges of conscience. Had he desired to recall the teaching and practice of the Catholic Church, how vastly different would have been his advice to the sorely tried in their moments of temptations—when prayer for God's help, true humility and earnest striving after a change of heart are alone efficacious.

Luther's fullest contempt for violations of the Decalogue is found in the famous letter he addressed from the Wartburg under date of August 1st, 1521, to his most intimate friend, Melanchthon, to encourage him with regard to possible sins of the past and prepare him to meet temptations in the future. The reader who is anxious to see the letter in its entirety can find it in Grisar's work, Volume III, page 196. His advice is couched in the following words: "Be a sinner, and sin boldly, but believe more boldly still. . . . We must sin as long as we are what we are . . . sin shall not drag us away from Him [Christ] even should we commit fornication or murder, thousands and thousands of times a day," provided the sinner only believed. Thus he repeats, against the traditional view of sin and grace, his teaching of justification by faith alone.

In his estimation, sin now must be regarded as something harmless in view of the satisfying Redemption of Christ by faith. This is the culmination of all his practical ideas of religion. "Be a sinner," he says, "sin boldly and fearlessly." The command embodied in the unauspicious words sets at naught all the laws of morality and gives wide scope to human freedom and to disorder. The thought of the degrading recommendation makes the blood run cold in the veins of decent, law-abiding people. In the face of the infamous suggestion, it is difficult to conceive how men with any pretentions to reverence for the Decalogue can be found to designate one who so unblushingly urges its violation as a "dear man of God." If the author of such an infamous suggestion as is involved in the words "sin boldly" was not a child of Satan, none ever labored so strenuously in advancing his soul-destroying principles.

The defenders of Luther do not deny the recommendation he addressed to Melanchthon. To hide its grossness, however, they, in the blasphemy of despair, have edited and interpreted the recommendation so as to give it a turn and a meaning altogether unwarranted and untenable. Luther said: "Be a sinner and sin boldly." His supporters, to hoodwink and deceive their followers, claim that the imperative mood used by Luther is not here to be read imperatively, and according to them, "Be a sinner and sin boldly" means, "even supposing thou art a sinner and dost sin boldly." This interpretation is ingenious, but like all their methods of defense to escape from the infamy of Luther's teaching, as Anderdon remarks, "the deploying of imperatives into subjunctives, suppositions, exaggerations, reductions *ad absurdum,* will never make the imperative mood read otherwise than as a clear, distinct injunction. Until some more formidable line of defense be invented, we must take Luther's words to mean, as they manifestly indicate, a recommendation, an exhortation and an injunction to mutiny, rebellion and disobedience to the Supreme Lawgiver, who directed all to observe and not disrespect His Commandments." Luther's pronouncement, "Be a sinner and sin boldly," has only one meaning, namely, a command to transgress the Divine Law, insult God and open up the way to the commission of crime and iniquity. If Luther knew his Bible as thoroughly as his advocates suppose, how could he, unless he was devoid of the elementary instinct of common propriety, advise his friend Melanchthon to provoke the divine justice by the commission of sin and expose him thereby to the willful risk of eternal chastisement? Had Luther been a true friend to Melanchthon and a trusted spiritual guide, he would have counselled him to cease to "sin," and not "to have strong sins," for only then faith in Christ brings consolation, joy and peace. Had he not been dominated by his unbounded self-sufficiency, he might have recalled with profit the divine warning so often repeated in Scripture: "Flee from sins as from the face of a serpent; for if thou comest near them, they will take hold of thee. The teeth thereof are the teeth of a lion, killing the souls of men. All iniquity is like a two-edged sword; there is no remedy for the wound thereof."

(*Ecclus.* 21: 1, 3). To recall these or other words of Scripture to Melanchthon would have been a kindness, but this was not Luther's way once his mind was made up to minimize, if possible, the influence of the Commandments in the lives of men.

When we consider his own behavior and the dangerous advice he gave his friends, we are led to believe that only one devoid of his senses or one morally weak could condone, palliate and defend sin, which is always contemptible both from a natural and a supernatural point of view, and is ever a base act of cowards who are too indifferent to conform their lives to the divine code of morality. Account as we may for Luther's suggestion to Melanchthon, the fact remains that he brazenly trifled with the soul-destroying principle of sin to spread corruption from that day to this in the body politic. The debasing teaching he shamefully advanced struck a mighty blow at the foundation on which all laws repose, and, as might be expected, a deplorable relaxation of principle among the deluded came along, as a matter of course, to curse the earth from that day to this. Following the example of Luther, many ever since have been loud in their praise of sin, and at times the more revolting it is the greater are the encomiums of it.

It cannot be denied that Luther taught that "good works are useless," that "they are sin," and, in fact, "impossible." In his *Babylonian Captivity* (chap. de Bapt.) he says, "The way to Heaven is narrow; if you wish to pass through it, throw away your good works." "Those pious souls," he says further, "who do good to gain the Kingdom of Heaven, not only will never succeed, but they must even be reckoned among the impious; and it is more important to guard them against good works than against sin." (*Wittenb.* VI. 160). Thus good works, the practice of piety, and the observance of the divine Commandments—the only way, according to Jesus Christ, which leads to eternal life—are in his estimation troublesome superfluities, of which

Christian liberty must rid us. Rather, according to this false teacher, they are invincible obstacles to salvation if one places the least reliance upon them. "Faith alone," said he, "is necessary for justification: nothing else is commanded or forbidden." "Believe, and henceforth you are as holy as St. Peter."

To bring these horrible doctrines, which sought to take from the Sacraments their efficacy and to throw saving grace into disrepute, was his avowed object. The utility and importance of the sacramental system of the Church once destroyed, it may easily be imagined what scope would be given to the passions and how the greatest excesses were likely to be committed. The influence exerted by the doctrine we have just mentioned immediately produced a great and widespread deterioration of morals, both public and private. Of this the writings of Luther's age and of that immediately following furnish incontestable proof. Out of many unsuspected Lutheran authorities we take one who was Luther's pupil and a boarder in his house, namely, John Mathesius. He complains of the spread of immorality, infidelity and oppression brought about through the introduction of the Reformation and states the cause of it all in these words: "Many false brethren, who flatter the people and ascribe all to the justification by faith, do not wish to hear anything of good works, but say openly: only have faith and do as you please, good or evil, it will not harm you as long as you are predestinated to be saved." The same notorious fact concerning the deterioration of morals is referred to in the sermons, correspondence, and other writings of the "Reformers," and those of the humanists, who, like Erasmus, at that time sided decidedly neither with the Reformers nor with the Church. So too do Hume, Robertson, Macauley, and Lecky, even while they, each in his own way, endeavor to disparage the Catholic religion.

Immediately on the preaching of this doctrine, crimes increased in number and enormity. In all classes frivolity and every kind of vice, sin and disgrace were much greater than formerly. Men quickly learned the lessons taught them both by the precepts and the example of their master. Setting up the rule unfolded to them for their guidance, they scoffed at and defied authority, secular and spiritual. In the name of "justification by faith alone," they dispensed themselves from performing good works, and without activity in the cause of goodness, they gradually fell into serious breaches of the divine Law. A rigid Pharisaical severity on certain points was united with utter license as regards many of the plainest obligations of religion and morality. The statute books of the several principalities of which Germany was then composed, of Belgium and the Netherlands, of France and Switzerland, and of England, the severe measures resorted to by the magistrates to repress general lawlessness, of which they complain in their official reports and declare themselves unable to check, furnish indisputable evidence directly to the point. But it is needless to multiply proofs. We call Luther himself as witness and give his own declaration as to the effects produced upon morality and religion by the new gospel of "faith without works."

"I would not be astonished," he says, "if God should open the gates and windows of Hell, and snow or rain down devils, or rain down on our heads fire and brimstone, or bury us in a fiery abyss as He did Sodom and Gomorrah. Had Sodom and Gomorrah received the gifts that have been granted to us, had they seen our visions and received our instructions, they would yet be standing. They were a thousand times less culpable than Germany, for they had not received the Word of God from their preachers. . . . If Germany will act thus, I am ashamed to be one of her children or speak her language; and if I were permitted to impose silence on my conscience, I would call in the Pope and assist him and his minions to forge new claims for us. Formerly, when we were the slaves of Satan, when we profaned the name of God . . . money could be procured for endowing churches, for raising seminaries, for maintaining superstition. Now that we know the divine word, that we have learned to honor the blood of our Martyr-God, no one wishes to give anything. The children are neglected, and no one teaches them to serve God."

"Since the downfall of Popery and the cessations of excommunications and spiritual penalties, the people have learned to despise the word of God. They care no longer for the churches; they have ceased to fear and honor God. . . . I would wish, if it were possible, to leave these men without preacher or pastor, and let them live like swine. There is no longer any fear or love of God among them. After throwing off the yoke of the Pope, everyone wishes to live as he pleases." (These and numerous other lamentations may be found in Walch ed.).

This declaration of Luther is significant, and testimonies from almost every writer of eminence who touches upon the state of society as regards religion and morals in every country where Protestantism had a foothold in the sixteenth and seventeenth centuries, might be adduced in confirmation of it. So notorious was the debauchery of the followers of Luther that it became a common saying when persons proposed to engage in drunkenness and revelry: "We will spend the day like *Lutherans*." "Drunkenness has come upon us like a deluge." (*Walch* XII, 788).

The new Gospel did not even make Luther himself better. He said: "I confess. . . that I am more negligent than I was under the Pope and there is now nowhere such an amount of earnestness under the Gospel, as was formerly seen among monks and priests." (*Walch,* IX. 1311). "If God," he says, "had not closed my eyes, and if I had foreseen these scandals, I would never have begun to teach the Gospel." (*Walch,* VI, 920).

"But it is not necessary," as a writer in the *American Catholic Quarterly Review* says, "to go back to past ages of the so-called Reformation to decide whether it has produced a real reformation as regards morality. It is only necessary to look upon facts existing all around us today. Protestantism has existed now for nearly four hundred years and has had ample time to show what improvement it can effect or has effected as regards to morality. Yet, notwithstanding all the efforts still made, here and there, to perpetuate the old traditional falsehood of the superiority of Protestantism over the Catholic religion in promoting morality, the most thoughtful and candid even of Protestants award the palm to Catholicity; and the general verdict of public opinion is fast confirming this decision. It is not necessary to refer to official statistics of crime and social immorality, which have been published and republished, analyzed, and exhaustively discussed by such non-Catholic writers as Laing, Mayhew, Wolsey, Bayard Taylor, Dr. Bellows, and many others, to prove that Protestant countries are not in advance of those where Catholicity predominates as respects morality.

"It is acknowledged by almost all who have any real knowledge of the subject that in point of purity of morals, Catholic Spain and the really Catholic part of the people of France and Italy are immeasurably above the people of Protestant Germany, Denmark, Sweden and Norway; and that judged by every test applicable to morality—female chastity, integrity and sobriety—Catholic Ireland is far in advance of Protestant Scotland. The inhabitants of Tyrol—during past centuries and today the most staunch and exclusive Catholic population in Europe—beyond all denial, stand above the people of Protestant Switzerland with regard to morality. The lazzaroni of Naples, for years the standing gibe and jest of Protestant travelers, are immeasurably less debased as regards morality than persons on the same social plane in England. Coming nearer home—for every act of brigandage, murder, or robbery in Italy and Spain, there might be truthfully recounted ten in the United States.

"This brings us still closer to our point. Compare the virtue and integrity here, in our country, and in England, of the persons who are under the respective influences of the Catholic religion and of Protestantism, and the general public voice ascribes superiority to the former. Where is the boasted morality of New England, the cradle and home of Puritanism? How stand, as regards social morals or honesty, the descendants of the 'Pilgrim Fathers'? And what are the moral consequences of their principles as they have permeated the public mind outside of persons who believe in and practice the Catholic religion? Witness the countless prosecutions for bigamy, for the violations of the obligation of the marriage relation, for adultery and seduction; the applications for divorces, and the scandals, frauds, etc. which crowd the records of our courts and the reportorial columns of the newspapers.

"It seems that God, in His justice, had determined summarily and at once to dispel the traditional delusion of the superiority of Protestantism over the Catholic religion in point of morals, and to refute once and forever the false charge, so long and persistently brought against the latter, by compelling people to open their eyes and look at the facts staring them in the face."

It is not a pleasant task to tell the story of hideous crime, no matter by whom committed. We would that there were no sin in the world to record. If we allude to the gross immoralities that followed everywhere among the peoples that adopted the soul-destroying principles announced by Luther, we do so with feelings of shame, and in self-defense against the gratuitous allegations of our adversaries. We certainly do not wish to prove that all Catholics avail themselves of the means their Church provides for attaining to sanctity of life, nor do we wish to excuse or palliate the corruption of morals sometimes found in their behavior. We cannot close our eyes to the painful fact that too many professing Catholics, far from living up to the teachings of their Church, are sources of melancholy scandal. "It must, however, be that scandals come," but their occasional occurrences among the members of the Church do not invalidate or impair the sacred and efficacious means she furnishes for holiness of life. We know that some Catholics are a disgrace to their religion and that they ought to be much better than they are, considering the potent means ever at their call. Yet, with Cardinal Gibbons, we will add, quoting his words in the *Catholic World:* "If we are not very much better than our neighbors, we are not any worse, and are not to be hounded down with the cry of vice and immorality by a set of Pharisees who are constantly lauding their own superiority, and thanking God they are so much better than we poor Catholics."

We have been careful in this paper to furnish the reader with Luther's own words describing his teaching on the absolute uselessness of all the hitherto, and even now generally accepted means for avoiding sin and helps for attaining sanctification. A cursory examination of the system he fathered shows it, as Fr. Johnston points out, to be absolutely "at variance with all Christian ideas on the subject both before his age and even now. Even a modern Protestant, by his devotion to prayer and penance and good works, practically repudiates this system of morality of a man whom he otherwise so blindly and inconsistently venerates as a great 'Reformer.' In fact, such a system is contradictory to even the most elementary psychology and everyday experience. It is at variance with the idea of penance and sin held by even the non-Christian religions such as Buddhism and Brahminism—as such, it is about the lowest and the most hedonistic in the whole history of religions. In a word it is unique. There is nothing in Christianity, ancient, medieval or modern, like it—nor in any other religion. Followed out to its logical conclusion, it can end only in unrestricted moral license. The reason that it is not followed out by Protestants is partly because they practically deny in practice the Lutheran faith they hold in theory, partly because they are, as a class, densely ignorant of the real crass Luther and Lutheranism; partly because their very common sense and sense of decency and weekday psychology save them from their own faith." (*Luther's Claim to Divine Mission*, 14).

From Luther's own words we learn the distincly heretical and truth-destroying character of his teaching which struck at the roots of man's relation with God. Faith with him, as Anderdon remarks, "was no longer what it had been through all previous Christianity, the supernatural grace, the gift from Heaven, by which man is enabled to accept and to retain a Revelation external to himself and in its fullness. It became simply a strong persuasion of one's individual acceptance with God. Faith as propounded by the Church contemplates God, and what He has said and done, warned and promised; faith as propounded by Luther regards the individual, who takes hold upon and appropriates to himself the results of what God has done. The essence of Catholic faith lies in God's catholic or universal truthfulness, projected in outline upon His Mystical Body, through all place and time. It is independent of individual minds and as high above 'religious opinions' as the heavens are above the earth. The Lutheran faith, so called, is a mongrel thing, partly personal belief, partly hope of acceptance, except that it rests on a personal assurance, and so is allied to presumption. Catholic faith is the mainspring of active obedience, 'working one's salvation' (*Phil.* 2:12); the Lutheran substitute is a principle of a dreamy acquiescence that contemplates "a finished work" on the part of the Saviour. Again, the Church teaches that faith on the one hand, and on the other hand love or the state of grace—though they have great mutual relations—are distinct gifts. The former may exist without the other, as in the case of every bad Catholic, who will be lost without true repentance for his personal sins, in spite of his Baptism and of the most unclouded faith. With Luther, faith does not imply distinct dogmatic truth; its creed is summoned up in this, 'I am a justified man; therefore I cannot lose my faith and fall from acceptance; therefore sin in me is not imputed as sin.'" This is Luther's teaching—novel, soothing, agreeable to human nature, if you will, but it is not Christ's nor that of His Church which is His organ of communicating supernatural truth and the means of acquiring sanctification.

Luther's teaching may appeal to such as decline to look things in the face and want the subjective in religion, in lieu of the objective dogmatic truth; but it can never appeal to the enlightened of God, who know that His will is their sanctification, and that they must labor in this life by good works, by prayer, by the observance of the Commandments, and the reception of the Sacraments, to make their calling and election sure. Faith and good works are the only terms on which men can purchase happiness here and hereafter; every other scheme is a deceit of Lucifer to draw souls away from the love and service of God.

This statement is not made without foundation. Read Luther's work against "The Mass and the Ordination of Priests" (*Erl.* 31, 311 ff.) where he tells of his famous disputation with the "Father of Lies" who accosted him at "midnight" and spoke to him with a deep, powerful voice," causing "the sweat to break forth" from his brow and his "heart to tremble and beat." In that celebrated conference, of which he was an unexceptionable witness and about which he never entertained the slightest doubt, he says plainly and unmistakingly that "the devil spoke against the Mass, and Mary and the Saints" and that, moreover, Satan gave him the most unqualified approval of his doctrine on justification by faith alone." Who now, we ask in all sincerity, can be found, except those appallingly blind to truth, to accept such a man, approved by the enemy of souls, as a spiritual teacher and entrust to his guidance their eternal welfare?

NOTES

1. The terms "justification" and "sanctification" both refer to the presence of Sanctifying Grace in the soul—that is, a participation in the Divine Life. (Cf. Appendix for the teaching of Trent on justification.) This is what Our Lord described when He spoke of the

vine and the branches: "Abide in me, and I in you. As the branch cannot bear fruit of itself, unless it abide in the vine, so neither can you, unless you abide in me. I am the vine; you the branches: he that abideth in me, and I in him, the same beareth much fruit: for without me you can do nothing." (*John* 15:4-5).

2. The Catholic Church teaches that only acts performed in the state of grace are meritorious for salvation, since only when a person is in the state of grace is he a living "branch" receiving divine life from the "Vine" which is Christ. (*Jn.* 15:5). Acts of virtue performed by a person in the state of mortal sin are "dead works"; they are useless for salvation and merit no supernatural reward—that is, an increase of sanctifying grace, and eventually Heaven. (Nevertheless, God may look upon such works, in His mercy, as a plea for forgiveness and grace.) In addition, every good act performed by a person in the state of grace is prompted by an "actual grace" from God, "actual grace" being a transitory supernatural help given to enable one to do good or avoid evil. Thus is the Christian completely dependent, in a twofold manner, on God in the performance of every good work.
3. For a man outside the state of grace this is true; but a man in the state of grace has within himself the very life of God, the principle of supernatural merit. His good works are not merely human works, nor simply actions of divine grace; rather, the good works of the just (those in the state of grace) are human-divine acts, supernaturally valuable and meritorious for salvation.
4. Fiduciary faith is confidence that one has been "saved" by being covered over or credited with the merits of Christ; this theory is Luther's invention. Dogmatic faith is belief in all the teachings of Christ. This is the Catholic meaning of "faith." Fiduciary faith is actually not faith; it is rather presumption, a perversion of the virtue of hope, which is the virtue by which a Christian trusts that God will give him eternal life and the means to obtain it.
5. Baptized children under the age of reason possess Sanctifying Grace and the "seeds," as it were, of faith, hope and charity; this is sufficient for them until such time as they are able to exercise these virtues and grow in grace.
6. Principally the Decalogue, the Ten Commandments.
7. "And Jesus answered him: The first commandment of all is, *Hear, O Israel: the Lord thy God is one God. And thou shalt love the Lord thy God, with thy whole heart, and with thy whole soul, and with thy whole mind, and with thy whole strength.* This is the first commandment. And the second is like to it: *Thou shalt love thy neighbour as thyself.* There is no other commandment greater than these." (*Mk.* 12:29-31).

CHAPTER 5

LUTHER ON THE CHURCH AND THE POPE

ONE of the most certain and best-established facts in the records of mankind is the existence of the Catholic Church, and her admirable career throughout the ages.

As the true Messias, Jesus had come to found the Kingdom of God on earth—that visible and universal kingdom, that new alliance, which, according to the prophets, He should inaugurate for all ages to come. And, in point of fact, Jesus founded this kingdom by instituting His Church. He foretold the persecutions that she would meet, and the continual struggles that she would have to endure in all the centuries; but He declared that the powers of the enemy would never prevail against His Church, because He will be with her, and she will last to the end of the world. And the Church, which has now existed for nearly twenty centuries, stands before all as an undeniable fact attesting the fulfillment of this promise.

The divinity of the Christian religion is a fact which all the efforts of sophistical criticism are powerless to deny or dispute. Witness its rapid and wonderful propagation, notwithstanding the thousands and thousands of obstacles that opposed it; its preservation unchanged amid continual terrible assaults; the testimony of millions and millions of martyrs who died for the faith; the sanctity of the Church in spite of the defects of some of her members; the existence of miracles, which illuminate the history of the Church, and even today occur before the eyes of unbelievers themselves; the excellence and sublimity of the morals and dogmas of the Christian religion, with which those of other faiths can bear no comparison; the adherence of the greatest intellects to the teachings of Christianity. Weigh all these facts and behold so many unanswerable arguments that demonstrate the divinity of the religion which Jesus Christ established in order that all men for all time should come to salvation. All considered, therefore, we may conclude with Richard of St. Victor: "O Lord! if we are mistaken, it is Thou who hast led us astray; because this Faith is proved by such signs and prodigies that Thou alone couldst work them."

Luther, in the earlier period of his life, realized that he and the rest of men could come to salvation only by the knowledge and practice of this Religion of which Jesus Christ is the Soul and the Founder. He knew, as demonstrated by Faith and reason, that Jesus Christ and true religion are to be found only in the Catholic Church, where alone the Master teaches, dispenses His graces and communicates His divine spirit. In common with every believer of his time, he was aware of the existence of this Church; and he recognized that this Church, as originally established in the land of his birth and as it had prevailed there for centuries, was in harmony with that prevailing throughout Christianity and dating back beyond all civil institutions, and was the one sole organization established by Christ and endowed by Him with perpetuity to preach His Gospel for the salvation of the world. As a layman he knew all this, as a priest he taught all this, and as a doctor of divinity he was ever prepared to advocate and defend all this against all comers. For years he continued true to his convictions and to all appearances exemplified them in his daily life. But, as time went on, he gradually became remiss in the discharge of his spiritual duties and little by little came to abandon them entirely; wherefore he lost the graces of his vocation, and in consequence his faith diminished and his allegiance to the Church weakened. By his own admission, as we have seen, he grew careless in the performance of his monastic duties and daily violated the plain and sacred obligations to which he had bound himself voluntarily by most solemn vows. Owing to the habitual neglect of prayer and meditation and the constant infraction of the rules of his Order, he went down the scale of perfection step by step, until, as is invariably the case in such conditions, his perception of divine truth waned and grew weaker day by day until finally he fell into a state of opposition and revolt against the eternal verities and the one true medium of their communication to mankind. Abandoning the light of Heaven which comes from persevering prayer, and carried away by his own self-sufficiency, he began to question, then to ignore, and finally to deny the divine authority of the Church in which he had been reared. He seemed to forget that the Church is the body of Christ, the individual Sacrament of unity with Christ and through Christ with God, and that "whosoever revolteth," according to the dictum of the Holy Spirit, "and hath not the doctrine of Christ, hath not God." But he cared little for so solemn a pronouncement and longed only for emancipation from the authority of the laws of God and of His Church to follow his own ever-varying caprice and fancy.

Possessed now by the spirit of disorder and opposition to law, and jealous of the authority of the Church and the God-given supremacy of her visible head, he conceived the idea of a new religion, which he thought in his vanity he was capable of formulating. Forthwith, without the shadow of a pretense of direct and divine commission, he began to construct what he foolishly considered a church, and then assumed the right to inflict and impose his self-made work upon his fellow men. In his wild scheme he aimed at getting rid of the Church's sacramental system and banishing altogether from men's minds the very idea of an outward and visible sign of an inward and invisible grace. He intended to take from men the only certain voice which, speaking in the name of God and representing Him, delivered infallible truth to the world and announced authoritatively the means whereby sanctification and salvation were to be secured. He purposed, in a word, to overthrow, annihilate and displace the Mother Church, and thus deprive men of her divine guidance unto truth, morality and life eternal. In his conceit he imagined that men should be left wholly to their own unaided and fallible reason, and hence he proclaimed the right of all, without any Church interference, to follow in matters of belief their own intellect as sole and final judge. In advancing this claim, so destructive to the authority of the Church, he asserted a right never before recognized; a right, let it be understood, never known under any other form of revealed religion; a right never allowed even under the Jewish theocracy; and a right hardly ever exercised among the more enlightened pagans. His program was one of the most daring in all human history. Though he had his misgivings about the propriety and success of his sacrilegious undertaking, yet he hardened his heart against these, and imagined that though many other "instigators of heresies and breeders of sects" in the fifteen hundred years before his time had failed in measuring their strength against the Church of Christ, he could not but triumph. His attitude was bold, defiant, arrogant, persecuting. He would overthrow and completely destroy the Church of his fathers. But the Founder of this Church had decreed that the powers of Hell would not prevail against His institution, and Luther, before he closed his eyes in death, saw that his protest was unavailing and that his self-made substitute for God's enduring work was doomed to meet the fate of all the other religious innovations that had scandalized preceding ages.

Luther came by degrees to feel that he was something more than Church or Pope or councils. In his vanity he put himself above all the great and learned lights of the Church and claimed to know more than all the schoolmen, Doctors and Fathers who in every age were noted for their clear, precise and exact exposition of God's revelation. To his way of thinking, all the great and saintly writers and defenders of the Church: Jerome, Chrysostom, Cyprian, Basil, Augustine, Thomas Aquinas and the rest, "fell into error" and were "untrustworthy teachers, pools out of which Christians had been drinking impure and loathsome water." In his mad ravings he called them "knaves, dolts, asses, and infernal blasphemers," "knowing very little about the Gospel, easily deceived by the devil and deserving to be in hell rather than in heaven." The majestic unity and the calm, unchanging enunciation of truth which characterized the writings of the Fathers in all the ages displeased, annoyed, and angered this false prophet. He would have none of them or their teachings, except when some fellow rebel against divine authority was in collision with him or when he had to appeal to some authority beyond himselt to refute an adversary, as for instance when he had to put down Zwingli. Otherwise he had no use for the recognized and authoritative exponents of the faith once delivered to the saints. They were in the way of the advancement of his nefarious scheme, and their influence and testimony to the uniform and universal belief of mankind throughout the ages should be destroyed. The Fathers and the Doctors were against his program; they were, one and all, "asses, rascals, beasts, Antichrists" and "unworthy of a hearing." He alone was right; he knew more than all of them put together; and, as they were "authors of impious things, empty declaimers, of no weight whatever, theological abortions, fountains of error," he thought he was called by Heaven to speak out and tell mankind it needed a new church, that the old one was alien to the world and must be destroyed, and that he, the "doctor of doctors," as he called himself, alone had the "doctrines from Heaven" which all henceforward must receive from his mouth lest they be "everlastingly condemned."

Luther now claimed more authority than any pope ever did. In his heart he knew that the work he was undertaking was unwarranted, unjustifiable and outrageously sacrilegious. But the spirit of rebellion against constituted authority, especially in the ecclesiastical order, took possession of him, and nothing now would stop him from sounding the trumpet of battle against the ancient Church, her teaching and her discipline. To escape the shame of his atrocity, he, as deceptive as he was subtle, began his work of destruction by mingling with the crowds to win disciples who were only too glad to "take revenge on Christianity for having so long interrupted the pleasures of the world." To these he preached rebellion and awoke that chord which responded in the heart of Eve to the Tempter's first whisper: "Why hath God commanded you?" Directing his shafts against the force of law, to give zest to his harangues, he spoke not "those things that are right," as Scripture enjoins, but "pleasant things," "errors" such as the populace who long to be deceived glory in, and hence, knowing the open road to an assured popularity and fame, he talked loudly and boisterously of the misdeeds, more or less real, of some of the members of the Church and of certain abuses which actually had crept into the Church.

This was a very clever and cunning way to inflame the passions of the lawless and the wicked, and to divert attention from his own heretical teachings and notoriously scandalous behavior. During all this time he was seemingly unconscious of his own faults, which sadly needed reformation and removal. He was, however, wide-awake and ever on the lookout for the shortcomings and the defects of the brethren in the household of the Faith in order to use these as a weapon against the Church and thus unfairly place responsibility where it did not belong. He seemed to take a special delight in keeping his nose fixed at the leak in the sewer and then rudely exposing the evils discovered in the lives of some whose personal conduct in certain directions was in conflict with the lofty and elevated teachings they professed. The illustrious deeds and the holy lives of the millions that were true to their holy calling were, for the moment, conveniently forgotten, and the corruption of the few that followed the misuse of wealth and power he emphasized and magnified for the outcry of men who themselves were anything but "reformed in the newness of their mind." The shortcomings of some, no doubt, presented then as now grievous stumbling blocks and tended to disedify. The Founder of the Church predicted that scandals would arise, but at the same time He was careful to warn all against using these as a motive for disloyalty and a basis for disobedience to legitimate authority. We do not wish to deny that some of the brethren, Luther himself for instance, were not always careful to exemplify in their lives the salutary morality which the Church ever and constantly preached to her members. It should be remembered, however, that whatever self-indulgence, pride, ambition and political profligacy existed now and then, were all traceable to a disregard for the Church's teachings and were committed in violation of her disciplinary regulations. The Church, therefore, could not rightly be held responsible for the misdeeds of her unfaithful children. Whatever abuses existed always sprang from the personal and not the official side of the Church; they were not inherent in the Church and did not originate in her essential constitution, nor grow out of it. It is only gross ignorance or malignity that attempts to make the Church responsible for the misdeeds and indiscretions of her unfaithful and degenerate members. It is remarkable, however, that in all matters of doctrine and morals not one among the unfaithful of all times ever directly or remotely set himself at variance as Luther did with the teachings and practices of historical Christianity. No bad Catholic before his day attempted to set up so false a Christianity; none ever so tampered with the original deposit of the True Faith; none ever dared assail the organization which God had established, and which He commanded all to obey and respect if they desired eternal life.

When Luther discovered that he could not frighten the Head of the Church, intimidate legitimate authority, and impose his special brand of reform, which was no reform at all, he was greatly disappointed and disturbed. Chagrined and wounded in his vanity, he grew litigious, vengeful and abusive. He had every opportunity in his chosen field, had he so willed, to seek out and minister to the lost and wandering sheep. Like many saintly souls in every age, he might by preaching, prayer and example have helped towards that reformation of abuses which the Church is ever attempting by canons of discipline—papal, provincial, diocesan—but this ministry of zeal and salvation, within the Church and not out of it, was not to his liking. What he wished was not the restoration of the lost and the reformation of the imperfect whose abuses he criticized, but the destruction of the sheepfold established by the One Great Shepherd of souls and the overthrow of His vicar's supreme authority. Little aware of his folly and carried away by an uncontrollable anger, he set to work not only to divide but to destroy the Kingdom of Christ and wreck the Bark of Peter.

The special weapons he used in his opposition against the Mystical Body of Christ and its representative on earth were calumny, abuse and misrepresentation. Though the Church has the right to have said of her nothing but what is true, yet Luther, in order to advance his nefarious scheme, twisted and altered and changed her well-known doctrines, which had remained intact and uncorrupted for centuries, to deceive the unwary masses unable to discern the malignant poison of heresy. Arrogating to himself more authority than any pope ever did, he falsely alleged that the Church founded by Jesus Christ was "corrupt in its very constitution"; that from the temple of God it had become "a synagogue of Satan"; that its visible head, the Pope, was "Antichrist," and that "the Papacy must be destroyed." He contended in a pamphlet that the Papacy is "an institution of the devil"; and he abused all Popes, Bishops, priests, monks, and Catholics in general, in the coarsest and most brutal manner. Possessed of a satanical hatred of all authority save what he claimed for himself, he imagined that the Church was all wrong and should be cast aside as a human invention, despite the fact that her Founder was Jesus Christ, who promised the assistance of the Holy Ghost to protect her from error and who declared He would preserve her to the end of time to spread the glad tidings of Redemption. Disregarding the magnificent unity of faith which had reigned during centuries before his day, the result not of ignorance or indifference, but of enlightened science and spiritual earnestness due to the powerful teachings of the missionaries and the profound expositions of the Scholastic theologians, he, in his brazen conceit, thought the time had come "to deliver Europe from the yoke of the Popes and the superstitions of an idolatrous worship." What he thought was needed in his day were *his* ways of explaining the truths and maxims of the Gospel, and *his* new doctrines, entirely different from and opposed to those which were taught and had been taught throughout historical Christianity. Thus his avowed object was to displace the Church, founded for all time by Jesus Christ, and in her stead rear up a new Christianity, form a new Scripture, prescribe a new faith and establish a new worship, something never dreamt of or recognized before his day. "The Bible," he alleged, "furnished the necessary instruction and authority for such an undertaking," and forthwith he declared that it and it alone, left to the caprice of individuals and interpreted without the traditional teaching of a Church divinely empowered to safeguard and explain it, was the sole and ultimate criterion of the Christian's faith. "The Bible and nothing but the Bible" became the familiar Protestant formula, which, as history tells, wherever it was followed out in practice, invariably resulted in confusion and produced as many religions as thinkers, or semi-thinkers, or no thinkers at all. An open Bible cannot render, and never will render, man's private judgment infallible. Freedom of interpretation means the destruction of all sure doctrine, the death-blow to truth handed down, the tearing asunder of religious union and the beginning of endless dissensions.

The life work Luther now proposed to himself had for its object the ignoble purpose of destroying the Church, disrupting the solidarity of united Christian belief, and leaving men without a safe guide as to the verities which the Almighty wished His subjects to know and the worship He required. The Reformer's genius, if we may dignify his spirit of destruction by that name, ended here. The Church, which in her appointment is as divine as the creation of the visible firmament of the heavens, he would not have; and yet to replace it or offer a worthy substitute, even were this possible, he of all men was manifestly incompetent. Ever vacillating, ambiguous, contradictory, he was utterly incapable of formulating a clear, well-defined, unhesitating system of belief to replace that of the old divinely established Church. It was a special characteristic of him, as every student of his life knows, to deny one day what he professed the day before. At one moment he would declare the Church infallible, and the next he would say it is fallible. He urged that all should submit to the Councils of the Church, and then that they must not. He maintained that the civil government had power over the ministers of religion, and then denied it. He admitted that there was a Hell, and afterwards questioned its existence. He taught that the Sacraments conferred grace, and advocated the contrary. He claimed that there were seven Sacraments, and then reduced them to two, increased them to three, and finally to five. He maintained each of the Sacraments, and denied five of them. In Baptism, he both admitted and denied that grace was conferred, and taught that Original Sin was effaced and that it was not. He maintained that there was a Purgatory and that we should pray for the dead, and then denied it.

These are only a few specimens of Luther's constant variation in teaching. They show how uncertain his attitude was regarding religious truth, and therefore how unfitted he was for the delicate task of framing a new profession of faith which could in any sense be presented and maintained before an exacting and intelligent world. His associates in rebellion recognized this uncertainty and often called attention to his lack of solid foundation in religious exposition. Cochlaeus says: "The seven-headed Luther everywhere contradicts himself and his own teaching." It is, moreover, a matter of history that when the meeting of the Diet at Augsburg made it necessary for the Protestant party to state distinctly its faith, Luther sinks to a secondary place. All knew that he was as unstable as water and could not be trusted to adhere to any pronouncement for the brief space of twenty-four hours. The Augsburg Confession, which is to this day the creed of the Lutherans, and printed in the beginning of some of their prayer books, is not the work of Luther. It was drawn up by Melanchthon, who corresponded with Luther, then at Coburg, but did not adhere to his views.

Fair-minded Protestant authors have all along admitted the woeful vagueness, inconsistency and perpetual contradictions everywhere noticeable in their hero's pronouncements on religious questions, but, strange to say, many of them do not consider his irreconcilable differences in dealing with eternal truth as real defects. They very cleverly but deceitfully evade the real issue by endeavoring to make their readers believe that his aberrations in doctrinal matters only show forth their formulator's wonderful intellectual versatility, vigor and wealth. These writers have eyes and see not that the contradictions so noticeable in their master's pronouncements on all matters religious unfit him to be in any sense a reliable exponent of Eternal Law and that his wild and reckless inconsistency in presenting his newfangled ideas, opposed entirely to all divine ordinances, disqualify him as a religious teacher and a spiritual guide to whom anyone could with safety entrust the care of his salvation. If the minds of such writers are not warped by prejudice, they should realize that when Luther set himself up as a religious leader and claimed a divine mission to teach truth, he should at least have been clear-headed enough to have given his hearers an exact, definite and consistent answer to any and all the vital problems affecting the interests of men's souls. This Luther did not and could not do so. He never knew for a moment what he was going to teach next. He despised the Church with her determined, fixed and unalterable declaration of truth, and thus, like unto "the heathen and the publican," his perception of divine truth became obscured, leaving him and all who were ever led by him, like "children," as St. Paul says, "tossed to and fro with every wind of doctrine." (*Eph.* 4:14). His "wickedness," to use the word of St. Paul at the end of the text just quoted to describe the promoters of false doctrine, taught men to "dissolve Jesus," deny the teachings of His Gospel and impose an impious travesty of Christianity that preaches "peace, and there is no peace." Look out on the Christian world today, with its hundred and more warring denominations,[1] and behold how few of the original articles of faith have survived among the disciples and followers of Luther.

Luther's advocates might, if their eyes are not filmed, read with profit the following words which their master penned when he had genuine misgivings at the outset of his apostasy. "How many times," he writes, "have I not asked myself with bitterness the same question which the Papists put me: Art thou alone wise? Darest thou imagine that all mankind have been in error for so long a series of years? I am not so bold as to assert that I have been guided in this affair by God. How will it be, if, after all, it is thou thyself who art wrong, and art thou involving in thy error so many souls who will then be eternally damned?" (*Latin Works,* Weim. ed., 8, p. 411 seq.). Some time after he wrote these words and reflected that "it is a terrible thing and full of danger to lift one's voice in the Church of God," he felt that he "could heartily wish to bury all in silence and pass a sponge over what he had written," knowing that he would "have to render an account to God for every heedless word." Compunction came too late. In spite of all his regrets he never had the courage to take in hand "the sponge" he spoke of to wipe out the slanderous scribblings and wanton perversions of truth he had penned against the Church of God and her infallible head. He went into eternity without, as far as we know, a sign of repentance, and, very likely, died as he had lived, blaspheming the Church which he had misrepresented and abused but which he could not either overthrow or destroy. Such an end was sad beyond expression. Would it not be well, whilst there is time, for all who, like him, revile, hate and misrepresent the Church and her doctrinal virtues and ethics, to carefully ponder over their master's mistake? The monomania of opposing the Church of Christ and decrying her authority over the souls of men is a disease that all afflicted therewith should rid themselves of at once, for it entails ruin for time and eternity.

Luther openly and unblushingly maintained that the Church founded by Jesus Christ had fallen into error in her teachings and that her doctrines needed change. This outrageous calumny has been assiduously circulated time and time again since its formulator first gave it to the world, and thousands upon thousands have been only too ready to believe it, notwithstanding its falseness, untenableness and, what is worse, its blasphemy against Christ and His Church. The noisy talk of degenerate demagogues who make an easy livelihood by spreading discontent among audiences that are only too ready to listen to everything defamatory of the Church cannot, however, silence truth or prevent the fair-minded and intelligent in the community from searching for it as it is in Christ Jesus and His Church.

On a little reflection, it will appear plain to the unbiased mind that what Luther declared concerning the Church could not be substantiated for the very good and solid reason that "if," as Preston, a distinguished convert from

Episcopalianism, says, "the Church had erred in her teaching of the Articles of Faith confided to her by her Divine Founder, then there never had been a Church, or if there had been a Church, it had not been the Church of Christ. The Church of Christ, if it be the Church of Christ, cannot err in matters of faith and morals, for the moment it errs, it is no longer the Church of Christ, but the Church of the devil. What can there be more plain than this? That cannot be called the Church of Christ which teaches error; but if the Church of Christ can teach error, then, according to the assumption, it is the Church of Christ and it is not the Church of Christ at one and the same time. It is the Church of Christ because, according to the assumption of the moment, it is so called; it is not the Church of Christ, because it teaches falsehood, and cannot, therefore, be the agent of God in any sense. The very idea of a Church having erred in faith destroys it root and branch, and leaves nothing whatever behind it. Again, this theory is open to another consideration. If the Church erred, then Christ broke His word, for He declared that it should not err, and He said to Peter on whom He built His Church: 'The gates of hell shall never prevail against my Church,' and 'I will guide it into all truth.' Now, if the Church erred, the gates of Hell *did* prevail against the Church, and Christ did not keep His promise. But you are to have a new Church and Christ is to be its author. But Christ has broken His work, according to the assumption of Luther and his followers, and, therefore, is not worthy of confidence. Then how can you trust Him again? And yet you are to believe, in one and the same mental act, that Christ broke His word and is not worthy of confidence and that He is worthy of confidence, and accept a new Christianity at His hands. Every logical mind will easily grasp the utter inconsistency of such theories as these." (*The Protestant Reformation,* 71, 72).

Whatever may be said, it is evident that the idea of the error of the Church in matters of faith and morals is suicidal to the Church itself. "The Church of God," says St. Paul, "is the pillar and the ground of truth." (*1 Tim.* 3:13). It holds up the truth to the nations, and on it the truth rests. Now break it down, and where is the pillar and the ground of truth? So when Luther taught that the Church had lapsed into error, and when his imitators continue his wicked work by constructing religious organizations which they know to be human and not divine, the work of man and not of God, each and all contribute their share in the work of crippling, dividing and destroying the Church Jesus Christ established as the organ of His truth for all time; and then, be it remembered, when this Church passes away from the minds of men, then will be obliterated the great bulwark of truth, piety and devotion. Eminent Protestants all along have admitted the influence of the Church on the nations' morality and civilization. "Withdraw that influence," the Rev. Dr. Boynton, a Congregational minister of Brooklyn, New York, says, "and there would be bedlam within a month."

The Catholic Church has always claimed Christ for her Founder and has proved her divine mission and her unchangeable teaching to the world. Eminent non-Catholic divines acknowledge this. From a vast number we select the late Dr. Briggs, a Protestant Episcopalian theologian of New York, who undertook to answer the question, "Who or what is a Catholic," in the *American Journal of Theology,* a periodical connected with Chicago University. "There can be no doubt," he writes, "that at the close of the third century 'Roman' and 'Catholic' were so closely allied that they were practically identical. In other words, connection or communion with the See of Rome was then, as now, a test and condition of one's Catholicity." Dr. Briggs further maintained that "the Roman Catholic Church of our day is the heir by unbroken descent of the Catholic Church of the second century." In his reading of early Christian literature he found the word "Catholic" to stand for three things: (1) the vital unity of the Church of Christ; (2) the geographical unity of the Church extending throughout the world; and (3) the historical unity of the Church in apostolic tradition.

Applying these tests to modern conditions, Dr. Briggs finds: "Geographical unity has been lost by the Protestant Churches, by the Church of England more than any other, for the Church of England is so strictly a national church that she is confined to the Anglo-Saxon race. She has not only no communion with the Roman Church, but she has also no communion with the sister national churches. . . . If we [the Episcopalians] would be Catholic, we cannot become Catholic by merely calling ourselves by that name. Unless the name corresponds with the thing, it is a sham and a shame."

The Catholic Church, then, has been well nigh two thousand years in this world of change, and at no age of her eventful history has her teaching been at variance with that of her Divine Founder. No reliable historian notes that after the death of the last of the Apostles a single change or increase ever took place in the Revelation or Deposit of Faith confided to the Church's keeping. Men, like Luther, accuse the Church of variation, and some, like Tochackert, go as far as to say that she manufactured new dogmas—for instance, the Immaculate Conception of the Virgin Mary and the infallibility of the Pope. Needless to say, all and every accusation of this nature is without the slightest foundation. To charge the Church with the manufacture of new dogmas is merely a scheme invented by designing men to deceive the unwary and prevent them from searching after the truth. The idea is rooted in misconception, bigotry and prejudice.

The Church does not tolerate, and never has in all the ages of her existence tolerated, novelty or newness of doctrine. She very wisely admits a progress, an amplification, and a development of her teaching for the fuller and better understanding and comprehension of divine truth. What has been announced from the beginning she cannot change and never has changed; what she had done and may do at some future time was, under the strain of controversy, the attacks of heresy or other causes, to increase the knowledge of the people regarding the fixed doctrines of Christ and bring out in clearer light and minuter detail the belief contained in the original Deposit of Faith handed down from Apostolic times. Dr. Mausbach, in the *Germania* of June 12, 1902, very pertinently observes: "As the germs of truth that lay dormant in the bosom of the early Church were, like the grain of mustard seed, to expand later on to the fullness of their life and growth, so it has come to pass that the simple and germinal elements of divine truth that appeared in the teachings of the Apostles have, at a later stage of the development of God's Kingdom, been more fully differentiated and more definitely related."

The Church has never assumed the right to formulate new teachings, manufacture new dogmas and impose new doctrines. She has, however, the right to define divine truth, to amplify it, and give it new and fuller explanation as necessity may demand. This right she exercises when she makes an infallible declaration concerning a dogma which is already a part of the original deposit of belief. These definitions of belief are not to be construed into other than formal and explicit declarations of the faith she held from the beginning. A new form of creed to safeguard her teaching can never with her imply a new doctrine. Progress in the understanding of the faith is her motto—but change, never. This view has been altogether ignored by those who are anxious to charge the Church with making a change in her teaching, but all scholars worthy of the name are agreed that she has been all along and is today in all doctrinal pronouncements exactly in accord with the truth which Christ commissioned her to deliver to the world. Heresy and schism there have been, but a mighty defender has at all times come forward to crush the head of error, and the Church has gone steadily on with her God-given mission to teach all things whatsoever Christ entrusted to her keeping. Surely there can be none so illogical as to deny the force of tradition. Yet tradition compels the admission of the Church's apostolic doctrine. This doctrine came by the blood and sacrifices of millions of martyrs to Luther's day, and it has remained intact and unchanged ever since to enlighten the minds and comfort the souls of men.

Bougaud in his remarkable work, *Il Cristianismo,* etc., pays the following tribute to the unchangeable character of the Church's teaching as embodied and epitomized in the Apostles' Creed. "For eighteen centuries," he says, "it has subsisted, not hidden away in some secret part of a temple, not rolled up in a bundle like a mummy, but thrown on the highways of humanity, sung in churches, repeated every day on the lips and in the hearts of millions and millions of mankind. And not only does it subsist to the shame of all things else, which are fading and unstable, but for eighteen centuries it has had to bear the brunt of the most formidable intellectual warfare ever seen. It had its beginning on the eve of Pentecost, and it has not yet ceased. And as the sword of the spirit is the most beautiful to be found in the world, who can tell the number and variety of attacks made against it by its enemies. Now it is in close quarters with the subtleties of Greek genius, as in the days of Arius, Nestorius, and Eutyches; now it meets the impetuous eloquence of a time both trivial and sublime, as in the epoch of Luther; again in this privileged country of the globe [France], where raillery kills with piercing witticisms, as in the period of Voltaire, or even in our days of scientific delirium, with the astonishing discoveries of science not rightly understood. Behold, for eighteen centuries this has continued: eighteen centuries of the most terrible intellectual warfare, maintained by the most choice intelligences. Now, what has been the effect of it? Has a single line of the symbol [Creed] been cancelled? No, the Creed subsists, unchanged, in its splendid integrity. It is like one of those beautiful obelisks of red granite brought from Egypt to the piazzas of Rome: the storms of four thousand years have not been able to break a fragment off them."

It is an incontrovertible fact that there is sham, individualistic religion unfortunately prevailing widely today. It had its origin in the rebellious heart of Martin Luther, the father of the Reformation. There and then originated the great gulf that divided the ideals, principles and ethics of the religion of the gentle Nazarene from the individualistic system which revived and re-established the selfish characteristics of paganism and which is falsely called by the name of Christianity today. Without right or sanction, Protestantism has promulgated doctrines unknown and unheard of for sixteen centuries after Christ established His Church. No wonder that many Protestant ministers today complain of the inconsistency of the religion that they avow. They realize that the terrible break of the Reformation opened up an enormous chasm which divides their belief from that which Jesus taught and gave His Church to communicate to the world. It could not be otherwise, for rebellion in matters spiritual, as often in things material, enervates, disrupts and destroys. Outside the Church today Protestant biblical scholars have gone almost completely and hopelessly away from the traditional Christ, true God and true Man. Dr. Loofs, a non-Catholic professor of Oberline College, Ohio, considers that the German Lutheran scholars are past the day of battle for the divinity of Christ, for among many the belief in the very Godhead and very manhood of Jesus Christ has been practically given up. By the denial of the divinity of Christ, they strike at the foundation doctrine of the Christian religion, and then the whole fabric of Revelation falls to pieces. The denial of the divinity of Christ involves the denial of the divinity of His Church, and in consequence men are left without a divine, infallible teacher to speak in God's name and with His authority.

If men who long for the true religion of Christ will only

throw off the veil of human respect, acknowledge their error and humbly accept what Luther rejected, they will have no further necessity to seek for what they want; for the Church, One, Holy, Catholic, and Apostolic, remains today to speak to all in the name and by the authority of her divine Founder, and shall remain through all future ages, as she was from the beginning, the sure fountain and arc of salvation, upholding by word and work the heavenly sanctions of law, divine, international, and social.

This Church is gradually becoming better known, and fair-minded men are coming in numbers to her defence. One of these is the Rev. T. B. Thompson of the Plymouth Congregational Church, Chicago. In a recent sermon he said: "It must be admitted in all fairness that popular ignorance, superficial knowledge and malicious slander have in many instances misrepresented the teachings of the Roman Catholic Church. To contemplate her history is to admire her. Reformation, wars, empires and kingdoms have been arrayed against her. After all these centuries she stands so strong and so firmly rooted in the lives of millions that she commands our highest respect. As an illustration, she is the most splendid the world has ever seen. Governments have arisen and gone to the grave of the nations since her advent. Peoples of every tongue have worshipped at her altars. The Roman Catholic Church has stood solid for law and order. Her police power in controlling millions untouched by denominations has been great. When she speaks, legislators, statesmen, politicians and governments stop to listen, often to obey. In the realm of worship, her ministry has been of the highest. In employing beads, statues, pictures and music she has made a wise and intelligent use of symbolism. Her use of the best in music and painting has been the greatest single inspiration to those arts, and her cathedrals are the shrines of all pilgrims."

Brother Thompson never uttered truer words than these. May the light spread till the minds of all will be illuminated with the glory and splendor of the truth as it is in Christ and in His Church!

Luther entertained not only a special hatred of the Church, but also a lifelong spirit of antagonism towards its Supreme Visible Head, the Pope. With him it mattered not that the Bible defined God's Church as "the pillar and the ground of truth"; he declared it, in his letter to Pope Leo X, to be "the jaws of Hell, kept wide open by the anger of God." His opposition toward the Head of the Church was equally pronounced. He knew that the Bible names Cephas [St. Peter] the "rock" and bids him "confirm the brethren," yet he dares in his *Comment on Galatians,* 5:20, to designate the Pope as "the general heresiarch and the head of all heresies." Thus to this erratic man, nothing was good or acceptable that came out of Nazareth. When the Holy See and its Supreme Ruler rose up before his mind, as they did constantly, he was aroused to frenzy, and it seemed as if "his heart was changed from man's." In denying the position and authority of the Successor of St. Peter, his language was always characteristically vulgar, abusive, and insulting. For one who claimed that his mouth was "the mouth of Jesus Christ," we are astonished at the vocabulary of insult and rancorous hate he constantly launched against the Successor of St. Peter. His maniacal ravings, which brushed aside the plain fact that the Holy See from the Apostles' days to his own had been recognized by the whole body of the faithful as the divinely constituted center of unity and truth, were especially marked in his work *The Papacy, an Institution of the Devil,* in which, "putting on cursing like a garment," as the Psalmist says, he did his utmost to malign and insult Catholics, and to abuse and deride their spiritual chief. Luther lived under the reign of four successive Popes, and he knew as well as any man of his day that not one of these, or any of their predecessors, ever tampered with the Faith of Jesus Christ, and they did not deserve to be designated as "heresiarchs." Moreover, to call the Vicar of Christ by the name of "heresiarch" was to incur the woe pronounced against those who "put darkness for light and light for darkness." (*Is.* 5:20). But we need not wonder at his attitude. No one becomes a greater enemy to God's Church than he who has left it; none reviles the amplitude of jurisdiction emanating from God Himself and embodied in the governor of all the faithful more than he who has fallen from it. *Corruptio optimi pessima* ["The corruption of the best is the worst"]. In Luther we have a flagrant example of St. Gregory's terrible saying about bad priests, that there "are no men from whom Our Lord receives greater injury."

The Reformer's abuse of the Head of the Church reaches its height in this frightful book published in Wittenberg, 1545. The text was illustrated by his friend, the famous painter Lucas Cranach, who, after the author's suggestions, filled it with a number of woodcuts, which in obscenity and vulgarity have never been surpassed. The purpose of this nasty work was to ridicule and defame the Papal office in the eyes of the lower classes. The following description of what Luther thought of "the Pope and his devil's kingdom" is furnished by Grisar and shows to what extremes the Reformer went to ensure the success of his work of destruction with the unthinking and vulgar rabble.

"The picture with the Furies, to which Luther refers, is that which represents the 'birth and origin of the Pope,' as the Latin superscription describes it. Here is depicted, in a peculiarly revolting way, what Luther says in his *Wider das Papstum vom Teuffel gestifft* [Against the Papacy, an Institution of the Devil], viz., the Pope's being born from the 'devil's behind.' The devil-mother is portrayed as a hideous woman with a tail, from under which Pope and Cardinals are emerging head foremost. Of the Furies, one is suckling, another carrying and the third rocking the cradle of the Papal infant, whom the draughtsman everywhere depicts wearing the tiara. These are the Furies Megaera, Alecto, and Tisiphone.'

"Another picture shows the 'Worship of the Pope as God of the World.' This, too, expresses a thought contained in the *Wider das Papstum,* where Luther says: 'We may also with a safe conscience take to the closet his coat of arms with the Papal keys and his crown, and use them for the relief of nature.' As a matter of fact, in this picture we see on a stool, decorated with the papal insignia, a crown or tiara set upside down on which a man-at-arms is seated in the action of easing himself; a second, with his breeches undone, prepares to do the same, while a third who has already done so is adjusting his dress.

"The picture with the title 'The Pope gives a Council in Germany' shows the Pope in his tiara riding on a sow and digging his spurs into her sides. The sow is Germany, which is obliged to submit to such ignominious treatment from the Papists; as for the Council which the Pope is giving to the German people, it is depicted as his own—the Pope's—excrement, which he holds in his hand pledging the Germans in it, as Luther says in the passage quoted above. The Pope blesses the steaming object while the sow noses it with her snout. Underneath stands the ribald verse:

> 'Sow, I want to have a ride,
> Spur you well on either side.
> Did you say *"Concilium"*?
> Take instead my *"merdrum"* [excrement].

'Here the Pope's feet are kissed' are the words over another picture, and, from the Pope who is seated on his throne with the Bull of Excommunication in his hand, two men are seen running away, showing him, as Köstlin says, 'their tongues and hinder parts with the utmost indecency.' The inscription below runs:

> 'Pope, don't scare us so with your ban;
> Please don't be so angry a man;
> Or else we shall take good care
> To show you the 'Belvedere.'

"Köstlin's description must be supplemented by adding that the two men, whose faces and bared posteriors are turned towards the Pope, are depicted as emitting wind in his direction in the shape of puffs of smoke; from the Pope's bull, fire, flames and stones are bursting forth.

"Of the remaining woodcuts one reproduces the scene which formed the title page to the first edition of the *Wider das Papstum,* viz., the gaping jaws of Hell, between the teeth of which is seen the Pope surrounded by a cohort of devils, some of whom are crowning him with the tiara; another portrays the famous pope-ass, said to have been cast up by the Tiber near Rome; it shows 'what God Himself thinks of popery'; yet another depicts a pet idea of Luther's, viz., the 'regard of the *"Papa satanissimus"* [Pope most satanic] and his cardinals,' i.e., their being hanged, while their tongues, which had been torn out by the root, are nailed fast to the gallows. 'How the Pope teaches faith and theology'; here the Pope is shown as a robed donkey sitting upright on a throne and playing the bagpipes with the help of his hoofs. 'How the Pope thanks the Emperors for their boundless favors' introduces a scene where Clement IV with his own hand strikes off the head of Conradin. 'How the Pope, following Peter's example, honors the King' is the title of a woodcut where a Pope (probably Alexander III) sets his foot on the neck of the Emperor (Frederick Barbarossa at Venice). It is not necessary to waste words on the notorious falsehoods embodied in the last two pictures. Luther, moreover, further embellished the accounts he found, for not even the bitterest antagonist of the Papacy had ever dared to accuse Clement IV of having slain with his own hand the last of the Staufens. Among the ignorant masses to whom these pictures and verses were intended to appeal, there were many who were prepared to accept such tales as true on the word of one known as the "man of God," the "Evangelist, the new Elias and the Prophet of Germany."

"In the *Historien des ehrwirdigen in Gott seligen thewren*

Mannes Gottes [*History of the Venerable Holy Man of God*], Mathesius says of Luther: 'In the year 1545 he brought out the mighty, earnest book against the Papacy, founded by the devil and maintained and bolstered up by lying signs; and, in the same year, also caused many scathing pictures to be struck off in which he portrayed, for the benefit of those unable to read, the true nature and monstrosity of Antichrist, just as the Spirit of God in the Apocalypse of St. John depicted the red bride of Babylon, or as Master John Huss summed up his teaching in pictures for the people of the Lord Christ and of Antichrist. 'The Holy Ghost is well able to be severe and cutting,' says Mathesius of this book and the caricatures. 'God is a jealous God and a burning fire, and those who are driven and inflamed by His Spirit to wage a ghostly warfare against the foes of God show themselves worthy foemen of those who withstand their Lord and Saviour. Mathesius, like many others, was full of admiration for the work." (Grisar., Vol. V., pp. 423, 4. 5).

Thus the first biographer of Luther shows his taste for the filthy and disgusting in his appreciation of one of the vilest and nastiest books that ever disgraced the pen of the Ecclesiastes of Wittenberg or of any other man before or since. Unlike Mathesius, decent men would consider it a less odious task to wade through sewage than go through the pages of this horrible book and its indecent engravings. It is with the greatest reluctance we refer to such an astounding production, but no account of Luther would be complete without reference to this book, which should never have been printed, for its filthy language and indecent illustrations show its author to have been anything but a "dear man of God," as his friends love to call him. Döllinger, when speaking of this book, said, "It must have been written under the influence of intoxicating drink, or of fury of mind bordering on madness." This celebrated writer had good grounds for the criticism he makes, for Hospinian, one of the contemporary reformers, declared

Luther to be "absolutely mad"; and men like Agricola and Catharinus, who knew the Reformer, openly referred to his well-known drinking habits, which at times approached intemperance, if not actual drunkenness.

In spite of all that Luther said and wrote against the Papacy, it is well to remember that nineteen hundred years ago and more, Jesus Christ, as foretold by the Prophets, was pleased to appear in this world to uplift, enlighten and save mankind. In the divine plan of Redemption, He, who was full of grace, life and power, was not to remain here below forever and continue in person the instruction and guidance of mankind in the way of eternal life. He is no longer visible on earth, but before He returned whence He came, He was mindful to organize, found and endow with perpetuity an hierarchical Church, which He made the depository of His teachings and which He empowered to instruct, govern and act in His name. This Church was to witness for Him until the consummation of the world, and her mission was to bring His doctrine, His worship, and His ministry down through the ages to all peoples and to all nations. In this system of divinely guaranteed authority which Christ established, the Master mercifully provided a safe asylum for the perpetuity, preservation and protection of His divine, saving, and ennobling teachings. Before ascending into Heaven, Christ was pleased to appoint a head over His society and to be vicariously represented on earth in the person of the Sovereign Pontiff, in whom the Church recognizes the most exalted degree of dignity, the full amplitude of jurisdiction, and power based on no human constitutions however venerable, but emanating from the Saviour Himself. As the true and legitimate Vicar of Jesus Christ, the Pope presides over the Universal Church. He is the father and governor in matters spiritual of all the faithful, of bishops and of all prelates, be their station, rank or power what they may. As the Church is never to perish, the rock on which it is built is never to perish—and that rock is the papal spiritual sovereignty. As the son of a king inherits the rights of his father, so each successor in the lineage of the spiritual children of Peter receives from Jesus Christ that high sovereignty and jurisdiction needed to rule and guide the Church for all time. "To thee I give the keys of the Kingdom of Heaven, and whatsoever thou shalt bind upon earth shall be bound also in heaven, and whatsoever thou shalt loose on earth, it shall be loosed also in heaven." (*Matt.* 16:19). And the Church, which is to endure to the end of time, is built upon a rock that can never perish. "Thou art Peter and upon this rock I will build my Church, and the gates of hell shall not prevail against it." (*Matt.* 16:18).

Thus, the papal spiritual sovereignty possesses three great distinguishing prerogatives: first, it is the rock upon which the impregnable Church is built; the crested billows may rise in storm and foam, but they break harmless at its feet; second, the Supreme Pontiff holds the keys; he makes the decrees to be obeyed on earth, and ratified in Heaven; third, he feeds with sound doctrine the lambs and sheep of the Church of God over which he rules. What the other Apostles received, Peter, the Pontiff of the Apostles, received in fullness and supremacy. "Where Peter is, there is the Church," says St. Ambrose. "Do you want to know who is the faithful Christian; ask him, is he in communion with Peter's successor?"

The Pope, then, is the mouth of the Church. Through him speaks the Mystic Body of Christ. When, acting as the Supreme Pontiff of the Universal Church, he defines a matter of faith or morals, he is infallible. The infallibility of St. Peter's Chair ever endures by virtue of Our Lord's prayer, "I have prayed for thee, that thy faith fail not, and thou being once converted, confirm thy brethren." (*Lk.* 22:32).

There is hardly a teaching of the Catholic Church that has been so grievously misrepresented by those who profess to be enlightened ministers of the Gospel, and so strangely misapprehended by our separated brethren, as the infallibility of the Pope. Non-Catholics have been taught, and many of them labor under the impression, that papal infallibility is a new doctrine of the Church, that it imparts to the Pope the extraordinary gift of inspiration, makes him impeccable, confers the right to trespass on civil authority, and even to play fast and loose with the Commandments of God. These and other equally ridiculous conceptions are presented in the most plausible and spicy manner to a gullible public, ever ready to swallow without a qualm any statement, no matter how preposterous, provided it reviles and injures the Church of the living God. The promoters of the campaign of misrepresentation are jealous of the Pope's authority, and, like the father of Protestantism, resort to every means, no matter how unfair, to throw obstacles in the way to keep people from entering the one sheepfold of the One great Shepherd of Souls. If, however, such a thing as Church unity could be effected among themselves and their hundred and more warring religious organizations, we imagine it would be no time before Protestantism would attempt to have a Pope of its own.

All who are anxious to know what papal infallibility really means are advised to consult the decrees of the Vatican Council held on July 18, 1870, over which Pius IX presided, surrounded by nearly 700 bishops gathered together from all over the world, representing more than 30 nations and more than 250 million Christians. In that general Council, the twentieth held by the Church, it was solemnly and officially defined that Catholics are bound to believe that the Pope is infallible only when he speaks *ex cathedra,* that is, from the chair of Peter: 1. in discharge of his office as supreme teacher of the Universal Church; 2. by virtue of his supreme Apostolic authority; 3. defining a doctrine, giving an absolutely final decision regarding faith or morals; 4. addressing the Universal Church; and 5. binding her to hold the doctrine he so defines.

When this doctrine is rightly understood, it means, to put it briefly, that God will keep the Pope from teaching error and falsehood, in faith and morals, when he acts as head of the Universal Church. The power of the Pope then is far from being, as so many suppose, arbitrary, absolute and despotic. It is rightly limited in many respects, and there is nothing in it to disturb or make anyone think that the Pontiff is at liberty to change the Scriptures, to alter the divine law or impose doctrines not contained in the original Revelation completed by Christ in the beginning of the Church. Acting in his private capacity, as a temporal sovereign or as Bishop of the diocese of Rome, the Pope, having free will and being human, can err in morals or in judgment. He is not impeccable, and it is false to allege that he claims to be. He cannot make right wrong or wrong right. His authority, like the Kingdom of Christ, is "not of this world." His jurisdiction belongs to spiritual matters, and is always for good, for truth, for the cause of Christ, for the welfare of souls, for the promotion of religion.

It is silly, then, in the highest degree of silliness, to be alarmed at the teaching of the Catholic Church on papal infallibility, and allege that this doctrine puts one's intellect and conscience in a state of thralldom and servitude. The privilege enjoyed by the Pope cannot be exercised arbitrarily. It is used only after study and prayer and regard for the welfare of the Universal Church, and then it must fulfill all the five conditions already enumerated and demanded by the dogma, as defined by the Vatican Council. Then papal decisions in faith and morals are so guided by divine providence, according to Christ's own promise, as ever to be infallibly true; and to the farthest extremities of the world every faithful Christian admits in his heart what every loyal son of the Church obeys in his act. It is not the man, remember, that is infallible, it is Jesus Christ; and Jesus Christ determines what that man, who holds the keys, shall teach when he "feeds the lambs and sheep" of his Master. Far then from arousing opposition, the doctrine of papal infallibility, which is the keystone in the arch of Catholic Faith, and which has preserved her marvelous unity of belief throughout the world from the beginning, ought to command the unqualified admiration of every reflecting mind.

The Papacy for well nigh two thousand years has been in this world where all things disappear, and never has a century passed in which the Popes have not conferred innumerable benefits on mankind. They enabled their followers to save the Christian religion when the wild pagans broke through the Roman army and swept down on Rome, laying waste with fire and sword, to the utter destruction of everything holy, ennobling and uplifting. No other organization could have met these savage peoples save that one organization, the Catholic Church. Without the Popes there would be no Christianity in the world today, for there would be neither authority, nor infallibility, nor unity. And could there be law without authority, revelation without certainty, in the midst of a society without unity? Every organization that accomplishes anything must have a dominant head, and even the United States, as great as she is today, would not last three months without a supreme ruler. Some complain that infallibility fetters the human mind, but they should remember that this infallibility regards subjects which the human mind unaided would never have discovered—or if discovered, could never, without infallibility, have trusted and reposed upon. Without infallibility, what thoughtful man could honestly declare his unhesitating and lasting conviction in an accurately worded profession of faith, declaring his hopes for the future and the means appointed by God whereby he may secure that future?

But the world is inconsistent. It is ever wearying of those who would serve it. It mistrusts its truest friends. It persecutes those who would help it. Jerusalem crucified Jesus Christ. The rulers imprisoned St. Peter in the midst of that city where his shadow has healed the sick and his words strengthened the withered limbs. All his successors for the first three hundred years sealed their profession of the Faith with their own blood. Thenceforward every Pope desired to pursue his heavenly mission in peace and quiet, but enemies of the Church arose to strike at the chief shepherd in the hope of involving the whole flock. The boldest and most daring of these was Martin Luther, who aimed to place himself on an equality with the Pope and to impose his personal views for the acceptance of mankind. During a long period of his life, according to his own testimony given in the preface to his Works, he was so besotted with the Papacy that he "would have killed or helped to kill anyone who rejected one iota of the Pope's teaching." But ambition and rebellious thoughts, after some time, agitated his mind; and growing restless, discontented, and dissatisfied in all that his earlier faith taught him to venerate, he yielded to the temptation "to make," as he says in a letter to the Augustinians of Wittenberg, "a stand alone against the Pope and hold him forth as Antichrist." Well might he write to the priest Leitzken: "Pray for me, for I grow more miserable every day. I am constantly drawing nearer to Hell." The pleadings of grace in his soul were hushed, and in a spirit of self-confidence never manifested by anyone before his day, he finally brought himself, as Alzog says, "to indulge the pleasing delusion that he himself was John the Evangelist, banished by Domitian to the island of Patmos: a second Paul or Isaias." Pride and "the prosperity of fools" led him on to destruction, and he who once wrote to Pope Leo X, "I acknowledge your voice as that of Christ who presides and speaks in you," turned in rankest hypocrisy and supreme effrontery to make out that the Sovereign Pontiff was "not the chief head of all Christendom," that "the time had come to cease to be the puppets of the Roman Pontiff," and that "the Papacy should be destroyed."

Leo X, like all his predecessors, who ever showed a

paternal love and an affectionate compassion for the wayward, labored to bring Luther to a realization of his sad condition, but to no purpose. Luther would no longer acknowledge the voice of the shepherd of the whole flock "as that of Christ," and this ingrate and lawless one, reckless in calumny, groundless in assertion, with the cursing and bitterness and deceit that filled his mouth, went throughout the land "determined," as he said, "to crush the Papacy" and bury it "under the weight" of his "thunders and lightnings." He was the first in all Christendom to raise the cry "No Popery." Why? Because he wanted no authority in religion save his own.

In the spirit of an apostate, he was now prepared to go to any lengths to vent his irrational hatred of the Holy See, the impregnable citadel of the communion of the true children of God. For nearly twenty years, he occupied himself in pouring forth a whole series of denunciations and insults against divine, ecclesiastical authority. His virulence and rage against the Holy See and its respected representative was so bitter and intense that "he could not," as we read in Hazlitt's Michelet, pp. 229-230, "pray without intermingling maledictions with his orisons." "If," he says, "I exclaim: Hallowed be Thy Name, I am, as it were, constrained to add: Cursed be the name of Papists and of those who blaspheme against Thee. If I say: Thy Kingdom come, I must put in: Cursed be the Papacy, and all the other kingdoms which are opposed to Thine. If I pray: Thy will be done, I rejoin: Cursed be the Papacy, and may their designs be overthrown who oppose Thy commands." (Consult *Luther on Prayer,* Erl. ed., 252, p. 254 f. 59, p. 22). The intensity of his bitterness towards the Head of the Church was especially manifested on leaving the Council of Schmalkalden, when he made the Sign of the Cross over the assembled crowds and cried out: "May the Lord fill you with hatred of the Pope." (Köstlin-Kawerau, 2, p. 390 f.).

Carried away by his wild aspirations for dominance, he

was convinced that he was to outlast the Papacy. In his insanity, he forgot, however, that the chair of Peter was like the Ark of the Covenant. No Uzzah ever touched it irreverently and remained unscathed. The keen-sighted Voltaire, another apostate, very aptly expressed this historic truth in the famous saying: "He who eats Pope, dies of it." The Cynic of Ferney read in the world's annals a truth to which Luther remained blind. "He remained blind to it," as Anderdon says, "because the evil passions to which he surrendered himself, his jealousy, his arrogance, and obstinate wrong-headedness and lust of dominion, and sensual downward tendencies, had caused the light that was in him to become darkness." (Ander, *Luther,* p. 123).

The keynote of his whole movement of Reformation is sounded in the Latin line he wrote on a piece of plaster at a banquet, "where the princes entertained him magnificently and regaled him with the finest Rhenish wine," and where, as Seckendorf tells, "he drank like a true German": *"Pestis eram vivus, moriens tua mors ero Papa,"* that is, "Living, I was your pest; dying, O Pope, I shall be your death."

The merry guests, delighted with his humor, sat down, and Luther "continued to vent his wit in sarcasms against his natural enemies, the Pope, the emperor, the monks, and also the devil, whom he did not forget, to the delight of the frivolous and bibulous company." As the boisterous and irreverent crowd rose from the table, a report of the death of Paul III reached them. Luther, delighted at the news, cried out, exultingly, "This is the fourth Pope I have buried: I shall bury many more of them." He that dwelleth in Heaven, however, laughed at the prediction. Luther was taken suddenly ill, and in spite of all the attention of his assembled guests, in a few hours he was called to the judgment seat of God to render an account of his long and bitter opposition to the Church and its legitimate representative. He "ate Pope and died of it."

Meanwhile, the Papacy—of which Luther was to be the

death and to see the end—what became of it? Let Lord Macaulay give answer. "The Papacy," he says, "remains: not in decay, not a mere antique, but full of life and youthful vigor. The Catholic Church is still sending forth to the farthest ends of the world missionaries as zealous as those who landed in Kent with Augustine: and still confronting hostile kings in the same spirit with which she confronted Attila. The number of her children is greater than in any former age. The acquisitions in the New World have more than compensated her for what she has lost in the old. Her spiritual ascendency extends over the vast countries which lie between the plains of Missouri and Cape Horn; countries which, a century hence, may not improbably contain a population as large as that which now inhabits Europe. Nor do we see any signs which indicate that the term of her long duration is approaching. She saw the commencement of all the governments and of all the ecclesiastical establishments that now exist in the world; and we feel no assurance that she is not destined to see the end of them all." (Macaulay, "Essay on Ranke's History of the Popes.").

Such is the estimate of a man whose prejudices were all against the Church of God. His common sense and acquaintance with facts, however, compelled him to laud her services and predict her perpetuity. Since his day hundreds upon hundreds, whose views of history were often distorted by prejudice, have admitted in all fairness that popular ignorance, superficial knowledge and malicious slander have in many instances misrepresented the teachings of the Catholic Church; and contemplating her marvelous career, her triumphs over wars, empires and kingdoms arrayed against her and her firm, consistent and persevering stand for law and order, they have declared that she is the most splendid institution the world has ever seen. They came to recognize that never has a century passed without the Popes conferring innumerable benefits on mankind, that they have literally been the civilizers and the evangelizers of the world, that during many centuries they denounced slavery and finally suppressed it, that they guarded the sanctity of marriage, encouraged learning and the arts, and that they alone have been able to make a periodical and lengthened peace between contending nations in Europe. These disinterested witnesses could not in fairness withhold the meed of praise so justly due the Papacy for its eminent and distinguished services to mankind. Indeed, mercy, justice and charity have ever flourished according to the extent of the papal influence.

A belief in the Lord and His teaching, and respect for His representative on earth, has ever been the real magnet that draws and holds the splendid loyalty of the Catholic people. Catholics know that their Church is the true Church of Christ, that it is international in character, that its comforting worship is the same for all throughout the universe, and that its head stands as an authority divinely guaranteed in all matters that pertain to faith and morals. They realize that divine truth, which was given for the universal benefit of mankind, could not be left without protection and was never intended to be a mere plaything in the hands of fallible men. They know that their religion antedates all man-made forms of belief and they can tell when, where, and by whom all the various religious denominations originated. They know that outside of God's own guarantee and everlasting endowment truth cannot be found, that other Christian churches cannot consistently claim succession from Christ Himself, and, therefore, their teaching is not the Christ-founded or guaranteed creed, and their religion cannot be as good, as true, as the religion of the Church founded by Jesus Christ Himself. With Catholics one religion is not as good as another. Truth cannot possibly admit error, and since perfect truth prevails with God alone, then in God's own Church only can the perfect truth be found. One religion would be as good as another if all religions were established by men. The Catholic religion was established by Christ Himself, and as He was God and Perfection itself, it is impossible to improve on His word or work. With Catholics the one religion is that of *the* Church founded by Christ, the Holy Catholic Apostolic Church of which Peter, the Fisherman, was the first Bishop at Rome. The line of his successors is *unbroken* down to the present ruler of the Holy See. Thus they are aware of the certainty of their position, and they are confident that as their Church came by the blood and sacrifice of millions of martyrs, and remained ever since to execute her heavenly mission, she will endure to the end despite the protest and opposition of the malicious who vilify and misrepresent her. The Catholic Church has stood adamant for nearly two thousand years, and no efforts of a lot of spiritual degenerates like Luther, Calvin, Zwingli and company will ever prevail against her.

This certainty of belief, as well as the solace and peace found in the Catholic Church under the headship of Peter's successors, was never offered by Luther to his followers in revolt or given by any of the various denominations that imitated their master in his rebellious course. The principle on which Luther started his new religion destroyed entirely, it its very inception, the possibility of any certainty of Christian creed and faith. The right of every individual to interpret the Scripture and judge for himself in all matters of religion was ruinous and destined to failure. "In theory, private judgment," as Preston says, "destroys both the creed and the possibility of faith. There can be no creed where each individual is the maker of his own faith. There can be no unity of faith where all matters of belief are referred to the individual judgment. One man is as good as another in finding out his faith and in interpretating Scripture, or tradition, or history; and more than that, this private judgment is not simply his privilege, but it is his duty. All are bound, even the ignorant and unlettered, to decide for themselves when there is no divine authority and divine witness, and thus you have as many creeds as there are individuals.

"Then, the principle of private judgment destroys the possibility of faith; for where there is no external authority there can be no exercise of faith, for, be it remembered, faith is the belief in that which God delivers to man. Now if God does not speak to the individual, he cannot exercise faith; and surely, no one is vain enough to say that his own judgment is to him a divine testimony. What each individual can prove on his own judgment is his own opinion, and his individual conception stands for what it is worth. But as for the voice of God, men must hear it from an external and an infallible authority before they can believe, for to believe is not to entertain an opinion, nor to know some truth by induction or logic, nor to search it out by science—but it is to believe it and receive it because God declares it to be so, and because, as the Sovereign Truth, He neither can deceive nor be deceived. On the private judgment theory of Luther there is no possibility of an external testimony." (*The Protestant Reformation,* p. 77-78).

Friedrich Paulsen, a non-Catholic writer, says: "The principle of 1521, viz., to allow no authority on earth to dictate the terms of faith, is anarchical; with it no Church can exist. . . .The starting point and the justification of the whole Reformation consisted in the complete rejection of all human authority in matters of faith. . . . If, however, a Church is to exist, then the individual must subordinate himself and his belief to the body as a whole. To do this is his duty, for religion can only exist in a body, i.e., in a Church." (*Gesch. des gelehrten Unterrichts vom Ausgang des M.A. bis zur Gegenwart* [History of the Learned Instructions from the End of the Middle Ages to the Present], 1^2, 1896, p. 213 f.). "Revolution is the term by which the Reformation should be described. . . . Luther's work was no Reformation, no 're-forming' of the existing Church by means of her own institutions, but the destruction of the old shape, in fact, the fundamental negation of any Church at all. He refused to admit any earthly authority in matters of faith, and regarding morals his position was practically the same; he left the matter entirely to the individual conscience. . . . Never has the possibility of the existence of any ecclesiastical authority whatsoever been more rudely denied." (*Ibid.,* p. 173).

Wherever Luther's cardinal principle of private judgment has been carried out in practice, it has invariably resulted in the destruction of the unity of the Christian Faith, and even of faith itself. Look at the condition of Christendom since this man first advocated the right of every individual to judge for himself in matters of religion. At the period of his revolt there was, with the exception of the Greek schism, only one faith in which all who called themselves Christians united. Now, if you look out beyond the pale of the Catholic Church, where can you find a semblance of unity, even in matters that might be called fundamental? And who among fallible men has the right to declare which are fundamental and which are not fundamental articles? Surely on every side are the variations of Protestantism. Its adherents, like its formulator, have contradicted themselves over and over again; pulpit stands against pulpit, and individual against individual, and sect against sect, and even in the same denomination there is not unity of faith. There is not, we believe, a single Protestant church in the whole world where the members of one single congregation are solidly united together in the unity of one certain faith. So, if facts count for anything, they proclaim the utter confusion which has resulted from Luther's effort to destroy the authority of the Church and the headship of the Pope. Even the Bible, called "the religion of Protestants," but which must be believed either on the authority of the Catholic Church or on no authority at all, has suffered at their hands; it has been torn into pieces; its supernatural character has been interpreted away, and some or all of it has been filched of inspiration. Some books are received, and some are not received. In many churches large portions of the Sacred Record are treated as the Father of the Reformation gave example in his day.

The great trouble with the Protestant belief all along has been its elasticity. In our day we count its denominations by the hundreds. On almost every street corner we face a church of a different persuasion, such as Lutheran, Episcopalian, Presbyterian, Methodist, Universalist, Latter Day Saints, etc., etc. The Protestant people are at constant variance with one another. They may for a time hold to the tenets and dogmas of the parent body from which they spring, but ever and anon, dissensions arise, and after a time the factions separate and announce a doctrine of their own and acknowledge no allegiance to any other sect or creed. If you doubt this, just investigate the discipline and the authority of any of the Protestant beliefs, and you will at once discover the truth of the statement. And yet, Protestants wonder at the steady and alarming decrease in their ranks and the consequent tendency of the day to abandon all religious profession. The reason is clear. They lack the great, essential unity of faith; they lack the dominant authority to satisfy their followers in the belief of the divinity of Jesus Christ and the true Church; and, as a result, their belief ceases to appeal to them, and they withdraw from active church participation.

It is astonishing how common it is nowadays to meet people who say they were brought up Lutherans, Baptists, Methodists or Presbyterians, but declare they no longer have any definite belief. They were taught that religion is a purely personal matter which each individual is competent to decide for himself, and in consequence they grow careless towards religious questions, and losing the sense of a positive obligation to God to seek the truth as it is in Christ Jesus and His Church, they turn away from their original creeds to join the ranks of the indifferent, the free-thinking, and the unbelieving. All Protestant denominations alike have been hit by these desertions. In this country alone, we face the appalling fact that out of nearly a hundred million people, there are fully sixty million who profess no religion whatever. This condition is sad beyond expression and should be the deep concern of every citizen having a love of his fellow man and the stability of the Constitution at heart, for so surely as Christianity lessens in the estimation of our countrymen, just so surely will the spirit of self-sacrifice on which it is founded disappear and lawlessness and anarchy reign. It should be remembered that Christianity does infinitely more than any other agency to preserve law and order and to bring contentment into the lives of the people.

Luther separated Christianity from the old and solid foundations upon which it had rested, and shutting it up within the covers of the Bible he changed the Christian church into a veritable "pandemonium where all dreams, all half-truths, and all errors disported themselves at ease and celebrated their Sabbath." As he rejected with indignation all historical and traditional data in matters of faith, and thereby kicked away the foundations of all fixed, solid and enlightened belief, there was nothing left for his followers but deism, naturalism, indifferentism or contempt of all revealed religion. He ventured to match his intellect against the Infinite Intellect, and the result was confusion and desolation. Church statistics point to the fact that his revolutionary work has been all along, and is now, with its multitudinous divisions of opinions and doctrines, a lamentable failure.

When Charles V saw and heard Luther at the Diet of Worms, he said, "That man would never make me a Protestant." He was right, and thousands upon thousands had cause enough to reach a similar conclusion. The lovers of novelty, however, the scoffers, the indifferent, and a large number of the ruling sovereigns who had their axes to grind, were not as keen in their judgment of the heresiarch as the loyal and faithful children of Holy Church, and they easily became the victims of the monster of impertinence, folly and pride. The weak, dissolute and rebellious of the day were ready to embark on the ways of innovation. For years the ranks of those who were captivated by Luther's absurdities and held in intellectual slavery by his abominable errors increased to an alarming extent and made giant headway, to the detriment of the true Faith throughout the land. God, however, was with His Church and would not suffer the rebellious to triumph.

Towards the year 1555, there came an amazing change, brought about by a great revival of religious life within the Church. Rapidly as Protestantism had spread in the beginning, its repulse was equally swift. While the apostate friar was raving against Rome over his beer in the Black Eagle Tavern, where he spent most of his evenings amid his dissolute disciples, and slanderously charging "the Pope and his crew," as he sarcastically designated them, "with hatred and dread of the very word, 'Reformation,'" the Council of Trent had met to restore to the purity and grave moral character of the ancient discipline and Church government whatever in the lives of clergy and people was contrary to that spirit and discipline—and also to renew and restate with great precision and detail the doctrines which had come down from the Apostles in order to oppose them to the errors and the innovations of the period. Thus Rome showed to the world that reformation is the very life of the Church. The voice of her chief Pastor now resounds throughout the Christian world, and the stray sheep—wearied, emaciated unto spiritual death, deceived by the false promises of liberty and emancipation which the hireling could not fulfill—return in humility and penitence to be nourished and fed as of old in the rich pasture of sound doctrine and of moral rectitude provided in the one sheepfold of the One great Shepherd of Souls. Luther's pre-eminence as the leader of a party of malcontents waned. Time showed him to be a deceiver, and the thoughtful who studied his revolutionary purpose, analyzed his wicked pronouncements, and witnessed his scandalous behavior concluded that they were neither economically, socially nor spiritually as well off as before the Lutheran brand of

Reformation had been proclaimed, and went back in masses to the Faith which in an evil moment they had abandoned. In the short interval of a decade, from 1555 to 1565, the Lutheran cause lost enormously, and ever since, as history and experience attest, it has gradually gone the way of all things human.

The revival of Catholicity at this period is one of the marvels of history, and the position it gained in those years has never since been lost. The Church, ever true to her sublime mission, redoubled her efforts in behalf of souls. Imbued with renewed vigor, she went out everywhere to remind the unfaithful of the misery and desolation of apostasy from God and the Christian Faith, with the result that thousands upon thousands hearkened to her appeals and submitted to her divine authority and saving influence. The conversion movement advanced with giant strides. Coming down to our own day, it is growing steadily as men realize more and more how their forefathers were robbed of the Faith by Luther, and as they apprehend that there is no logical middle ground between the Catholic Faith and the purely agnostic philosophy of which Protestantism is the parent. In Germany conversions are numerous; and the population, by virtue of a superior birth rate, is steadily shifting towards a larger Catholic parentage, so much so that even non-Catholic writers admit that in less than a century the fatherland will have a preponderance of Catholics. In England, Scotland and Wales conversions average eight thousand a year. In the United States they run close to forty thousand a year. The movements now going on in the Church of England, in the Episcopal Church of America, and in other denominations clamoring for unity will inevitably lead many more into the ranks of the one, true Church established by Jesus Christ.

In the past the Catholic Church has achieved victories in the face of the world's greatest opposition, and she will continue to achieve victories until the whole Christian world will be Catholic. Her mission is to realize the prayer of her Founder that there shall be One Faith, One Fold, One Shepherd. She desires all who as yet do not believe in Christ to become Christians and enter into communion with the one Church which Christ established, in order to glorify God by the universal acceptance of the institution founded by His divine Son and to convert, sanctify, and save souls. Her aim is to prepare men for Heaven, to bring them to a knowledge of God, the love and service of Christ and the practice of virtue, to administer to them grace-giving Sacraments and to offer up the adorable sacrifice of the Mass for their benefit. Outside the sphere of faith, morals and discipline, she has no desire and makes no claims to enter, no matter what stories her enemies may circulate to her detriment. She knows her business too well to dabble in things that lie outside of the object for which she was established, and hence in all matters which are purely temporal, purely political, purely secular, she neither claims nor exercises jurisdiction. Her authority relates to religion only, and hence all who go about telling the people that the object of the Church in her desire to advance Catholicity is to enrich her treasury and to see her head, the Pope, become king or emperor or supreme civil potentate of the universe, are only helping the devil to deceive the ignorant, foment strife, and perpetuate the grossest of calumnies. These maligners of the Church and the Papacy who fatten on deception are like their father Beelzebub, "liars and the truth is not in them."

The bigoted disturbers in our midst may decry the fact that every Catholic the world over recognizes the Pope as the supreme head and final judge of matters religious, but they should understand that this loyalty is based on the knowledge that the Catholic Church is the true Church of Christ and the only one that makes the word "Catholic" mean what it is intended to mean. By close observation, they will discover that the Pope's power and authority are modest indeed when contrasted with that of many of the sovereigns of the day, who are not satisfied with the mere temporal rule of their respective countries, but claim also supreme spiritual dominion over their subjects. Is it not a fact that the King of England is the recognized head of the church in that land, and that this church is the fountainhead of the American denomination? Is it not a fact that the Czar of Russia is the head of the Russian Orthodox Church and that Russians acknowledge him as supreme in matters spiritual? Is it not a fact that the Emperor of Germany is the head of the Prussian Lutheran Church and that all Lutherans in Prussia recognize the Kaiser as their spiritual chief? What have the bigots to say to this? Can they disprove these facts that are patent to everyone who runs? Do they ever allude to these conditions in their harangues against the Catholic Church and her legitimate representative? Do they ever charge the Englishman, the Russian, or the Prussian in America with disloyalty to the Stars and Stripes because in the profession of their respective creeds they manifest allegiance in spiritual matters to foreign potentates? Do they ever tell their deluded audiences that Luther and his followers were the framers of the principle that created the State Church? Do they ever tell that the so-called reformers held that kings rule by divine right, that they were autocrats, and therefore could do as they willed in things spiritual as in things temporal? Do they ever tell how Luther flattered the princes till they became the aides of his religious movement? Do they ever tell that Luther was a consummate politician, willing to sacrifice any principle for political expediency? Do they ever tell how, when he foresaw that his innovations were sure to lead to civil war, he openly and boldly proclaimed the right and duty of armed resistance in the cause of his new doctrines? Do they ever tell that he was the very one to urge the secular power to repress Catholicity as a rebellion, that he labored to excite the populace to resort to arms to spread his reformed doctrines and impose them by force on an unwilling community? Do they ever tell how the secular supremacy, advocated by the leaders of the reform movement, became unlimited in its claims and more arrogant in its assumptions than the Byzantine despotism of the Lower Empire?

To these burning questions the bigots give no answer, for the reason that they know as little about these matters as they do about the Church and her respected head—whom they imagine they are especially called on, like their master Luther, to denounce, oppose and persecute. A course of solid reading might help them to dispel their malice and correct their ignorance. Investigation will show them one thing at least—that all who live in glass houses should be mindful not to throw stones at their neighbors. In the meantime, we advise the bigots who claim a monopoly of patriotism to possess their souls in peace and to rest assured that the Catholic Church will never adopt, but will always oppose the principle which Luther fathered and gave to his religion, namely, the subservience of the Church to State domination.

Of one thing we may all be certain, that come what will, the Catholic religion, which is not and does not aspire to become a state religion, shall remain for all time in all her truthfulness, beauty and strength, because she is the one universal religion established by God to endure to the consummation of the world; and that, moreover, when the chronicles of this creation close, in its last page shall be recorded the perpetuity and endurance of the Roman Pontiff. Do not forget that amidst the terrors of the world's closing scenes, one voice, ever gentle, constant, patient, hopeful, shall travel around the earth, bringing peace to every Christian heart; it will be the voice of the last Pope for the last time blessing the world. Then and then only will the Church Militant cease her existence on earth and pass to the glory of the Church Triumphant in Heaven.

NOTES

1. According to the *Encyclopedia of Religion,* in 1980 there were 7,889 distinct Protestant denominations in 212 nations.

CHAPTER 6

LUTHER AND THE BIBLE

DURING the last three hundred years and more it has been widely and persistently proclaimed that Luther was the discoverer, the first translator and the only correct interpreter of the Bible. Ever since the so-called Reformer threw off the authority of the one true Church of Christ and set himself up in its place, the story went the rounds that when he was appointed librarian of his convent he "discovered among the dangerous and prohibited books" a copy of the Sacred Scriptures, carried it off to his cell, devoured it and was "converted." The story was first put into circulation by Mathesius, Luther's pupil and a boarder in his house. It fascinated the simple, and many, ignorant of the facts, came to believe that Luther exhumed and dragged into the light of day the Holy Book that had lain for many dark ages in the dungeons and lumber rooms of Popery. Had Luther really accomplished such a notable feat, we should have just reason to sound his praises and offer him the expression of our deepest gratitude. But we are constrained, however disappointing it may be to his admirers, to declare in the interests of truth that the tale bearing on Luther and his discovery of the Bible has no foundation in historic fact and is entirely unworthy of credence. It is a fabrication pure and simple. It was invented to throw dust into the eyes of the illiterate and to fan the flames of senseless bigotry. Whenever and wherever it is repeated, it has only one object in view, viz., to mislead the unwary into the belief that Rome hated the Bible, that she did her best to destroy it and that she concealed it from her people lest it should enlighten their supposed blindness.

Of all the accusations laid at the door of the Church, this one must appear to any person who does not willfully shut his eyes to facts as the most ludicrous, and the truth is, it is ridiculed and put down by the learned as too silly to deny. It has been refuted and repudiated hundreds of times, and yet so venomous or ignorant are the propagators of error that they continue with brazen effrontery to keep it in continual circulation. The story will not down. It is difficult to convince the ignorant of its preposterous falsity, and it continues to be repeated in hostile circles for the vile purpose of catering to the low susceptibilities of those who never question the veracity of the false teacher. Although the story continues to be told, the truth is that the Church never hated the Bible, never persecuted it, never tried to blot it out of existence and never kept it from her people.

She has been the parent, the author and maker under God of the Bible; she has always been the only effective and consistent preserver of the Bible; she guarded it through the ages from error and destruction; she has ever held it in highest veneration and esteem, and has ever grounded her doctrines upon it; *she alone* has the *right* to call it *her book* and *she alone* possesses the Bible in all its fullness and integrity.

This proud claim is not an idle boast. It is a fact which cannot be controverted. Serious and impartial students of the question are all in agreement on this point, and so true is this that no scholar of repute would today dare risk his reputation by giving to the public the silly and groundless stories circulated concerning the Church in her relation to the Bible and the inferences the unwary draw therefrom. To prove that Luther and his followers had little or no reverence for the Bible, that they changed and falsified it, that they tampered with it and deliberately mistranslated numerous passages to buttress the new religion of Protestantism, is a much easier task than to show that the Catholic Church was ever afraid of the Bible, that she ever tried to keep the Scriptures away from the people and that there ever was a time in her history when she was not most anxious to copy, print and put editions of the Holy Book into the hands of the faithful.

That Luther did not discover and was not the first to give the Bible to the people in the latter's own language is easily proved.

Fr. Lucian Johnston, in an able review of Grisar's work, says: "Luther as well as every other man of education of his day was accustomed to the Scriptures from his youth. Like thousands of others in any other schools, he was a regularly appointed professor of Scripture. It was precisely this position as teacher of Scripture in his monastery that gave the outlet to his peculiar views. Had the Bible been as unknown as the popular biography supposes, Luther might not have developed as he did along Scriptural lines. Here again Luther's maturer memory played him tricks. He fell back for excuses upon the supposed lack of Scriptures, just as he did upon the presence of abuses, when, as a matter of fact, there is no evidence from his own earlier works to prove that these things exercised any material effect upon his early mental development."

"Luther's studies," according to McGiffert, a non-Catholic writer, in his biography of the Reformer published in 1912, "embraced the writings of the Church Fathers and particularly the Bible, to which he was becoming more and more attached. It was in his twentieth year, he tells us, that he first saw a complete copy of the Scriptures in the university library of Erfurt. He had hitherto supposed they embraced only the lessons read in the public services and was delighted to find much that was quite unfamiliar to him. His ignorance, it may be remarked, though not exceptional, was his own fault. The notion that Bible reading was frowned upon by the ecclesiastical authorities of the age is quite unfounded." The Scriptures "were read regularly in church, and their study was no more prohibited to university students of that day than of this."

Professor Vedder of Crozer Theological Seminary, a non-Catholic author, in his work on the Reformation published in 1914, says: "The most recent writers are inclined to discredit the story of his [Luther's] finding the Bible—as inherently incredible. They point out the facts regarding the circulation of the Bible, both Latin and vernacular, and tell us that Luther must have taken great pains to keep himself in a state of ignorance, if we knew no more about the Bible than this anecdote implies. . . .The real difficulty is not so much with the incident, as with the inferences that have been drawn from it. Protestant writers have often seized on the occurrence as proof of the darkness of the times, of the indifference of the Church to the instruction of the people in the Scriptures, and have by comparison exalted the work of the reformers in their translation and circulation of the Scriptures. What the incident actually proves is merely Luther's own personal ignorance. If he did not know that the passages which he had heard in church did not constitute the whole Bible, there were nevertheless in Germany many who did know this." (*Vedder,* pp. 5-6).

The notion that people before the Reformation did not possess the Scriptures, and that Luther was the first to translate them into the common language of the country, is not only a mistake, but a stupid blunder. Every layman who has read history knows that the Church in the olden days translated the Scriptures from the Hebrew and Greek into Latin for the benefit of her children. Latin was not then a dead language and an unknown tongue. It was a common language among the educated and was known, spoken and written almost universally in Europe. In those days reading was a sign of a certain degree of scholarship and erudition, and it would have been hard to have found any man capable of reading who was not also capable of understanding Latin. The groundwork of all school learning was the knowledge of the Latin language. Dr. Peter

Bayne, a Protestant, says in the *Literary World,* Oct., 1894: "Latin was then the language of all men of culture, and to an extent probably far beyond what we at present realize, the common language of Europe: in those days tens of thousands of lads, many of them poor, studied at the universities and learned to talk Latin. The records of the proceedings in the courts of law were in those days in Latin, and the wills of dying persons were commonly in the same tongue. As Latin was the prevailing language of the time, most people who knew it would certainly prefer to use the authorized Vulgate to any vernacular version."

The Rev. Charles Buck, a virulent Protestant, says: "Both old and new Testaments were translated into Latin by the primitive Christians: and while the Roman Empire subsisted in Europe, the reading of the Scriptures in the Latin tongue, which was the universal language of the Empire, prevailed everywhere." ("Bible" in *Theological Dictionary,* by Rev. Charles Buck).

"No book," says *The Cambridge Modern History,* p. 639, "was more frequently republished than the Latin Vulgate, of which ninety-eight distinct and full editions appeared prior to 1500, besides twelve others which contained the *Glossa Ordinaria* or the Postils of Lyranus. From 1475, when the first Venetian issue is dated, twenty-two complete impressions have been found in the city of St. Mark alone. Half a dozen folio editions came forth before a single Latin classic had been printed. This Latin text, constantly produced or translated, was accessible to all scholars: it did not undergo a critical recension." In fact the Bible in its Latin dress, observes Mons. Vaughan, "was just as accessible to the people as it would have been if it had been in English. Neither more nor less. Lay this fact to heart namely: Those who could read Latin could read the Bible, and those who could not read Latin could not read anything."

Whilst the Vulgate was in general use we know that translations into the vernacular of the various peoples were also made and read. In Germany, not to mention Italy, France, Spain, Denmark, Holland, Norway, Poland, Bavaria, Hungary and other countries before the days of printing, we know that Raban Maur, born in Mainz in 776, translated the Old and New Testament into the Teutonic, or old German, tongue. Some time later, Valafrid Strabon made a new translation of the whole Bible. Huges of Fleury also translated the Scriptures into German, and the monk Ottfried of Wissemburg rendered it into verse. In Germany prior to the issue of Luther's New Testament in 1522, no authority enumerates fewer than fourteen editions in High German and three in Low German. "Those in High German," says Vedder, "are apparently reprints of a single MS. [manuscript] version, of which two copies are still preserved, one in a monastery of Tepl, Bohemia, the other in the library of the University at Freiburg in the Breisgau. The former, known as the Codex Teplensis, has recently been printed and is accessible to all scholars." The library of the Paulist Fathers of New York City contains, at present, a copy of the ninth edition of a German Bible profusely illustrated with colored wood engravings and printed by A. Coburger at Nuremberg in 1483, the very year in which Luther was born. In the year 1892 the Protestant historian Wilhelm Walther published in Brunswick a book under the title, *The German Translation of the Bible in the Middle Ages,* in which he proves that previous to the year 1521, before Luther ever thought of translating the Bible into the German language, there existed seventeen editions of the whole Bible in German, besides an almost countless number of German versions of the New Testament, the Psalms, and other parts of the Bible. He gives the following list of pre-Lutheran editions of the whole Bible in German, viz: Edition Mentel, Strassburg, A. D. 1466; edit. Eggenstein, Strassburg, 1470; edit. Pflanzmann, Augsburg, 1473; edit. Zainer, Augsburg, 1473; edit. Sorg, Augsburg, 1480; two editions of Köln (Cologne) by Quentel, 1480; edit. Koburger, Nuernberg, 1483; edit. Grueninger,

Strassburg, 1485; edit. Schoensperger, Augsburg, 1487; edit. Schoensperger, Augsburg, 1490; edit. Arndes, Luebeck, 1494; edit. H. Otmar, Augsburg, 1507; the Swiss Bible, Basel, about 1474; edit. Zainer, Augsburg, 1477; and edit. S. Otmar, Augsburg, 1518.

The Protestant historian, Ludwig Hain, enumerates in his work, *Repertorium Bibliographicum,* Stuttgart, 1826, ninety-eight editions of the whole Bible in Latin which appeared in print before the year 1501.

Sixty copies of as many different editions of Latin and vernacular Bibles, all printed before 1503, were to be seen at the Caxton Exhibition in London, 1877; and seeing is believing. The *Church Times,* a Protestant journal, under date of July 26, 1878, writing of the list of Bibles in the catalogue of the Caxton Celebration, 1877, published by H. Stevens, says: "This catalogue will be very useful for one thing at any rate, as disproving the popular lie about Luther *finding* the Bible for the first time at Erfurt about 1507. Not only are there very many editions of the Latin Vulgate long anterior to that time, but there were actually nine *German editions* of the Bible in the Caxton Exhibition earlier than 1483, the year of Luther's birth and at least three more before the end of the century." Mr. H. Stevens writes in the *Athenaeum* of October 6, 1883, p. 434: "By 1507 more than one hundred Latin Bibles had been printed, some of them small and cheap pocket editions. There had been, besides, *thirteen editions of a translation of the Vulgate into German,* and others into other modern languages.... Among the most interesting additions latest made (to the Grenville Library in the British Museum) is a nearly complete set of fourteen grand old pre-Luther German Bibles, 1460-1518, all in huge folios except the twelfth, which is in quarto form." These facts any student can verify by a visit to the British Museum, where most of the Bibles alluded to are to be seen.

The *Athenaeum* of December 22, 1883, contains an article on "The German Bible before Luther" in which it is shown that what Geffeken calls "the German Vulgate" was in common use among the people long before Luther's time; that Luther had evidently the old Catholic German Bible of 1483 before him when making his translation, and that consequently it is time we should hear no more of Luther as the first German Bible translator and of his translation as an independent work from the original Greek."

The Protestant Professor Lindsay, in his partisan work on the Reformation published in Edinburgh in 1908, admits that "other translations of the Bible into the German language had been made long before Luther began his work." He says, moreover: "It is a mistake to believe that the medieval Church attempted to keep the Bible from the people."

Hallam, the non-Catholic historian, in his work on the *Middle Ages,* chap. 9, part 2, says: "In the eighth and ninth centuries, when the Vulgate had ceased to be generally intelligible, there is no reason to suspect any intention in the Church to deprive the laity of the Scriptures. Translations were freely made into the vernacular languages, and, perhaps, read in churches. . . . Louis the Debonair is said to have caused a German version of the New Testament to be made. Otfrid, in the same century, rendered the Gospels, or rather, abridged them, into German verse. This work is still extant."

The well-known Anglican writer, Dr. Blunt, in his *History of the Reformation* (Vol. I. pp. 501-502), tells us that "there has been much wild and foolish writing about the scarcity of the Bible in the ages preceding the Reformation. It has been taken for granted that the Holy Scripture was almost a sealed book until it was printed in English by Tyndale and Coverdale, and that the only source of knowledge respecting it before them was the translation made by Wyckliffe. The facts are . . . that all laymen who could read were, as a rule, provided with their Gospels, their Psalter, or other devotional portions of the Bible. Men did, in fact, take a vast amount of personal trouble with respect to the productions of the Holy Scriptures, and accomplished by head, hand and heart what is now chiefly done by paid workmen and machinery. The clergy studied the Word of God and made it known to the laity; and those few among the laity who could read had abundant opportunity of reading the Bible either in Latin or English, up to the Reformation period."

Long before the art of printing was invented, about 1450, the monks, friars, clergy, and even the nuns of the Catholic Church spent their lives in making copies of the Bible in vellum, so that it might be preserved, multiplied and scattered far and wide for the benefit of all readers. Their labors in this direction were constant, unceasing, and tireless. Through their industry and perseverance in reproducing the sacred pages from century to century, every church and monastery and university was put in possession of copies of the Bible. The Bishop and Abbots of those days encouraged the work and were zealous propagators of the Scriptures. They required, moreover, all their priests to know, read, and study the Inspired Word. Councils like that of Toledo, held in 835, issued decrees insisting that Bishops were bound to inquire throughout their dioceses whether the clergy were sufficiently instructed in the Bible. In some cases the clergy were obliged to know by heart not only the whole Psalter but, as under the rule of St. Pachomius, the New Testament as well. From time immemorial, the Church always used a great portion of the Bible in the celebration of the Mass, in the Epistles and Gospels for 365 days of the year, and in the Breviary, which she enjoined her priests to recite daily.

The Sacred Scriptures were always a favorite subject of study among the clergy; and a popular occupation was the writing of commentaries upon them, as all priests are aware from having to recite a great many of them every day, ranging from the time of St. Leo the Great and St. Gregory down to St. Bernard and St. Anselm. The Scriptures, besides, were read regularly to the people and explained frequently both in church and school, through sermons, instructions and addresses, so that the faithful were steeped in, and permeated through and through with the inspired Word of God. Paintings and statuary and frescoes and stained glass windows were used in the churches to depict biblical subjects and fix on the people's memories and understandings the doctrines of faith and the great events in God's dealings with His creatures since the beginning of the world. Through these and other means, all, from the king down to the humblest peasant, came to know and understand the great and saving truths of religion as found in the Bible. The Scriptures were made so familiar that the people could repeat considerable portions from memory, and their frequent reference thereto by way of passing allusion is considered now very puzzling to those who are unacquainted with the phraseology of the Vulgate. Their ideas seemed to fall naturally into the words of Scripture, and the language of the Bible passed into the current tongue of the people.

One of the best evidences of the medieval attitude and practice in the matter of Bible-reading is furnished in the *Imitation of Christ* by Thomas à Kempis, published about the year 1425. À Kempis, who was a monk in the Archdiocese of Cologne, had himself made a MS. copy of the Bible. In the first book, chapter I, of the *Imitation,* there are some useful directions about reading the Holy Scriptures:

"All Holy Scripture should be read in the spirit in which it was written. Our curiosity is often a hindrance to us in reading the Scriptures, when we wish to understand and to discuss, where we ought to pass on in simplicity. . . . If thou wilt derive profit, read with humility, with simplicity, with faith, and never wish to have the name of learning."

In the eleventh chapter of the fourth book he says: "I shall have, moreover, for my consolation and a mirror of life, Thy holy books, and above all Thy most holy Body for my especial remedy and refuge. . . .Whilst detained in the prison of this body I acknowledge that I need two things, food and light. Thou hast therefore given to me, weak as I am, Thy sacred Body for the nourishment of my soul and body, and Thou hast set Thy word as a light to my feet. Without these two I could not live; for the Word of God is the light of my soul and Thy Sacrament is the Bread of Life. These also may be called the two tables set on either side in the storehouse of Thy holy Church."

"The medieval mind, as here laid down in the greatest work of the Middle Ages, does not," as Desmond remarks, "seem to raise any questions as to whether it is wise to read the Bible or as to whether the Bible is difficult to procure. These matters are evidently not even contemplated as possible issues: on the contrary, the excellence of Scripture reading and its necessity as 'the light of the soul' are dwelt upon. Be it remembered, too, that this manual of à Kempis came at once into the hands of the laity as well as the clergy, for it went into the vernaculars of every nation in Europe only a few years after its first publication."

An enlightened Protestant writer, the Rev. Doctor Cutts, in a work published by the Society for Promoting Christian Knowledge, observes: "There is a good deal of popular misapprehension about the way in which the Bible was regarded in the Middle Ages. Some people think that it was very little read, even by the clergy: whereas, the fact is that the sermons of the medieval preachers are more full of Scripture quotations and allusions than any sermons in these days, and the writers on other subjects are so full of Scriptural allusion that it is evident their minds were saturated with Scriptural diction, which they used as commonly, and sometimes with as great an absence of good taste, as a Puritan of the Commonwealth."

The *Quarterly Review* for Oct., 1879, dealing with Goulburn's Life of Bp. Herbert de Losinga, says: "The notion that people in the Middle Ages did not read their Bibles is probably exploded, except among the more ignorant of controversialists. But a glance at this volume is enough to show that the notion is not simply a mistake, that it is one of the most ludicrous and grotesque of blunders. If having the Bible at their finger's ends could have saved the Middle Ages teachers from abuses and false doctrine, they were certainly well-equipped. They were not merely accomplished textuaries. They had their minds as saturated with the language and associations of the Sacred Text as the Puritans of the seventeenth century."

Another Protestant writer, Dr. Maitland, in his valuable work *The Dark Ages,* page 220, says: "To come, however, to the question, Did the people in the Dark Ages know anything of the Bible? Certainly, it was not as commonly known and as generally in the hands of men as it is now, and has been almost ever since the invention of printing—the reader must not suspect me of wishing to maintain any such absurd opinion; but I do think that there is sufficient evidence (1) that during that period the Scriptures were more accessible to those who could use them, (2) were, in fact, more used, and (3) by a greater number of persons, than some modern writers would lead us to suppose."

On page 470 the same author observes: "The writings of the Dark Ages are, if I may use the expression, made of the Scriptures. I do not merely mean that the writers constantly quoted the Scriptures, and appealed to them as authorities on all occasions—though they did this, and it is a strong proof of their familiarity with them; but I mean that they thought and spoke and wrote the thoughts and words and phrases of the Bible, and that they did this constantly and habitually, as the natural mode of expressing themselves." And again, he says: "I have not found anything about the arts and engines of hostility, the blind hatred of half-barbarian kings, the fanatical fury of their subjects, or the reckless antipathy of the Popes. . . . I know of nothing which should lead me to suspect that *any* human craft or power was exercised to prevent the reading the multiplication, the diffusion of the Word of God." (1. 6, pp. 220-1).

Dr. Maitland in his work, p. 506, discounts the absurd story as told by D'Aubigné of Luther "discovering" a Bible for the first time when he was twenty years old. He says: "Before Luther was born, the Bible had been printed in Rome, and the printers had the assurance to memorialize his Holiness, praying that he would help them off with some copies. It had been printed, too, at Naples, Florence, and Piacenza; and Venice alone had furnished eleven editions. No doubt, we should be within the truth if we were to say that beside the multitude of manuscript copies, not yet fallen into disuse, the press had issued fifty different editions of the whole Latin Bible, to say nothing of Psalters, New Testaments, or other parts. And yet, more than twenty years after, we find a young man who had received a 'very liberal education,' who 'had made great proficiency in his studies at Magdeburg, Eisenach, Erfurt,' and who, nevertheless, did not know what a Bible was, simply because 'the Bible was unknown in those days.'"

Proofs without number might easily be adduced to show that the Bible was known, read and distributed with the sanction and authority of the Church in the common language of the people from the seventh to the fourteenth century. Enough, however, have been given, and we hope these will carry some weight with intelligent and well-disposed non-Catholics. The contention of the ignorant and bigoted who would have the simple and unlettered believe that Rome hated the Bible and did her best to keep it a locked and sealed book is so utterly absurd and stupid that all honest and patient researches of distinguished scholars flatly and openly oppose it by accumulating evidence from the simplest facts of history. Instead of misrepresenting the Church, it would be more consistent with honor and truth to proclaim from the housetops the debt all owe to the pious and untiring labors of the monks and nuns and clergy of the Middle Ages who saved the written Word of God from extinction, and without whose precious and distinguished services, the world today would not rejoice in its possession. When will our dissenting brethren see things as they are? When will they be candid enough to read history aright? When will they, in the presence of the Church's jealous guardianship of the Bible from the beginning, rid themselves of the silly mouthings of anti-Catholic bigots in declaring that Luther was the very first to give his poor languishing countrymen the Bible in their own tongue, a book which as a student in Erfurt he knew was held in high esteem and which as a monk and priest he was obliged by rule to have known, studied and recited for years? To maintain that Luther knew not and could not find any Bibles except the one he was supposed to discover as librarian of his convent, is to brand him as a liar. It is interesting now to recall what Zwingli, the Swiss Reformer, who made many false boasts for himself, once said to Luther: "You are unjust in putting forth the boastful claim of dragging the Bible from beneath the dusty benches of the schools. You forget that we have gained a knowledge of the Scriptures through the translations of others. You are very well aware, with all your blustering, that previously to your time there existed a host of scholars who, in Biblical knowledge and philological attainments, were incomparably your superiors." (*Alzog*. III, 49).

The Catholic Church reigned supreme for more than fifteen hundred years before Luther introduced his special conception of the Bible. During this long period the Church had it in her power to do with the Bible what she pleased. Had she hated it, she could easily have dragged into the light of day every copy then in existence and, were she so disposed, could have destroyed and reduced all to ashes. But did she do this? The truth is that the Catholic Church, ruled by the Pope, instead of getting rid of the Bible, saved, preserved and guarded it, all through the centuries from its institution and formation into one volume in 397 A. D., to the sixteenth century. All along she employed her clergy to multiply it in the Greek and Hebrew languages, and to translate it into Latin and the common tongues of every Christian nation that all might read and learn and know the Word of God. She and she alone, by her care and loving watchfulness, saved and protected it from total extinction and destruction. Where was Protestantism when the Roman Emperor Diocletian issued a decree to burn the churches and destroy the copies of the Scriptures? Where was Protestantism when the Huns, the Vandals, the Turks and Saracens invaded the Christian countries and threatened to wipe out every vestige of Christian culture and civilization? Protestantism began with Luther about the year 1520, some 1,200 years after the promulgation of Emperor Diocletian's decree. Had the Catholic Church not carefully guarded, transcribed and preserved copies of the Bible in the olden days, there would have been nothing left for Luther or any others to translate.

The Catholic Church alone, from the beginning, defended the blessed Word of her Divine Founder and her inspired writers. This fact is entirely ignored in the mendacious chatter of ranting spouters and ignorant writers whose tongues and pens are steeped in gall and vinegar when they deal with matters Catholic. In spite of modern education and the findings of history, this particular class, from bigoted motives, continue to impose on their dupes and insist without warrant that the Church and her rulers made war, long and persistent, upon the Bible—and that, were it not for "the Founder of Protestantism," the good Book would still be chained to church and monastery walls, as directories are seen today in hotels and other public places. Of course, Martin Luther must be glorified for his supposed achievement. He translated the Bible—or what pretended to be the Bible. His mutilation of the Holy Book and the amputation of several of its members make little or no difference to his admirers. It was great work, one of the chief and most important labors of his life, and according to them deserves a distinguished place on the roll of immortal achievements. With this and similar inaccuracies and misstatements, they forthwith hail him as "the hero of the Bible." The title pleases the multitude and fascinates all who are ignorant of the facts. It is amazing how easily most of the people are most of the time deceived. To tell these benighted souls that Luther was not "the hero of the Bible" would astonish, alarm and shock. The truth is, however, that he has no claim to such honorable distinction, for, as every scholar knows, he docked and amended and added to the Bible, as he would, so that he made the Word of God become the word of man by making it the word of Dr. Luther. He sacrificed accuracy and mistranslated the Bible with deliberate purport and intention, in order to fit it to his false theories and to make it serve to buttress his heresies. His "evangelical preaching," denouncing the time-honored spiritual order, and advocating abolition of ecclesiastical science and the rejection of the Sacraments, required a substitute for the "undefiled Word of God." He produced the needed substitute in his false and mutilated version, and for the sacrilegious achievement his followers call him a "hero." All the heroes of the Bible we know of were never guilty of the liberties he took with the Word of God. They revered and respected every word and thought of the Bible. They neither took from nor added thereto—as was befitting God's message to mankind. To call Luther's version, which is a monstrous forgery, the Word of God is nothing less than criminal and blasphemous.

Luther began his version of the Scriptures in German during his residence at the Wartburg. He had just been ordered by Charles V, who saw it was impossible to convince him of his errors, to leave Worms under an imperial safeguard. After going some distance from Worms, the imperial protector was dismissed and then, according to a previous arrangement, a party of friends—not a band of hostile armed men, as is ignorantly told—appeared upon the scene, took him from his wagon, mounted him on a horse and conducted him in the silence of the night to the ancient and historic castle of Wartburg. To ensure his incognito in this place selected for his retirement, he put aside his monk's habit, donned the dress of a country gentleman, allowed his hair and beard to grow and was introduced to those about not as Martin Luther, but as Squire George. This was the second time he changed his name. The first time, as we have seen, was about 1512, long after he entered the University of Erfurt, where he was enrolled among the students not as Luther but as Lüder, by which name his family was known in the community from time immemorial. The change was perhaps pardonable, for Lüder has a vile signification, conveying the idea of "carrion," "beast," or "low scoundrel." The second assumed name, Squire George, was a decided improvement on Lüder.

The Castle of Wartburg, where Luther spent ten months in retirement, unknown except to some friends who were in the secret, was full of historic and inspiring memories. It was once the residence of the gentle and amiable St. Elizabeth, and was on this account suggestive of the holiest recollections. To live within such precincts might be considered a privilege and one well calculated to stimulate to holiness and sanctity of behavior. The place, however, was little to the liking of the so-called "courageous apostle," who was designedly seized upon by pre-arrangement with the Elector of Saxony and who was constantly protected by his friends whilst disguised as a country magnate under the assumed name of Squire George. He would have much preferred to be out in the open to continue his revolutionary movement publicly and among the masses, but his intimates decreed he should remain in solitude in the hope that the storm which his wild teachings provoked might, after a while, blow over. His stay in the Wartburg from May, 1521, to March, 1522 was, according to his own account, a time of idleness, despair and temptation. Remorse of conscience tormented him. "It is a dangerous thing," he says, "to change all spiritual and human order against common sense." (De Wette 2.2 10 q.). On November 25th, 1521, he wrote to the Augustinians in Wittenberg: "With how much pain and labor did I scarcely justify my conscience that I alone should proceed against the Pope, hold him for Antichrist and the bishops for his apostles. How often did my heart punish me and reproach me with this strong argument: 'Art thou alone wise?' Could all the others err and have erred for a long time? How if thou errest and leadest into error so many people who would all be damned forever?" (De Wette 2-107). He often tried to rid himself of these anxieties, but they always returned. Even in his old age, a voice within, which he believed to be the voice of the devil, asked him if he were called to preach the Gospel in such a manner "as for many centuries no bishop or saint had dared to do." (*Sammtliche Werke, [Collected Works]* 59, 286: 60. 6. 45). Not only was he tormented by remorse of conscience in regard to his revolutionary work, but he was sorely tried by the devil, whom he thought he saw in every shape and form. Writing to his personal friend, Nicholas Gerbel, he says: "You can believe that I am exposed to a thousand devils in this indolent place." He told another friend, Myconius, that in the Castle of Wartburg, "The devil in the form of a dog came twice" to kill him. (Myconius, Hist. Reform. 42). "Throughout life," Vedder remarks, "he was accustomed to refer whatever displeased or vexed him or seemed to hinder his work to the direct agency of the devil, in whom he believed with rather more energy than he believed in God. So now, instead of blaming his mode of life and changing it, he ascribes all his troubles to Satan. He even seems to have imagined that he had personal interviews with the devil." (Vedder, p. 169). From his hiding place he writes to Melanchthon, who of course was in the secret of his retreat, to inform him of his doings and says: "It is now eight days that I neither write anything nor pray, nor study, partly by reason of temptations of the flesh, partly because vexed by other cares. I sit here in idleness and pray, alas! little, and sigh not for the Church of God. Much more am I consumed by the fires of my unbridled flesh. In a word, I who should burn of the spirit, am consumed by the flesh and by lasciviousness." (De Wette, 2:22). His was a most lamentable state whilst confined at the Wartburg. No wonder he produced a Bible full of malicious translations. A victim of fleshly lust and one in constant contact with Satan could hardly be expected to treat the undefiled Word of God with reverence. What reliance can be placed on a translation of the Bible made under such unfavorable circumstances?

Luther, in a letter to his friend Lange dated December 18, 1521, announces his intention to translate the New Testament into German. On March 30, 1522, he writes to Spalatin, another friend, to tell that he has completed the work and placed it in the care of a few intimates for inspection. This leaves little more than ten weeks for the completion of what he hoped would "prove a worthy work." After some revision, the translation was ready for the press and given to the public on September 22, 1522. The whole work was done in great haste and, as might be expected, suffered in consequence. The faults and imperfections everywhere in evidence are numerous and unpardonable. The rapidity with which the work was produced by both author and publisher borders on the marvelous. "It would be difficult," observes Vedder, "to believe that a complete translation would have been made by a man of Luther's limited attainments in Greek and with the imperfect apparatus that he possessed in the short space of ten weeks. . . . Any minister today who had the Greek course of a college and seminary is a far better scholar than Luther. Let such a man, if he thinks Luther's achievement possible, attempt the accurate translation of a single chapter of the New Testament—such a translation as he would be willing to print under his own name—and multiply the time consumed by the two hundred and sixty pages. He will be speedily convinced that the feat attributed to Luther is an impossible one. What then? Is the whole story false? That too is impossible—the main facts are too well attested. The solution of an apparently insoluble contradiction is a very simple one: Luther did not make an independent translation: he never claimed that he did: none of his contemporaries made the claim for him. It is only his later admirers who have made this statement to enhance his glory, just as they have unduly exaggerated for the same purpose the paucity of the Scriptures and the popular ignorance of them before Luther's day. We now know that both these assertions are untrue to historic fact and have misled many unwary persons into inferences far indeed from the truth. The two assertions are so intimately connected that in showing either to be unfounded, the other is also and necessarily controverted." (Vedder, p. 170).

The same Protestant professor tells us that "the version *Codex Teplensis* was certainly in the possession of Luther and was as certainly used by him in the preparation of his translation. This fact, once entirely unsuspected and then hotly denied, has been proved by the 'deadly parallel.' It appears by a verse by verse comparison that this old German Bible was in fact so industriously used by Luther that the only accurate description of Luther's version is to call it a careful revision of the older text. . . . He had a better text than had been available to former translators. . . . The old German Bible had been translated from the Vulgate and had followed it slavishly. Luther proposed to use the original Greek and Hebrew Scriptures as the basis of his work. For the New Testament he had the second Basel edition, 1519, of Erasmus, in which many of the misprints of the first edition had been corrected. He did not fail to consult the Vulgate and sometimes followed that version, which in some passages was made from an older text than that of Erasmus."

When Luther finished the translation of the New

Testament, he, with the assistance of many friends such as Melanchthon, Spalatin, Bugenhagen, Cruciger, Justus Jonas and others, undertook the completion of the entire Bible, which was published in German in 1534. This work, which occupied so many years, was not entirely to his liking. It needed to be altered still more and fitted more exactly to suit his new teachings and more especially his main doctrine, that nothing could be required to be believed that is not explicitly laid down in the Bible. It never occurred to him that this much cherished dogma, if accepted, must be rejected, for it is not itself explicitly laid down anywhere in the Bible. This inconsistency did not, however, trouble him. Intent only on urging his false views, he never stopped in his work, but went on changing and altering the original translation until his death. No fewer than five editions of the complete work were issued during his lifetime. After 1545, when the final text was published, numerous unauthorized reprints, abounding in more changes, were given to the public, so that, as Vedders says, "a critical recension finally became necessary. This was accomplished about 1700 by the Canstein Bible Institute, and that edition became the *textus receptus* of the German Bible, until its recent revision by a committee of distinguished German scholars. This revision is now published at the Francke Orphanage, Halle, and is rapidly superseding the original 'Luther Bible.'" We wonder, were poor Luther alive today, what epithet the master of vituperation would fling at the "distinguished German scholars" who had the boldness to give their revision, and not his Bible, to the world.

Luther's translation was genuinely German in style and spirit. He wanted to make it thoroughly German and to make the sacred authors read as though they had been written in German. In this he had no little difficulty. "Great God," he writes, "what a labor to employ force to make the Hebrew poets express themselves in German." To attain his end he often sacrificed accuracy and "allowed himself," as McGiffert says, "many liberties with the text, to the great scandal of his critics." He boasted that his version was better as a translation than the Vulgate or Septuagint. The earlier translations were faithful to a nicety and much more literally correct, but their German, being in a formative state, was "harsh and crude and occasionally somewhat obscure." At that time dialects were many and various, so that people living only a short distance apart could scarcely understand one another. Though Luther did not create the German language, he labored in conjunction with the Saxon Chancery to reform, modify, and enrich it. His efforts were not without results. He had a large, full and flexible vocabulary which he used with force in his translation, where is displayed the whole wealth, power and beauty of the German language. He wished to make his Bible really a German book and understood by all alike. He did not want the people, as he said, "to get their German from the Latin as these asses," alluding to his predecessors, "do." He gave them German, simple, idiomatic, racy, colloquial, classical, and as his Bible sold for a trifle, it was purchased by many, read widely and exercised a decided influence in giving the whole country a common tongue. We cannot deny that his translation surpasses those which had been published before him in the perfection of language, but while we admit this, we cannot but regret that he failed with all his beauty of diction to give what his predecessors valued more than all else—a correct, faithful and true rendition of "the undefiled Word of God." His work is praised as the first classic of German literature, but the distinction can never blind the scholar to its many and serious imperfections and faults, and its arbitrary additions and changes maliciously introduced to favor his individual and fanciful teachings as against those of the Church sacredly held and constantly adhered to from the beginning of Christianity.

Jerome Emser, a learned doctor of Leipsic, made a critical examination of Luther's translation when it first appeared and detected more than a thousand glaring faults.

He was the first who undertook to show the falseness of the translation and to correct its errors; he published a very faithful version, in which all the passages that had been falsified in the other may be easily seen. Luther did not like this exposure of his work by his learned antagonist, and the only reply he made was to launch out his usual volley of insulting and abusive epithets. "These popish asses," said he, "are not able to appreciate my labors." (Sackendorf, Comm. L. I. sect. 52). Yet even Sackendorf gives us to understand that, in his cooler moments, the Reformer availed himself of Emser's corrections and made many further changes in his version.

Martin Bucer, a brother reformer, says that Luther's "falls in translating and explaining the Scriptures were manifest and not a few." (Bucer, *Dial, contra Melanchthon*). Zwingli, another leading reformer, after examining his translation openly pronounced it "a corruption of the Word of God." (*Amicable Discussion,* Trevern, 1, 129—note). Hallam says: "The translation of the Old and the New Testament by Luther is more renowned for the purity of its German idiom than for its adherence to the original text. Simon has charged him with ignorance of Hebrew; and when we consider how late he came to the knowledge of that or the Greek language, it may be believed that his acquaintance with them was far from extensive." (Hallam, *Historical Literature,* I. 201). "It has been as ill-spoken of among Calvinists as by the Catholics themselves." (*ibid.*). It is now, as might be expected, grown almost obsolete, even in Germany itself. It is viewed as faulty and insufficient in many respects. In 1836, many Lutheran consistories called for its entire revision.

The errors in Luther's version were not those of ignorance, but were a willful perversion of the Scriptures to suit his own views. A few examples will suffice to prove our contention. In *Matt.* 3:2, he renders the word "repent," or "do penance" by the expression "mend," or "do better."

Acts 19:18: "Many of them that believed came confessing

and declaring their deeds." Lest this should confirm the practice of confession, he refers the *deeds* to the Apostles, and renders "they acknowledge the miracles of the Apostles." These errors were afterwards corrected by his followers. The expression "full of grace" in the Annunciation of the Blessed Virgin, he renders "thou gracious one." *Romans* 4:15: "the law worketh wrath," he translates, "the law worketh *only* wrath," thus adding a word to the text and changing its sense.

Romans 3:28: "We account a man to be justified by faith without the works of the law" he renders by the interpolating of a word: "We hold that a man is justified without works of the law by faith *alone*." His answer to Emser's exposition of his perversion of the text was: "If your Papist annoys you with the word [*alone*], tell him straightway: Dr. Martin Luther will have it so: Papist and ass are one and the same thing. Whoever will not have my translation, let him give it the go-by: the devil's thanks to him who censures it without my will and knowledge. Luther will have it so, and he is a doctor above all the doctors in Popedom." (*Amic. Discussion,* 1, 127). Thus Luther defends his perversion of Scripture and makes himself the supreme judge of the Bible. His work, faulty and erroneous, places the true Lutheran in a serious dilemma. He needs the Bible for his salvation—and yet he cannot be sure that Luther has given him a version possessing any binding force.

Luther translated and altered the Sacred Word by the freedom of his opinions. His irreverent work did not stop here. As he rejected the authority of the teaching Church, he had no guide but his own whim and took upon himself to expunge from the canon of Inspired Writings those of the Old Testament known as Deuterocanonical Books, although they had always been received by the Oriental churches and especially by those who occupied the Holy Land, and who, consequently, had preserved the books continuously. In his prefaces to these books he gives at length his opinion as to their character and authority. The result was that they were published as "Apocrypha," or books profitable for pious reading, but no part of the Sacred Text, because not inspired by the Holy Ghost. The catalogue in the edition of 1534 gives as "Apocrypha," Judith, Wisdom, Tobias, Ecclesiasticus, the two books of Maccabees, parts of Esther, parts of Daniel and the prayer of Manasses.

But even for the books he chose to retain, he showed little or no respect. Here are some examples of his judgments on them. Of the Pentateuch he says: "We have no wish either to see or hear Moses." "Judith is a good, serious, brave tragedy." "Tobias is an elegant, pleasing, godly comedy." "Ecclesiasticus is a profitable book for an ordinary man." "Of very little worth is the book of Baruch, whoever the worthy Baruch may be." "Esdras I would not translate, because there is nothing in it which you might not find better in Aesop." "Job spoke not as it stands written in his book, but only had such thoughts. It is merely the argument of a fable. It is probable that Solomon wrote and made this book." "The book entitled 'Ecclesiastes' ought to have been more complete. There is too much incoherent matter in it. It has neither boots nor spurs; but rides only in socks, as I myself did when an inmate of the cloister. Solomon did not, therefore, write this book, which was made in the days of the Maccabees of Sirach. It is like a Talmud, compiled from many books, perhaps in Egypt at the desire of King Evergetes." "The book of Esther I toss into the Elbe. I am such an enemy to the book of Esther that I wish it did not exist, for it Judaizes too much and has in it a great deal of heathenish naughtiness." "The history of Jonah is so monstrous that it is absolutely incredible." "The first book of the Maccabees might have been taken into the Scriptures, but the second is rightly cast out, though there is some good in it."

The books of the New Testament fared no better. He rejected from the canon the Epistle to the Hebrews, the Epistle of St. James, the Epistle of St. Jude and the Apocalypse. These he placed at the end of his translation, after the others, which he called "the true and certain capital books of the New Testament." He says: "The first three [Gospels] speak of the works of Our Lord, rather than of His oral teachings; that of St. John is the only sympathetic, the only true Gospel and should undoubtedly be preferred to the others. In like manner the Epistles of St. Peter and St. Paul are superior to the first three Gospels." The Epistle to the Hebrews did not suit him. "It need not surprise one to find here," he says, "bits of wood, hay and straw." The Epistle of St. James, Luther denounced as "an epistle of straw." "I do not hold it," he said, "to be his writing, and I cannot place it among the capital books." He did this because it proclaimed the necessity of good works, contrary to his heresy. "There are many things objectionable in this book," he says of the Apocalypse; "to my mind it bears upon it no marks of an apostolic or prophetic character. . . . Everyone may form his own judgment of this book; as for myself, I feel an aversion to it, and to me this is sufficient reason for rejecting it." (*Sammtliche Werke* [*Collected Works*], 63, 169-170). At the present day and for a long time previously, the Lutherans, ashamed of these excesses, have replaced the two Epistles and the Apocalypse in the canon of the Sacred Scriptures.

Luther declared time and again that he looked upon the Bible "as if God Himself spoke therein." "Yet," as Gigot says, "inconsistently with this statement, he freely charges the sacred writers with inaccurate statements, unsound reasonings, the use of imperfect materials and even urges the authority of Christ against that of Holy Writ." In a word, as is admitted by a recent Protestant writer: "Luther has no fixed theory of inspiration: if all his works suppose the inspiration of the Sacred Writings, all his conduct shows that he makes himself the supreme judge of it." (Rabaud, p. 42). His pride was intense. He conceived himself directly illuminated by the Holy Ghost and second only to the Godhead. In this spirit of arrogance and blasphemy, he did as he willed with the Sacred Volume, which had been handed down through the centuries in integrity, truth, and authority. The old and accepted Bible he knew in his professorial days was an awkward book for him when in the period of his religious vertigo he rebelled against the Church which had preserved, guarded, and protected it during the previous fifteen hundred years. It went straight against his heresies, and he would not have it as it had been handed down in integrity and completeness. He twisted, distorted, and mutilated it. He changed it, added to and took from it, to make it fit his newly found teaching. He feels abundantly competent, by his own interior and spiritual instinct, to pronounce dogmatically which books in the canon of Scripture are inspired and which are not. Nothing embarrasses him. To make his Testament more Lutheran, though less scriptural, was his object. Reverent scholars decried his arbitrary handling of the Sacred Volume. He, however, cared little for their protests. In his usual characteristic raving, he cries out: "Papists and asses are synonymous terms." He will have his changes in the Sacred Text, right or wrong. "Here one must yield not a nail's breadth to any, neither to the angels of Heaven, nor to the gates of Hell, *nor to St. Paul,* nor to a hundred emperors, nor to a thousand Popes, nor to the whole world; and this be my watchword and sign: *tessera et symbolum.*" [watchword and sign].

The Inspired Word of God was nothing to Luther when it could not be made to square with Lutheranism. He is prepared to assume the whole responsibility for the changes he made, and believes he has the faculty of judging the Bible without danger of error. He believes he is infallible. "My word," says he, in an exhortation to his followers, "is the word of Christ: my mouth is the mouth of Christ." And to prove this, he indulges in a prophecy: he proclaims that "if his Gospel is preached but for two years, then Pope, bishops, cardinals, priests, monks, nuns, bells, belltowers, masses—rules, statues and all the vermin and riff-raff of the Papal government will have vanished like smoke." Luther with all this flourish of trumpets proved himself a false prophet. The Church that he thought would "vanish like smoke" is still in existence and now as ever cries out in the words of her Founder: "There will rise up false Christs and false prophets and they shall show signs and wonders to seduce, if it were possible, even the elect. Take ye heed, therefore: behold I have foretold you all things." (*Mark* 13:22-23).

Not only did Luther knowingly make additions to the text and expunge from the canon some of the Inspired Books, but he distorted the meaning of several passages by interpretations that were erroneous and nothing short of blasphemous. He even went so far as to accuse the Divine Author of *playful mendacity,* of *irony,* when no other sense of the Inspired Words would suit the Lutheran cause. "This champion of *free inquiry,*" says Alzog, the historian, "was obliged to go whither the logical deductions of his system would lead him: and he did not halt at difficulties. There were Scripture texts plainly against his theory of the inherent slavery of the human will: but even these he set aside by an *ipse dixit* [his own dictum], distorting them from their natural sense and obvious meaning by blasphemously asserting that God, in inspiring the passages in question, was *playfully mendacious,* secretly meaning just the reverse of what He openly revealed; and that the Apostles, when speaking of the human will and actions, gave way to an impulse of unseemly levity and used words in an ironical sense." (Alzog, Vol. III, p. 227).

"To do," said Luther, "means to *believe*—to keep the law by *faith.* The passage in Matthew: Do this and thou shalt live, signifies *Believe this* and thou shalt live. The words, *Do this,* have an ironical sense, as if Our Lord should say: Thou wilt do it tomorrow, but not today; only make an attempt to keep the Commandments, and the trial will teach thee the ignominy of thy failure."

This illustration, one out of many, shows Luther's unscrupulous method of distorting the plain and evident meaning of the Inspired Word of God. What he did with this text, he did with hundreds of others. In the most reckless and unblushing manner, this self-appointed expositor twisted backwards and forwards the Sacred Word at will to force it to conform to his special whims and fancies. When he had shorn the Bible of its proportions and changed it in the direction of his new religious theories, he had the daring and the boldness to call his work the work of God. Like all other heretics, he made himself an infallible authority, and as such insisted that his special version be received as the work of God. He knew full well that he had mutilated, distorted, and perverted the Bible, but what cared he, when, in his folly, he wanted his word to be taken for the Word of God. His new religious system was formulated and based exclusively on the Scriptures—not, however, on the Scriptures known to the world for so many centuries before, but the Scriptures as translated, interpreted and understood by the "Founder of Lutheranism."

This travesty of the Divine Revelation, falsified in most of its lines and stripped of its divine character, he gave to the people on his own authority to be henceforward their sole means of salvation and their guide in judging for themselves in all matters of faith. To spite the authority of the Church and advance his destructive theories, he constituted everybody, man or woman, young or old, learned or unlearned, wise or foolish, absolute judges of the meaning of the Bible. This arbitrary act pleased the unthinking multitudes, who now with lamentable folly began like himself to reject the authority of the Church established by God and to substitute, therefore, the authority of man, human, fallible, blasphemous and bent on the destruction of the Christian creed and of divine faith. Through the fluctuations of passion and the inconsistencies of the human intellect, divisions and parties and sects began to abound on all sides as a result of widely different interpretations, until the Inspired Word of God, made the text-book of party strife, lost all its divine character and sank to the level of the human mind.

The work begun by Luther was followed up with ardor by those whom he led into rebellion against the Church. Beza, Zwingli, Calvin and a host of other malcontents claimed the same power and authority as Luther, to be supreme judges of the interpretation and meaning of the Scriptures. In their hands the Bible, without note or comment, without an infallible voice to which men may listen, became the fruitful source of disunion, the foundation of enormous and conflicting errors, and the destroyer one by one of nearly all the principal truths of revealed religion. It is really painful to read the lamentations of the Protestant writers of those days over the utter and inextricable confusion in which nearly every doctrinal subject had been involved by the disputes and contentions consequent upon the introduction of the individual interpretation of the Bible. "So great," writes the learned Christopher Fischer, superintendent of Smalkald, "are the corruptions, falsifications and scandalous contentions which, like a fearful deluge, overspread the land, and afflict, disturb, mislead and perplex poor, simple, common men not deeply read in Scriptures, that one is completely bewildered as to what side is right and to which he should give his adhesion." An equally unimpeachable witness of the same period admits that "so great, on the part of most people, is the contempt of religion, the neglect of piety and the trampling down of virtue, that they would seem not to be Christians, nothing but downright savage barbarians."

Luther sowed the wind and reaped the whirlwind. He saw the miseries of the distracted Reformation he brought into life and was plunged into the deepest despair. Losing all control of himself, he would at times berate with severest, even unbecoming language, all who dared to put into practice the principle of private judgment. In one of his frequent exhibitions of temper he cried out: "How many doctors have I made by preaching and writing! Now they say, Be off with you. Go off with you. Go to the devil. Thus it must be. When we preach they laugh. . . .When we get angry and threaten them, they mock us, snap their fingers at us and laugh in their sleeves." (Walch VII. 2310). What other treatment could he expect? He taught them to decide for themselves the meaning of the Bible, and as his teaching led to the creation of as many creeds as there were individuals, he had none to blame but himself. According to his own principle, the opinions of any of the rabble were as good as his in finding out their faith and in the interpretation of the Scripture. When he did away with divine authority and rejected a divine witness in dealing with the Bible, it ill became him to lecture his own children for imitating his example.

"There is no smearer," he said, "but when he has heard a sermon or can read a chapter in German, makes a doctor of himself and crowns his ass and convinces himself that he knows everything better than all who teach him." (Walch V. 1652). "When we have heard or learned a few things about Holy Scripture, we think we are already doctors and have swallowed the Holy Ghost, feathers and all." (Walch V. 472). Mark how this erratic man speaks of the third person of the Blessed and Adorable Trinity. Will the Bible Christian approve the blasphemous language? Does this show his mouth was the mouth of Christ? We will not wait for an answer, as we would learn more from Luther concerning the failure of his cherished teaching. "This one," he says, "will not hear of Baptism, that one denies the Sacrament, another puts a world between this and the last day: some teach that Christ is not God, some say this, some say that: there are about as many sects and creeds as there are heads. No yokel is so rude but when he has dreams and fancies, he thinks himself inspired by the Holy Ghost and must be a prophet." (De Wette III, 61). Seeing his power and authority to control the masses gone, he now in a spirit of disappointment sarcastically remarks: "Noblemen, townsmen, peasants, all classes understand the Evangelium *better than I or St. Paul;* they are now wise and think themselves more learned than all the ministers." (Walch XIV, 1360). Thus Luther himself testifies to the utter failure of the cardinal principle of his so-called Reformation.

As early as 1523, when Carl von Bodmann heard that Luther declared the Bible's authority is to be recognized as far only as it agrees with one's "spirit," he asked the very pertinent question: "What will be the consequences of the Reformer's principle about the interpretation and value of the Sacred Scriptures? He rejects this book and that as not apostolic, as spurious, because it does not agree with his spirit. Other people will reject other books for the same reasons; and finally, they will not believe in the Bible at all and will treat it like any profane book."

Von Bodmann's words seemed to have in them the ring of prophecy. The outlook for the honor, dignity and authority of the Bible among the followers of the Reformer was indeed gloomy. Luther saw the injurious results of his principle of private interpretation. Depressed by the thoughts of what the future would unfold, he said to Melanchthon one day whilst at table: "There will be the greatest confusion. Nobody will allow himself to be led by another man's doctrine or authority. Everybody will be his own rabbi: hence the greatest scandals." (Lauterb. 91). Just so. He opened the floodgates of infidelity, and nothing but ruin and disaster to countless souls might be expected in consequence.

Luther's system contained in itself the germs of infidelity and paved the way for the Rationalists who, in Germany, hardly surpass their master. Everyone knows what the general influence of the Reformation on Biblical studies in Germany has been. The Rationalism which it generated prevails still to an alarming extent throughout almost the whole of the first theater of Protestantism and is daily working havoc amongst all classes. "This system," as Spalding says, "which is little better than downright Deism, has frittered away the very substance of Christianity. The inspiration of the Bible itself, the integrity of its canon, the truth of its numerous and clearly attested miracles, the divinity and even the Resurrection of Christ and the existence of grace, and everything supernatural in religion have all fallen before the Juggernaut-car of modern German Protestant *exegesis* or system of interpretation. The Rationalists of Germany have left nothing of Christianity, scarcely even its lifeless skeleton. They boldly and unblushingly proclaim their infidel principles through the press, from the professor's chair and from the pulpit. And the most learned and distinguished among the present German Protestant clergy have openly embraced this infidel system. Whoever doubts the entire accuracy of this picture of modern German Protestantism, needs only open the works of Semmler, Damon, Strauss, Eichorn, Michaelis, Feuerbach, Bretschneider, Woltman, and others." (*Prot. Reform.*, Vol. 1, pp. 311, 312).

The following extract from the sermons of the Rev. Dr. Rose, a learned divine of the Church of England, presents a graphic sketch of these German Rationalists: "They are bound by no law but their own fancies; some are more and some are less extravagant; but I do them no injustice after this declaration in saying that the general inclination and tendency of their opinions (more or less forcibly acted on) is this: That in the New Testament, we shall find only the *opinions* of Christ and the Apostles adapted to the age in which they lived, and not eternal truths: that Christ Himself had neither the design nor the power of teaching any system which was to endure; that when He taught any enduring truth, as He occasionally did, it was without being aware of its nature; that the Apostles understood still less of real religion; that the whole doctrine both of Christ and the Apostles, as it was directed to the Jews alone, so it was gathered from no other source than the Jewish philosophy; that Christ Himself erred (!) and His Apostles spread His errors, and that consequently not one of His doctrines is to be received on their authority; but that, without regard to the authority of the books of Scripture and their asserted divine origin, each doctrine is to be examined according to the principles of right reason before it is allowed to be divine."

Since these words were written some forty or more years ago, the higher critics have multiplied to an alarming extent, and the boldness of the extravagances in which they constantly indulge in regard to the treatment of the Inspired Word is a scandal to all lovers of the Bible. The Scriptures, in their estimation, are no more sacred than any other writings. They not only subject them to the most unreasoning criticism, but strive by every means known to erratic and unscientific minds to question their inspiration, undermine their authority, and underestimate their saving teachings. Too proud to "stand in the old paths" designated by Mother Church, they take to the "new one struck out by Luther"; and with *private judgment* for guide, and under the guise of liberty of thought, they attack the "open Bible," now exposed to the vagaries, passions and humors of individual readers, and not only abuse but despoil and strip it of its ancient beauty, sacredness, and authority. How could an "open Bible," with a perception of it hermetically sealed, and an erring "private judgment," meet with other than destruction and lead to "perdition," as St. Peter declares. From a book of life, they make it a book of death. They vaunt their zeal for it only to compass in its rejection.

As we recall the extraordinary and almost incredible developments of the principle of private judgment, which supports a hundred contradictory systems of religion, we are forcibly reminded of what St. Paul writes of the ancient philosophers, that they "became vain in their thoughts" and "thinking themselves wise became fools." The sad aberrations of the so-called learned bibliomaniacs of the various countries furnish palpable evidence of the necessity of a divinely appointed guide in religious matters.

The Bible manifestly contains and teaches but one

religion. Truth is but one. There is but one revelation and, therefore, but one true interpretation of that volume which is its record. The Catholic Church, which existed before the New Testament, which made the Bible, which selected the books and settled and closed the Canon of Holy Scriptures, has alone in her possession the key to the true meaning of the Sacred Oracles of which she was the guardian in all ages and under all circumstances. The same Holy Spirit which founded the Church and inspired the Scriptures made her the authorized interpreter of the Divine Word, and the same Holy Spirit, as He promised, has ever abided in her to guard and protect from all possibility of error in penetrating and expounding the book of life and salvation. God could not do less than safeguard His work. He would not have His children "tossed to and fro and carried about with every wind of doctrine, by the wickedness of men, in craftiness, by which they lie in wait to deceive." (*Ephes.* 4:14). God therefore established the Church to be a witness to His revelation. He made her the external and infallible authority to declare that the Bible is His word and is inspired by Him. With the Church, the Bible is a book of life. Her infallible interpretation guarantees unhesitating certainty in all matters of faith and morals, that peace and not dissension, certainty and not confusion, unity and not division may prevail amongst men of good will. Without this Church there is no witness to the Revelation or Redemption of Christ, and no other divinely constituted teacher of the Word of God.

Today there are outside the Catholic Church numbers of good, plain, intelligent men who love divine truth and are anxious to know it as it was announced in the beginning by the Master, in all fullness and perfection. They love the Bible, but have grown tired of being tossed about by every wind of doctine as set in motion by any new-fledged divine with a superficial education who imagines that he has received a call from Heaven to inaugurate a new religion. They know that in the Scriptures there are "some things hard to understand," that "many wrest them to their own perdition," and that they [the Scriptures] do not contain all the truths necessary for salvation. They feel that the Scriptures *alone* cannot be a sufficient guide and rule of faith, because they cannot, at any time, be within the reach of every inquirer. They know it is impossible for anyone to learn his faith from the Bible alone. The feeling grows on them that their edition of the Bible has been mutilated, that it has been tampered with, that it has rejected what the Holy Ghost has dictated, that it has deliberately cut out what God had put in. Then they recall the solemn warning contained in the closing words of the Apocalypse: "If any man shall take away from the words of the book of this prophecy, God shall take away his part out of the book of life and out of the Holy City and from these things that are written in this book." The arbitrary act of the Reformers in changing the Word of God fills them, as well it might, with horror and distrust. They must not, however, be discouraged. They must learn to put aside their old-time prejudices and arouse their perceptions to see that what they call "the Church of Rome," which they were taught hated the Bible, is indeed the Church of Jesus of Nazareth and holds sacred and uncorrupted every verse of the Gospel. They must be taught that all who would know God, and who would learn what God is, in all His beauty and His truth, must know Him in His Incarnate Son and humbly follow the solemn command to "hear the Church," which He made "the pillar and ground of truth," under the awful penalty of being reckoned "with heathens and publicans."

Once this Voice is recognized, as right reason and faith demand, men of good will, earnest and sincere, will become filled with the sure knowledge of God and His Revelation, as it is in Christ and His Church, and peace shall possess their souls. They will return to the Church of their fathers whence they were beguiled by the false teachings of unscrupulous and crafty men, and discover that whilst she fearlessly leaves the whole Scriptures as they were given her in the beginning in their original, untouched majesty, yet she pours upon them a full stream of light, which draws out into life and beauty and salvation their minutest shades of meaning—a light which they have sought in vain to draw from Luther and his erroneous principles of biblical interpretation.

CHAPTER 7

LUTHER, A FOMENTOR OF REBELLION

LUTHER was a regularly ordained priest of the Catholic Church and "his lips," according to Holy Writ, should "keep knowledge" for all who would "seek the law at his mouth; because he is the angel of the Lord of Hosts." In assuming the sacred office of the priesthood, his mission was not only to the religious, but to the social order, for both are from God their Founder. Like all priests before and after his time, he understood that his duty was not only to acquire, but to keep that knowledge which was necessary for all who sought the law at his mouth, in order to teach the things men should render to God and the things they should render to Caesar. The mission of the priest, as the keeper and expositor of divine knowledge and heavenly truth, is not merely to the individual, but to the nation in its corporate capacity. This was manifestly the will and the design of Christ when He commissioned His Apostles to go and teach the nations all things whatsoever He had commanded. This Gospel embodies all knowledge and all truth, and its message, which is one of peace and good will, is intended to promote among the peoples the blessings of tranquillity, good feeling and fraternal union.

"Anointed," as Luther was, "to preach the Gospel of peace," and commissioned to communicate to all the knowledge which uplifts, sanctifies and saves, it is certainly pertinent to ask what was his attitude towards the ministry of the divine word, and in what manner did he show by speech and behavior the heavenly sanctions of law: divine, international and social?

As we draw near this man and carefully examine his career, we find that in an evil moment he abandoned the spirit of discipline, became a pursuer of novelty, and put on the ways and the manners of the "wolf in sheep's clothing" whose teeth and claws rent asunder the seamless garment of divine knowledge which should have been kept whole for the instruction and the comfort of all who were to seek the law at his lips. His words lost their savor and influence for good, and only foulness and mocking blasphemy filled his mouth, to deceive the ignorant and lead them into error, license and rebellion against both Church and state. Out of the abundance of a corrupt heart this fallen priest, who had departed from the divine source of that knowledge which is unto peace, shamelessly advanced theories and principles which cut at the root of all order, authority and obedience, and inaugurated an antagonism and a disregard for the sanctity of law such as the world had not known since pagan times. His Gospel was not that of the Apostles, who issued from the upper room of Jerusalem in the power of those "parted tongues, as it were of fire." His doctrine, stripped of its cunning and deceit, was nothing else, to use the words of St. James describing false teaching, but "earthly, sensual, devilish"; so much so, that men of good sense could no longer safely "seek the law at his mouth" and honestly recognize him as "the angel of the Lord of Hosts" sent with instructions for the good of the flock and the peace of the nations. Opposed to all law, order and restraint, he could not but disgrace his ministry, proclaim his own shame, and prove to every wise and discerning follower of the true Gospel of peace, the groundlessness of his boastful claims to be in any proper sense a benefactor of society, an upholder of constituted authority and a promoter of the best interests of humanity.

Luther, like many another framer of religious and political heresy, may have begun his course blindly and with little serious reflection. He may have never stopped to estimate the lamentable and disastrous results to which his heretofore unheard-of propaganda would inevitably lead. He may not have directly intended the ruin, desolation and misery which his seditious preaching effected in all directions. "But," as Verres aptly says, "if a man standing on one of the snowcapped giants of the Alps were to roll down a little stone, knowing what consequences would follow, he would be answerable for the desolation caused by the avalanche in the valley below. Luther put into motion not one little stone, but rock after rock, and he must have been shortsighted indeed—or his blind hatred made him so—if he was unable to estimate beforehand what effect his inflammatory appeals to the masses of the people and his wild denunciations of law and order would have." He should, as a matter of course, have weighed well and thoroughly the merits or demerits of his "new gospel" before he announced it to an undiscriminating public, and wittingly or unwittingly unbarred the floodgates of confusion and unrest. Deliberation, however, was a process little known to this man of many moods and violent temper. To secure victory in his quarrel with the Church absorbed his attention to the exclusion of all else, and, although he may not have reflected in time on the effects of his revolutionary teachings, he is nonetheless largely responsible for the religious, political and social upheaval of his day which his wild and passionate harangues fomented and precipitated. Nothing short of a miracle could have prevented his reckless, persistent and unsparing denunciations of authority and its representatives from undermining the supports by which order and discipline in Church and state were upheld. As events proved, his wild words, flung about in reckless profusion, fell into souls full of the fermenting passions of the time and turned Germany into a land of misery, darkness and disorder.

Luther conceived himself to be a religious teacher of no ordinary standing. In his self-exploitation, he time and time again boasted that his word was "the word of Christ" and that his mouth was "the mouth of Christ." Holy Writ tells us that "the words of the Lord are pure words; as silver tried by the fire, purified from the earth, refined seven times"; but the great biblical scholar as Luther imagined himself to be must not have been acquainted with this pronouncement, for we find in his utterances on all vital religious and social questions such falsity and rudeness of speech as were never before voiced by the most depraved of mortals. His mouth could hardly be the mouth of Christ, as he claimed, for we find it most unbecomingly glorying in holding up all things holy, sacred and venerable to unceasing ridicule and scorn. As all who are familiar with his utterances know, he roared like an enraged animal against the Church which the Master founded, and impudently declared her to be "the jaws of Hell, kept wide open by the anger of God." In the vilest and bitterest terms he denounced the head of the Church, who governed in Peter's place, and asserted him to be "Antichrist," "the man of sin," "the general heresiarch," "the chief of all heresies," and the one who "deserved to be torn in pieces with hot glimmering pincers." Nor was he more respectful towards the episcopate of the Catholic Church, against which he declaimed like a madman. If you consult his *Treatise Against the Priestly Hierarchy* you will discover for yourself how he indulges in the very wildest expression of passionate abuse against the Sacrament of Holy Orders. Ulenberg says this incendiary volume has the appearance of being written "not with ink, but with human blood." In this work Luther is not ashamed to call the successors of the Apostles "hobgoblins of the devil," and because they would not adopt and follow his teaching he wanted them "wiped off the face of the earth in a great rising." "Whoever," he cries out, "shall assist and lend his personal influence, means and reputation that the episcopate be destroyed and the rule of bishops exterminated, is a beloved son of God, a true Christian, an observer of God's commandments and wars against the ordinance of the devil." (Erl. 28, 178).

Decency prevents us from quoting further from his malicious work, written to weaken and destroy the very order to which its author was indebted for his priesthood. Suffice it to say that only one who had fallen from the grace of his state could thus recklessly encourage the destruction of the episcopate and openly commend sacrilege and murder as means for the mob to become, as he declares, "the true sons of God and the right kind of Christians." It is almost unthinkable that anyone using this passionate and extravagant language would dare insist that his mouth was "the mouth of Christ," and yet Luther was so persuaded of it that he prophesied that if his gospel "is preached but for two years, then Pope, bishops, cardinals, priests, monks, nuns, bells, bell-towers, masses. . . rules, statues and all the riff-raff of the Papal government will have vanished like smoke." The prediction, as might be expected, was never fulfilled. The Church went on calmly and serenely in the discharge of her heavenly mission, as if the false prophet and his satellites had never existed.

The tirades which Luther hurled incessantly against the Church and her ministers were only preludes to those he aimed against secular government and its legitimate representatives. The seeds of discord he so lavishly sowed in the soil of the Church were gradually but effectively introduced into that of the state. It could not be otherwise. He was naturally of a belligerent temperament and an enemy to all existing institutions, laws and ordinances that were not in agreement with his ever-changing policies. The most cursory examination of what he called his "new gospel" proclaims this characteristic and shows most convincingly the mighty difference existing between its spirit and that announced by the primitive Church. In its every line is written large the grant of liberty to violate all law and to disregard all authority, save his own. Did he not set the example of disobedience to legitimate rule by rejecting the authority of the head of the Church and declaring, "Popery is an institution of the devil?" Did he not spurn God Himself when he admitted the authority of the devil, who "argued in favor of his doctrine of justification by faith alone and against Mary and the Saints"? Did he not, without warrant or proof, proclaim his own authority as that of an Evangelist, who was not even to be judged by an angel? Did he not reject several portions of the inspired word of God and falsify others by additions and suppressions to make them express his teaching of justification by faith alone? Did he not show throughout his excommunicated career the utmost recklessness concerning the most fundamental laws of God and an insufferable arrogance and intolerance towards all who refused to submit to his dictation? Did he not maintain that the poor man "has ample reason to break forth with the flail and the club"—and when the peasants did break forth with the flail and the club and his advice to lay these down was ignored, did he not order everybody "to strike in. . . . to strangle and stab, secretly or openly—for in the case of a man in open rebellion everybody is both chief justice and executioner"?

In Luther's estimation his "new gospel," which was a gospel of rebellion and not of law and order, was paramount to all else. He wanted it, with all its incendiarism, to be made known and proclaimed in all directions. In supplicating his fellow rebels to "spread and aid others to spread his new gospel," he exhorted all to be mindful in carrying out his designs to "teach, write and preach that all human establishments are vain." (See Hazlitt, p. 375). This was his ultimatum, and none in the community must be at liberty to disregard or ignore it. In case any were found bold enough to oppose the spread of the new gospel, he ordered that they should be treated with the utmost severity. No quarter was to be given to the violators of his commands. He decreed in the most dictatorial manner that all who opposed his religious program were to be "denied all rights, all power, all authority and like wolves were to be shunned and avoided." Imagining himself to be the sole keeper of all heavenly blessings, he promised in his famous "Bull," "the grace of God as a reward to all who would observe and carry out" his new and rebellious injunctions.

To respect, honor and obey legitimate authority, whether ecclesiastical or civil, had always been a sacred precept of the Catholic Church. With St. Paul she ever proclaimed what he wrote to Titus: "Admonish them to be subject to authorities and powers, and to obey at a word; to be ready in every good work, to speak evil of no man, not to be litigious, but gentle, showing all mildness to all men." For centuries the Church upheld by word and work the heavenly sanctions of law and order, and whether men would hear, or whether they would forbear, her voice has ever been true to that of the Master, who said: "The Scribes and the Pharisees have sat in the chair of Moses. All things, therefore, whatsoever they shall say to you, observe and do, but according to their works do ye not; for they say and do not." (*Matt.* 23:2-3). Obedience to the state is not an institution of modern establishment, nor is it solely one of man's establishment. Obedience to law, obedience to the respresentative of law, to Caesar, is a divine institution, for God Himself taught respect for civil authority when He bade the Pharisees, "Render to Caesar the things that are Caesar's, and to God the things that are God's." Civil allegiance was thus raised from a mere natural obedience to a meritorious obedience, one which demanded for the law and which brought its own rewards and punishments. It created a new type of citizenship founded upon law and order and absolute obedience. God's way is the way of discipline, of order and of respect for dominion, and His Church will not suffer departure therefrom in dealing with legitimate authority, even when exercised by a Nero or by any of his cruel imitators. Luther, as might be expected from his revolutionary tendencies, set himself very distinctly against this supernatural teaching and, in spite of all evangelical injunctions, followed his own way;

and that way was to decry law, preach sedition and heap abuse upon the rightful representatives of authority, civil and ecclesiastical.

In the second part of a work he wrote, *On Authority,* etc., he expresses his views on the extent to which men are obliged to obey. To the question, "How far does worldly authority extend?" he replies in this strange manner: "But do you want to know why God has ordained that the temporal princes should make such shameful mistakes? I will tell you. God has handed them over to their wicked hearts and will make an end to them." In the same work he raises the objection: "There must be an authority even among Christians," and his answer is, "Among Christians there ought not to be and there cannot be any authority. But they are all at the same time subject one to another."

This was a pet doctrine of Luther, and while its wicked teaching is most untenable and anarchical, it need not surprise anyone who is in the least familiar with his revolutionary tendencies. It was characteristic of him to "despise dominion and blaspheme majesty," and as he constantly set himself against all law, restraint and ordinance, he could not consistently do otherwise than declare that "there ought not to be and there cannot be any authority." What dire results this wicked teaching brought to Church and state ever since it was first announced would require volumes to record.

This open profession of the doctrine of license led Luther to exemplify it in his own behavior. Every opportunity was seized upon to show his contempt for dominion. He took a special delight in holding up the representatives of authority to ridicule and in exposing their faults, real or imaginary, in the most glaring colors, till disregard for dominion gradually spread all over the country. Hardly a ruler of the period escaped his railing speech. Unmindful of St. Paul's wise advice "not to be litigious, but gentle," he denounced the reigning emperor as a "tyrant" and called him "a mortal sack of worms." "Here," he says, "you see how the poor mortal sack of worms [*"Madensack"*], *the Emperor,* who is not sure of his life for a moment, shamelessly boasts that he is the true, supreme protector of the Christian faith." (*Erlanger Ausgabe,* XXIV, 210). In a like spirit of hatred and opposition, he declared that the princes were "mad, foolish, senseless, raving, frantic lunatics." In his work *On Authority,* etc., he says: "You must know that from the beginning of the world a wise prince is *a rare bird,* and still more so a pious prince; they are generally *the greatest fools or the worst rascals on earth;* therefore, as regards them we may always look out for the worst and expect little good from them." Addressing the princes, he says, "People cannot, people will not, put up with your tyranny and caprice for any length of time." In another work written in 1524, entitled *Two Imperial, Inconsistent and Disgusting Orders Concerning Luther,* the antagonism of the disgruntled "Evangelist" against the princes is expressed in extremest bitterness. He says: "From the bottom of my heart I bewail such a state of things in the hearing of all pious Christians, that like me they may bear with pity such *crazy, stupid, furious, mad fools . . . May God deliver us from them, and out of mercy give us other rulers. Amen."*

It is evident from the few quotations given above that Luther believed in freedom of speech, which is a very good thing under approved conditions, but the use he made of it was little calculated to foster in the people respect for authority and willingness to obey it. The fact is that his wholesale denunciations of the Emperor and the other rulers of the period, and his unsparing criticisms of existing conditions, tended to sow the seeds of sedition among the discontented elements of society, to promote a revolutionary tendency, and to arouse into activity the dormant prejudices and passions of the lower orders against their rulers.

The inflammatory power of the violent expressions found in his writings and addresses should never have been used unless he intended to inaugurate a rising of the masses to destroy all order and government. Erasmus, speaking of the crowds who assembled to hear Luther and his preachers expound their new-fangled notions of Christian liberty, says: "I saw them coming from these sermons with threatening looks, and eyes darting fire, as men carried beyond themselves by the fiery discourses to which they had just listened. These followers of the Gospel are even ready for a conflict of some kind, whether with polemical or material weapons, it matters little." (Alzog, Vol. III, pp. 219, 222). Bezold, a non-Catholic, in his history of the German Reformation issued in 1890, referring to Luther's violent productions, says: "He should never have written in such a way had he not already made up his mind to act as leader of a Revolution. That he should have expected the German nation of those days to listen to such passionate language from the mouth of its 'Evangelist' and 'Elias' without being carried beyond the bounds of law and order was a naiveté only to be explained by his ignorance of the world and his exclusive attention to religious interests." Concerning the effects of such language upon the people, the same historian wrote as late as 1908: "How else but in a material sense was the plain man to interpret Luther's proclamation of Christian freedom and his extravagant strictures on the parsons and nobles?"

The evil consequence of holding up the rulers of the nation to ridicule and denouncing them as "tyrants" and "persecutors" did not entirely escape Luther's own attention. As early as 1522, in his *Advice to All Christians,* etc., he writes: "It seems as if a rebellion is going to break out. . . and the whole clerical body are about to be murdered and driven out, if they do not prevent it by an earnest, visible change for the better. For the poor man, in excitement and grief on account of the damage he has suffered in his goods, his body and his soul, has been tried too much and has been oppressed by them beyond all measure, in the most perfidious manner. *Henceforth he can and will no longer put up with such a state of things, and, moreover, he has ample reason to break forth with the flail and the club as Karsthans threatens to do.*"

Luther did not have long to wait to see his fears realized. The incentive to rebellion, which he had long instigated and developed, was at last realized in the tremendous outbreak of the "Peasants' War" which was led by fanatics of Münzer's persuasion in the year 1525. The peasants were for the most part a quiet and peaceful class, and at first had little thought of rebelling against their rulers. They suffered much, however, from unjust oppression, which prevailed at the time to a large extent in many parts of Germany. They had many and great grievances to endure. Naturally they wanted their complaints heard, their wrongs remedied, and the request for a modicum share of liberty conceded. A manifesto setting forth their demands was drawn up and scattered all over the country. There is little doubt that most of what they claimed was founded in strict justice and might easily have been granted by the rulers. Vedder says: "That the ideals and demands of the peasants were substantially just is conceded by practically every modern writer of the period and is tacitly confessed by subsequent legislation in Germany, which has virtually conceded every one of their demands and more."

The proposals of the peasants published in the "Twelve Articles" of the "Manifesto" give unmistakable proofs of the religious character of their demands of justice. Luther tells us that what pleased him best in the Peasants' Articles was their "readiness to be guided by clear, plain, undeniable passages of Scripture." It was believed by those who drew up the petition for redress that all the claims, even those relating to the tithes, to hunting, fishing, forest rights, etc., could be proved from Holy Scripture. The peasants were willing to be advised, but they said they would not abandon their claims unless they were refuted "with clear, manifest, undeniable texts of Scripture." The First Article demanded liberty to preach the Gospel and the right of congregations to elect and depose their parish priests. The Third Article declared: "There are to be no serfs, *because Christ has liberated us all.*" In presenting their requests, they at the same time made it plain that they reserved to themselves the right to make in the future such additional demands as they might come to recognize as being in accordance with Holy Scripture. Thus a higher warrant was bestowed upon the complaints and demands concerning secular and material matters. The preaching of the "new gospel" supervened in addition to the consideration of the oppression of the peasantry.

To all petitions for a more equitable adjustment of the lamentable conditions existing among the common people, most of the rulers turned a deaf ear. Unfortunately, instead of listening patiently and sympathetically, the princes not only refused to consider the demands made on them and afford relief, but they added insult to injury by treating their subjects with the utmost harshness and severest cruelty. A strong desire for retaliation now filled the minds of the aggrieved and despised peasants. Fancying they were helping the new gospel, they thought it lawful to rise against those masters who had been represented to them as tyrants and persecutors of the Word of God. Forthwith the standard of revolt was everywhere raised, and on it was inscribed the talismanic word—Liberty.

At the breaking out of the rebellion, when the greater part of Germany was thrown into arms, fierce fanaticism and wild extravagance dominated the minds and spirits of the insurgents. In the disastrous conflict, the heavy oppression and the many disabilities under which the masses had labored for years were for the most part entirely forgotten, and in their place was substituted an uncontrollable passion for complete liberty as outlined in Luther's "gospel of freedom," under the mistaken approbation found in biblical passages for equality among the classes and a juster distribution of property. Luther was the "man of the Evangel [Gospel]," and on him the eyes of the great number of the peasants were directed when the rising unfortunately took place. The new preaching, proclaimed by word of mouth and in writings, readily fostered among the excited masses the most fantastic and impossible notions of a society in which they were to be in complete and undisputed control. The passions of the multitude were stirred up to the highest pitch. They purposed to overthrow the whole political and social structure as it then existed. They wanted to efface all inequalities in property, employment and rank. In the new social order which they aimed to establish there were to be "no rulers or subjects, no rich or poor, no cities or commerce, but all should live in primitive simplicity and perfect equality."

The fanatical ministers, who harangued the peasants and urged them on to execute their extravagant and impractical scheme, made bold to tell their dupes that it was "God's will" they should everywhere "kill and destroy without mercy until all the mighty were laid low and the promised Kingdom of God established." Münzer, who led the insurgent troops, and all his radical associates, according to McGiffert and hundreds of other non-Catholic authors, "appealed to Luther's gospel and quoted his writings in support of their program. They called themselves his followers and declared it their purpose to put his principles into practice. And whatever was true of the leaders, by the great mass of the peasants themselves it was doubtless honestly believed that Luther was with them and they could count on his sympathy and support." (McGiffert, p. 252).

The unrest brought about by the preaching of the apostasy came quickly to a head, and the catastrophe foreseen filled all with alarm. The rising spread terror on all sides as the insurgents attempted to revenge their wrongs by bloodshed. The passions of the crowd were thoroughly aroused, and the flames of insurrection were kindled all over the country.

At this time, Luther, who was thoroughly alarmed, wrote

a pamphlet with the purpose of keeping the insurgents within limits. In this work entitled *An Exhortation to Peace* (Erl, 24, 257 ff.), he urges the peasants to keep quiet and renounce all desire for revenge, and appeals to the rulers to show a modicum of mercy and to grant at least some few measures of relief. His endeavor at this time to stop the full outbreak of the revolution was no doubt sincere; but his interposition in favor of order came too late and lost all its force by reason of his own blundering in the use of language which tended not to check, but to develop most effectively the growth and advancement of the revolutionary spirit. "Had Luther," observes Grisar, "been endowed with a clear perception of the position of affairs, and seen the utter uselessness of any attempt merely to stem the movement, he would not at this critical juncture have still further irritated the rebels by the attacks upon the gentry into which he allowed himself to break out and which were at once taken advantage of."

Luther's *Exhortation to Peace* consists of two parts, one addressed to the princes, the other to the peasants. In the first part of this work, he throws once more the blame on the princes and then cries out: "Your government consists in nothing else but fleecing and oppressing the poor common people in order to support your own magnificence and arrogance till they neither can nor will endure it. The sword is at your throat; you think you sit fast in the saddle and that it will be impossible to overthrow you. But you will find that your self-confidence and obstinacy will be the breaking of your necks." "You are bringing it upon yourselves and wish to get your heads broken. There is no use in any further warning or admonishing." "God has so ordained it that your furious raging neither can nor shall any longer be endured. You must become different and give way to the word of God; if you refuse to do it willingly, then you will be forced to do it by violence and riot. If the peasants do not accomplish it, others must."

In the second part of the same work he addresses the

peasants and exhorts them not only to suffer in a Christian manner, but to be ready to endure even persecution and oppression willingly. This special pleading came with strange grace from one who was instrumental in raising the call to arms, and as might be expected, its effect was destroyed by fresh attacks against the ruling classes. He says, for instance: if they, the lords and princes, "forbid the preaching of the gospel and oppress the people so unbearingly, then they deserve that God should cast them down from their thrones, as they sin mightily against God and man, nor have they any excuse." Luther fancies he already sees the hands stretched out to execute the sentence and concludes his address by saying to the princes: "Tyrants seldom die in their beds; as a rule they perish by a bloody death. Since it is certain that you govern tyrannically and savagely, forbidding the preaching of the gospel, and fleecing and oppressing the people, there is no comfort or hope for you, but to perish as those like you have perished."

The foregoing is the merest summary of Luther's pamphlet *On Peace.* From the few quotations we have furnished it is clear that his ill-timed and imprudent language was little calculated to inspire confidence and promote the interests of peace between the two parties who were at daggers' points. Whilst we believe that he desired, when the outbreak was begun, that all should desist from violence and preserve order, yet we cannot forget that his excitement and his anxiety to advance the interests of his special gospel interpretation so overcame him as to induce him to use language in denunciation of the injustice of the princes which could not fail to bring into fullest play the aroused passions of the oppressed and sorely tried peasants. The ideas of gospel freedom, which he set forth in such inflammatory terms, stuck too fast in their memory and imagination to be displaced by any later pronouncements, especially when these were coupled with fresh attacks against their oppressors. Henceforth no appeals to keep order and observe law were of use to extinguish the fire already enkindled in their souls. All they thought of now was what pleased them in Luther's denunciations of their wrongs, and, hence, all advice to have nothing to do with rebellion or revolution was spurned and contemned.

Luther is now thoroughly vexed. He is angered because the common people, whom he felt he owned body and soul, were no longer willing in his changed mood to listen to his advice and submit to his further dictation. To his mind such conduct in any man or any body of men was an unpardonable crime. But he had instilled into their minds his new "biblical" ideas of freedom, and, like the docile disciples they proved themselves to be for a time, they considered his teachings favorable to their movement, affording them "ample reason to break forth with the flail and the club." To abandon these ideas now that they were cognizant of his shifting position was a course they were altogether unwilling to pursue. He had taught them to use their own judgment in the interpretation of the Bible, and they felt they were entirely within their rights when they differed from him and set up a view of their own, one which especially agreed with their leanings and tendencies. This they would not relinquish at his command. They refused to heed his appeal to lay down their arms. Up to this time Luther had made common cause with the peasants, but now that they claimed a right to think for themselves and to frame doctrines of their own making, gaining an evil name for his gospel because of the frightful atrocities everywhere perpetrated in its name, he forthwith changed his attitude towards them and immediately presented himself in a new aspect, that of a cruel and relentless oppressor.

Imagining that the warlike disturbances which prevailed on all sides were the work of the devil, Luther thought it high time, as he considered himself his chief foe, to oppose his Satanic Majesty and prevent him from inflicting further injury on himself and compromising still more the cause of his evangel. "If," he says, "the devil devoured him in the struggle, the result would be a belly cramp." Whilst his excitement increases as he sees his influence in the ranks of the peasants decline (and his fancies at the time concerning "signs in the heavens and wonders on the earth" "foreboding no good," grow), sanguinary encounters were the order of the day. The insurrectionary party spread rapidly over Swabia, the Rhine provinces, Franconia, Thuringia, and even approached his own Saxony. Everything was upside down. Luther became thoroughly alarmed. What he saw and heard of the atrocities in the insurgent districts filled him with fear and dread. He "now asked himself," says Grisar, "what the new evangel could win supposing the populace gained the upper hand, and also, how the rulers who had hitherto protected his cause would fare in the event of the rebels being successful in the Saxon Electorate and at Wittenberg." Passionate rage, not discriminating justice, decided his course of action. Assuming the role of a cruel and relentless oppressor, he treacherously turns upon the poor peasants as if they were not his own spiritual progeny whom he led into the trap, and loudly clamors for the princes to turn out in force to exterminate all who had taken up the sword against them. In the fury of his wrath at the horrors of the armed rebellion, he seemed to forget that he had ever been the relentless enemy of the princes, that he had incessantly rebuked them for their tyranny, and that he had brazenly denounced them as "the greatest fools and the worst rascals on earth." So bitter was his hostility towards the very people whom, as Osiander, the non-Catholic historian, says, he "flattered and caressed while they were content with attacking the bishops and the clergy," that he now calls upon the rulers, regardless of his former antipathy toward them, to act in the most vigorous and relentless manner for their complete suppression and extermination. Thus, from the rebels, whose cause he once espoused and encouraged, he turns in basest perfidy and meanest sycophancy to ally himself entirely with their oppressors.

At this juncture he wrote a terrible tract entitled *Against the Murderous and Rapacious Hordes of the Peasants* (Erl. 24, 287, ff.) to urge the civil authorities to crush the revolution. This tract was issued about May 4, 1525. In a copy preserved at the British Museum, London, we find these heartless words: "Pure deviltry is urging on the peasants; they rob and rage and behave like mad dogs." "Therefore let all who are able, mow them down, slaughter and stab them, openly or in secret, and remember that there is nothing more poisonous, noxious and utterly devilish than a rebel. You must kill him as you would a mad dog; if you do not fall upon him, he will fall upon you and the whole land."

In this tract Luther claims that the peasants are not fighting for his new teaching, nor serving the evangel. "They," he says, "serve the devil under the appearance of the evangel. . . I believe that the devil feels the approach of the Last Day and therefore has recourse to such unheard of trickery. . . Behold what a powerful prince the devil is, how he holds the world in his hands, and can knead it as he pleases." "I think there is not a single devil now left in Hell, but they have all gone into the peasants. The raging is exceedingly great and beyond all measure."

He therefore calls upon the princes to exert their authority with all their might. "Whatever peasants," he says, "are killed in the fray, are lost body and soul and are the devil's own for all eternity. The authorities must resolve to chastise and slay so long as they can raise a finger: Thou, O God, must judge and act. It may be that whoever is killed on the side of the authorities is really a martyr in God's cause. A happier death no man could die. The present time is so strange that a prince can gain Heaven by spilling blood easier than another person can by praying."

Luther does not forget to exhort the evangelically-minded rulers to remember to offer the "mad peasants," even at the last, "just and reasonable terms, but where this is of no avail to have recourse at once to the sword." Before this, however, he says: "I will not forbid such rulers as are able to chastise and slay the peasants without previously offering them terms, although it is not according to the Gospel."

He is not opposed to indulgence being shown those who have been led astray. He recommends that the many "pious-folk" who, against their will, were compelled to join the diabolical league, should be spared. At the same time, however, he declares that they, like the others, are "going to the devil. . . For a pious Christian ought to be willing to endure a hundred deaths rather than yield one hair's breadth to the cause of the peasants." "It has been said," Grisar further remarks, "it was for the purpose of liberating those who had been compelled to join the insurgents that he admonished the princes in such strong terms, even promising them Heaven as the reward for their shedding of blood; and that the overthrow of the revolt by every possible means was, though in this sense only, 'for Luther a real work of charity.'" This, however, is incorrect, for he does not speak of saving and sparing those who had been led astray until after the passage where he says that the princes might gain Heaven by the shedding of blood; nor is there any inner connection between the passages; he simply says: "There is still one matter to which the authorities might well give attention. Even had they no other cause for whetting their sword against the peasants, this [the saving of those who had been led astray] would be more than sufficient reason." After the appeal for mercy towards those who had been forced to fight, there follows the cry: "Let whoever is able help in the slaughter; should you die in the struggle, you could not have a more blessed death." He concludes with Romans 13:4 concerning the authorities, "who bear not the sword in vain, avengers to execute wrath upon him that doth evil."

"While his indignant pen stormed over this murderous paper, Luther had been thinking with terror of the consequences of the bloody contest, and of the likelihood of the peasants coming off victorious. He writes: "We know not whether God may not intend to prelude the Last Day, which cannot be far distant, by allowing the devil to destroy all order and government, and to reduce the world to a scene of desolation, so that Satan may obtain the 'Kingdom of this world.'"

Such is the brief summary Grisar makes of this tract *Against the Murderous and Rapacious Hordes of Peasants,* which was written to hound on the authorities to slay in cold blood their misguided subjects and "choke them like mad dogs."

All along, from the time this tract was first issued till the present, every non-Catholic writer of note has been loud in denouncing and condemning its passionate tone and cruel teaching. Among the latest in our own day we present the following estimates. Lindsay, an ardent supporter of the Reformer, in 1908 says: "In this terrible pamphlet Luther hounded on the princes to crush the rising. When all is said that can reasonably be said in explanation of his action, we cannot help feeling that the language of this pamphlet is an ineffaceable stain on Luther, which no extenuating circumstances can wipe out. It remains the greatest blot on his life and career." (Lindsay's *Luther,* p. 186). McGiffert, writing in 1912, says: "The tract seemed over-harsh and cruel, even to many of his friends." (McGiffert, p. 256). Vedder, writing in 1914, says: "The passionate violence and bitterness of this pamphlet constitutes to this day an ineradicable blot on the name and the fame of Luther, for which his admirers attempt various lame apologies, but no defense. His conduct is the more condemnable when we recollect that he was the son of a peasant, that his sympathies should naturally have been with the class from which he had risen, and that in thus taking without reservation the side of the princes, and becoming more violent in words than they were in deed, he was acting the renegade. But no stones should be cast at him today by those men who have come up from the lower ranks and obtained professional standing or business eminence and now for hire take the side of corporate wealth and special interests against the rights and welfare of the plain people from whom they sprang. Even Luther's friends were shocked by this pamphlet and remonstrated with him." (Vedder, p. 244).

Luther's advice to "strangle" the peasants, to "stab them secretly and openly, as they can, as one would kill a mad dog," was fulfilled to the letter. He thought that "God gave rulers not a fox's tail, but a sword," and "the severity and rigor of the sword," he says, "are as necessary for the people as eating and drinking, yes, as life itself." The time, in his estimation, had come "to control the populace with a strong hand," and the rulers must resort to "the severity and rigor of the sword." "Like the mules," he says, "who will not move unless you perpetually whip them with rods, so the civil powers must drive the common people, whip, choke, hang, burn, behead and torture them, that they may learn to fear the powers that be. The coarse, illiterate Mr. Great I am—the people—must be forced, driven as one forces and drives swine and wild animals." (El. ed. 15, 276). This is a most astounding utterance; but apart from its heartlessness and lack of consideration of the common people, it shows the way Luther preached liberty and democracy, a liberty and democracy which meant absolutism and despotism armed with all its iron terrors in government, and through which, for nearly two centuries after, the nations of Europe were oppressed and tyrannized.

The insurgent bands fought under the name of the "Christian Evangelical Army." They struck for what they had come to call "Gospel liberty," and they counted confidently upon supernatural aid in their blind and reckless undertaking. They had the spirit and the courage of the boldest of warriors, but they were unprepared for the mighty contest. They were undisciplined and lacked adequate military training. As might be expected in the circumstances, all their attempts to overcome the thoroughly equipped forces of the confederated princes were in vain. The struggle went on with vigor and intensity, but defeat met the insurgents at every turn. At last the hostile enemies met in May 1525 on the memorable field of Frankenhausen. Before the battle, Münzer, the leader of the peasants, excited his troops by an enthusiastic appeal, and, confident of success, he promised his followers that he would "catch all the bullets aimed at them" in his sleeves. His prediction failed in its realization. The enemy's fire came thick and fast and so thinned the ranks of the peasant forces that they were obliged to flee in utter confusion. Münzer, who fell mortally wounded, was taken and publicly executed. In his last hours he recanted his errors and was reconciled to the Church of his fathers. He died exhorting the people to hold fast to the true Catholic Faith. To his last breath he accused Luther, whose fanatical teachings he had unfortunately imbibed and advocated, of having been the cause of all his misfortunes. With the death of Münzer, the insurrection ended. The confederated chiefs scored victory. Their triumph hushed the voice of the poor peasants crying out for redress of grievances in their blood. The civil powers obeyed Luther. They wielded the sword unsparingly. They drove the common people before them like mules; they whipped, choked, hung, burnt, beheaded, tortured and slaughtered to teach them to "learn to fear the powers that be." The result of the rebellion, thus stifled in the blood of the common people, was a weakening of the democratic principle and a strengthening of the arm of power.

In the short time the rebellion lasted, the peasants were slaughtered like sheep. It is computed that more than a hundred thousand men fell in the field of battle. Cities were leveled to the ground; churches, monasteries and asylums were burned. Immense treasures of painting, sculpture and other works of art were destroyed. All manner of excesses were committed, and general disorder prevailed. The rights of property, of life and of liberty were ruthlessly trampled underfoot. Wholesale massacre and sacrilege, unheard of in the Catholic Middle Ages, were the order of the day whilst the war lasted. Had the insurgents triumphed, Germany would have relapsed into barbarism; literature, arts, poetry, morality, faith and authority would have been buried under the same ruin. This was the greatest tragedy of the age and surpassed in magnitude any ever seen in Germany before. The dire results it occasioned did not, however, in the least disturb Luther. When the war ended and the Reformer saw the last of the crowd which he had exhorted the princes to slaughter for carrying out his own pet principles, he celebrated their funeral, as Osiander tells us, "by marrying a nun" he helped to escape from her convent. This reminds us of Erasmus' significant remark, that while Luther was reveling in his nuptials, "a hundred thousand peasants were descending to the tomb." The massacre of the poor victims of his "Evangel of freedom" was evidently a matter of little concern to the holy (?) man, the ex-priest, Martin Luther and his Katie Von Bora, the Adam and Eve of the "new gospel" of concubinage.

The voice of all history proclaims that Luther was the cause of the insurrection of the peasants and of their subsequent massacre. Protestant writers for the last four centuries have declared that he was the firebrand who alternately stirred up peasant against prince and prince against peasant. Intelligent non-Catholic minds of his own day denounced him as the instigator of the rising and accused him of being the cause of all the subsequent bloodshed. Besides Osiander, whom we quoted above, we have, for instance, Hospinian and Simon, two careful observers of the times who looked upon him as the disturber of the peace and the promoter of revolution. Hospinian says, addressing Luther: "It is you who excited the peasants to revolt." Simon asserts the same thing: "We leave to Lutherans to ponder over the outlandish and sanguinary factions which they excited some years ago in order to introduce and recommend their doctrines." Ulrich Zasius, the jurist, who at one time had been inclined to favor Luther, wrote in the year of the revolt to his friend Amerbach as follows: "Luther, the destroyer of peace, the most pernicious of men, has plunged the whole of Germany into such madness that we now consider ourselves lucky if we are not slain on the spot." Cochlaeus, estimating the number of the slaughtered peasants at one hundred and fifty thousand, does not exaggerate when he declares that "on the day of Judgment, Münzer and his peasants will cry out before God and His angels, 'Vengeance on Luther.'" Erasmus, who was closely observing Luther, reproached him with having fomented the rebellion "by his libels against the monks and shaven crowns." When Luther wrote that he believed there was "not a single devil now left in Hell, but that they had all gone into the peasants," and that a prince "now might better earn Heaven by bloodshed than by prayer," Erasmus promptly answered him in these memorable words: "We are now reaping the fruit of your spirit. You do not acknowledge the rebels, but they acknowledge you, and it is well known that many who boast of the name of the evangel have been instigators of the horrible revolt. It is true you have attempted in your grim booklet against the peasants to allay this suspicion, but nevertheless you cannot dispel the general conviction that this mischief was caused by the books you sent forth against the monks and bishops, in favor of evangelical freedom, and against the tyrants, more especially by those written in German." (Hyperaspistes, Opp. p. 1032).

As time went on, numerous authors other than Luther's contemporaries wrote on the important topic; and they, cognizant of all the testimony in the case, proclaimed in the interests of truth the Reformer's undoubted agency in bringing about the "Peasants' War." Plank, an eminent Protestant writer and defender of Luther, says: "It is but too evident that this revolution was prepared by the reform agitations, and that by such agitations the minds of the people were deluded by such a swindle which otherwise would not have inflamed so many minds at once." (Plank, *Entstch. Des Prob. Lehb.*). Karl Hagen, an eminent Protestant historian, writes: "Even Luther. . . in his earlier writings, contributed to foster the rebellious feeling among the people; for once he actually incited the German nation to bathe itself in the blood of the Papists, and he declared that they would do a thing agreeable to God who would make away with the Bishops, destroy churches and convents! He 'called . . . the princes . . . impious, miserable rascals . . . silly fools,' whose tyranny and caprice people neither could nor would put up with for any length of time. Was it surprising that this judgment of the Reformer concerning the reigning powers remained uppermost in the minds of his readers, and that on the other hand they doubted the correctness of his doctrine of unconditional obedience?" (K. Hagen, *Deutsche Geschichte,* etc. pp. 183-184). Lindsay, in his *Luther and the German Reformation,* page 169, says: "When we consider the causes which produced the Peasants' War, it must be acknowledged that there was an intimate connection between that disastrous outburst and Luther's message to the German people." McGiffert, whilst he does not wish to hold his hero responsible for the tremendous uprising of 1525, nevertheless makes the following significant admission on page 250: "His [Luther's] attacks upon many features of the existing order, his criticisms of the growing luxury of the wealthier classes, his denunciation of the rapacity and greed of great commercial magnates and of the tyranny and corruption of rulers both civil and ecclesiastical, all tended to inflame the populace and spread impatience and discontent. His Gospel of Christian liberty also had its effect." Vedder, on page 242 of his work on Luther, says: The peasants "became conscious that they had rights, that they might rise, and that their inherited condition was a hindrance to them. At this time Luther came preaching that the Pope was a tyrant, imposing unjust, useless, even injurious laws upon the people; that the bishops were doing the same thing;

and that the rulers, in addition to the wrongs that they themselves inflicted, were protecting and upholding the Pope and the bishops. Those among the poorer classes who believed Luther came to feel that the rulers were their enemies and God's enemies. That they had this feeling is proved by their conduct, by their publications and the testimony of all. That Luther's teaching helped to produce and intensify it is equally clear."

But why multiply evidence to prove our contention? The most conclusive argument is furnished by Luther himself, who accepted the responsibility for the wide slaughter of the peasants. On one occasion in later years, looking back upon the events of the unhappy rising, he declared that he was completely at ease concerning the advice he had given to the authorities against the peasants, in spite of the sanguinary results. "Preachers," he says, in his usual drastic mode of expression, "are the biggest murderers about, for they admonish the authorities to fulfill their duty and to punish the wicked. I, Martin Luther, slew all the peasants in the rebellion, for I said they should be slain; all their blood is upon my head. But," he blasphemously added, "I put it upon the Lord God by whose command I spoke." Thus his usual persuasion, viz., that he was God's instrument, is made use of.

Luther's cruel pamphlet against the "murderous peasants" caused such an amount of criticism and complaint among his friends and followers that he thought himself called upon to answer the "wiseacres who wished to teach him how he should write" and to vindicate all he advocated in his previous publications. This he did in an "open letter," which he issued when the revolt was practically suppressed and peace was partially assured. A careful perusal of this work, which was written not under pressure of excitement, but in cold blood and after due deliberation, shows that he recants nothing of what he taught before, but brazenly repeats the offense and, in spite of the scandal caused, even takes pleasure in using stronger language than any he had already uttered. In his endeavor to justify himself, he boldly maintains that it was quite right for him to say that "everybody ought to strike into the peasants, strangle them, stab them by stealth or openly as they can, as one would kill a mad dog." This is his deliberate opinion concerning his former work, as he clearly declares in the following passage: "Therefore my little book against the peasants is quite in the right and shall remain so, even if all the world were to be scandalized at it." (*Erlanger Ausgabe,* XXIV, 299). "Here, as in many other places where Luther has to defend his standpoint against attack," Köstlin, a non-Catholic, says of this writing, "he draws the reins tighter instead of easing them. Here he no longer sees fit to say even one word in behalf of the peasants, notwithstanding the real grievances which had caused the rising."

It was characteristic of Luther never to admit that he was in the wrong. He says of himself: "To the best of my judgment, there is neither emperor, king nor devil to whom I would yield: no, I would not yield even to the whole world."

His dislike for the peasants on account of their disagreement with his general views was deep-rooted, and on every available occasion he manifested this feeling in vilest denunciation. In speech and writing, he poured forth bitterest words of anger against them. "A peasant is a hog," he says in 1532, "for when a hog is slaughtered it is dead, and in the same way the peasant does not think about the next life, for otherwise he would behave very differently." (Schlaginhaufen, *Aufzeichnungen,* p. 118). At the same period he says: "The peasant remains a boor, do what you will"; "they have," so he remarks, "their mouth, nose, eyes and everything else in the wrong place." "I believe that the devil does not mind the peasants"; he "despises them as he does leaden pennies"; he thinks he can "easily manage to secure them for himself, as they will assuredly be claimed by no one." (Cordatus, *Tagebuch,* p. 127). "A peasant who is a Christian is like a wooden poker." (Cordatus, *ibid.,*

p. 131). To one who was about to marry he wrote: "My Katie sends you this friendly warning, to beware of marrying a country lass, for they are rude and proud, cannot get on well with their husbands and know neither how to cook nor to brew." (*Briefe,* ed. De Wette).

"The peasants as well as the nobles throughout the country," he complains in 1533, in a letter to Spalatin, "have entered into a conspiracy against the evangel, though they make use of the liberty of the gospel in the most outrageous manner. It is not surprising that the Papists oppose us. God will be our Judge in this matter! Oh, the awful ingratitude of our age, we can only hope and pray for the speedy coming of our Lord and Saviour (the Last Day)." (*Briefwechsel,* 9, p. 333).

The violent invective which Luther hurled against the "murderous peasants" in the year 1525 had a lasting and disastrous effect not only on the Reformation, but on the Reformer himself. All fair-minded Protestant historians, writing of this period, acknowledge that his former popularity and his influence over the crowd were gone. Up to this time he seemed to have the greater number of the discontented behind him, but now that his power over them was weakened, owing to his fickle and vacillating nature, he was obliged (in the presence of his changing tactics) more and more to seek the assistance necessary to maintain his preachments in the camp of the princes. His shifting from the peasants to the authorities caused no small amount of adverse criticism, and in consequence he was denounced and even branded as a "hypocrite" and "slave of princes" by many of the discontented. All were against him and some even, as he says himself, "threatened him with death." "The springtime of the Reformation was over," says Hausrath. "Luther no longer passed from one triumph to another as he had during the first seven years of his career. He himself says: 'Had not the revolted peasants fouled the water for my fishing, things would look very different for the Papacy.' The hope to overthrow completely the Roman rule in Germany by means of a united, overwhelmingly powerful, popular movement had become a mere dream." (Hausrath, *Luthers Leben,* 2, p. 62).

Luther was fully aware of the disastrous consequences of his evil teachings. He recognized that the common people, as a result of his doctrines, lost many rights and privileges which they had previously enjoyed, and that they were no longer disposed to look upon him as a leader worthy of confidence and support. The crowds that heretofore followed him in rebellion were gradually decreasing in numbers, and there were grave fears that the safety and progress of his pet schemes were in danger of complete collapse. To preserve and keep his evangel in prominence was the problem that confronted him. It called for a speedy and practical solution. As he was a consummate politician, ever ready to sacrifice any principle for political expediency, he had no difficulty in rising to the emergency. Having abandoned the people whom he had at one time believed had the right of armed resistance to authority, he sees now the need he has in his shaky position of the strong arm of the secular power. Putting aside all his innermost convictions regarding an independent Church free from secular control, he now in cowardice and weakness determines to place his whole reliance for the propagation of his evangel on the princes he once denounced and condemned. This vacillating character, who once repudiated all authority in religion and rejected that of Pope and emperor, now falls back on it as embodied in the princes of the period. Under the pressure of circumstances and in spite of his better judgment, he accepted Erastianism as a practical solution of a difficult problem and forthwith inaugurated the typical State Church, a Church which soon after became the tool and instrument of civil power and which eventually was absorbed by it. "The State," Grisar says, "had stood sponsor to the new faith on its first appearance, and, whether in Luther's interest or in its own, the State continued to intervene in matters pertaining to the Church. This interweaving of politics with religion failed to insure to the new Church the friendly assistance of the State but soon brought it into a position of entire subservience in spite of the protests of the originators of the innovations." (Grisar, III, p. 29). "The Catholic Church" observes Fr. Johnston, "had preferred to lose a nation—England—rather than abandon her principles: Luther won over the larger part of his nation—Germany—by abandoning his own principles."

As Melanchthon had foreseen, the most insupportable tyranny took the place of the promised freedom of faith and conscience, in consequence of state absorption of Church interests. According to the execrable maxim of the Lutheran creed, "*Cujus regio, ejus religio* ["Whoever's reign, his religion"], which was formally enunciated by the rulers and theologians of that church assembled at Passau soon after Luther's death and which gained wide acceptance, the religion of each province depended on the caprice of its reigning prince. "He that owns the country owns the Church, and he that makes your laws for you has a right to make your religion for you." There never was a theory more odious, both in the light of civil and of religious liberty. If the prince chose to go over to the Reformers, his subjects had to go with him. In one instance, that of Pfalz, the religion of the people was changed arbitrarily four times within eighty years by reason of this principle. Catholic worship was forbidden, Catholic priests were banished, and if any resisted the new order of things, he was robbed of his goods, expelled from the land, or subdued by imprisonment, hunger, tortures and threats of death. In some cases the territories of Catholic rulers were forcibly seized and Protestantized by Protestant princes. Dukedoms and kingdoms became "Lutheran," or "Sacramentarian," or "Calvinistic," or adopted some other phase of Protestantism, according to the dictates of the prince or duke or king who ruled them. This is simply a historical fact and cannot be disproved.

"It is also undeniable that, with few exceptions, the almost countless Protestant 'confessions' and 'declarations of belief' of the sixteenth century were submitted to the approval of secular rulers and enforced by them. This is the fact as regards the Augsburg Confession, which is the fundamental declaration of belief of the Lutherans; the Heidelberg Catechism, the most generally accepted formula of belief of the 'Sacramentarians' or 'followers of Zwingli and Calvin' or, as they style themselves, the 'Reformed' churches of France, Switzerland, Germany and Holland; and it is notoriously true with regard to the 'Thirty-nine Articles' of the 'Established Church of England.'"

"Where the Reformers dared attempt it, as in Switzerland, they fused the secular and spiritual authority together and established a theocracy. Where they dared not attempt this, they placed themselves sycophantly at the feet of secular rulers as in England and Germany." (*Cat. Quarterly Rev.* Vol. IX, 154-155).

According to the Reformers, the individual was the sole and all-sufficient judge in religious matters, amenable to no authority and quite competent to pass upon the law of God, to interpret and expound it, to admit or reject portions of it, according as his "reason" should dictate. The leaders, it is true, confined this principle to revelation. But more logical minds soon extended it to other matters, and thus ambitious secular rulers whose hearts were set on self-aggrandizement and the extension of their royal prerogatives, following the example of the "Reformers," set up their own private judgment as the supreme tribunal for the determination of all matters, ecclesiastical or political, within their respective domains. The "Reformers" practically confined the so-called right of private judgment each one to himself and his followers; but soon, too, they virtually surrendered it to the secular princes who protected them, with the result that there was instituted a policy which, as systematized and further carried out later on, culminated in the almost entire demolition of the institutions of constitutional government and of the safeguards of civil liberty in all Protestant countries and in most of the Catholic centers of Europe during the sixteenth century, the seventeenth and far on into the eighteenth. One of the most famous historians of modern times, Guizot, once Prime Minister of France, referring to this, says in his Lectures on Civilization in Modern Europe: "*The Emancipation* [!] of the human mind [by the 'Reformation'] and absolute monarchy triumphed simultaneously in Europe." Reserving the word "emancipation," Guizot's startling statement of the fact is true.

During the one hundred and fifty years that followed the so-called Reformation, Europe went back as regards civil liberty almost to the absolutism of Caesar Augustus and his successors. All who have but glanced at the political history of Europe in the sixteenth century, and later on, must know that the ancient liberties of the people were crushed and temporal rulers were virtual despots. Passing over England with its tyrannical sovereigns, its alternately sycophantic and rebellious Parliaments, its revolutions and restorations, it is only necessary to cite Protestant Prussia, Denmark and Sweden. Nor does the fact that the statement applies also to France and Spain weaken in the least the force of our argument. Their peoples were Catholic; in Spain exclusively so, in France by a vast majority. Their rulers were professedly Catholics, but quickly learning the lessons of the Reformers they were anything but Catholic in their political policy, and in their actions as regards both Church and State they were behind no other temporal sovereigns of the period in extending their royal prerogatives and breaking down all the ancient guarantees of constitutional liberty in their respective dominions, despite the remonstrances and protests of successive Sovereign Pontiffs of the Church. In belief they were Catholics; in the exercise of political power they acted according to their own imperial "private judgment," defying alike the authority of constitutional civil law and that of the wise and sane teachings and rulings of the Church of God. As notable examples you will recall Francis I of France, Charles V of Spain, Prussia and the Netherlands—Catholics in belief, but Protestants in their political policy. Then came Louis XIV of France, whose famous dictum, *"I am the State,"* was carried out by him to a despotic extent with regard also to ecclesiastical affairs. Albrecht of Brandenburg, who was called by his contemporaries "the Attila of the Reformation," pursued the same tyrannical course. By sacrilegious plunderings and invasions, he established a despotism which has descended as a part of his patrimony to his successors on the throne of that country. In no region in Europe has despotism been so thoroughly systematized as to Church and State as in Prussia.

"Thus, from the very outset of the Reformation onwards, that movement," says a writer in the *Am. Cath. Quarterly Review,* "has not promoted civil liberty, but has retarded its progress. It taught no true principle respecting human rights and civil institutions that was not previously known and taught by the Catholic Church, her doctors and theologians, long years ago. It introduced principles of disorder and confusion, which inevitably led to anarchy on the one hand and tyranny on the other." (Vol. IX, 156-157).

No other result could be expected. In its fundamental principle the Reformation denied authority, encouraged individualism, and promoted resistance to established government. When this centrifugal principle brought in insubordination, uprisings and popular revolts, the Reformers went to the other extreme and justified absolutism and the use of despotic means in the government of the people. So Protestantism, while tending inevitably to destroy popular rights, at the same time strengthened the arbitrary rule of the civil powers.

"Wherever," Archbishop Spalding observes, "the Reformation had penetrated and had uplifted its 'fiery cross,' protracted civil wars had everywhere marked its progress, and bloodshed by brother armed against brother in fratricidal strife had everywhere stained the soil of Europe. Its career might have been traced by the dismantled or burning churches, the ruined monasteries and the smoking libraries, which it usually left behind it—the dismal trophies of its victory over the old religion. It had unsettled society, and it threatened the change or destruction of existing dynasties. No government any longer rested on a secure foundation; what was strong today might be tottering to its fall tomorrow. And the new political order, which was to rise on the ruins of the old, however flattering soever to popular liberty were its promises, did not really result, at least in the vast majority of cases, in any greater extension of popular freedom."

"The political tendency was rather, on the contrary, in the opposite direction. To strengthen their party, the reformers almost everywhere threw themselves, body and soul, into the arms, or rather under the feet of the new kings and princes who had acquired riches by the spoliation of the old Church, and had obtained increased political consequence and power by the protection of the new gospelers. This protection generally consisted in that utter enslavement of religion which so often results from the union of Church and State, and which is almost always a necessary result whenever the spiritual as well as the temporal power is lodged in the same hands. This was invariably the case wherever the Reformation triumphed in Europe."

"The idle boast," observes Dr. Corcoran, "that political liberty has any connection with Martin Luther or his Reformation is sufficiently disproved by the fact that the liberties of Germany were effectually lost after Lutheranism had brought Germany under its influence, and nowhere more thoroughly than in Scandinavian Europe, where it became supreme without a rival." This was noticed more than two hundred years ago—1692—by an acute observer, Lord Molesworth, British Ambassador to the Court of Copenhagen, who not only observed the fact, but discovered its reason. "In the Roman Catholic religion," he says, "there is a resisting principle to absolute civil power from the division of authority with the head of the Church of Rome. But in the North, the Lutheran church is entirely subservient to the civil power, and the whole of the northern people of Protestant countries have lost their liberties ever since they have changed their religion for a better." (Quoted by Laing, *Notes of a Traveler*). Mr. Hallam says: "It is one of the fallacious views of the Reformation, to which we have adverted in a former page, to fancy that it sprang from any notions of political freedom, in such a sense as we attach to the term."

Luther, then, deserves no praise at the lips of any well-informed people for any influence his teachings may have exercised on civil or religious liberty.[1] All the rhetoric expended in lauding him as a great liberator is worse than wasted. Every attempt to hold him up as the advocate of "freedom of conscience" and the promoter of "religious liberty" is intended either to lead the ignorant into error or confirm the delusions of existing prejudice. The enemies of God and His Church may glorify to their hearts' content the father and founder of an evangel that was not the Lord's, but the voice of all true history testifies that his only claim to remembrance rests on the fact that he pushed freedom of thought or assertion and pride of understanding to an extreme limit by his revolutionary break with the Christian traditions and the established faith of fifteen centuries—a merit, if we can call it such, which he shares in common with every heretic, innovator, or reformer who has troubled the Church of Christ, from Alexander the Coppersmith or Simon Magus, down to George Rapp and Joe Smith, one of the few Americans who figured as a founder of a "new religion." This has made him a hero forever with all infidels, materialists and unbelievers of every class, for they feel, and they are logically right, that he was their precursor, the first to make possible the overthrow of the Christian "superstition" and open the way for the triumph of reason and the new era of light that they imagine is to succeed Gospel darkness. But the most ardent devotees and admirers of this false hero must, if they are thoroughly acquainted with his teachings, admit that he knew nothing of religious liberty or freedom of conscience, much less believed in it, as we understand the phrase. No doubt, he used his private judgment freely enough, indeed with rationalistic boldness, in regard to the Scriptures, but did he ever dream that it was a right belonging to all Christians, that the Protestant crowds whom he drew out with him from "the bondage of the Roman Antichrist" possessed that right, or that his own followers and fellow-religionists had the privilege of following their own private view in any religious matter whatever? His practical teaching was everlastingly to the contrary.

All men were free to differ from the Pope, to reject his teaching, to curse him to the lowest depths, were even invited and encouraged to slay him like a wolf or robber, and wash their hands in his blood and that of his cardinals and other adherents—but they must not dare to differ from Luther, who never doubted his own personal inspiration and his own infallibility. Piously believing himself to be an authoritative judge, both of the meaning and of the authenticity of Scripture, did he not compel, with unrelenting rigor, all his friends and disciples to subscribe to his doctrinal views, and even to his capricious changes of opinion? Did he not, when some, like Carlstadt, Lemnius, Wicel, Agricola, Schwenkfeld and others, rebelled against the shameful slavery in which he held them, make them the objects of his relentless hate and enmity? Did he not manifest his tyrannical and revengeful spirit against the peasants who differed from him when he urged the princes to "choke like mad dogs" the unhappy victims whom his own teachings had led into their evil courses? Did he not hate all who presumed to dissent from his opinions and follow a religious belief of their own, and as in the case of the

Sacramentarians, Zurichers and others, did he not call them fanatics and factious sectarians, his sworn enemies, soul-murderers, damned blasphemers, lying mouths with hearts thoroughly possessed by the devil? Did he not damn to Hell's lowest depths his own dissenting Protestant brethren, and did not the shocking condition of his intolerant mind make him look upon Jew and Catholic as such outlaws that judicial murder or private assassination were lawful and commendable in their case?

But it is useless to ask any more questions. The well-informed know that Luther's gospel in practice was the gospel of hate toward all who conscientiously refused to accept it. Menzel declares that "this intolerant hatred was as truly a part of the religion of the reformers as belief in the infallibility of the Church was for Catholics." Is it any wonder that a gospel, good only inasmuch as it afforded a plausible shield and cover to its framer's bitter intolerance, should lead its upholders to persecution for conscience's sake and move its blind dupes to rioting, violence and the horrors of war?

European history for the last three hundred years and more is little besides a record of the trampling underfoot of almost every element of popular government and the imposition of the intolerable yoke of absolute despotism, with union of Church and State, on the necks of the suffering multitudes. In the good old times the people, as John Quincy Adams said of the Swiss cantons in a speech he once made at Buffalo, "loved liberty and therefore remained Catholic." Every important element of free government, popular representation, trial by jury, exemption from taxation without the consent of the governed, *habeas corpus,* and the great fundamental principle that the people have certain inalienable rights, were generally recognized and firmly established. All these blessings Catholics enjoyed for centuries before the Reformation was even dreamt of. With its advent seditions and tumults, civic factions and religious dissensions, distrust among those who had been hitherto united as brethren appeared on all sides and paved the way for the omnipotence of the princes when absolute and uncontrolled despotism reigned on the one hand, and dreadful anarchy on the other.

Scherr, an enemy of the Catholic Church, puts the blame on Luther for the absolute despotism and union of Church and State in every place in Germany where the Reformation obtained a solid footing. In his *German Culture,* Third edition, page 260, he says: "Luther was the originator of the doctrine of unconditional surrender to civil power. That two and five make seven he preached, that you know. But if the civil government should proclaim that two and five are eight, then you must believe it against your better knowledge and sense. That explains why so many German princes took so kindly to the servile policies of Lutheranism."

That shifty position of Luther inaugurated a period of revolution on the one hand and tyranny and absolutism on the other, so that ever since, governments and subjects are at all times at swords' points and can never regain their balance until the cause of the evil is removed.

When in this age of ours revolution walks like a destroying angel among the nations of the earth and breathes death from its nostrils among the peaceful inhabitants thereof; when the rulers upon their thrones are unsafe; when in this very land of liberty, calling itself Protestant, a Booth strikes down the most peaceful of men, the kindly Lincoln; a Guiteau destroys the useful life of a Garfield; when at the dawn of the twentieth century a ruler chosen by his fellow citizens is murdered by the hands of the assassin Czolgosz while enjoying the quiet hospitality of a sovereign state; and when you ask for the reason that produced such murderous outrages, we bid you turn to Luther and his rebellious teachings announced and embodied in the work falsely styled "Reformation," producing the result of a deformation. Luther is its father, the sixteenth century its cradle, and autocracy its protector and high priest.

If the world today rejoices in such liberty as it possesses, it is indebted, be it remembered, to no principle or tendency born of the religious upheaval of the sixteenth century. Luther taught, preached and exemplified in action the propriety and the need of civil and religious persecution. All his followers in rebellion, Calvin, Beza, Gustavus Vasa and the rest, believed in and advocated the right and duty to persecute for civic and religious convictions. The policy of all the Reformers and of all the nations that became Protestant was from the beginning guided by this belief and was always marked by the immediate promulgation of laws against Catholics and dissenters. Civil and religious liberty came only after the Reformation movement had run its disastrous course. Freedom of conscience is a *reaction* rather than a *result.*

It is well to remember that when Christ organized His Church, He commissioned her not only to save each individual in the human family from the wrath to come; but He commanded her to teach the peoples, in their organized capacity, that God is Sovereign Lord over all, that righteousness exalteth a nation, and that the body politic, no less than the individual body, must be kept pure, undefiled and uncorrupted. This saving teaching the Catholic Church has always and unflinchingly proclaimed from her pulpit, in the confessional, and in the schoolhouse. The nations that heeded the lesson and the governments that did not dispute the authority of the teacher became the powerful empires and kingdoms of the world, the framers of a system of jurisprudence which has never been excelled, the husbandmen of a civilization that was most glorious and enduring, the benefactors of humanity and the patrons of art and science—everything that adorns human life and makes for the uplift and ennobling of society. Those docile nations received their strength, their influence and their support from the Church, whose protector in turn they were.

But in the sixteenth century a most disastrous calamity swept over Christendom. The old bonds of religion and authority were broken. Civil government became envious of God's sovereignty and forthwith aided and manipulated a fearful and blighting heresy which demoralized national life, stimulated revolution and encouraged lawlessness. Then rebellion against the Church of Christ became a dogma of civil authority, and the aim of subjecting her to civil power was openly and shamelessly advocated. The new goddess of liberty, "the sovereignty of the people," with an extinguished light in her hand, was proclaimed the Queen of the World; and while the people were enticed by her coquettish ways to worship at her shrines, the rulers forged the chains for the victims which they were to lead away captives.

Ever since the rebellion of Luther, genius and learning, wit and satire, eloquence and poetry, sophistry and specious reasoning have been employed to ridicule, destroy and stamp out of the mind and action of men the principle of divine and human authority. Protestant Christianity squeezed it out of its system; it has been driven out of domestic life; and it is treated with scorn in governmental circles. Indeed there is today little or no regard for legitimate authority, either in the home or in organized society. The authority entrusted to the head of the family is almost entirely discarded. The person of the chief magistrate of city, state or nation is treated with disrespect, and the tribunal of justice is hailed with contempt. Majesty is no longer attached to law. This denial of authority has demoralized all conception of respect for superiors, for property rights, and for individual liberty; and the very foundation stones of the national structure are being moved one by one, so that the structure itself is in danger of tottering and of falling asunder. The general aversion to the guidance of legitimate and divinely established law, which Luther's loose and immoral teachings introduced into the world and which have come down to our day, must be removed if domestic happiness and national prosperity would bless the land, its homes and its people. It is only when men render to God the things that are God's and to Caesar the things that are Caesar's that there shall be brotherly love, a common feeling of kinship and a readiness to stand shoulder to shoulder, one for all and all for one, forming one powerful army, and that the uplift, advancement and sanctification of mankind shall bless the earth. "Unless the Lord," as the Holy Spirit says, "keep the city, he watcheth in vain that keepeth it." (*Ps.* 126:1).

Luther and his Protestantism, on the contrary, proclaimed the false doctrine of the Divine Right of Kings and the unequalled absolutism of rulers, and, as might be expected, freedom was destroyed, sedition promoted, and the security not only of all kinds of property but even of human life was endangered.

When we consider Luther's teaching and practical behavior and that of his fellow instigators of rebellion regarding civil and religious liberty, and see how they struck at the free institutions brought down from the Middle Ages, only to introduce in their stead a reign of centralized despotism from which we are but slowly recovering, we may well and justly say with the Protestant Hallam: "It is strange to see men, professing all the time our modern creed of charity and toleration, extol these sanguinary spirits of the sixteenth century." (*Const. History,* Vol. I, ch. III, p. 147).

NOTE

1. See Note 1 on page 305 for an explanation of "religious liberty" and "freedom of conscience."

CHAPTER 8

LUTHER ON FREE WILL AND LIBERTY OF CONSCIENCE

WHEN God created man, He united to a material body a spiritual soul endowed with faculties that not only proclaim his dignity and nobility, but tell him that he is to be eternally happy or miserable according to the good or bad use he makes of these gifts in this world. One of the principal perfections with which man is endowed is the faculty of free will. After his own existence, there is no truth he realizes more vividly in his inner consciousness than the possession of free will. Through this faculty man's soul is enabled, according to its liking, to do what it pleases, act or not act, decide in such or such a manner, and among different impressions, choose one and attach itself to it in such wise that it becomes insensible to every other, as occurs so often in the phenomenon of abstraction, where the mind, exclusively occupied with one object, hears nothing, feels nothing, sees nothing that is passing around it.

This faculty of free will differentiates man from all other creatures that surround him. Whilst matter is blindly submissive to the action of external agencies, and other creatures obey a superior immutable will which constrains them always and everywhere to execute its commands, it is man's God-given privilege to think, reason and will freely. His soul acts or does not act; it wishes or it does not wish; it chooses or does not choose; while doing one thing it perceives perfectly well that it might do another instead. If the action is good, the soul experiences joy; if bad, remorse; for it feels that it is free not to act improperly. There is no one among us unacquainted with the sentiment of pleasure or pain which follows the commission of a good or a bad action. This sentiment we could not experience if we had not been free to act as we choose; we could not then merit either recompense or chastisement. Without free will we should move as mere machines. All things would be equal, since all things would be compulsory. In this condition it would be absurd and unjust to punish vice and reward virtue; or rather, there would be neither good nor evil, neither vice nor virtue. Accordingly, God would be unjust in rewarding some and punishing others; but if God were unjust, He would no longer be God; He would no longer be anything; the world would be an effect without a cause. Such is the abyss, Gaume tells us, into which all fall after a few steps if they deny the free will of the soul.

The liberty or freedom from interior necessity or compulsion we enjoy as thinking and reasonable beings is the subjective basis of all moral, religious, civil and social order. On this inestimable privilege of self-determination the Catholic Church has always laid great stress, and has ever uniformly and consistently considered it as the foundation of all man's worship of God and all communication with Him. In His merciful designs He willed that "all men be saved and come to a knowledge of the truth." To help them to fulfill His will and to acquire eternal happiness, He gives His grace to all without exception. In the bestowal of His heavenly assistance to man, God leaves him entirely free to receive or to reject it. Man's freedom of choice ever remains in this life his own peculiar possession to do with it whatsoever he pleases and select for himself a right or a wrong course regarding his eternal destiny. Whilst God is ever ready to assist man to arrive at a wholesome and unfettered decision, yet He will not overrule, dominate, or derange the will of man to deprive it of its freedom of choice between good and evil. God made man without his cooperation, but, as St. Augustine says, "He will not save him without it." Man, in cooperating with God's grace, does not thereby lose his freedom of will. Under the action of His grace man retains all his power of freedom, and therefore, all the efforts he makes in the salvation of his soul are "as an act organically one, effected equally by God's grace and by his free cooperation." "Free-will," as St. Augustine aptly remarks, "is not destroyed because it is assisted by grace; it is assisted because it has not been destroyed."

To this basic truth of sane reason, the pillar of all religious belief, Luther was decidedly and unalterably antagonistic. It mattered not to him that the vast majority of the human race believed in the freedom of the human will and manifested on every page of history since the world began acknowledgment of the sense of duty and the force of the requirements of the moral order. In spite of the general belief of mankind, the teaching of Scripture and the doctrine of the Catholic Church on man's power of choice for what is good, he gradually came to hold and to advocate that man does not possess freedom of will, and is, therefore, incapable of either merit or guilt in the sight of his Creator. Moving along the old lines of his distaste for good works and for so-called self-righteousness, he came to exaggerate the results of Original Sin with regard to doing what is good, and imagined that the Fall of our first parents warped and obliterated the freedom of moral choice by giving rise to concupiscence and the movements of inordinate passion. The false conception he formed of the corruption of human nature by Original Sin and concupiscence led him on to the denial of all liberty on man's part for doing what is good and to the adoption of the idea of "the imputation of the merits of Christ as a cloak to cover and hide all iniquity." The Catholic doctrine, which holds that free will had not been destroyed by Original Sin, and that in one who acts aright, it is not interfered with by God's grace, he thought "did not allow to free will its full rights, since it ostensibly does all and obliterates every free deed in the domain of salvation."

Original Sin, which the Catholic Church attributes to the voluntary weakness of man and the artifice of the seducer, he had, as we shall show further on, the temerity to attribute to the Thrice-Holy God.

In scanning Luther's works issued from 1516 to 1524, we frequently discover certain emphatic statements on the question of man's free will which give a clear insight into his trend of thought and show plainly his intention to develop his new theories and to make them the core and kernel of all his teaching. From out of the vast number of the false assertions he made during this period, we present the following: "Everything happens of necessity"; "Man, when he does what is evil, is not master of himself"; "Man does evil because God ceases to work in him"; "By virtue of His nature God's ineluctable concursus determines everything, even the most trivial," hence "inevitable necessity" compels us in "all that we do and everything that happens"; "God alone moves and impels all that He has made," nay, "He decrees all things in advance by His infallible will," including the inevitable damnation of those who are damned. These assertions indicate clearly and unmistakably his position and feeling regarding the doctrine of human will and the liberty of the thinking being. Although his views are as false as they are blasphemous, they surprise none familiar with his unscriptural teaching on justification by faith alone, which totally deprived human action of all moral character and mankind of all moral responsibility. In order to give some appearance of logical coherence to his new system of religion based on the general corruption of human nature due to Original Sin, it is easy to understand how naturally he came to deny the freedom of the human will, to excuse human culpability and to minimize human responsibility. In his estimation man's will was totally depraved and, therefore, possessed no self-determining power. Fathering this view of man's will, which destroys all moral liberty, he thus revived and reproduced in a somewhat new form the ancient Gnostic and

Manichean error and forthwith made this teaching the fundamental doctrine of his new system of belief. So confident and assured was he of the soundness and correctness of his position regarding man's will that he wanted none to attack or dispute his favorite teaching, for to do so "would," as he says, "place the knife at his throat."

To those who have been taught all along that Luther was the one great champion of human liberty, it must come as a shocking surprise to learn for the first time that their hero persistently denied free will in man and considered it, to use his own words, "a mere empty name." It is true that at times in some of his practical writings and instructions he makes it appear as though the Christian were free, with the help of grace, to follow the path of salvation. He expresses this view in his exposition of the Penitential Psalms, the Our Father and the Ten Commandments. In his sermons on the Decalogue he even calls the opinion "godless" that any man is forced by necessity to sin and not rather led to commit it by his own inclination. "All that God has made is good, and thus all natural inclination is to what is good." In his tract *On the Freedom of the Christian Man,* written in October, 1520, he teaches that the Christian is "free lord of all and subject to none." Thus, in such works as he intended for the furtherance of the Christian life, he speaks to the faithful as though they still enjoyed moral freedom of the will and liberty of choice. But when we glance at his *Commentary on Romans,* the *Resolutions* on the Leipzig Disputation and the *Assertio omnium articulorum,* written in defense of his condemned propositions, we find his language is the very reverse of that used in his sermons, expositions and practical writings. These works do not pass over his denial of free will in silence. They are most outspoken in opposition to free will and contain in substance all the strictures embodied later on in his treatise entitled *Slave Will.* In one of the works just named Luther says: "The world has allowed itself to be seduced by the flattering doctrine of free will, which is pleasing to nature." If any point of his teaching, then certainly that of the "captive will" is to be accounted one of the "most sublime mysteries of our faith and religion, which only the godless know not, but to which the true Christian holds fast." (*Assertio*, etc., pp. 95, 158).

This statement of Luther shows how close to his heart was his pet teaching on the absence of free will in man. But whilst he and many of his ardent followers were satisfied with the strange pronouncement, there were millions who did not consider his "captive will" as anything but degrading and demoralizing. From the beginning, its announcement and tendency to unsettle moral conditions were discerned by the enlightened in the community, and the prevailing convictions of humanity resented the insult embodied in the teaching. Opposition was met with in almost all quarters. Many, even in the wide circle of his own readers, were startled at his bold attacks on free will, and not a few, considering his inconsistency on the point—now admitting and again denying the faculty of man's freedom, and weighing the consequences of his final adoption of the "captive will" as one of the "most sublime mysteries" of his "faith and religion," abandoned his cause and refused longer to be associated with his movement. The promulgation of his views on free will caused widespread scandal and opened the way to the licentious for the commission of the grossest violations of law, divine and civil.

"Capito," Grisar says, "declared himself openly against Luther's theories concerning the absolute enslavement of the will. The humanist Mosellanus (Peter Schade), a great admirer of the Wittenbergers, spoke so strongly at Leipzig against the propositions deduced from Luther's teaching on predestination to Hell that the latter was warned of what had occurred. Many who had previously been favorably disposed to Luther were repelled by his teaching on the enslaved will and fell away then or later, for instance, the learned naturalist George Agricola."

Luther, during a period of seven or eight years, labored

with all his energy, by writing and preaching, to destroy in the hearts of the people the traditional teaching of the Church on the important question of free will, justification and pardon. His efforts were not without results among the ill-informed, the lovers of novelty, and the rebellious. The confusion and disorder which followed everywhere as a consequence of his demoralizing teachings threatened to undermine the very foundations of society itself.

Among the vast number who grew alarmed at the frightful condition noticeable on all sides was Erasmus, whom Luther endeavored by flattery to win over to his side and whom he called the "Glory and Hope of Germany." This man was a prolific author and wrote in the most fluent Latin. He enjoyed great fame in the domain of learning and, by common consent, was the first authority of the day on classical and critical studies. Justly renowned for his general literary culture and familiarity with religious and historical questions, he was just the man the occasion required to hold Luther up to the world in his true colors and help to diminish the corruption then everywhere rampant on account of the Reformer's loose doctrine. Though timid by nature and preferring any other task to attacking Luther, he launched forth in 1524, at Basle, his work *De libero arbitrio diatribe* [*Discourse on Free Will*], which administered a severe blow to Luther and enlightened all on the fallacy and dangers of the religion of the "enslaved will." Many cultured laymen, such as Duke George of Saxony, Ulrich Zasius and Martin Lipsius, expressed their approbation of Erasmus' work in defense of free will. Melanchthon, Luther's closest friend, praised the moderation with which the champion of free will treated the subject. Even Luther himself admitted the kindness displayed by Erasmus in this work. According to Vedder, a non-Catholic writer of our own day, "This great scholar [Erasmus] had little difficulty in pointing out Luther's errors and in showing that his doctrine of the will is incompatible with reason, experience and the general tenor of

Scripture." In a tone of studied moderation and without a trace of bitterness, "Erasmus," to use the words of Grisar, "dwelt with emphasis and success on the fact that, according to Luther, not merely every good, but also every evil must be referred to God; this was in contradiction with the nature of God and was excluded by His Holiness. According to Luther, God inflicted eternal damnation on sinners, whereas they, insofar as they were not free agents, could not be held responsible for their sins; what Luther had advanced demanded that God should act contrary to His eternal Goodness and Mercy; it would also follow that earthly laws and penalties were superfluous, because without free will no one could be responsible; finally, the doctrine involved the overthrow of the whole moral order."

In pointing out the practical difficulties of Luther's reckless assertions, Erasmus called on the heresiarch to reply to his arguments, which may be briefly summed up as follows: "If the will of man is not free to choose the good, who will try to lead a good life? Will not everyone find a ready excuse for all sins and vices by saying: I could not help falling? What is the meaning of God's law, if the people for whom it was made cannot obey? The whole legislation of God becomes a farce and a mockery if man has not the power to observe it. How, finally, can God punish or reward those who cannot choose between good and evil, but merely do what they must?" These were practical questions, but Luther never attempted to deal with them seriously.

"Erasmus, in defending free will," writes A. Taube, a Protestant theologian, "fights for responsibility, duty, guilt and repentance, ideas which are essential to Christian piety. He vindicates the capacity of the natural man for salvation, without which the identity between the old and the new man cannot be maintained, and without which the new life imparted by God's grace ceases to be a result of moral effort and becomes rather the last term of a magical process. He combats the fatalism which is incompatible with Christian piety and which Luther contrived to avoid only by his want of logic; he vindicates the moral character of the Christian religion, to which, from the standpoint of Luther's theology, it was impossible to do justice." (A. Taube, *Luther's Lehre über die Freiheit,* etc. Göttingen, 1901, p. 46).

Although the work of Erasmus reached Luther in September, 1524, it was not until late in the following year that a reply was issued. The troubles of the Peasants' War and his marriage to a kidnapped nun engrossed his attention to the exclusion of almost everything besides. He was inclined at first to treat his opponent's attack with contempt, but when Katherine Von Bora represented to him that his foes "might see in his obstinate silence an admission of defeat," he began his reply and composed it, as he himself admits, in excessive haste. To this work he gave the title *De servo arbitrio*—"On the Enslaved Will," or "On the Servitude of the Will," which was borrowed from a misunderstood saying of St. Augustine. In this famous volume Luther defined his position on the absence of free will and expressed his matured convictions that man is absolutely devoid of freedom of choice, even in the performance of works not connected with salvation and moral acts generally. Luther was very proud of this work. He thought it was unanswerable and defied Erasmus, and even the devil, to refute it. Notwithstanding the high estimate he conceived of this treatise, it is well-known that many in his own day regretted its issue, for as Köstlin-Kawerau remarks, "It was a stumbling block to his followers, and attempts were made to explain it away by all the arts of violent exegesis." Kattenbusch says, in the preface of his study on this work, that "quite rightly it caused great scandal and wonder." Vedder, another Protestant author, says, "Though this is by far the most decent of all his controversial writings, his 'Slave Will' cannot be commended to controversialists for their imitation. He cannot deny himself the pleasure of an occasional mean fling, and a bitter ephithet bursts forth from him now and then, as if it were unawares, while a tone of ill-suppressed rage is heard through the whole." (Vedder, p. 230).

The tone of this book is indeed violent, but what is worse, the doctrine it advances is debasing and wantonly demoralizing. As one wades through its dismal pages, it is impossible to refrain from asking how any man claiming, as Luther did, to be a religious reformer, could pen anything so revolting and so shocking to the common sense of the Christian heart as the wild, reckless and unfounded assertions that fill it from cover to cover.

It is not possible in a chapter like this to give a full review of Luther's work on "Slave Will." To set forth completely the whole theory of his enslaved will would require volumes. In the limited space at our disposal we can only offer the reader a few extracts, which embody his teachings and are fairly representative of all the views he held on the subject. In order to remove any suggestion of bias in the matter, we quote the non-Catholic Vedder's findings. "Luther," he says, "grounds this doctrine of the will in the nature of God." He then quotes the following from the Reformer's work on "Slave Will": "The omnipotence of God makes it, that the wicked cannot evade the motion and action of God, but, being of necessity subject to it, he yields. . .God cannot suspend His omnipotence on account of his aversion, nor can the wicked man change his aversion. Wherefore it is that he must of necessity continue to sin and err, until he be amended by the Spirit of God. To the objection that this contradicts our ideas of goodness and justice, Luther declares that whatever God wills is right, purely because He wills it; God is that being for whose will no cause or reason is to be assigned as a rule or standard by which it acts, seeing that nothing is superior or equal to it, but it is itself the rule of all things. For if it acted by any rule or standard, or from any cause or reason, it would no longer be the will of God. Wherefore, what God wills is therefore not right because He so wills. A cause and reason are assigned for the will of the creature, but not for the will of the Creator, unless you set up, over Him, another Creator." "Luther thus treats us," says Vedder, "to the ultimate absurdity of his system, a God who is wholly irrational, and acts without any reason, or else He could not be God." Is not this evidence enough to brand Luther as an out and out enemy of God and man, and rank him among the vilest teachers the world ever produced?

At the end of his work on "Slave Will" the irreverent author sums up all he had written and appeals to God's rule and to His unchangeable predestination of all things, even the most insignificant; likewise to the empire of the devil and his power over spirits. In the most shameful manner and without a blush, he revives the old Persian idea of two eternal principles of good and evil contending continually for the possession of man. With a slight variation of the ancient debasing doctrine of Manes, he declares that man is the merely passive subject of a contest between God and the devil. To make his meaning evident, he, to the amazement of all, compares man to a beast of burden who is compelled to move in whatever direction the rider may require.

"Man," he says, "is like a horse. Does God leap into the saddle? The horse is obedient and accommodates itself to every movement of the rider and goes whither he wills it. Does God throw down the reins? Then Satan leaps upon the back of the animal, which bends, goes, and submits to the spurs and caprices of its new rider. The will cannot choose its rider and cannot kick against the spur that pricks it. It must go on, and its very docility is a disobedience or a sin. The only struggle possible is between the two riders, who dispute the momentary possession of the steed, and then is fulfilled the saying of the Psalmist: 'I am become like a beast of burden.' Let the Christian, then, know that God foresees nothing contingently, but that He foresees, proposes and acts from His internal and immutable will. This is the thunderbolt that shatters and destroys free will. Hence it comes to pass that whatever happens, happens according to the irreversible decrees of God. Therefore, necessity, not free will, is the controlling principle of our conduct. God is the author of what is evil in us as well as of what is good, and, as He bestows happiness on those who merit it not, so also does He damn others who deserve not their fate." (*De Servo Arbitrio,* in op. lat. 7, 113 seq.).

This parable summarizes the whole of Luther's teaching on the vital and all-important subject of man's free will. It expresses in the most deliberate manner his matured conviction on the question; and so sure is he of the soundness of his view that he declares it to be the very core and basis of religion. "Without this doctrine of the enslaved will, the supernatural character of Christianity cannot," so he says, "be maintained; the work of redemption falls to the ground, because whoever sets up free will cheats Christ of all His merit; whoever advocates free will brings death and Satan into his soul." "To me," he says in another passage, "the defense of this truth is a matter of supreme and eternal importance. I am convinced that life itself should be set at stake in order to preserve it. It must stand, though the whole world be involved thereby in strife and tumult, nay, even fall into ruins."

The last words in Luther's book on "Slave Will," Grisar says, "even exceed the rest in confidence, and the audacity of his demand that his work should be accepted without question almost takes away one's breath. 'In this book I have not merely theorized; I have set up definite propositions and these I shall defend; no one will I permit to pass judgment on them, and I advise all to submit to them. May the Lord Whose cause is here vindicated,' he says, addressing himself to Erasmus, 'give you light to make of you a vessel to His honor and glory. Amen.'"

No one has ever attempted to deny the existence, authenticity and authorship of this book. Some of Luther's admirers, however, have endeavored to defend the grotesque theses advanced in this famous work and give them a meaning altogether foreign to their expression, development and spirit. But all their arts of "violent exegesis" cannot hide or remove from the pages of this work the hard, offensive, soul-destroying teaching it formulates. No amount of enthusiasm for Luther's standpoint can ever wipe out the degrading doctrine of despair announced within its covers. To apologize for the detestable teaching by claiming that "it was essentially Lutheran" will never down the scandal and wonder it gave rise to. All who are honest and fearless of consequences must admit in frankest terms that Luther's teaching on free will, as expounded in his book, and explicitly making God the author of man's evil thoughts and deeds, cannot but lend a mighty force to the passions and justify the grossest violations of the moral law. Indeed, the enemy of souls, as Anderdon remarks, "could not inspire a doctrine more likely to effect his wicked designs than Luther's teaching on the enslavement of the human will."

When we stop to reflect on Luther's favorite parable, we cannot help asking ourselves what sort of a man was he and what did he think would likely be the effect on the simple and untrained mind of his singular doctrine and its concomitant despair? Is not the man portrayed in his teaching? Does not his teaching show the confusion of his mind and the lack of an exact logical system? And does not his whole theory, born of personal motives and fashioned to suit his own state of soul, show clearly enough that it could not be approved of Heaven or help to righteousness? Think of what this erratic man, with all his presumptuous belief in himself, says, and then judge for yourselves whether or not his doctrine on the enslaved will should become, as he wished, the common conviction of all the faithful, which none can do without, and which he made the very basis of his new Christianity. What man in his senses would subscribe to such an audacious demand

and accept such a singular innovation without questioning its inconsistency, obscurity and confusion? When he says, "If you happen to have Satan for a rider, you must go as Satan wills and there is no help for it," does he not debase man and make him a mere tool, a machine, an automaton? Likening him to a "beast of burden," does he not maintain that man is utterly powerless "by reason of his fallen nature" to lead a godly life, and merit by the practice of virtue the rewards of eternal happiness? Does he not say: "It is written on the hearts of men that there is no freedom of will," that "all takes place in accordance with inexorable necessity,' and that even "were free will offered him, he should not care to have it"? But does not all this contradict the Spirit of God when, speaking in the Book of Ecclesiasticus, He says: "Before man is life and death, good and evil; that which he shall choose shall be given him." (*Ecclus.* 15:18).

Luther, unfortunately for himself and others, would have none of this teaching; and though it is God's own doctrine, he, in his extraordinary self-confidence, boldly and blasphemously maintained that man has not the power to choose between "life and death, good and evil." Thus "the law of liberty," as St. James declares, "the law by which all shall be judged," is ruthlessly and brutally brushed aside by the arbitrary pronouncement of this deluded man to make way for the spread of his false, degrading and fanciful concept of liberty, the liberty of the horse bridled, bitted and spurred, the horse that must obey his rider, whichever of the two contending riders represented in his profane parable occupies the saddle. "It is," he says, "either God or the devil that rules; man has no freedom of choice and is absolutely devoid of responsibility for his acts. Having lost free will, man cannot observe the precepts of the Decalogue; he cannot master his passions; he must sin as long as he lives." "As God pushes him, then he does something not through free will, but by the power of God; and when the devil pushes him, then he does something not through free will, but by the power of Satan who takes possession of him. When the devil takes possession of some man or leaves him, it is only by that arbitrary will by which God wills that a certain number shall be damned and a certain number shall be saved. Then the conclusion is simply this: that those who are to be saved are to be saved without any regard to their good works and that they *will* be saved; that there is nothing in Heaven or earth that can keep them from being saved. Why, then, should they undertake to do anything themselves? It matters not to them; they will be saved anyway whatever they do. And, as for those unfortunate ones who are left behind and are to be damned, how idle for them to kick against the arbitrary decree! They must perish anyway, and as they must perish, they ought to say to themselves: 'Let us eat and drink and be merry, for tomorrow we die.' "

The foregoing is only a part of the infamous and degrading teaching propounded without a blush in Luther's work on the enslavement of the human will. There is much besides in this scandalous volume of such a despicable nature that we would be ashamed to present it to the public unless forced to do so in the interests of truth. This, like almost all of Luther's writings, is full of pitch, and in reading his works, one is bound to look well to his hands lest they be soiled.

Luther's teaching on the loss of free will was, on account of its novelty and the license it encouraged, soon taken up and zealously advocated by many who loved error rather than truth. Among those who advocated the oracle of the fiery apostle, we will name only a few of his most prominent supporters.

Melanchthon comes first in order. He was Luther's mild, gentle and most obsequious friend. In December of 1521, he published a work entitled *"Loci Communes Rerum Theologicarum,"* which was the technical exposition of Lutheranism at that time. In this work the disciple of Luther gives clear and full expression to his master's teaching. "All that happens," Melanchthon says there, "happens of necessity in accordance with the divine predestination; there is no such thing as freedom of the will." As might be expected, he inveighed in his work against the Catholic theologians, whom he accused of having borrowed from philosophy and imparted into Christianity the impious doctrine of liberty, a doctrine absolutely opposed to Scripture. It is also to the philosophy of Plato, according to him, that we are indebted for the equally pernicious word, "reason." It is of interest to remark that the author of this work later on, when freed from the tyranny of his master, came to a more correct view, making no secret of his rejection of Luther's determinism.

Another promoter of Luther's doctrine on free will was Ulrich Zwingli, who in the course of time was denounced by the friends of the Reformer as a "false prophet, a mountebank, a hog, a heretic." This advocate of the new doctrine of Luther was ordained for the diocese of Constance, Switzerland in 1506. From the opening of his career he was noted for his light-mindedness, frivolity and slavery to sensual pleasures. When his familiarity with a woman of notorious and profligate character became public, he was obliged to resign his care of souls. In 1522 he had the audacity to write to his bishop to demand a general permission for priests to marry. In this letter he candidly acknowledged his many and grievous lapses. "Your Lordship," he writes, "knows very well how disgraceful my conduct heretofore has been and how my crimes have been the ruin and scandal of many." The bishop, of course, was powerless in the matter, but Zwingli, nothing daunted, dispensed himself and took to himself a widow, one Anna Reinhard, with whom he had lived for many years, without leave of either Church or state. A character of this sort was prepared to lend himself to the propagation of any protective doctrine, no matter how immoral. Following the lines of his leader he wrote a brutal book, *On Providence,* in which he repeats at every page that "God leads and forces man into evil; that he makes use of the creature to produce injustice, and that yet he does not sin; for the law which makes an act sinful does not exist for God, and, moreover, He always acts from right and supremely holy intentions. The creature, on the contrary, although acting involuntarily under the divine guidance, sins, because he violates the law and acts from damnable motives." Without a blush this "reformer" brutally declares: "I will indulge my sinful desires and, whatever I shall do, God is the author of it. It is by the ordination of God that this man is a parricide and that man is an adulterer." Such was the teaching and practice of the man who his friends call the "Eagle of Helvetia" and praise as "full of noblest chivalry."

Another of the wretched number who lent assistance to spread the harrowing teaching on the loss of free will in man was John Calvin, who was born at Nayon, France, in 1509, three years after Zwingli's ordination. He, too, studied for the Church, but was obliged to leave the seminary early on account of his immoral and revolutionary proclivities. After advocating Luther's teachings at the Sorbonne, Paris, he departed in 1534 for Basle, where he wrote his *Institutes of the Christian Religion.* Later on he betook himself to Geneva, where he gathered disciples and set up his special brand of worship in 1538. Overbearing, cruel and despotic in character, he meted out the direst vengeance to all who dared to controvert or assail his false preachments. His barbarous treatment of Balsec, Ameaux, Gruet, Gentilis, and Servetus, the latter of whom he seized and burned at the stake, himself an eye-witness to the holocaust, is a well-known fact of history. Such was the man who himself was branded with the infamous mark of the galleys for having committed a crime of so shameful a character that it cannot be named here. This vindictive and licentious ally of Luther evolved from the teachings of his master the gruesome system of an absolute predestination by which God, from all eternity, has irrevocably destined some to goodness and eternal happiness, and others to evil and eternal misery. He taught that "free-will no longer had an existence" and that "God was the author of man's sins." "For reasons," he says, "incomprehensible to our ignorance, God irresistibly impels man to violate His laws, that His inspirations turn to evil the heart of the wicked, and that man falls, because God has thus ordered it." These are beautiful assertions to fall from the lips of one who claimed to be a reformer. Satan himself could hardly formulate a dogma more designed to insult God and deceive the souls of men. No wonder that the Protestant minister, Mr. Pouzait, writing of Calvin's theological system, declared it to be "the most horrible ever conceived by any human being." His death was as sad as his life was indecent.

The last one we shall refer to here who espoused Luther's views on free will was the mellifluous Theodore of Beza. When Calvin died in 1564, in the fifty-sixth year of his age, after a life of tyranny over both the bodies and souls of men, Beza, who was his disciple and who wrote his history, succeeded to the leadership of the gloomy religionism which his master introduced into Geneva as a substitute for the Catholic religion. Of this man, Hesshuss writes: "Who will not be astonished at the incredible impudence of this monster, whose scandalous life is known throughout France?" This estimate sums up all we care to know about him. His teaching, like his life, is horrible and disgusting. Wishing to explain absolute predestination, which Calvin had taught as an incontrovertible but profoundly mysterious dogma, he boldly affirms that God has created the largest portion of men only with the object of making use of them to do evil; and then gives as a reason for it that God, in the creation of the universe, designed to manifest His justice and His mercy; but how could this end be attained with creatures who, remaining innocent, would need no pardon, nor merit any punishment; God then ordains that they should sin; He saves some, and here His compassion is seen; He condemns others, and behold His justice. The end that God proposes to Himself is evidently just and holy; consequently, the means must be the same. Thus the disciple goes farther in blasphemy than the master, but, like all others in rebellion in his day, Beza makes the action of justification and spiritual regeneration a mere mechanical movement of man under the irresistible influence of God. In his system, as in that of all the other reformers, there is no room, as in Catholic doctrine, for casting off the degradation of sin, freeing one's self from the tyranny of passion and the corrupt love of creatures, and following in the footsteps of Jesus Christ and in the way of His Commandments.

In presenting to our readers a condensed and necessarily imperfect summary of facts regarding the teaching and standing of the chief lights of the Reformation, we would not be understood as wishing to reflect upon the character or conduct of the present professors of Lutheran and Calvinistic doctrines, many of whom are men estimable for their civic virtues. It is not our fault that the truth of history will not warrant a better showing for those who played a public and conspicuous part in the great religio-political drama of the sixteenth century. Their life and acts and teachings are all matters of public and official record, open to closest scrutiny and investigation. The facts cannot be concealed, and all who know these must honestly confess that the work of the leaders of the Reformation was one of sorrowful darkness, despair and disintegration. One and all were enemies of the Church God established for all men and for all time. They labored under the hallucination that they were serving God by impressing their individual character and system of salvation upon their deluded and unthinking followers, but in reality, they were ministers of Satan, as their abuse of God's Church and their scandalous treatment and perversion of His Revelation to mankind abundantly show. The principles they fathered sapped the very foundations of the true worship of God and destroyed all moral sense in man. The evil effects of their destructive propaganda were noticeable everywhere in their own day and passed down to successive ages, bringing in their train an immorality, a lewdness and a licentiousness that have hardly been equalled in the worst days of paganism. The teaching of these lawless ones is rampant even today. It is substantially that which is now put forth by our modern materialists, who brazenly contend that the human will is devoid of self-direction and self-determining power, as is a feather subject to the action of different currents of air. Thus the evil done by the so-called Reformers in their day and generation lives after them to discredit their mission and their authority and to warn all to beware of their false teaching and their pernicious example.

It is pitiful to know that in this enlightened age there are numbers in our midst who still claim Luther as the friend of liberty and a defender of the rights of reason. These men are unwilling to read his works, which as every scholar recognizes, present a dismal and low estimate of human nature and do not, therefore, entitle him to be considered in any legitimate sense as an apostle of humanity, of human liberty, of human dignity or inherent worth. Religious bigotry, which controls and dominates all their natural impulses of decency and honor, prevents them from seeing the insult Luther's teaching presents to human freedom and its disastrous effects upon true religion and real Christian morality. In the words of the Holy Spirit of Truth we cry out: "O ye sons of men, how long will ye be dull of heart? Why do you love vanity and seek after lying?" If you love truth and sincerely desire enlightenment, open up the pages of Luther's work on "Slave Will" and discover for yourselves at first hand that he spoke very little of liberty, and that he had no conception of it other than as what we call "license," the license to resist and to rebel against all legitimate authority, ecclesiastical and civil. In that work you will find that he maintained with all his force that man is a hopelessly corrupt being, as devoid of all spiritual freedom as a mere animal, utterly incapable of doing good, the sport of either a devil that mocks him or of a God that damns without mercy. Is not such a teaching calculated to make the blood run cold in the veins of men attuned to the truth as it is in Christ and His Church? Examine the book carefully and see for yourselves how the principle he lays down as gospel truth not only attacks, but destroys a possession and an attribute of man which has ever been held sacred and which is dear to the human heart, namely, human liberty. When you become acquainted with his horrible teaching, you will not wonder that to him the word "liberty," which excites a thrill and stirs the deepest feelings of the soul, had little or no significance.

The truth is that Luther rarely spoke or wrote of liberty in the sense in which we know and realize the God-given boon. It is a well-known fact of history that he did not favor that freedom of thought which later became the vogue among his progeny. Liberty, as he understood the word, was solely for himself, but not for others. With him it was a personal matter. All men were free to differ with the Pope, to reject his teaching, to curse him to the lowest depths, were even invited and encouraged to slay him like a wolf or robber, and wash their hands in his blood and that of his cardinals and other adherents, but they must not dare to differ from Martin Luther. Sir William Hamilton, a non-Catholic writer says: "The great reformer had an assurance of his personal inspiration of which he was, indeed, no less confident than of his ability to perform miracles. He disclaimed the Pope, he spurned the Church, but varying in all else, he never doubted of his own infallibility." His autocracy, as is well known, allowed no discussion, and his intolerance knew no limits. The tyranny that dominated his propaganda was the natural result of his false and unheard-of theories. Theory, as everyone knows, is the cause of practice, and therefore it is evident that from a corrupt theory, corrupt conduct will flow. Luther advanced the false theory that man did not possess free will, and by consequence was deprived of personal liberty; and thus holding tenaciously to his false theory, he could not save himself from its corruption—and, naturally, he became not the advocate, but the enemy of all liberty, civil and religious.

Non-Catholics, as a rule, are not familiar with the degrading teachings which Luther expounded in his infamous work on "Slave Will." They have never been given an opportunity to study this volume at first hand and find out for themselves the destructive principles therein advocated. Their ignorance of the facts has been taken advantage of, and they have been made to believe that their leader, who declared man's will to be a "slave will," was the real and only one who promoted liberty in the sixteenth century, by breaking the fetters of religious bondage and securing for all perfect freedom of conscience and thought. This view has been repeated so often by the maligners of truth that they have come to imagine that as soon as the people of Europe got the Bible—Luther's Bible, mistranslated, changed, and altered—they abandoned the Mother Church, rushed into the new man-made form of religion of their own accord, and at once established civil and religious liberty for everybody. The story is fascinating. It tells against Rome, and therefore thousands upon thousands have been deceived into giving it credence. What, however, is the hard, cold, plain truth in the case?

History, when truly and fully written, proves that all the notions entertained by our separated brethren on this matter are but the lying artifices of the mischievous, intended to deceive, and that whenever and wherever Luther's abominable principles and his Protestantism triumphed, they succeeded by violence, torture, persecution and the power of wicked princes against the struggles, the protestations and the manifest will of the people. Everywhere that they attained control of the government, which they invariably sought, they overthrew religious liberty and imperiously imposed their new-fangled beliefs on the country and on the people thereof. This may seem a very strong statement, but the facts of history confirm it most abundantly. In advancing this statement, we do not seek to appeal to prejudice or stir up hatred. We aim to tell the truth, the whole truth and nothing but the truth, to enlighten those who love justice and to defend our forefathers in the Faith who were always and in all places the real upholders of the liberties of the people, and without whose struggles and sacrifices we would not now be in the enjoyment of these inestimable blessings.

According to the time-honored teaching of the Catholic Church, religious liberty guarantees to every man the right to worship God according to the dictates of his conscience without thereby incurring any civil penalties or disabilities whatever.[1] The Catholic Church has not only proclaimed this doctrine from the very beginning of her existence, but she has, moreover, faithfully adhered to it in practice all through the course of her marvelous existence. No one who is familiar with her career can gainsay this statement. "It is an axiom," wrote the late Archbishop Kenrick of Baltimore, "that the worship of God must be voluntary in order to be acceptable. Liberty of conscience was claimed by Tertullian for the Christians as a right grounded on the very nature of religion. 'It is,' said he, 'a right and a natural privilege that each one should worship as he thinks proper; nor can the religion of another injure or profit him.' Neither is it a part of religion to compel its adoption, since this should be spontaneous, not forced, as even sacrifices are asked only of the cheerful giver. The duty of worshiping God conformably to His revealed will being manifest, every interference with its discharge is a violation of the natural right which man possesses to fulfill so solemn an obligation. The use of force to compel compliance with this duty is likely to result in mere external conformity, which, without the homage of the heart, is of no value whatever." This is the uniform teaching of the

Catholic Church. "If at any time," as Cardinal Gibbons states, "encroachments on these sacred rights of man were perpetrated by professing members of the Catholic faith, these wrongs, far from being sanctioned by the Church, were committed in palpable violation of her authority."

Luther was by no means ignorant of this teaching and practice of the ancient Church, which he singled out for abuse and misrepresentation. During his preparation for the priesthood and after his ordination, he familiarized himself with all that was to be known on the important topic. He knew as well as any priest or layman of his day that, whilst Christ, His Apostles, and their legitimate successors in the divine mission of teaching and preaching the truths of revelation enjoined obedience on all, under the penalty of being ranked with heathens and publicans, they, however, did not intend and never meant to stifle or to crush all rational liberty and all rational investigation. He knew that their insistence on the acceptance of the eternal verities had for purpose the cultivation of the truest and highest independence of conscience and of thought by perfect submission to God's teaching, thus saving men from being "tossed about by every wind of doctrine," and that personal freedom of thought and fallible judgment in religious matters leads inevitably to the destruction of "the faith once delivered to the saints." The "Truth," as St. John says, "shall set you free." Luther knew and, in his earlier days, taught and insisted that in obeying the Church and her authorized ambassadors, men obeyed Him who founded and commanded her to teach all things whatsoever He had directed. He knew, too, that whilst in the clear, plain, explicit teaching of revelation, obedience was strictly enjoined to preserve truth in all its original purity; in other matters that were not essential, a reasonable latitude was always wisely allowed. He knew all this, but gradually becoming restless under the restraint of divine limitations, which he construed as servility of intellect, and nursing the unwholesome thought that men were absolutely free to decide by their private judgment whether they would receive or reject the eternal verities, he, conveniently, in his state of antagonism to divine authority, forgot his earlier beliefs, and grew pugnacious, rebellious and seditious. No longer willing to recognize and submit to the conservative principle of Church authority, which up to his day held the religious world in the unity for which Christ prayed and willed, this proud man forthwith determined to oppose, persecute and malign the institution which Christ enjoined all to obey and respect, and to which during fifteen hundred years millions upon millions of the brightest, ablest and the most intelligent minds had given glad and willing loyalty and submission.

As had been the case with all other heresiarchs who preceded him, Luther used the weapons of which Hell availed itself to inaugurate "sects" and "dissensions," in order to burst asunder the time-honored bond of Christian unity. An adept in lying, which every student knows he approved by his teaching and example, he went forth in bold effrontery to make his hearers believe that the Church had bound its members hand and foot, body and soul, and that they were not allowed even to reflect or think for themselves. The time had come, he thought, to strike and free mankind from what he called the degrading yoke of the Papacy and to restore to them their "Christian liberty." He told them that those who professed the old religion were groaning under a worse than Babylonian captivity and that all who would rally under his banner of reform would be brought back from exile into the beautiful land of Israel, there to worship in freedom and in peace near the Sion of God. In the desire to accomplish his wicked project he never thought how like he was to Antichrist, the one who sets up a false Christ or a false Christianity or draws away many from the true. No. He thought that the Pope, whom Jesus Christ made the head of His society, was Antichrist; that the Church was ruthlessly trampled underfoot by his followers and especially by his ministers; that the liberties of the world were entirely crushed in Catholicism. The Church, her ruler, her teachings, were all, according to him, corrupted; and this instigator of revolt, who himself spurned authority and declared the Decalogue had little or no binding force on Christians, exhorted all to arise in their strength to break their chains and to sever their connection with Rome forever. The saving and restraining influence of Church authority was to be spurned as wholly incompatible with freedom, and each one henceforth was encouraged to invest himself with sovereign power and unrestricted liberty in dealing with all matters of religion. Thus, under the enticing name of freedom, men were promised that they would realize the brightest visions of liberty and the blessing of true and independent manhood.

But the credentials for all this? Did the new doctrine of private judgment, which was to bring about "the emancipation of the human mind," result in the blessings it announced with such a flourish of trumpets? Did the insurrection against the power established by God in the spiritual order, wherein existed, in principle and practice, true independence of conscience and thought, compensate for the profound and degrading subjection of the intellect and the adoption of the thoughts and words of the impudent and low buffoon who dogmatized in taverns amid the fumes of beer and outraged in his fury that same liberty he pretended to secure for his companions in rebellion? Is it not true, as all ages attest, that whoever throws off the yoke of legitimate authority will be punished with slavery; and the more legitimate the authority, that is, marked with the divine seal, the more complete and degrading the servitude? Men who refuse to obey God and those whom He authorizes to rule in His name, are invariably led, as the blind, by fools, or bound by executioners. Mark how all this was literally realized in the case of the Reformer and his followers in rebellion against the Church of God.

Luther stood before the world in the attitude of a liberator, but when we draw near, we discover his doctrine is license and his behavior its exemplification. We were prepared to think, when he freed himself and his blind followers from the duty of obedience to Rome and presented his "new gospel," proclaiming the principle of private judgment as the broad basis of his system of Christian liberty, that it would at least have guaranteed its followers real freedom of thought and of judgment in all matters of belief. Surely we might expect that after having indignantly rejected the wise and wholesome principle of Church authority as incompatible with liberty, he would not attempt to enthrone again this selfsame principle in his new system of belief, much less to impose it as an obligation on those whom he had cajoled and seduced to leave the Church of their fathers to embrace one of his own making.

Yet this course, absurd and inconsistent as it manifestly proved, was the very one he adopted, and the one adopted, as Spalding says, "without one exception, by the numerous sects to which the Reformation gave birth. If there be any truth in history, the reformers were themselves the most intolerant of men, not only towards the Catholic Church, but towards each other. They could not brook dissent from the crude notions on religion which they had broached. Men might protest against the decisions of the Catholic Church; but woe to them if, following out their own private judgment, they dared protest against the self-constituted authority of the new-fangled sects."

The tyrannical and intolerant character of Luther, the father of the Reformation, is a fact admitted by all candid Protestant writers. Roscoe, for instance, in his *Life and Pontificate of Leo X,* justly censures "the severity with which Luther treated all those who unfortunately happened to believe too much on the one hand, or too little on the other, and could not walk steadily on the hair-breadth line which he had presented." This distinguished writer, whose pen has so glowingly depicted the bright literary age of Leo X, makes the following appropriate remarks on this glaring inconsistency: "Whilst Luther was engaged in his opposition to the Church of Rome, he asserted the right of private judgment with the confidence and courage of a martyr. But no sooner had he freed his followers from the chains of Papal domination than he forged others in many respects equally intolerable; and it was the employment of his latter years to counteract the beneficial effects produced by his former years."

For a time Luther was almost omnipotent, and exercised his self-constituted power to persecute with relentless fury. No sooner, however, did his followers in revolt recover from the first enchantment of his personal influence and the intoxication of their insurrection against the Holy See, than they began to quarrel with their leader and with each other, just, we suppose, to give an object lesson in dissension and illustrate practically their widely heralded and inconsistent system of liberty. Their controversies, bickerings and wranglings, all the result of their glorious new gospel of so-called Christian liberty, are matters of historical record and put down to the shame of Protestantism.

Luther set himself up against all law, restraint and ordinance, and his disciples soon followed his example. As he attacked the most essential truths of Christianity, we must not wonder that his followers, trained in the principles of private interpretation, used their right to construe the verities of religion as their individual judgment dictated. The path to unity, which freedom of thought and of judgment in matters of religion was supposed to establish, was soon trodden down and rendered desolate by the divergent views of its misguided followers. In the work of construction its builders maliciously destroyed and recklessly frittered away the eternal verities—so much so, that scarcely one saving truth of revelation remained as a basis of their belief. One and all rejected the Church, "the pillar and the ground of the truth"; one and all spurned the authority of the Church's legitimate head; one made God the author of sin; another made the Almighty unalterably determine the ultimate fate of each man beforehand from all eternity; "one," to use the words of Luther in his letter to the Christians of Antwerp, "rejected Baptism; another the Eucharist; another strikes out revelation from his creed; one says this, the other that; there are as many sects as heads; everybody wishes to be a prophet." When the Founder of Protestantism saw his path of unity winding in so many directions and his self-assumed infallibility ignored, he grew disconsolate, threatening and abusive. On page 292 of the *Tischreden* [*Table Talk*] we find what this man, who was supposed to have freed his followers from the chains of papal domination, thought of his false brothers and fellow heretics who would no longer suffer his domination and intolerance. "If," he says, "they would not listen" to him, "so much the worse for them; in the end, they would be seen with the worthies whom they resembled, all burning in Hell together." Surely no Pope of Rome was ever so uncharitable as to voice such wholesome condemnation.

But the tyranny and intolerance of Luther did not stop in mere denunciation of those who dared to exercise the liberty of differing from him in his opinions. All who ventured to question his infallibility in religious matters were made to feel the heavy weight of his habitual and never-ceasing intolerant vengeance. From the number of the many victims of his brutal conduct, we will recall a few glaring examples. One of the victims of Luther's violence was his most favored disciple, Melanchthon, a learned but weak, timid, obsequious character. "This man was incapable of bearing any contradiction," says his friend Baumgartner. "He veered with every wind, and whilst timidly a disciple of the Reformer, he was secretly a Calvinist." In a letter Melanchthon wrote to his friend Camerarius, he tells of Luther's brutal conduct towards him. "I am," he says, "in a state of servitude, as if I was in the cave of Cyclops, and often do I think of making my escape." Deploring Luther's outbursts of temper, he says, "I tremble when I think of the passions of my master; they yield not in violence to the passions of Hercules." He testifies, moreover, that Luther occasionally inflicted on him personal chastisement. According to Goschler, this disciple "gave himself up to all manner of oaths, and contumelious speeches which dismayed everyone." He lacked, however, the courage to break the chains of servitude with which his cruel master had bound him hand and foot. Happy, indeed, he would have been had he followed the example of Staupitz, Ulenberg and others among Luther's quondam friends who were wise in time and returned to Catholic unity, the "City that could not be hid" containing "the light of the world" to which the heresiarch had shut his eyes.

Andrew Bodenstein, more generally known by the name of Carlstadt, was another victim of Luther's intolerance. According to Audin, this man's vocation was to "blacken paper; to throw ink on the head of Luther or his disciples, his delight and amusement." In his study of the Bible, using his right of private judgment, he reached totally different conclusions from Luther as to the lawfulness of images, the Real Presence, infant baptism and other questions. Having the courage of his convictions, he began to disseminate his special discoveries and tried to win proselytes to his views and opinions. This proceeding angered Luther, who could brook no opposition. "You are my enemy, my adversary," said Luther to Carlstadt. "It is true," retorted the other: "I am the adversary and enemy of everyone who will oppose God and fight against Christ and the truth." "May I see you broken on a wheel," said Luther on taking leave of him. "And may you," retorted the latter, "break your neck before you get out of the city." Luther never forgot this unpleasant altercation with his old professor. In the bitterness of his heart he there and then swore vengeance against his antagonist and ever after left nothing undone to have him banished from Wittenberg, the citadel of the Reformation. His spite followed his former disciple in his wanderings from place to place. Reduced to the direst misery through the never ceasing pursuit of Luther, Carlstadt wrote to his friends Krautwald and Schwenkfeld, two Lutheran theologians, to tell of his distress and said: "I shall soon be forced to sell all in order to support myself, my clothes, my self, all my furniture. No one takes pity on me; and I fear that both I and my child shall perish with hunger." Luther hunted his "enemy and adversary," as he called Carlstadt, up and down the country in the most relentless manner until finally the victim of his abiding vengeance expired, a miserable outcast, at Basle in Switzerland.

To these victims of Luther's intolerance we may add Strigel, who was imprisoned for three years for maintaining that "man was not a merely passive instrument in the work of his conversion"; Hardenberg, who was banished from Saxony for having been guilty of some leaning towards the Calvinistic doctrines on the Eucharist; and Zwingli and the Sacramentarians, who, Luther declared, "were heretics who had broken away" from him, and "ministers of Satan, against whom no exercise of severity, however great, would be excessive."

Luther not only persecuted individuals, but also large bodies of dissenters who organized themselves to resist his authority and disseminate doctrines opposed to his. Prominent amongst the rebels from the Lutheran ranks were the Anabaptists, who received their name from their custom of baptizing over again those who had been already baptized in infancy. Thomas Münzer, the leader of the sect, and his preachers gave themselves out for prophets in Thuringia and other places, and ran like madmen through the streets of the cities and towns exhorting and summoning all to be re-baptized. In their reckless propaganda they sacked churches, destroyed altars and trod underfoot the images of Christ and His saints. Not only men, but even women ran wildly from place to place and flung themselves on the ground, cursing and praying by turns. The rabble were invited to join "the thousand years' reign of Christ" they imagined had come when "God would destroy all tyrants from off the face of the earth." They promised possession of every enjoyment to all who would join their ranks and help in downing all constituted authority. A frightful condition of things ensued. Polygamy even was introduced, and the most scandalous excesses were openly committed without fear or shame. None of their prophets, Matthiesen, a baker of Haarlem, Boekelson, a tailor from Leyden, whilst they agreed in putting forward a free inquiry into the meaning of the Bible as the fundamental principle of their teaching, would tolerate any other interpretation than his own.

Luther could not endure this new sect, which his teaching on private judgment brought into being. He manifested his opposition toward it in a synod convened at Hamburg on the 7th of August, 1536, composed of deputies sent by all the cities which had separated from the Mother Church. The object of the synod was to devise means for exterminating the adherents of Münzer and his new religion. The animus of this synod is manifested in one of its decrees, which runs as follows: "Whoever rejects infant baptism, whoever transgresses the orders of the magistrates, whoever preaches against taxes, whoever teaches the community of goods, whoever usurps the priesthood, whoever holds unlawful assemblies, whoever sins against faith, shall be punished with death. . . . As for the simple people who have not preached or administered baptism, but who were seduced to permit themselves to frequent the assemblies of the heretics, if they do not wish to renounce Anabaptism, they shall be scourged, punished with perpetual exile and even with death, if they return three times to the place whence they have been expelled." Not a single protest was raised against this cruel decree. It received the unanimous approbation of the assembled delegates. When the bigamist, Philip of Hesse, was apprised of the intolerant views of the synod, he remonstrated with Luther, but to no purpose. The excommunicated Saxon monk sent the Landgrave a letter to soothe his scruples of conscience on the severity of the official decree of the synod and therein openly defended persecution on Scriptural grounds. "Whoever," he wrote, "denies the doctrines of our faith, aye, even one article which rests on the Scripture, or the authority of the universal teaching of the Church, must be punished severely. He must be treated not only as a heretic, but also as a blasphemer of the holy name of God. It is not necessary to lose time in disputes with such people; they are to be condemned as impious blasphemers." No comments are here needed. Luther's doctrine, as given to this synod, it is obvious, is entirely opposed to freedom of conscience and in favor of religious persecution.

Every student of history knows that Luther treated with an insufferable arrogance and downright intolerance all who refused to submit to his wild, erratic and destructive pronouncements. He was as intolerant towards the leaders and followers of the new sects that sprang up and differed from him as he was against the Mother Church and her adherents. "As I am now," he says, "near the grave, I will bring this testimony and this glory with me before the judgment seat of my dear Lord and Saviour, Jesus Christ, that with all my heart I have condemned and avoided the enthusiasts and the enemies of the Sacraments, Carlstadt, Zwingli, Oecolampad, Stenckfeld, and their disciples in Zurich and wherever they may be." "I would," he goes on to say, "far sooner be cut into pieces or burnt a hundred times over, than be of one opinion or of one mind with Stenckfeld, Zwingli, Carlstadt, Oecolampad, and whoever else they may be, the wicked enthusiasts, or agree with their teaching." Of Zwingli and his colleague, Oecolampad, he wrote that "they had a devilish, super-devilish, blasphemous heart and lying lips." All this and more of the same kind of reproach showed the love the Reformer entertained for those who deserted his cause and inaugurated sects of their own making. Zwingli replied to Luther and told him, "We do thee no injustice when we reproach and condemn thee as a worse betrayer and denier of Christ than the ancient heretic Marcion." Zurich also answered the leader of revolt by the mouth of Campanus: "It is as certain that Luther is a devil as that God is God."

But this glorious defender of religious liberty is not satisfied merely with persecuting those who refused to submit to his authority and infallibility. Just to show how dear to him was the principle of liberty of conscience, he inaugurated a campaign of intolerance against the Jews such as was never surpassed in severity or cruelty before or since. Not content with calling them by the most opprobrious names, "assheads," "lying mouths," "devils' children," "devils," "young devils, damned to Hell," he consoles himself with the thought that "they will be tormented, not in upper Hell nor in middle Hell, but in Hell's deepest depths." He tells how they ought to be treated by Christian princes: how he would treat them, if he had the power. "What," he writes, "are we to do with this rejected, damned people of the Jews?. . . I will give my honest advice."

"First, their synagogues or schools are to be set on fire and whatever will not burn, is to be covered and heaped over with earth, so that never again shall one find stone or cinder of them left.

"Secondly, their houses are likewise to be broken down and destroyed, for they do exactly the same in them as they also do in their schools. Therefore they may perhaps be allowed a roof or a stable over them, as the Gypsies are, in order that they may know they are not the lords in our country as they boast to be. . . .

"Thirdly, all their Prayer Books and Talmuds are to be taken away from them, in which such idolatry, lies, curses and blasphemies are taught.

"Fourthly, their Rabbis are to be forbidden under pain of capital punishment to teach any more. . . .

"Fifthly, the Jews are to be entirely denied legal protection when using the roads in the country, for they have no business to be in the country. . . .

"Sixthly, usury is to be forbidden them, and all their cash and their treasures of silver and gold are to be taken away from them and to be put aside to be preserved. And for this reason, all that they have (as was said above), they have stolen and robbed from us through their usury."

Further on in his work *About the Jews and Their Lies,* edition 1543, he addresses himself to the princes in these words: Burn their synagogues. Forbid them all that I have mentioned above. Force them to work and treat them with every kind of severity, as Moses did in the desert and slew three thousand. . . . If that is no use, we must drive them away like mad dogs, in order that we may not be partakers of their abominable blasphemy and of all their vices, and in order that we may not deserve the anger of God and be damned with them. I have done my duty. Let everyone see how he does his. I am excused."

The implacable hatred of Luther towards the Jews stands out in bold and unfavorable contrast with the consistent, uniform, kind consideration of the Catholic Church and her rulers towards that oppressed people. It is well known how, in the Middle Ages, the Jews were constantly and uniformly protected by the Popes, even in Rome itself, where they had, and still have at the present time, a special quarter of the city allotted to them. Rome has always been the asylum and home of this oppressed people, as Voltaire himself acknowledges, and Avignon, because it was for a long time the residence of the Popes, shares with the Eternal City this honorable distinction.

The Jews themselves bear witness to this fact. In the "great Jewish Sanhedrin" held in Paris in the year 1807, and in the session of the fifth of February of that year, the following resolutions were placed upon record of that Jewish assembly: "At divers times the Roman Popes have given protection and refuge in their territories to the persecuted Jews from all parts of Europe. Toward the end of the seventh century St. Gregory defended them in all Christian countries. In the tenth century the Spanish Bishops resisted the ill treatment of the Jews by the people, and Pope Alexander II congratulated them on their courageous attitude. In the twelfth century St. Bernard defended them, and Innocent II and Alexander III protected them. In the thirteenth century Gregory IX averted a threatening disaster against them in England, as well as in France and Spain, as this Pope commanded under the penalty of excommunication that no one do violence to their conscience or interfere with their holy days. Clement V facilitated for them the means of education. Clement VI gave them an asylum in Avignon, when they were persecuted in the whole of Europe. It would be easy to enumerate many other kind promulgations in favor of the Jews. The people of Israel, ever unhappy and almost ever persecuted, never had the opportunity nor the means to acknowledge their gratefulness for the many benefits received. Since 1800 years, this is the first opportunity afforded to express the feelings of our heart. . . .The deputies of the French Empire and of the Kingdom of Italy in the Hebrew Synod, full of gratitude for the many kindnesses and protection granted the Jews by the Catholic clergy, do resolve that the expression of our feelings be incorporated in the records of this day, that it forever remain in authentic testimony of the gratitude of the Jewish people." (*Lettre aux Isrelites sur l'attitude qui leur convient de prendre à l'egard de la souverainté temporelle du Pape*).

Another testimony to the attitude of the Church and her head towards the oppressed Israelites was furnished in the reply of Benedict XV to the American Jewish Committee, which in a letter to the Pope under date of December 30, 1915, cited instances in Poland by which Jews "have been marked for special persecution and have been subjected to oppressive measures not borne by compatriots of other creeds." Among other things the petitioners wrote: "With all due veneration, we now approach the Supreme Pontiff for succor in this the bitter hour of our need, knowing the exemplary humanity for which your Holiness is justly distinguished. . . .We recall with admiration and gratitude that on many occasions in the past some of the revered predecessors of your Holiness have, under like conditions, extended protection to those of the Jewish faith in the interest of right and justice. Appreciating the transcendent importance which the entire civilized world attaches to any utterance from so exalted a source of morality and wisdom as that which your Holiness represents, we confidently express the hope that timely action be taken by the Vatican to the end that the suffering under which millions of our brethren in faith are weighed down may be terminated by an act of that humanity to which your Holiness is so passionately devoted, and that the cruel intolerance and the unjust prejudice which have been aroused against them may forever vanish before this glorious exercise of your supreme moral and spiritual power."

To this communication, signed by the most prominent representatives of the Jewish people of America, the Pope's Cardinal Secretary of State replied in a letter "breathing the Christlike spirit of peace and love, reminding all of the principles of natural right to respect all men as brethren, which should be observed and respected in relation to the children of Israel, as it should be to all men, for it would not conform to justice and religion itself to derogate therefrom solely because of a difference of religious faith."

Herman Bernstein, commenting on this letter in *The American Hebrew,* says: "Among all the Papal letters ever issued with regard to the Jews throughout the history of the Vatican, there is no statement that equals this direct, unmistakable plea for equality for the Jews and against prejudice on religious grounds. The Bull issued by Innocent IV, declaring the Jews innocent of the charge of using Christian blood for ritual purposes, while a remarkable document, was, after all, merely a statement of fact; whereas, the present statement by Pope Benedict XV is a plea against religious prejudice and persecution.

All this shows Rome's attitude towards the oppressed. How different it is from that of Luther, as evidenced by his own utterances in his infamous work *About the Jews and their Lies,* which brand him beyond power of contradiction as an oppressor, a tyrannical anti-Semite.

A volume might be filled with indubitable facts to prove the intolerant spirit of Luther and of the various sects which his rebellion originated. The quarrels, hostilities and jealousies that constantly arose among one and all made them a prey to the fiercest dissensions. They anathematized and persecuted each other with the most virulent hatred and indulged in the coarsest and vilest invective. The ultra-Lutherans and the Melanchthonians mutually denounced each other and even refused to unite in the rites of communion and burial. The Flaccianists and the Strigelians, the Osiandrians and the Stancarians and many other new sects persecuted one another with relentless fury. The Lutherans, according to Professor Fecht, denounced and excluded the reformed Calvinists from salvation. The Calvinists roused up the people against the Lutherans, who in turn mildly and charitably designated their enemies as "the sons of the devil." Zwingli complained of Luther's intolerance when he was the victim of its violence—but when he became almost omnipotent in Switzerland, he and his followers threw the poor Anabaptists into the Lake of Zurich, enclosed in sacks, and mocked them at the same time with the inhuman taunt that they were merely "baptizing them by their own favorite method of immersion."

The other reformers were not a whit better than Luther in regard to toleration. The injury done their cause by their bickerings, disunions and hostilities did not escape their own notice. Calvin, for instance, fully aware of the disastrous results accruing from the specious principles of universal liberty by which the Reformers had allured multitudes to their standard, wrote to Melanchthon: "It is indeed important that posterity should now know of our differences; for it is indescribably ridiculous that we, who are in opposition to the whole world, should be, at the very beginning of the Reformation, at issue among ourselves." Melanchthon wrote in answer that "the Elbe with all its waters could not furnish tears enough to weep over the miseries of the distracted Reformation."

The whole fabric of the Reformation threatened to fall to pieces at its very rise through the internal divisions and differences which Calvin in his letter to Melanchthon was so anxious "posterity should not know." One thing alone was able to save it from destruction, namely, the civil power, whose influence and assistance the leaders in religious rebellion very soon learned to seek and obtain. The lawless anarchy into which Protestantism in its various forms had sunk made it necessary, if it would survive, to place the new religions under the protection of the degenerate princes of the times, who, as Melanchthon admits, "had in view neither the purification of Christianity, the diffusion of learning, the exalting of a creed, nor the improvement of morals; but only interests that were miserable, profane and earthly, adjudicating to themselves the treasures of the cloisters and religiously keeping the jewels of the churches." The influence of the leaders of reform being on the wane owing to their dissensions, quarrels and intolerance, they saw clearly that their only hope of promoting further their power and ascendency was to invoke the interposition and backing of the temporal power, without which their movement would be as inevitably suppressed as had been the commotions of the Hussities at a previous period.

Luther, who was by no means, as Frederic von Schlegel says, "an advocate for democracy," began to "assert the absolute power of rulers," and "zealously upheld," as Menzel, the Protestant historian says, "their princely power, the divine right of which he even made an article of faith." "Thus," he continues, "through Luther's well-meant policy, the Reformation naturally became that of the princes, and, consequently, instead of being the aim, was converted into a means of their policy." Not satisfied with catering to the vanity of the princes, Luther, who in his heart despised dominion and blasphemed majesty, appealed to their cupidity by promising them the spoils of sacrilege. "Your power," he said to the German princes, "emanates from God alone; you have no master on this earth; you owe nothing to the Pope. Mind your own affairs and let him mind his. He is the Antichrist predicted by the prophet Daniel; he is the man of sin. . . .You, princes and nobles, owe him neither first fruits nor services for the abbeys he has bestowed upon you. The abbeys are as much your property as the game that runs on your lands. The monasteries in which these pious hypocrites live are dens of iniquity, which you must root out, if you would have God bless you in this life or in the next." (Audin, Vol. II, 186, 188).

At the beginning of Luther's rebellion, he denied the principle of authority, then encouraged individualism, and, finally, promoted resistance to established order and rule. When this centrifugal principle, which is the very basis of the Reformation, brought on insurbordination, uprising, and popular revolts, he and other leaders went to the other extreme and justified absolutism and the use of despotic means in the government of the people. So Protestantism tended inevitably to destroy popular rights and liberty, and, at the same time, strengthened the arbitrary rule of princes, who, lording it with rods of iron over both the bodies and souls of their subjects, crushed out eventually all freedom, both civil and religious.

Hallam, who lived and died a Protestant, furnishes the following testimony in his great work, *The Introduction to the History of Literature*, Vol. I, p. 200, Sec. 34. He says, "The adherents to the Church of Rome have never failed to cast two reproaches on those who left them; one, that the Reform was brought about by intemperate and calumnious abuse, by outrages of an excited populace or by the tyranny of princes; the other, that after stimulating the most ignorant to reject the authority of their Church, it instantly withdrew this liberty of judgment and devoted all who presumed to swerve from the line drawn by law to virulent obloquy, and sometimes to bonds and death.

These reproaches, it may be a shame to us to own, can be uttered and cannot be refuted."

The favorite plan of establishing and reinforcing the Reformation when it began to wane and totter was by violence on the ruins of Catholic institutions. The Reformers supported the princes in trampling on the liberties of the people, and in return, the princes supported the new beliefs. The result was that absolute monarchy prevailed wherever the Protestant party dominated. Jurieu, the celebrated Calvinist minister, quoted by Audin and Alzog, makes this acknowledgment: "Geneva, Switzerland, and the free cities, the electors, and the German princes, England, Scotland, Sweden and Denmark got rid of Popery and established the Reformation by the aid of the civil power."

The vast majority of the people wanted to be and remain Catholics, but the state forced the new religions on them in these countries against their will, and progress was made only by the influence of civil power. The priests of the Catholic Church were killed off and hunted like criminals; the laity were converted by the rack, the thumbscrew, the dark cell, the *peine forte et dure,* fines, imprisonment, banishment, stripes, the headman's axe, the gallows and the disemboweling knife. Their property was confiscated, and convents, abbeys, priories, monasteries, churches, passed into the hands of greedy potentates and their servile courtiers. Such were the methods and means invariably resorted to by the leaders of Protestantism to foist the new religion on the people. Was this toleration or oppression?

Plain men may well look round them, and ask if these things can be. But all this is no hideous misquotation or misrepresentation. The facts are only too evident. Non-Catholic writers, as a rule, describe Luther and his work in the most glowing and favorable terms. Many others, however, better informed and more enlightened, have, in all fairness and candor, humbly apprehended that the free exercise of private judgment was most heartily abhorred by the first Reformers except only where the persons who assumed it happened to be exactly of their way of thinking.

The late Protestant bishop Warburton gives the following character of the pretended advocates of civil and religious freedom: "The Reformers, Luther, Calvin, and their followers, understood so little in what true Christianity consisted that they carried with them into the reformed churches that very spirit of persecution which had driven them from the Church of Rome." The Protestant historian Hallam also tells the truth when he says in his *Constitution History,* page 63: "Persecution is the deadly original sin of the Reformed churches, that which cools every honest man's zeal for their cause in proportion as his reading becomes extensive."

Gibbon, in his *Rise and Fall of the Roman Empire,* Ch. 54, says: "The patriot reformers were ambitious of succeeding the tyrants whom they dethroned. They imposed with equal vigor, their creeds and confessions. They asserted the right of the magistrate to punish the heretic with death."

Strickland, in her *Queens of England,* says: "It is a lamentable trait in human nature that there was not a sect established at the Reformation that did not avow, as part of their religious duty, the horrible necessity of destroying some of their fellow creatures on account of what they severally termed heretical tenets."

Guizot, in his *History of Civilization,* pp. 261-262, says: "The Reformation of the sixteenth century was not aware of the true principles of intellectual liberty. . . . On the one side it did not know or respect all the rights of human thought; at the very moment it was demanding these rights for itself it was violating them towards others. On the other hand, it was unable to estimate the rights of authority in the matters of reason."

Macaulay, in his *Essays*, Hampden, says: "Rome had at least prescription on its side. But Protestant intolerance, despotism in an upstart sect, infallibility claimed by guides who acknowledge that they had passed the greater part of their lives in error, restraints imposed on the liberty of private judgment at the pleasure of rulers who could vindicate their own proceedings only by asserting the liberty of private judgment—these things could not long be borne. Those who had pulled down the crucifix could not long continue to persecute for the surplice. It required no great sagacity to perceive the inconsistency and dishonesty of men who, dissenting from almost all Christendom, would suffer none to dissent from themselves; who demanded freedom of conscience, yet refused to grant it; who execrated persecution, yet persecuted; who urged reason against the authority of one opponent, and authority against the reason of another."

Lecky, in his *Rationalism in Europe,* Vol. I, p. 51, ed. 1870, says: "What shall we say of a church that was but a thing of yesterday; a church that had as yet no services to show, no claims upon the gratitude of mankind; a church that was by profession the creature of private judgment, and was in reality generated by the intrigues of a corrupt court, which nevertheless suppressed by force a worship that multitudes deemed necessary to salvation; which by all her organs and with all her energies persecuted those who clung to the religion of their fathers? What shall we say of a religion which comprised at most, but a fourth part of the Christian world, and which the first explosion of private judgment had shivered into countless sects, which was nevertheless so pervaded by the spirit of dogmatism that each of these sects asserted its distinctive doctrines with the same confidence, and persecuted with the same unhesitating violence, as a church which was venerable with the homage of twelve centuries?. . . So strong and so general was its intolerance that for some time it may, I believe, be truly said that there were more instances of partial toleration being advocated by Roman Catholics than by orthodox Protestants."

The foregoing quotations from reliable Protestant authors show how the Reformers believed in the rights of conscience and how they practiced religious liberty. It is, moreover, a remarkable fact that their followers have been guilty of persecution wherever they have had the power, not only against the Catholic Church, but against one another; and their intolerance, though greatly mitigated, is even at the present enlightened day far from being extinct.

But have not Catholics, who boast that persecution is not, and never has been a doctrine of their Church, persecuted in times past? We do not deny it; but we answer that they did so as individuals and in direct opposition to the teaching of their Church. "Yet every impartial person," as Abp. Spalding says, "must allow that the circumstances under which they persecuted were not so aggravated, nor so wholly without excuse, as those under which they were themselves persecuted by Protestants. The former stood on the defensive, while the latter were in almost every instance the first aggressors. The Catholics did but repel violence by violence, when their property, their altars and all they held sacred were rudely invaded by the new religionists, under pretext of reform. Their acts of severity were often deemed necessary measures of precaution against the deeds of lawless violence, which everywhere marked the progress of reform. They did but seek the privilege of retaining quietly the religion of their fathers, which the reformers would fain have wrested from them by violence. They were the older, and they were in possession. Could it be expected that they would yield without a struggle all that they held most dear and most sacred? There were extenuating circumstances, which, though they might not wholly justify their intolerance, yet greatly mitigated its malice; while the reformers could certainly allege no such pretext in self-vindication." (*Prot. Reformation,* Vol. p. 336).

The Catholic Church has always favored religious liberty and is today its most ardent defender and supporter.[2] Facts are more convincing than arguments; and Catholics are willing that, as to religious liberty, they be put to the test laid down by the Bible: "By their fruits ye shall know them." It is a fact that in this day and hour the Catholic countries of Europe are far in advance of the Protestant countries in respect to religious independence. There is not one Catholic government on that continent which persecutes its subjects for conscience's sake, and there is not one Protestant country in which Catholics enjoy equal rights and privileges with the members of the established religion. In England, Catholics are merely tolerated; in Switzerland, they suffer from religious disabilities; in Sweden, Holland, Denmark and Prussia, their conscientious convictions are discriminated against; and as for Russia, their treatment is notoriously contrary to the demands of justice and of Christian charity. On the contrary, in all Catholic countries, without any exception, where there is not and never was a governmentally established church, the great principle of universal toleration is sedulously exercised, and all, Catholics and Protestants alike, enjoy the blessings not only of religious but of civil rights and privileges. There is no room under Catholic teachings and principles for intolerance and persecution.

The accusation that Catholic doctrine teaches that no faith is to be kept with heretics is totally unfounded. The religion of Catholics obliges them to respect the rights of others, and any apprehensions as to the danger of their violating their sacred duty towards those of an opposite faith are the result of vain fears, which no honest mind ought to harbor. Catholics desire to live together with their Protestant neighbors quietly and peaceably, each and all worshipping God as their conscience honestly directs.

Catholics, it should be remembered, were the first in America to proclaim and to practice civil and religious liberty. While all the English colonies in the New World were practicing persecution, while Protestants of one sect were everywhere intolerant of every other sect, the colony established by Lord Baltimore in Maryland granted civil and religious liberty to all who professed different beliefs. From this abode of happiness and good will towards all, the principle of freedom spread until there was hardly a colony on this broad continent that did not make universal toleration a settled law of the land. The glory of being the first to raise the banner of civil and religious liberty in this country belongs to Catholics, and none can deny or rob them of it. This glory is all the greater because at that very time the Puritans of New England and the Episcopalians of Virginia were busily engaged in persecuting their brother Protestant for conscience's sake; and the former were moreover enacting proscriptive "blue laws" and hanging "witches." Ever since that far-off day and before, when Columbus planted the Cross, the emblem of Christianity, upon American soil, Catholics have stood side by side with men of every creed in every human effort to make this the grandest and the freest nation in the world. Throughout all these years the country grew and developed because there has been good fellowship, mutual respect and hearty cooperation for the common good.

But alas, here in the morning of the twentieth century, here at a time when we have reached a perhaps unparalleled plane of general intelligence, at a time when we have lived together as neighbors and friends long enough to become well acquainted; when we have mingled together in social and business and fraternal life—here in such an era we have thousands of misguided men foisting themselves upon peaceful communities, scattering the seed of discord and religious hate and pouring forth their vile abuse of everything Catholic. They are not content to have civil and religious liberty for themselves, but desire to deny it to Catholics, as is proved in many instances, especially by the fact that no Catholic can be elected President of the United States, no matter how competent he may be.[3] To advance their wicked purposes, they go about with flag in hand, which they stain with their dirty fingers, to form Know-Nothing societies like the Patriotic Order of Sons of America, the Junior Order of United American

Mechanics, the Order of Independent Americans, the Luther League, the Guardians of Liberty, etc., etc., all pretending to be patriotic, but really persecutors and bigots; all pretending to support American institutions, but really trampling on the Constitution, which prohibits the establishment of any religion or the requirement of any religious test for public office; all pretending to favor religious liberty, but really plotting to violate it whenever Catholics are concerned.

The flame of bigotry, which these malicious societies are now so vigorously fanning throughout the length and breadth of this great country, cannot last for long. Their creatures are being condemned on all sides. Ex-President Taft has dubbed them "Cockroaches" and President Wilson brands them as "Swashbucklers." Only ignorant fanatics are duped by the unclean birds of prey. Our Protestant fellow citizens are levelheaded enough to see that Catholics are just as keen for their country's welfare and glory as they themselves, just as ready to defend it, work for it and shed their blood for it as any in the land. They recognize that there is no just ground for any opposition to Catholics, and as they are not fools, they are not going to swallow the foul, calumnious and filthy accusations against Catholics by which bigots, knaves and fanatics would destroy the mutual trust and understanding between citizens of a common country and with a common cause. Their mentality is still sound, and their hearts are in the right place. They believe that all citizens irrespective of nationality and creed must be friends, and to them no other relation is conceivable. They are aware of the specific objects of the evil-doers, their insincerity and the utter lack of religion that exists among them; and so they have come to consider the promoters of bigotry, the calamity howler, the alarmist and those editors who are bent on filling their pockets by publishing the lying and the riot-breeding literature that stirs up hatred and enmity between Protestantism and the Catholic Church, as a menace to civilization, to government, to the brotherly feeling that all of all faiths should strive to cultivate.

The end of the hellish work of hatred is in sight, and all decent, fair-minded and intelligent Protestants are daily becoming more disgusted with the methods of vilification, mendacity and slanderous insinuation, which most of the breeders of hatred get from Luther, who was dismissed from the Catholic Church because he preached heresy and practiced iniquity. The best amongst non-Catholics are determined to be no longer taken in by such frauds and gross swindlers, and they feel the time has come for a closer union of Protestants and Catholics to combat the real evils of the day, the evils that are bringing disaster to our American civilization. "The great enemy which the State, which Catholics and Protestants alike have to resist and vanquish by education," as Dr. Brownson remarks, "is the irreligion, pantheism, atheism, and immorality, disguised as secularism, or under the specious names of science, humanity, free religion, and free love, which not only strike at all Christian faith and Christian morals, but at the family, the State, and civilized society itself."

The learned publicist further remarks: "The State cannot regard this enemy with indifference. . . .The American State is not infidel or godless, and is bound always to recognize and actively aid religion as far as in its power. Having no spiritual or theological competency, it has no right to undertake to say what shall or shall not be the religion of its citizens; it must accept, protect, and aid the religion its citizens see proper to adopt, and without partiality for the religion of the majority any more than the religion of the minority; for in regard to religion the rights and powers of minorities and majorities are equal. The State is under the Christian law, and it is bound to protect and enforce Christian morals and its laws, whether assailed by Mormonism, spiritism, free-lovism, pantheism, or atheism.

"The modern world has strayed far from this doctrine,

which in the early history of this country nobody questioned. The departure may be falsely called progress and boasted of as a result of 'the march of intellect'; but it must be arrested, and men must be recalled to the truths they have left behind, if republican government is to be maintained and Christian society preserved. Protestants who see and deplore the departure from the old landmarks will find themselves unable to arrest the downward tendency without our aid, and little aid shall we be able to render them unless the Church be free to use the public schools—that is, her portion of them—to bring up her children in her own faith and train them to be good Catholics. There is a recrudescence of paganism, a growth of subtle and disguised infidelity, which it will require all that both they and we can do to arrest."

It then behooves all who love liberty to stand together unto the destruction of the enemies of our glorious republic.

The descendants of Luther and the modern exemplars of his spirit of hatred would do well to remember that the Catholic Church was born, brought up, and maintained through persecution. If, indeed, she had no longer adversaries, her members would need to despair of the promises of her divine Founder. It would be impossible for her to pass through severer ordeals than she has in her past, and especially at the time of the so-called Reformation. Experience has proved, over and over again, that the powers of Hell, however determined in doing so, cannot extirpate Catholicism by force from the midst of the peoples and the nations. The Church thrives under persecution, for to suffer for Christ's sake is a signal honor, and martyrdom is a crown of glory. The Christians, as Lactantius says, "conquer the world not by slaying but by being slain." Men are so constituted that they do not really love that which costs them no sacrifice. Just as the soldier, who has suffered for his country, holds it in deeper affection, so the child of the Church loves her the more if he has had to suffer on her account. As long as struggle and opposition continue, the Church will live and flourish. There is so much vitality in her that all her haters can harm her little. Ever so many—Nero, Julian, Henry VIII, Luther, Calvin, Zwingli and their deluded imitators—have gone to their graves after living a life of fierce opposition to everything Catholic, and still the Church lives on, proving over and over the statement of Gamaliel to the Jewish council: "If this be the work of men, it will come to naught. But if it be of God, you cannot overthrow it." The temporary harm which those inflict who indulge in attacks against the Church, of whose history, teaching and precepts they are ignorant, is more than offset by the ultimate good. Divine vitality permeates the whole Church, and no persecution, however frightful or excruciating, can prevail against her. The Master is with her. The enemy cannot conquer. She is Heaven-protected and will remain, in spite of all opposition, to the end of time to preach to mankind, as she ever did in the past, the inestimable blessings of civil and religious liberty.

NOTES

1. In the author's entire discussion about the right of "religious liberty" or "freedom of conscience," the reader should be aware that he is using the expression loosely and that he is referring basically to the person's inherent or inalienable *civil* right to "freedom of conscience." Strictly speaking, and this is the teaching of the Church, the individual most emphatically *does not* possess *moral* "freedom of conscience." For the Catholic Religion maintains that it is the one, true religion revealed by God through His Son and the Second Person of the Blessed Trinity, Jesus Christ, who is True God and true man, and outside of this Religion or Faith or Communion or Church—which Christ identified with Himself personally and which St. Paul calls "the Mystical Body of Christ"—no one can be saved ("Without me you can do nothing"—*John* 15:5). Further, the Roman Catholic Church identifies herself as the Mystical Body of Christ *visible* in the world, in which is contained, on the one hand, as the teaching authority commissioned by God, the entirety of truths needed to be known for salvation, and on the other hand, the instruments of grace (the Sacraments) instituted

by Christ Himself to confer the necessary spiritual helps to salvation which we all need to assist us on the way of life (for example, "Except you eat the flesh of the Son of Man, and drink his blood, you shall not have life in you," *John* 6:54, referring to the Sacrament of the Eucharist).* Now, when the non-Catholic individual is presented the truth contained in the doctrines of the Catholic Church, he does not possess the *moral* "freedom of conscience" to refuse to believe them and to refuse to join this Church which God has instituted as the means for his salvation. ("He that believeth and is baptized, shall be saved: but he that believeth not shall be condemned." *Mark* 16:16). For the doctrines of the Church are divinely revealed, do not contradict common-sense judgment, are according to right reason, are (as far as the mind can verify them) completely logical, never disagree with the human conscience, appeal to the intellect, satisfy the will, are beautiful, noble and ideal, and are given upon the authority of God Himself (which divine authority He has verified with miracles and confirmed by prophecies). As a result of the total veracity of the doctrines of the Catholic Church, founded upon the revealed word of God Himself, the individual human being does not, as stated, possess the *moral* right to "freedom of conscience" and to refuse the acceptance of his mind and the adherence of his will to these truths. For the truth demands that man's mind receive the truth and his will accept it and that he conform his life to it—as being in keeping with his very nature as God has constituted his nature, and to the will of Almighty God for his salvation.

However, by contradistinction, the human being, by reason of his free will, possesses the *ability* or the *freedom* to reject truth, although definitely not the (moral) *right* to do so, for it is axiomatic (that is, immediately evident to the mind) that error does not possess *moral* rights. *Morally* considered, therefore, man does not have a "right" to reject the truth which the Catholic Faith is, and the Catholic Church in her teaching denies that he has any such *moral* "right," as being against the privilege of truth to demand its own acceptance. But definitely, man has the *ability* or the *power* or the *"freedom"* to reject the truth, by reason of possessing the faculty of free will. And political governments must allow him the *political* "freedom" or the *civil* "right" to make this choice. Therefore, *politically* considered, the matter is entirely different: the Church would maintain that people *must* be given the *civil* "right" to "freedom of conscience," or they will be denied, in effect, the use of their free will with which the Creator endowed them and which, along with their intellect, constitutes and distinguishes them as man—that is, as creatures made in the "image and likeness" of God. (*Gen.* 1:26).

Consequently, and to restate the matter briefly, the Catholic Church promotes the *civil* "right" of "freedom of conscience" to all people, but would deny that they have the *moral* right to it. *Nor are we in this discussion denying the Catholic Church's teaching of "Baptism of Desire," which many conservative-minded people today deny by confusing it with the broader notion of "no salvation outside the Church." One must understand precisely what the Catholic Church means by the term "Catholic Church." (See paragraph 1 of this note.)

2. See Note 1 above explaining the sense in which the term "religious liberty," as used by the author, must be understood.
3. Until recent times this situation prevailed as an unwritten rule in the United States.

CHAPTER 9

LUTHER AS A RELIGIOUS REFORMER

EVER since the day when the Saxon monk's hammer on the church door at Wittenberg sounded the signal for rebellion against spiritual and ecclesiastical authority, Luther's admirers have persistently and uniformly held him up before the world as a "great religious reformer." Their hero, in a highly sensitized imagination, fancied that he had a direct divine mission to reform the Church of Christ, and that, as he said, he "was by God's revelation called to be a sort of anti-pope." Men after his own heart, deluded, proud in intellect and revolutionary in tendency, gave willing credence to the self-asserted prerogative, and, believing without question his pretended claim to be true, they blindly chanted his praises and invited all to unite with them in paying him tribute. In all courtesy, but with entire frankness, we make bold to say that did these men make a profound and exhaustive study of Luther's writings and acts, they would soon cease their laudations and discover for themselves how his life and teaching were distinctly and openly at variance with any conception of a "God-inspired man" and a true "spiritual leader."

The title "religious reformer" is a proud and significant one. To wear it with honor, it is not enough merely to apply it to oneself; nor is it becoming in others to confer it on anyone unless the subject is distinguished for virtue and the purpose he has in view is the restoration of relaxed discipline, as well as the renewal of the standard of holy living to its pristine purity. From the beginning, all who have arisen from the midst of their brethren charged with a distinct message from God to assail corruption and to raise men from earth to Heaven began their noble and sacred mission by first improving and reforming themselves. It is rightly expected that the moral leader of his generation should walk in that "holiness without which no man shall see the Lord." The true reformer, as Anderdon remarks, "should be as Elias, or the Baptist, in his moral height and personal detachment; as Nathan, in his rebuke of licentious and murderous sin; as Daniel, in his fastings, in his self-affliction, in his tearful supplications for God's people." He must, in a word, be able to say with St. Paul: "Be ye followers of me, as I also am of Christ." "Be ye followers of me, brethren, and observe them who walk so as you have our model." It is plain, then, that anyone who sets himself up to be a moral leader should first begin by reforming himself, for it is only then that men become impressed, subdued and reclaimed. The irresistible persuasiveness of an upright and holy life, backed by the intrinsic truth of the real reformer's preaching, alone carries conviction and brings about a loving compliance with divine injunctions—the sure and sole foundation of all reformation worthy of the name.

When we turn now to Luther and ask him why he claimed to be a religious reformer and why he posed as one entrusted by Heaven with a great and holy mission, we are not only astonished, but dumbfounded, to discover that his title was self-assumed and without warrant; and that, moreover, his qualifications for the work of reform were of such a nature as to impress the wise with the conviction that he received no call from Heaven to inaugurate and carry out a moral rejuvenation in either Church or State. Unlike the saintly preachers of God's truth of all times, he was in no way ever under a sense of his own personal need of improvement, and was in consequence utterly incapable and unfitted to elevate unto righteousness any among the brethren. As an inspired instrument of God to work out with success a genuine religious reform, he stands out as the supreme contradiction in the history of all we know concerning Heaven's dealings with fallen nature in relation to its uplift and improvement.

Everyone who is in the least familiar with the literature of the so-called Reformation, and especially with that part of it which touches on the life of the pretended Reformer, must appreciate his utter lack of constructive genius, his depraved manners and utterances, and his perversity of principle coupled with falsity of teaching. He has nowhere and at no time given his hearers a complete, methodical and reasoned synthesis of God-given doctrine. He is inconsistent, illogical: he is not afraid to contradict today the statements of yesterday. It is, then, absurd beyond the power of expression to imagine that anyone so noted as Luther for the ungovernable transports, riotous proceedings, angry conflicts and intemperate controversies that made up the greater part of his life, could be an instrument of God to bring about and to effect a moral and religious reform. To discover the notes of a messenger of God in one who had so little regard for merely ordinary proprieties and whose language was usually so coarse and disgusting that to quote it one would need to saturate the atmosphere with antiseptics and avoid coming into collision with the civil authorities, presupposes a partiality amounting to blindness. That he was a deformer and not a reformer is the honest verdict of all who are not blind partisans and who know the man at close vision for what he was and for what he stood sponsor.

It has long since been said by Cicero that "most men are determined in their views by their mental and spiritual condition." This was undoubtedly the case with Luther—and what that condition was on moral questions, on matrimony, on the dignity of man and on kindred matters, we learn from himself. His own utterances, his doubts, his terrors and those compunctious visitings of a disturbed conscience, which seem at one time at least to have made his life a torture, prove conclusively that he was not a God-inspired man and had no claim to be considered even an ordinary reformer or spiritual guide.

In studying Luther, we must remember that his cardinal dogma when he abandoned Catholic teaching was that man has no free will, that he can do no good, and that to subdue animal passion is neither necessary nor possible. He insisted that the moral law of the Decalogue is not binding, that the Ten Commandments are abrogated and that they are no longer in force among Christians. "We must," he says, "remove the Decalogue out of sight and heart." (De Wette, 4, 188). "If we allow them—the Commandments—any influence in our conscience, they become the cloak of all evil, heresies and blasphemies." (*Comm. ad Galat.*, p. 310). "If Moses should attempt to intimidate you with his stupid Ten Commandments, tell him right out: chase yourself to the Jews." (Wittenb, ad. 5, 1573). Having thus unceremoniously brushed aside the binding force of the moral law, we do not wonder that he makes the following startling and shameless pronouncements. "As little as one is able," he says, "to remove mountains, to fly with the birds (*Mist und Harn halten*), to create new stars, or to bite off one's nose, so little can one escape unchastity." (*Alts Abendmahlslehre,* 2, 118). Out of the depths of his depraved mind, he further declares: "They are fools who attempt to overcome temptations [temptations to lewdness] by fasting, prayer and chastisement. For such temptations and immoral attacks are easily overcome when there are plenty of maidens and women." (Jen. ed. 2, p. 216).

The filthiness embodied in this pronouncement is shocking. When we note the unbecoming language in which he couches his degrading teaching, how, we must ask ourselves, can its author be called "a messenger and a man of God"? Would his warmest advocates dare in this day and generation to repeat his words, either in private or in public? Would any Lutheran minister of the period be so lost to shame and common decency as to quote these in the presence of his family or sound them from his pulpit?

Would any man using such language in our day be a welcome guest at the table of any of the ministers belonging to the seventeen different brands of Lutheranism? Could any man uttering such filthy speech possibly enter into matrimony imbued with those high ideals which are the glory of Christianity, so as to enable him to become a model husband or father, and to inspire his neighbors to practice domestic virtue? Why, then, call Luther a reformer—one who would not in our times be regarded fit to be entrusted with police duty in the worst slums of our cities, much less to be made the presiding officer of a vice purity committee? Like Bullinger, the Swiss reformer, we stand aghast at what he calls Luther's "muddy and swinish, vulgar and coarse teachings." The indelicate and grossly filthy expression of this man's views on Christian morality reminds us of the apt saying of St. Matthew (12:37): "By thy words thou shalt be justified, and by thy words thou shalt be condemned."

It is not an agreeable task to attack a man's moral character, but Luther's mouth is to blame for the exposition of the corruption that seemed to be down deep in his heart. This so-called physician of souls, while he cannot "heal himself," must yet needs manifest himself, as "raging waves of the sea," foaming out "his own shame"; because his tongue and his devices were "against the Lord, to provoke the eyes of His Majesty." It is well, perhaps, that he should proclaim his sin "as Sodom, and not hide it," for the interests of humanity and to save "men of good will" from his poison. The serpent's rattle made itself distinctly heard in his unholy utterances; and though he presumed to be the "doctor of doctors" and declared all besides "asses and rascals," his expression of the moral views he entertained shows beyond peradventure that he was not a man in any way fit to lead others unto reformation and sanctity of life.

After Luther's break with Rome and when his piety grew cold, he gained a bad name for himself owing to his loose teachings on morality and his general lightness of behavior.

To say the least, his pronouncements on delicate questions were rather lax, and, as might be expected, his conduct and example could not but have been in keeping with them. It is well known that he was pretty generally and often openly accused by his enemies, both Catholic and Protestant, of extremely grave moral delinquencies. No doubt there was considerable exaggeration in the accusations brought against him, but it nevertheless remains true that many of his faults and failings against morality cannot be denied or gainsaid. As a matter of fact, he was openly blamed for his well-known and imprudent intimacy with Katherine Von Bora before his marriage; and Melanchthon severely censured him for his lack of personal dignity, his loose behavior and coarse jests in the company of his intimates and even in the presence of the nuns he helped, in violation of Germanic law, to escape from their convents.

Hieronymus Dungersheim, an eminent theologian of Leipzig, indignant at his conduct, which little became one who thought he was called to reform the Church and the age, puts this question in his "Thirty Articles" to Luther: "What are your thoughts when you are seated in the midst of the herd of apostate nuns whom you have seduced and, as they themselves admit, make whatever jokes occur to you? You not only do not attempt to avoid what you declare is so hateful to you (the exciting of sensuality), but you intentionally stir your own and others' passions. What are your thoughts when you recall your own golden words, either when sitting in such company, or after you have committed your wickedness? What can you reply, when reminded of your former conscientiousness, in view of such a scandalous life of deceit? I have heard what I will not now repeat from those who had converse with you, and I could supply details and names. Out upon your morality and religion; out upon your obstinacy and blindness! How have you sunk from the pinnacle of perfection and true wisdom to the depths of depravity and abominable error, dragging down countless numbers with you! Where now is Tauler, where the *Theologia Deutsch* from which you boasted you had received so much light? The *Theologia* condemns as utterly wicked, nay, devilish through and through, all that you are now doing, teaching and proclaiming in your books. Glance at it again and compare. Alas, you 'theologian of the Cross'! What you now have to show is nothing but the filthiest wisdom of the flesh, that wisdom which, according to the Apostle Paul (*Rom.* 8: 6), is the death of the soul and the enemy of God."

The Leipzig University professor then goes on to refer to the warning which Luther himself had given against manners of talking and acting which tempt to impurity, and continues as follows: "And now you set aside every feeling of shame, you speak and write of questionable subjects in such a disgraceful fashion that decent men, whether married or unmarried, cover their faces and fling away your writings with execration. In order to cast dishonor upon the brides of Christ you (in your writings), so to speak, lead unchaste men to their couches, using words which for very shame I cannot repeat."

To the testimony of this distinguished writer regarding Luther's unseemly behavior we might add that of many other reliable authors, but the foregoing is representative of all who lost respect for the man and who strongly protested against his flagrant violations of decency in speaking and treating of sexual questions.

That he was consumed by the fires of fleshly lust he admits himself. Even when engaged in the translation of the Bible, as we related in another place, Luther, in the year 1521, while living in the Wartburg—to which place this "courageous Apostle" had fled in the disguise of a country squire and lived under an assumed name—wrote to his friend Melanchthon to say: "I sit here in idleness and pray, alas, little, and sigh not for the Church of God. Much more am I consumed by the fires of my unbridled flesh. In a word, I, who should burn of the spirit, am consumed by the flesh and by lasciviousness." (De Wette, 2, 22).

In the *Table Talk* he is recorded as saying: "I burn with a thousand flames in my unsubdued flesh: I feel myself carried on with a rage towards women that approaches madness. I, who ought to be fervent in spirit, am only fervent in impurity."

Luther further tells that while a Catholic, he passed his life in "austerities, in watchings, in fasts and praying, in poverty, chastity and obedience." When once reformed, that is to say, another man, he says that as it does not depend upon him not to be a man, so neither does it depend upon him to be without a woman; and that he "can no longer forego the indulgence of the vilest natural propensities." (*Serm. de Matrim.* fol. 119).

"He was so well aware of his immorality," as we are informed by his favorite disciple, "that he wished they would remove him from the office of preaching." (Sleidan, Book II, 1520).

But the remedies for all this. Did he struggle and make issue with temptations? Did he rebuke the devil and his onslaughts, or did he, like one deprived of the power of resistance, allow himself to become an easy prey to the wiles and the machinations of the tempter? Alas, he tells us that instead of being prepared for the attacks of the enemy of his soul, he prayed little in the hour when he was "consumed by the fires of his unbridled flesh." How, then, could he expect to come off victorious in the unequal and terrible struggle?

Lutherans often relate how, when their hero was attacked by the devil, he hurled an inkstand at the arch enemy. This was an ingenious method of defense, but something more effectual was urgently required in the unpleasant circumstances. The ordinary useful and consecrated means for repelling Satan's onslaughts, such as prayer, penance and the use of the Sacraments, were not, however, agreeable to Luther's tastes. Fancying himself to be a wonderful physician of souls, he, in his resourcefulness, conceived new means and new methods which he thought would surely be helpful in the uncomfortable and dangerous meetings with his Satanic Majesty. What, think you, are they? Does he prescribe prayer, fasting, and the crucifixion of the flesh for the mastering of passion and the overthrow of the enemy of salvation as the Master ever enjoined? No. His ways are not the ways of the Lord. "They are fools," he says, "who attempt to overcome temptations by fasting, prayer, and chastisement. For such temptations and immoral attacks are easily overcome when there are plenty of maidens and women."

How now can anyone believe the exponent of such teaching to be an inspired man of God? Is it not horrible to think that anyone in his senses could give utterance to such unbecoming language and prescribe such indecent methods for the overthrow of unruly passion? Did the corruption of his mind, as is plainly evidenced in his speech, induce to laxity of behavior and lead him to exemplify his teaching in grave moral delinquencies? Corrupt teaching begets corrupt action, and hence it is difficult to believe that anyone holding such principles and "consumed by the fires of his unbridled flesh" could wholly escape in his own case the exemplification of his unhallowed pronouncements. But whether or not he used his own avowed remedies in temptations to lewdness, of one thing we are certain—namely, that his conduct after he left the Church was often open to just criticism. By his own admission, he made no scruple of drinking deeply in order to drive away temptations and melancholy, and whilst his enemies may have gone too far in charging him with gross immorality, there is, however, much in this direction which cannot be ignored or excused. His ghastly utterances, his bubbling over with obscenity, his boiling spring of sensuality were known to all, and it could not be wondered at if men thought that these defects could only be explained and partially defended on the ground of an abnormal sexual condition which was supposed to have been heightened by licentious irregularities.

In the *Analecta Lutherana* by Theodore Kolde, there is

a medical letter of Wolfgang Rychardus to Johann Magenbuch, Luther's physician, dated June 11, 1523, taken from the Hamburg Town Library, which is of a character to make one wonder on reading it whether Luther did not at one period suffer from syphilis, at any rate in a mild form. On this delicate matter anyone may, if further information be desired, read Grisar, Vol. II, pp. 162-164, where all the details of the question are carefully and learnedly discussed.

With Luther's nasty writings and sayings at hand, coupled with the accusations of his friends and intimates regarding the looseness of his behavior, it is sheer recklessness and consummate audacity to hold him up to public gaze as a teacher and model of morality. His admirers may canonize him as the forerunner of revolution, as the apostle of socialism, as the liberator of human thought, but the insult is too great, and the deception too easily discovered, when once the "Reformer" is spoken of in connection with morality.

Many a time and oft when Luther was in the monastery he heard the inspired words, "Make your bodies a temple of the Holy Ghost." That is the great aim of the Christian religion. Christianity met paganism full of corruption and of impurity; it came to conquer immorality by spirituality. It alone inculcated the idea that the greatness of man must consist in becoming master of his passions, and of his animal nature. It ever insisted that even the flesh must be sanctified. This idea took hold of the minds of men and was so deeply rooted, that on all sides the orders of those who by vows practiced chastity and perpetual virginity began to multiply. This thought of chastity, both in the single and married life, the Church impressed upon all of her children in all generations. Around the nuptial chamber, she placed the Sacrament of Matrimony as a sentinel, and upon the bosom of the virgin, she placed the laurel of her loving approval and motherly benediction. Woman was elevated and became the true companion of her husband, the educator of her children; and the maiden, the virgin, became the cherished object of knightly courage and protection. Chastity was the motto written across the Christian horizon and engraved on the shield of the chevalier.

To change all this, to deify indecency, decry celibacy and virginity and dishonor the married state, was Luther's satanic desire and diabolical purpose. The evil effects of his destructive work have cursed the world during the past four hundred years, and even in our own day we find it has penetrated our homes to work havoc there through the divorce mill[1] and to tell men they are powerless, in the midst of the allurements of life, to resist animal proclivities. For many today, chastity in the single and married state is purely a matter of law, a matter of social etiquette, an external thing, something which is decried as an impossibility and as an encroachment upon natural demands.

Luther, horrible to relate, with the Gospel in his hand, taught his disciples, male and female, in the world and in the cloisters, that no man or woman could be chaste in primitive, much less in fallen nature. "Chastity or continence," said this vile man, "was physically impossible." In the most brutal frankness, he writes without a blush the following lines to a number of religious women: "Though," he says, "the womenfolk are ashamed to confess it, yet it is proved by Scripture and experience that there is not one among thousands to whom God gives grace to keep entirely chaste. A woman has no power over herself. God created her body for man and to bear offspring. This clearly appears from the testimony of Moses (*Gen.* 1: 28), and from the design of God in the construction of her creation." "The gratification of sexual desire was nature's work, God's work," as he cynically calls it, "and, as necessary, aye, much more so, than eating, drinking, digesting, sweating, sleeping," etc. (De Wette II, 535). We dare not repeat all he enumerates in his filthy catalogue. "Hence," said he, "to vow or promise to restrain this natural propensity is the same as to vow or promise that one will have wings and fly and be an angel, and morally worth about as much as if one were to promise God that he would commit adultery."

The way in which this "glorious evangelist" explains his beastly theories in his coarse Latin and in his still coarser German is such that it cannot be given here, "so full is it," to adopt Hallam's mild language, "not only of indelicacy but of gross filthiness." No defense can be set up for the indecencies of his expression, which no Christian ear could listen to. He had the advantage of a monastic training which should have had a refining influence over his whole life, and no matter what hatred he bore the Church and her teachings, he should not have forgotten that his speech should be that of a gentleman and not that of a denizen of the underworld. The pity is that cudgel or other weapon was not lifted in threat against the theological pretender who taught, in virtue of his new gospel, that all women, Catholic or Protestant, outside those that contracted marriage, are necessarily unclean and impure. If Protestants hearing Luther's language can keep cool and restrain their indignation, it only shows how far religious bigotry can control all natural impulses of decency and honor.

From the beginning of the world, men were taught to place a high value on personal purity and were directed to present their bodies a living sacrifice, holy, pleasing unto the Lord. This lesson was thoroughly impressed upon society; and the holy of all times, even the virtuous sages of paganism and the professional votaries of false gods, believed that continence was not only possible, but acceptable to the Deity. The Incarnation of God, and of a God conceived and born of a spotless Virgin, elevated the holy teaching to a still higher degree; and the sacred lives of Jesus and Mary, becoming the ideals of Christian behavior, caused religion to open up peaceful retreats the world over for generous souls, free agents, followers of evangelical counsels, to give strongest expression thereto for the sake of the Kingdom of Heaven, and of love of virginal continence. Enchanted by the example of the Saviour, men and women wished and strove to be as He was, and as a direct consequence, Christian celibacy and virginity blessed the world to teach it to rise triumphant over the passions of the human heart. When one is convinced that there is nothing here below really worthy of lasting regard, who has a right to prevent him from vowing to make God the eternal object of his love and affection?

Luther knew full well the especial esteem the Church always entertained for celibacy, for virgin souls and for the state of consecrated continence. Sympathizing with this spirit of Holy Mother Church, he himself went forth from kindred and father's house, from the surroundings and sweet ties of family affection, from the innocent inducements that open out before a young heart, to consecrate his life in holy chastity and to dedicate it to the service of Him who is alone without blemish. Then he did not express himself openly and declare chastity was impossible and a mere delusion, that licentiousness was permissible and natural, and that the gratification of the flesh was the aim of man. Far from it. On many occasions before his break with the Church we find him, as some of his Protestant supporters will be surprised to learn, extolling the religious calling and declaring it as "more pleasing in the sight of God than the marriage state . . . better on earth as having less care and trouble, not in itself, but because a man can give himself to preaching and the Word of God . . . whosoever wishes to serve the Churches . . . would do well to remain without a wife." In this Luther was right. He was in accord with a conviction common to men of all times, of all places and of all religions, that there is a manifest incompatibility of the priestly office with sexual relations with women even in the bonds of marriage. He understood the Church's wisdom in not allowing her priests to marry, as is apparent from the fact that a wedded clergy must necessarily be separated from the queen of virtues and the mother of great self-devotion, charity, profound study, and all that wins favor from God and man. Hampered by the ties of family and the cares of wife and children, how could the ambassadors of Christ ever fulfill the sublime commission entrusted to them by the great Eternal Priest who said: "Go, teach all nations"? How could they, as St. Paul says, "think of the things of God," be free to devote themselves entirely to His service and afford example to the people, unless they led celibate lives?

In spite, however, of all earlier pronouncements on voluntary chastity for Christ's sake, "Luther at bottom," as Father Johnston remarks, "hated the very idea of virginity. The reason that he extols it at times was because he could not explain Paul's plain praise of the same in First Corinthians. Fundamentally he was driven to depreciate it most of the time and to conceive a positive diabolical hatred of celibacy, in particular: driven to disparage virginity by his strange pessimistic theory of the hopeless depravity of man and lack of freedom of the will; driven to hate celibacy because of its connection with his own onetime and hated priesthood and possibly because of the gibes of his Catholic opponents at his haste to wed."

Luther in his heart of hearts had a low conception of male and female virtue and did not believe chastity outside of wedlock possible, except in such rare cases as amount to a miracle of divine interposition. "Chastity," he says, "is as little within our power as the working of miracles. He who resolves to remain single should give up his title to be a human being and prove that he is either an angel or a spirit." "As little as we can do without eating and drinking, so it is impossible to do without women." "The reason is that we have been conceived and nourished in a woman's womb, that from woman we were born and begotten; hence our flesh is for the most part woman's flesh and it is impossible to abstain from it." (*Tischr.* 2, s. 20 S. 27).

We omit out of decency to quote more of Luther's vile

utterances on this delicate subject. The thoughts that filled his depraved mind and reflected on the greater part of mankind led him on, after his excommunication, to strive with diabolical energy to eradicate from the people's hearts the love for and belief in the possibility of chastity outside of wedlock. He now sets himself up very distinctly against the supernatural counsel which the Master proposed to those who "will to be perfect" and who, with largeness of heart, are "able to contain it." He knew that Christ surrounded Himself with virgins. He knew that His forerunner, St. John the Baptist, was a virgin; His foster father St. Joseph was a virgin; His mother Mary was a virgin; all of His Apostles, except St. Peter, were virgins, who had "left all things to follow Him," and it is a tradition of the Church that St. Peter too observed continency from the time that he obeyed the call of the Lord to be "a fisher of men." He knew that St. Paul, too, was a virgin. He knew that from the apostolic times onward the conviction grew in the Church that men who exercised Christ's office and priesthood at the altar and handled His sacred Body thereon were called on to practice the highest form of chastity and to consecrate their virginity to God of their own accord, confident in divine help for the fulfillment of the requirements of their holy and exacting calling. Luther knew all this and yet, in the perversity of his will and in spite of his better judgment, he deliberately closed his eyes to the facts, hardened his heart and resisted the counsels of the Lord.

Christ, speaking of virginity, not by way of command, but by way of counsel, said, "He that can take it, let him take it," and that His grace will be all-sufficient to overcome the infirmity of nature. Luther, in unbounded blasphemy, contradicts this divine utterance. He will no longer acknowledge such preaching. He, the doctor of doctors, considers it all folly and declares most emphatically that "it is impossible for anyone to live single and be continent." To his distorted mind, the vow of chastity was an "impossible vow," "an abomination" and "worse than adultery." In his desire to abolish and get rid of it, he is not ashamed to appeal "to priests, monks and nuns, who find themselves capable of generation," to violate their sworn promises and abandon their freely chosen state of celibacy. Unless they follow his advice, he considers nothing remains for them but "to pass their days in inevitable self-gratification." "Parents," he said, "should be dissuaded from counselling their children to adopt the religious state, as they were surely making an offering of them to the devil." (Wittemb. V, 124). Thus with shameless effrontery, he declaimed like a maniac against religious vows, and so bitterly antagonistic was he that he went so far as to declare that "the day has come not only to abolish forever those unnatural vows, but to punish, with all the rigor of the law, such as make them; to destroy convents, abbeys, priories and monasteries and in this way prevent their ever being uttered." (See Wittenb. 2, 204 B.). To all this, every libertine from Luther's day down to the present would respond with a hearty "Amen." Not so, however, the clean of heart, who appreciate the invaluable services that the religious, male and female, have rendered the world in all ages and climes in every department of life.

The great exemplar of virginity was the Lord Jesus Christ. The dissolute nailed Him to the Cross. Ever since, persecution has been the lot of the clean of heart. Luther and his followers had not the courage to continue to make sacrifices, conquer their passions and bring their unruly bodies into subjection to divine law and heavenly grace, and imagining others to be as weak, depraved and cowardly as themselves—no longer men enough to bear their self-imposed yoke of chastity—they even charged with a horrible hypocrisy the imitators of the virginity of Christ, whose glorious history is in veneration among the pure of heart the world over. In refusing to believe in the possibility of virtue and self-control and in persecuting the aspirants after perfection, they only prove to the disgust of the decent of all times that they have reached the lowest limits of brutality.

Luther, however, had a remedy for all the abominations he conjured up in his filthy mind against celibacy and virginity. In a most disgusting sermon, which he should have been ashamed to preach at Wittenberg in 1522, he advanced in the crudest and most shocking manner his conviction that Matrimony is obligatory on every individual. "Chastity," he says, "is an abomination." "Religious vows are impossible to keep," and "He who desires to remain single undertakes an impossible struggle." The gracious ways of Providence and the free choice of individuals to determine their state of life are as nothing to the Founder of Lutheranism, who now decrees Matrimony for all as the only remedy against the violence of corrupt and unruly passion. The words of God, "Increase and multiply," found in Genesis 1:28, he thought "are not simply a precept, but much more than a precept; they enjoin a divine work which is just as necessary as eating, drinking, digesting, sweating, sleeping, etc." After alluding to the words of Christ recorded in Matthew 19:12, "and there are eunuchs who have made themselves eunuchs for the kingdom of heaven," he says: "He that does not find himself in any of the classes referred to ought to think of Matrimony forthwith . . . If not, you cannot possibly remain chaste . . . you cannot withdraw yourself from that word of God, 'increase and multiply,' if you will not necessarily and continually commit the most horrible crimes." (Wittenb. Vol. V. 119 B.). In a letter written to Reissenbusch, he repeats his claim that "chastity is as little within the power of man as are other miracles and favors of God." Then he asks his friend, "Why do you hesitate and trouble yourself so much with serious reflections? It must and shall and will be ever thus, and things will not be different. Put such thoughts out of your mind and behave courageously, by entering into wedlock. Your body demands and requires it; God wills it and urges you to it. How will you get over this? . . . Every day we see how difficult it is to observe conjugal chastity in

Matrimony, and should we, outside of that state, resolve on chastity, as if we were not human beings and possessed neither flesh nor blood?" (De Wette II, 637 seqq.).

The motives which Luther urged to induce all to enter wedlock were evidently far from being in accord with those which the Almighty intended in the consecration of the union of both sexes. But as he held Matrimony to be a worldly thing, denied its sacramental character, and refused to acknowledge it to be a type of that great sacrament which is between Christ and His Church, we need not be astonished that he urges an additional motive to those already advanced for maintaining the obligation of marriage. Here it is, genuinely stamped with the usual Lutheran brand and bearing the marks of the Reformer's abiding hatred against the Pope. To the single, he now cries out: "Though one may have the gift to live chastely without a wife, yet one ought to marry to spite the Pope, who insists on celibacy and forbids the clergy to marry." (*Tischr.* II, c. 20 S. 3). Marry and spite the Pope. Do not mind whether you are called or not called to the married state. Rush into it. Do not weigh the consequences. The Pope insists on safeguarding one of the evangelical counsels, and he must not be suffered to do so longer. The way to weaken his influence and destroy his holy work is for all to marry. The motive was truly ingenious and in every way worthy of the inventive powers of the Reformer. Needless to say, the strange advice was not generally heeded, for then and now most men have other and higher reasons than spiting the Pope for their entrance into married life.

Luther, notwithstanding the evident folly and weakness of his advice, still kept harping on the Pope. In spitefulness and in hatred of celibacy, he is now carried beyond himself and urges the violation of the laws of the Church which are framed for the safeguarding of marriage in the general councils of Christendom. "To understand his course the better," Fr. Johnston reminds us, "we should know that there were many secretly in favor of his new doctrines but bound to clerical celibacy, such as priests, nuns, and the Knights of the Teutonic Order. That these should have followed Luther's example and repudiated their vows and married openly, was comprehensible and from their standpoint not at all surprising. But that is not what many of them did. Instead they were keeping concubines, or at least were secretly marrying in a way that legally amounted to the same." Now what is the advice that Luther gave such offenders? He tells them to contract such secret marriages and counselled certain parish priests living under the jurisdiction of Duke George or the bishops to "marry their cook secretly." In a letter addressed to the lords of the Teutonic Order dated March 28, 1523, Luther writes as follows: "Again I say that if it should happen that one, two, a hundred or a thousand and more Councils should decree that a priest should wed or do anything else that the word of God commands or forbids, then I would expect God's mercy and much more for him who kept one or two or three females all his life than for him who weds a wife in accordance with such a decree. Yea, I would command in the name of God and advise that no one should wed according to such a decree upon the penalty of the loss of his soul, but that he should live in celibacy and, if this is not possible, that he may rely on God's mercy and not in despair in his weakness and sinfulness." (Wittenb. 6, 244). A little further on he repeats that "one who keeps a female commits less sin and is nearer to God's grace than a man who would take a wife by permission of a Council."

As we read the disgusting words addressed to the nobility of the Teutonic Order approving and counselling concubinage and secret immortality, we are amazed beyond the power of expression, and the blush of shame rises to our cheeks. The fact that Luther counselled such secret illicit unions in defiance of ecclesiastical and civil law and considered them holier than those that honorably and openly complied with the regulations of the General Councils of Christendom, makes his advice and recommendation all the more abhorrent and detestable. His apologists may try to explain away his advocacy of concubinage, but his filthy words remain to confront them at every turn and to tell the world that in base wantonness and blasphemy they have never been equalled or surpassed by the most depraved of mortals. It is only preachers and writers like himself, men lost to all appreciation of marital propriety, who attempt to excuse the brazen manifestation of their master's corruption of moral sense and dare call this advocate of concubinage and illicit matrimonial unions a "reformer" and a "servant of the Lord." Men of sense, men who take Luther's words as they read and consider the filth, obscenity, moral corruption and infidelity that constantly fill his pronouncements on the holy state of single and married life, are not deceived. The evidences of his depravity are so overwhelming and convincing that they are forced to the conclusion that this shameless advocate of brazen prostitution could not be and was not a "messenger of the all Holy God." To the clean of heart the idea is preposterous. As one thinks of this man's efforts to degrade humanity, it makes him feel almost ashamed to belong to the same human family.

It is an awkward thing for a man without credentials to charge himself with the public conscience and to assume the position of an evangelist without discharging the high obligations inseparably attached thereto. Luther was very proud of the pretended light which he thought he was spreading through his novel and immoral teachings. He delighted to tell his admirers how, through his efforts, religion had been made accessible to all. Before his time, he said: "Nobody knew Christ. . . nobody knew anything that a Christian ought to be familiar with. The Pope-asses obscured and suppressed all knowledge of heavenly things." They were nothing short of "asses, big, rude, ignorant asses," and especially in all matters pertaining to Christianity. "But now," he continues, "thanks to God, men and women know the catechism, they know how to live, to believe, to pray, to suffer and to die." (Walch XVI. 2013).

This was a proud boast of Luther, and well might he feel elated did the wonderful change he conjured up in his vivid imagination actually come about. Of enlightenment, as conceived by him, there was a plenty. It was not, however, the enlightenment which the "Pope-asses," as he calls the Vicars of Christ's Church, had furnished the world for its uplift and sanctification. They, in their long rule of the Church of God, were never so unmindful of their sacred mission and the high obligations attached thereto as to proclaim that the Decalogue had no longer any binding force, that vows made to God might be disregarded, and that fornication, divorce and concubinage were permissible to every blackguard who violated the sacred relations of the married state. If an opprobrious name were in order and if it were permissible to confer such on one who earned it as well as Luther did, then it is not the Pope, but himself he should have called an "ass," for it was his braying that announced to men and women the new enlightenment in the indecencies and gratifications of animal passions that degraded humanity, offended Christian sensibilities and ruined souls for time and eternity.

But, it is time to get acquainted with a little more of the special kind of "enlightenment" Luther furnished the world and of which it was ignorant until "his blessed gospel" (?) announced it for the delectation of the lawless and the dissolute in society. In the *Babylonian Captivity,* which was issued in 1521, he denied the sacramental character of Matrimony, and thereafter, especially in a filthy sermon delivered at Wittenberg in 1522, for which he should have been stoned out of the pulpit, he gave utterance to sentiments which did not contribute to raise wedded life in public esteem. His aim seemed to be to destroy the sanctity of marriage and thereby work the destruction of the social order organized by God, whose cornerstone is the family. Religion, civil order, manhood and womanhood are there matured and fostered and protected and started upon the way of duty and civilization. If the wells are poisoned, disease will spread everywhere; if the home is defiled, the whole of life is profaned and corrupted; if the sacred bonds of the home and the ties of the family are weakened, the demons are unchained and let loose upon humanity. It is for this reason that the Catholic Church with diligence and perseverance watched over the holy state of Matrimony, which Christ elevated to the dignity of a Sacrament, making it a union never to be dissolved. "For better, for worse, till death do us part," was the motto of Christendom. But Luther steps forward, with "his evangel" in hand, and both in theory and practice condemns the divine commandment: "Let every man have his own wife and let every woman have her own husband." He proclaims instead the permissibility of bigamy, and of the system of polygamy on the installment plan through divorce, a system which naturally opened the floodgates of sensuality and threatened the very existence of society. According to his new teaching, any man who is tired of his wife may leave her for any reason whatsoever, and, forthwith, the marriage is dissolved and both are free to marry again. "The husband may drive away his wife; God cares not. Let Vashti go and take an Esther, as did the king Ahasuerus." (Wittenb. V, 123). Does not such a permission open the gates to successive polygamy, free love and legalized prostitution?

Luther was an out-and-out believer in polygamy. To say that he did not "counsel" polygamy, or that he advised that it should be kept secret as a sort of matter of "conscience," is utterly beside the facts. When Brück, the Chancellor of the Duke of Saxe-Weimer, heard that Carlstadt in 1524 advocated polygamy, he consulted Luther on the new and pernicious teaching. The Reformer, not in the least abashed, openly and distinctly stated: "I confess that I cannot forbid a person to marry several wives, for it does not contradict the Scripture. If a man wishes to marry more than one wife he should be asked whether he is satisfied in his conscience that he may do so in accordance with the word of God. In such a case the civil authority has nothing to do in the matter." (De Wette II, 459). Many other clear statements wherein Luther sanctions polygamy might be reproduced here, but the one given above will suffice for the present.

It is certain that Luther not only advocated the vile teaching of polygamy, but, that he also sanctioned it in specific cases—notably that of the Landgrave Philip of Hesse. This potentate was one of the most licentious men of his day, and in consequence of his excesses suffered from a violent secret malady. In a petition addressed to Luther, supplicating permission to take an additional wife, he stated that he "lived continually in adultery" and that he "neither could nor would abstain from impurity." This unfaithful man knew of Luther's free views on Matrimony and appealed to him to obtain his heart's desire, not only, as he said, "to escape from the snares of the devil," but "to ease his conscience in case he died on the battlefield in the cause of the Lutheran gospel." Luther was sorely perplexed. He dared not repudiate the principle of polygamy he had adopted from the very commencement of his Reformation, and yet he feared to sanction the promulgation of a general law allowing polygamy to all on account of the scandal and difficulties it would occasion. The Reformer had hoped, as he said, that Philip of Hesse would "take an ordinary, honest girl and keep her secretly in a house and live with her in secret marital relations." (Lauterbach's Diary, Seidman, 196). "The secret marital relations," he maintained, "of princes and great gentry is a valid marriage before God and is not unlike the concubinage and matrimony of the Patriarchs." (*Tischreden,* Vom Concubinat der Fürsten). The interesting penitent, apparently so tender of soul, was not, however, to be thwarted in his shameful designs. He knew that bigamy was a crime, punishable with death according to German law, and in order to avoid most serious consequences, which in less turbulent times would eventuate to his discomfort, he felt it was to his interest to have some approbation of authority for his shameful petition for a double marriage and thus offer a sedative to his conscience in the thought that he lived in lawful wedlock. The dissolute prince urged his indecent proposition until finally Luther and all of his Wittenberg theologians shamefully acceded to his request and granted him permission to take a second wife during the lifetime of the first, with the sole condition that she should not be publicly recognized. The document which expresses the grant of dispensation, accompanied with a representation of the difficulties of the case and under condition of its being kept secret, was written by Melanchthon and covers about five pages of De Wette, a Professor of Protestant Divinity at Basle. This document, signed by Luther and seven of his associate theologians, amongst other things, says: "If your Highness has altogether made up your mind to marry another wife, we declare under an oath that it ought to be done secretly. . . . No conditions or scandals of any importance will be the consequence of this (of keeping the marriage secret), for it is nothing unusual for princes to have concubines; and although the reason could not be understood by ordinary people, nevertheless, more prudent persons would understand it, and this modest way of living would please more than adultery. . . nor are the sayings of others to be cared for, if our conscience is in order. Thus and thus far only do we approve of it." "For what was allowed in the law of Moses concerning marriage, the Gospel does not revoke or forbid. . . . Your Highness has, therefore, not only the decision (testimonium) of us all in case of necessity, but also our foregoing consideration." "That is to say: We allow the marriage, but at the same time we wish you also to consider whether it would not be more advisable to give up all thoughts of the double marriage."

Philip of Hesse, having obtained the sanction he wanted, cared little for the singular advice of the reformed theologians. The document granting him the longed-for dispensation was issued on December 10, 1539, and Philip of Hesse launches out with the approval of the Father of the Reformation and his associates on his course of concubinage and adultery a few months later, early in 1540. Philip's wife, the daughter of the Elector, gave a written consent to the ignominious arrangement after the unfaithful husband "had clearly proved to her that the double marriage was not against the laws of God." In return, she was promised that she would always have the distinction of being the chief wife, and only her children were to have a right to the honors and political privileges of the father. In keeping with the whole disgusting proceedings the Rev. Denis Melander, one of the eight who signed the letter granting the dispensation, and who had three wives living, officiated at the shameful and scandalous ceremony of handing over to Philip his chosen concubine. "Melander," as Verres remarks, "was the right man in the right place, and he might be depended upon to dwell in the wedding sermon on the peace of conscience with which this matrimonial alliance might be entered into and to inveigh against the Papal tyranny which had for so long a time curtailed the carnal freedom of Christians."

Shortly after the unholy alliance of Philip with Margaret Von der Saal, a lady of honor to his sister, the secret of their union became public, and the scandal occasioned widespread consternation in the newly formed Lutheran camp. When Melanchthon discovered that the news of the double marriage was spread broadcast, "he sickened almost to death with remorse" on account of the sanction he had given to it. The less impressible Luther, however, was not so easily overcome as his truculent partner in the loathsome and illegal transaction. To deny the truth was an end devoutly to be wished for, as Luther was afraid of the evil consequences to the public who would come to learn of the Prince's double marriage. In his anxiety to prevent the blame from being attached to his name, he pretended in speech and in letters to his intimate friends that he knew absolutely nothing about the whole affair. After consultation with Bucer, who was the chief agent in the arrangements, and some other intimates, it took a short time for Luther to decide that the rumor of the permission given to Philip to take a second woman and the farcical marriage should be met with a flat contradiction; "for," as he said, "a secret *yes* must remain a public *no* and vice versa." (De Wette—Seidemann, VI., 263). Then Luther went so far as to declare: "What would it matter if, for the sake of greater good and of the Christian Church, one were to tell a good, downright lie?" (Lenz. Briefwechsel, I, 382).

No doubt Luther was heartily ashamed of granting to Philip the dispensation, which he issued through human respect and in order to prevent the loss of a powerful ally in the advancement of the cause of the new gospel. The Landgrave, however, wanted no 'big lie' to be told about the concession made in his behalf, and he threatened to expose Luther, who was trying to reverse himself before the public. "You will have to remember," Philip said to Luther, "in case you withdraw your approbation, that we should be forced to put before the accusers your written memorial and your signature to show what [concubinage] has been allowed to us." This threat threw Luther into a state of wild anger. "I have this advantage," he said: "that your grace and even all devils have to bear witness and to confess: first, that it was a secret advice; secondly, that with all solicitude I have begged to prevent its becoming public; thirdly, that if it comes to the point, I am sure that not through me it has been made public. As long as I have these three things I would not advise the devil himself to start my pen. . . I am not so much afraid for myself, for when it is a question of writing I know how to wriggle out of the matter and to leave your grace in it—a thing which I do not mean to do if I can help it." (De Wette—Seidemann VI, 273). The unpleasant matter, which caused widespread scandal, was in a short time gotten over—and peace being re-established between the unholy combatants, the polygamous Philip and his vile counselor became the closest friends.

Here we may be permitted to remark that it is a matter of common knowledge that Luther's relations with truth, honesty and uprightness were not always what might be expected from one who claimed that his mouth was "the mouth of Christ." Not to speak of his general attitude of misrepresentation of everything Catholic, we have his frank admission of his readiness to make use of what he calls "a good downright lie" "in the complication consequent on Philip's bigamy and his invitation to the Landgrave to escape from the dilemma in this way." It is as clear as daylight that the Reformer not only believed in lying and duplicity, but that he was, moreover, prepared to make any and every sacrifice to uphold the same. To the specimens of Luther's teaching given above, we have only, in confirmation of what we allege, to add one out of many of his celebrated utterances, viz., that "in order to cheat and to destroy the Papacy, *everything is allowed against the deception and depravity of the Papacy*." (De Wette, 1, 478). If a Catholic, especially a Jesuit, had ever played fast and loose with truth as Luther did, what an outcry, and justly so, would be raised! In order to divert attention from Luther's behavior regarding the obligation of speaking with truth and honesty, our enemies, in the hope of fanning the passions and hatreds of the purblind, ignorant, prejudiced classes in the community, are constantly insinuating and charging that it was not the Reformer, but the Jesuits, who were the real propagators and defenders of the infamous, absurd and damnable principle that "the end justifies the means." That calumny will not down, although it and a thousand others have time and again been exploded. However, no scholar today, no person of sane mind, can be found to give the infamous insinuation a moment's attention, for the good and sufficient reason that the absurd doctrine is not and never was held by Jesuits or any other Catholics. It is incumbent on non-Catholics to name the Jesuit who announced the despicable principle that "the end justifies the means." Let them name the time, the place, the circumstances of such an announcement. If they can give proof, however meager, for the alleged charge sustaining such teaching, the grateful thanks of every God-fearing man, woman, and child in the community will be theirs. This, however, no one can do. Great scholars have undertaken that task and found their labors to be in vain. Grownup men of intelligence who have made any research on the subject are no longer frightened by the silly bugbear invented to deceive and inflame the passions of the ignorant and dishonest of heart. The malicious charge, unfounded and incapable of proof, is thrown out in many quarters merely to hide and save from view its real author, propagator and defender. Whilst Luther did not actually formulate the words embodying the absurd principle, the teaching he announced and the action he adopted were always and ever in the direction of the end justifying the means. To Luther and to no one else may be traced directly and unerringly the fatherhood of this unsavory, unhallowed, unmanly and un-Christian principle. Until non-Catholic preachers and writers can produce a single utterance directly or indirectly verifying the principle they allege against the Jesuits, the unanimous verdict of an honest and impartial public will condemn the calumniators to silence.

The double marriage of Philip, and the relation of the Reformer to the bigamy of his powerful disciple, was made the occasion of a remarkable speech in this country in the House of Representatives on January 29, 1900. (*Cong. Record,* Vol. 33, p. 1101). Congressman Roberts of Utah, charged with polygamy, which he could not deny and for which he was not allowed to take the oath of office, called the attention of the country to Luther. "Here," he said, "in the resident portion of this city you erected—May 21, 1884—a magnificent statue of stern old Martin Luther, the founder of Protestant Christendom. You hail him as the apostle of liberty and the inaugurator of a new and prosperous era of civilization for mankind, but he himself sanctioned polygamy, with which I am charged. For me you have scorn, for him a monument." And he cited, as well he might, passages from Luther's writings to support his views. How truly wonderful is the perversity of human nature. That same man who bears witness in favor of Mormonism, which is a new development of private judgment in religious matters among us in America, and is in direct hostility to the groundwork of our society—and in the full sense of the word, to our civilization—is cited on occasions and hailed by Lutherans and other clergymen in our cities in the twentieth century as the one whom the German nation has to thank for their home life and their ideals of married life. Let the wives and mothers of America ponder well the polygamous phase of the Reformation before they say "Amen" to the unsavory and brazen laudations of the profligate opponent of Christian marriage, Christian decency, and Christian propriety. Compare the teachings of Luther on polygamy with those of Joseph Smith, the Mormon prophet and visionary, and see their striking similarity. Mormonism in Salt Lake City, in Utah, which has brought so much disgrace to the American people, is but a legitimate outgrowth of Luther and Lutheranism. No wonder that the wretched institution of divorce followed to degrade womanhood and revive the usages of barbarism.

Numerous respectable Protestants who know Luther in his historical setting admit that he cared little or nothing for the sacramental character of marriage; and that from the lofty eminence of a once Catholic pulpit, in the presence of men and woman, married and unmarried, young and old, he positively sanctioned adultery in the clearest and most unmistakable manner. It is true that he only allows it in certain given circumstances and that he requires the previous approval of the community, but the stubborn fact remains that he unhesitatingly sanctioned it.

Karl Hagen, a celebrated Protestant historian, says: "He

[Luther] went so far as to allow one party to satisfy his propensities out of wedlock that nature might receive satisfaction. It is quite evident that his view of matrimony is the same as prevailed in antiquity and again appeared in the French Revolution." We beg to note that the high ideal of home life and the married state that the Reformer so openly and brazenly taught the German nation, and which his imitators so strongly and lovingly uphold before an unsophisticated public, is, by the Protestant testimony just cited, the same as existed among the pagans of old and later on in the French Revolution, whose forerunner was Luther.

Returning for a moment to the adulterous marriage of Prince Philip of Hesse, to which bigamous alliance Luther gave his sanction, we wish to remind the reader that according to Köstlin, the most prominent modern champion of the Reformer, "This double marriage was not only the greatest scandal, but the greatest blot in the history of the Reformation and in the life of Luther." (Köstlin, 2, 481, 486). We may add with Fr. O'Connor, S.J., that "the blot is so great as to blot out every possibility of one ever looking upon Luther as a Reformer sanctioned and commissioned by Almighty God. For marriage is one of the most important and most essential elements both of the social and religious order. And God would not allow a Reformer really chosen by Himself to trample under-foot the law concerning the unity of marriage, which was promulgated by Christ, the first born Reformer of the World."

Luther preached and wrote much on the universal obligation of marriage. He was anxious that all should enter wedlock, because his low estimate of human nature led him to believe that "no man or woman could remain chaste outside of matrimony." Holding such views, it is rather surprising that he waited until his forty-second year to give practical effect to his teaching—by marrying a nun who broke her enclosure before breaking her vows. Within the circle of his scheme of ecclesiastical Reformation, Luther included the marriage of priests and monks, and as he was one, why should he not put his own views into practice, join the crowd of the lawless ones, and present his infamy to the public for imitation?

But, if we still have any regard for divine things, then we cannot forget that Luther, in order to wed, had to commit an act of infidelity towards God and disregard his vow of celibacy. No excuse can be offered to palliate or condone his infidelity.

The sacred obligations of vows are frequently mentioned in the Bible and are of divine institution. These vows are clothed with a solemn character and are forever binding. If the God in which Lutherans profess to believe is not a myth, but a personal God, to whom we sustain certain relations and with whom certain relations can be formed, then, as a Protestant writer puts it: "The idea involved in a vow was that of a definite contract or covenant entailing a whole series of after consequences depending upon the condition being fulfilled, a promise and an acceptance mutually sealed by which both parties in the covenant were affected. Even as God comes forth out of Himself to make a covenant with His creatures and confirms it by an oath, so may man go forth from himself, sealing the covenant by his promise." (Carter, *The Church and the World*).

In the very first epochs of the history of God's people, vows—free, deliberate promises made to the Almighty of something of superior excellence—received a special divine sanction. Let the maligners of vows turn to the twenty-eighth chapter of Genesis and they will read of Jacob's vow, the first of which a record has come down to us, while the blessings he afterwards received proved that his vow was looked upon with divine favor. In the one hundred and thirty-first Psalm, David "vowed a vow" to build a temple to God, and how acceptable such a vow was to the Divine Majesty we learn from the seventh chapter of the second Book of Kings. The tenor of many other passages in the Old Testament shows that one of the special ways by which the Jewish people honored and worshipped God was the taking of vows. All along from the beginning, the taking of vows had received among them, time and again, the divine sanction; to it they had recourse when pressed by calamity or when demanding particular favors, or again when striving to make amends for past obstinacy. They felt, and they knew revelation, that the sacrifice of the will through the obligation of a solemn promise was most acceptable to the Lord. Of this they had a suggestive proof also in the exactness with which He required the fulfillment of vows. "When thou hast made a vow to the Lord, thy God," it was said in the twenty-third chapter of Deuteronomy, "thou shalt not delay to pay it, because the Lord, thy God, will require it. And if thou delay, it shall be imputed to thee for a sin."

The practice then of taking vows to God comes down to man from the tradition of primitive revelation. The Mosaic dispensation confirmed that practice anew, and Christ, the Lord, ratified the moral teaching of the past, blessing with an especial grace all those who aspired to follow Him more closely by an entire offering of themselves to the divine goodness by solemn engagement or vow.

Luther was a member of a religious order and a priest of the Catholic Church. Of his own free choice, for the greater love of Christ and as a means to reach perfection, he engaged to practice chastity and bound himself to it by solemn promise. He knew that his consecration to the religious calling had a deep significance, and he knew, moreover, as a professor of Scripture, that it was laid down in Numbers 30:2, that "he who takes a vow shall not break his word; he shall do according to all that proceedeth out of his mouth." Having taken the vow to live his life in the observance of celibacy and having failed to keep the covenant and contract he solemnly made with God, his infidelity was nothing short of the commission of a most grievous sin. And not only was the violation of his vow an offense against the law of God, but it was a crime against the laws of the state then existing. In his day not only the Church, but the state also prohibited priests from marrying. The reader is requested to remember this point in dealing with Luther's marital venture. To violate law—divine, ecclesiastical and civil—never disconcerted this instigator of revolution, upholder of adultery and defender of bigamy, divorce and polygamy. It came easy to this "lawless one" to offend against legitimate authority, but in violating the laws of God and disregarding his vow of chastity by taking a partner unto himself, he committed an act of perfidy, and his union, even from a legal standpoint, was no marriage. Katherine Von Bora was only his companion in sin, and the children brought into the world through the unholy alliance were illegitimate children.

This is sad reading, but there is no help for it. Luther claimed to be a "reformer" and as such he must be inexorably judged. Think you now that the man whose teachings and whose behavior run counter to the laws of God, of His Church and of the state deserves for a moment to be considered a "reformer?" All law-loving citizens protest against such an outrage.

Luther, of course, has his defenders, and they are not devoid of ways and means to support his evil doings at all costs. In this specific case they claim, notwithstanding all Scriptural teaching to the contrary, that their master had a right to break his vow of celibacy, because "it was a sin in him to take such a vow." Mark the last words, and then reflect on how they hold him up as the great and only impeccable one. But, passing this over for the moment, we ask who is to be the judge of his right to break a vow and by what code of laws was such a vow made to the Lord God not binding and of perpetual observance?

The reasons that impelled Luther to marry, as gathered from his writings, are enumerated by Grisar as follows: 1. Because it was necessary to shut the mouth of those who spoke evil of him on account of his relations with

Bora. 2. Because he was obliged to take pity on the forsaken nun. 3. Because his father wished it. 4. Because the Catholics represented Matrimony as contrary to the Gospel. 5. Because even his friends laughed at his plan of marrying. 6. Because the peasants and the priests threatened him with death, and he must therefore defy the errors raised by the devil. 7. Because God's will was plainly apparent in the circumstances. Melanchthon's reason, viz., that man is impelled to marriage by nature, Luther does not himself bring forward. But whatever may have been his motives, the fact remains that he established himself with one escaped nun and lived with her as faithfully as he could. This sacrilegious breaking of vows by monk and nun cannot be condoned by ingenious excuses, and we object to his defenders calling his alliance with Katherine "Matrimony" and speaking of it as "family life." This view might be regarded as "slander," as "papistical malice," because his admirers, closing their eyes to the facts, do not want the truth to prevail. But there is no "slander" or "papistical malice" in the statement. Indeed, we wish we were not under the necessity to record it. If there be any blame in presenting this version, remember it does not belong to us, but to no less an authority than Melanchthon, Luther's co-laborer and intimate friend. A letter written by this "light of the Reformation" to Camerarius gives all the proof needed to support the contention. This letter runs as follows:

"Greetings: Since you have probably received divergent accounts concerning Luther's marriage, I judge it well to send you my views on his wedding. On the thirteenth of June, Luther married unexpectedly Bora without giving any information beforehand to his friends. In the evening he invited to a dinner the Pommer (Bugenhagen), Lucas, the painter, and Appel, and he (Luther) performed the usual ceremony. You will perhaps be amazed that he can be so heartless in such times when noble people live in trouble, and that he should lead a more easy life and thus undermine his usefulness when Germany stands in need of his judgment and ability. But, I believe, that it came about in this manner. He (Luther) is light-minded and frivolous to the last degree; the nuns pursued him with great cunning and drew him on. Perhaps all this association with them has rendered him effeminate, or inflamed his passions, noble and high-minded though he be. He seems after this fashion to have been drawn into the untimely change in his mode of life. It is clear, however, that the gossip concerning his previous criminal intercourse with her (Bora) was false. Now the thing is done it is useless to find fault with it, or to take it amiss, for I believe that nature impels man to Matrimony. Even though this life is low, yet it is holy and more pleasing to God than the unmarried state. I am in hopes that he will now lay aside the buffoonery for which we have so often found fault with him, for a new life brings new manners, as the proverb runs. And since I see that Luther is to some extent sad and troubled about this change in his way of life, I seek very earnestly to encourage him that he has done nothing which, in my opinion, can be made a subject of reproach to him. He would, indeed, be a very godless man who, on account of the mistake of the doctor, should judge slightingly of his doctrine." (Sessions of the Academy of Munich, 1876, p. 491. Original in Chigi Library in Rome).

From this letter it is quite evident that the ideals and motives which prompted the "Reformer" to marry were so low, so degrading, so pagan, that they vexed and worried his friends and intimates, who were by no means candidates for canonization and were not proof against the pleadings of the devil's advocate. Melanchthon acknowledges that Luther's nature and "former buffoonery" compelled him to this union with Katherine Von Bora. His remarks in the letter as to certain rumors no doubt concern suspicions which were cast upon Luther's relations with Bora before their marriage. His conduct with Bora previous to wedding her called forth from both friends and enemies severe and apparently well-grounded criticism. Luther himself admits that his marriage was hastened precisely because of the talk that went the rounds concerning him and Bora. Bugenhagen said tht "evil tales were the cause of Dr. Martin's becoming a married man so unexpectedly." And Luther himself wrote to his friend, Spalatin, that "I have shut the mouth of those who slandered me and Katherine Bora." It is not proven that he was openly immoral with her before marriage, but it is certain that there was so much talk going on about his intimacy with the ex-nun that he thought it advisable to marry her sooner than he had expected. Melanchthon, in his letter to Camerarius, says that he took his Katie in haste and unbeknown to his friends. Was this union even according to civil law valid? The jurists of those days and of his own following did not recognize the marriage as valid. Even we in "free America" have not progressed as far as that.

Melanchthon, though he did not object to Luther's marriage on principle, was nevertheless anything but edified by his action. In his letter to Camerarius, he states that the "Reformer" was rather sad and disturbed on account of his entrance upon the new state of life. Did the voice of conscience denouncing the unholy alliance have something to do with his depressed and forlorn condition? We expect his partisans to reply in the negative, but we fail to see how anyone who had so grossly violated the holy laws of the religious state and of marriage could possess peace and rest of soul, unless his heart was closed to all appeals of divine suggestion. Petticoat government in the case of ex-priests never leads to Paradise. No wonder, as his friend Melanchthon tells us, he was depressed in spirit and sore of heart.

Heretofore we have seen to some extent how Luther, by precept and example, defiled religion, disregarded morality, and appealed to all of the evil propensities that flesh contains. It is now time to speak of the shameless brutality and indescribable vulgarity that habitually in public and private characterized his utterances, which were of such a low, gross, filthy nature that they would startle even a pagan. Almost all of his biographers admit that his language was invariably coarse and vulgar, imprudent and impetuous, but their description falls short of the reality, because they are either loath to offend their readers or are afraid to expose the man in his real character. If the old saying be true that "out of the abundance of the heart the mouth speaketh," then what must we think of Luther's heart, when from the depth of it he threw out with its every pulsation such utterances as to give a veritable nausea to refined and decent manhood? This foul-mouthed evangelist has forever on his tongue the words, "Hell, devil, damn, rascal, thief, fool, ass, villain" and many others that cannot be repeated to ears polite. Hell and the devil seem to have ever been uppermost in his thoughts, for there are no words that occur so frequently in his books.

In 1541 Luther published a dirty little tirade entitled *Hans Wurst.* It was directed against Henry, Duke of Brunswick, who had the courage to attack the Reformer and tell him what he thought of his ways and doings. Though this book is of small compass, the devil's name is mentioned no less than one hundred and forty-six times. Perhaps the same thing may be true of the words "lie," "liar," etc. Amongst the names he applies to his adversary we give a few like "dirty fellow," "the devil of Wolfenbüttel," "a damned liar and villain," "the donkey of donkeys," "that damned Harry," "devil Harry" and "Harry devil," "whose name stinks like the devil's dirt," "an arch-assassin and bloodhound whom God has sentenced to the fire of Hell and at the mention of whose name every Christian ought to spit out." He addressed the Duke as follows: "Thou beautiful image of thy hellish father," and asks "how could such a blockhead presume to write a book, until you have heard a. . .of an old sow. Then you may open your mouth and say: Thanks to you my beautiful nightingale: here is a text which is meant for me." He tells Henry that the Church from which he apostatized is "the devil's Church," "a whore-church of the devil," "an arch-whore of the devil," "an infernal school and a stench den of the devil," "an infernal whore and the devil's last and most abominable bride," "the devil's brother." Thus "damned," "devil" and "whore" are choice words found in nearly every line of this mad production, and the pity is that he mixes the sacred word of God constantly in his revolting filth. In vileness of language and bitterness of hate this book has no equal. We defy any Protestant to read Luther's *Hans Worst* without coming to the conclusion that its author was mentally deranged and that his coarse invective was the production of a raving madman. No wonder that Zwingli, notorious, immoral and corrupt himself, speaking of Luther's eloquence, says, "The time for the word of God to prevail is far off, for there is too much heard of 'enthusiast,' 'devil,' 'knave,' 'heretic,' 'murderer,' 'rebel,' 'hypocrite,' and like cussing, dirty words."

It is said by Luther's admirers that his vulgarity was the fault of his time. Perhaps it was, but may not the statement be highly exaggerated? To say that his vulgar speech was the fault of his age seems to carry with it an insult to the German nation which was so far advanced in the sixteenth century that it was well-known for its reverential and respectful use of language. Even if it were true that the ordinary classes were less choice in their expressions than in our days, it is not too much to expect that one who posed as a "reformer" should at least use the speech of an educated gentleman. The excuse alleged for Luther's abominations will not hold good, for history tells us that many of his friends and intimates of those days were shocked and disedified by his constant use of the most brutal and unseemly language. We can prove by one quotation, and there are hundreds to the same effect, that his own contemporary, Bullinger, the Swiss Reformer, who was neither a "Papist" nor a "saint," stood aghast at what he calls Luther's "muddy and swinish, vulgar and coarse teachings." "Alas," he says, "it is as clear as daylight and undeniable that no one has ever written more vulgarly, more coarsely, more unbecomingly in matters of faith and Christian chastity and modesty in all serious matters than Luther. There are writings by Luther so muddy, so swinish, Schemhamphorasch, which would not be excused if they were written by a shepherd of swine and not by a distinguished shepherd of souls." (*Wahraffte Bekanntniss*, B. 1, 9). With such testimony and that of many others equally reliable, it is useless for the Reformer's apologists, unless they regard the people as coarse and devoid of intelligence, to consider his abominations and indecencies of speech as the fault of the times in which he lived. The truth is, it was the fullness of his heart that was perpetually bursting through all bonds of conventional propriety and decency.

The cesspool seems to have been the garden that furnished his choicest flowers of rhetoric. To be plainer still, "It is a fact," Fr. Johnston says, "that Luther's usual talk took its imagery most often from the privy. In this connection, perhaps, it is significant that Luther admitted that it was precisely in the privy of the monastery that he received from God the revelation of his famous doctrine about justification by faith alone. 'By the grace of God, while thinking on one occasion in this tower over those words, "The just man lives by faith alone," the Holy Ghost revealed the Scriptures to me in this tower.' Protestant biographers have naively attempted to show that this place was not the monastery toilet; but there is no reasonable doubt."

"This is significant," the same learned writer continues, "for, as above noted, it is simply amazing how habitually Luther made use of the imagery suggested by such a place. When he wishes to vomit his wrath against the Pope or the Cardinals, his favorite word is that word which indicates the contents of a privy. I forbear from repeating it. This particular word (the common popular English word for evacuations) is constantly on his lips. Repeatedly he says that if the Pope should send him a command to appear before him: "I should. . .upon his summons." "I—— sarcastically said that 'no lawyer should speak till he hears a sow.'" The reader can find plenty of other instances of the use of this word in Grisar Vol. III, 226, 232, 235, 298. Concommitant with the use of this filthy word is the use of another signifying that portion of the human body which functions the same. Those expressions I cannot repeat here. See for yourself Grisar, e.g., 111, 229, where he tells the devil to "kiss——."

"The vomits of the human stomach are also a frequent word wherewith to express his rage against his enemies. For instance, he says that the Pope 'vomits' the Cardinals. Again the 'monks' are 'the lice placed by the devil on God Almighty's fur coat.' 'No sooner do I pass a motion but they smell it at Rome.' Then note this specimen of stable boy's wit apropos of the 'Pope-ass' mentioned before. 'When I (the Pope-ass) bray, hee-haw, hee-haw, or relieve myself in the way of nature, they must take it all as articles of faith, i.e. Catholics.' That other filthy word common to people who suit their language to privies was also constantly on his lips, employed in endless variations."

"The most amazing aspect of this vulgarity is that Luther brings the very name of God into conjunction with just such coarse expressions. Thus in trying to explain how far God is or is not the author of evil, he says: 'Semei wished to curse, and God immediately directed his curse against David. God says, "Curse him not and no one else." Just as if a man wishes to relieve himself I cannot prevent him, but should he wish to do so on the table here, then I should object and tell him to betake himself to the corner.'"

The reader may consult Grisar's monumental work on Luther if he is anxious to learn more about the filthy, scandalous, and indecent utterances of this vile man. To all who have hitherto known little of his actual obscenity and vulgarity of speech, the study suggested will be not only surprising, but illuminating. After such an inquiry, no honest man with any pretention to decency would be found in the ranks of those who trample on the truth and insist in spite of such glaring faults that this man was an "instrument of God" for the reformation of society.

It is appalling that men should take this filthy talker, whose hopelessly dirty language indicated the morally diseased state of his mind, as a guide to expound Eternal Law, and that they should hang upon his words, hold him up for imitation and entrust to him their salvation. It is pitiable but true that men have eyes and see not, they have ears and hear not, they have hearts and feel not. Oh! that the eyes and the ears and the hearts of our separated brethren, if their faculties are not blunted, would come to recognize the unspeakable character of the heresiarch's utterances, his obscene remarks, his vulgar jokes, his habitual nasty references to sexual matters, and discover in time that this open, brazen and shameless violator of all conventional decency could not in any sense have been raised up by the All-Holy to lead men to the Kingdom of Heaven.

However outrageous to Christian feeling and abhorrent to Christian principle was his habitual filthy talk, it is far surpassed in vileness and obscenity when he treats of womanhood, a fertile theme for his dirty tongue and pen. On this subject he was quite at his ease and allowed himself singular license. In the *Colloquia* no fewer than a hundred pages are devoted to the fair sex. In this work he surpasses himself in vulgarity and shows his brutality in indecent references to women. No one could quote him in this respect without the blood rushing to his head. His warmest biographers are ashamed of his vulgar and unmanly references to women. The filthy expressions he recorded in his books were so habitual with him that he even used them in his own home before his companion and the children. "Certainly," Fr. Johnston says, "no Protestant woman can read them without—I will not say utter shame and womanly horror—but without indignation that any man, above all a spiritual leader and cleric at that, could speak of her sex with such ordinary common familiarity and coarseness and vulgarity and downright obscenity; that could joke at her sex in its most sacred and venerable moral and physical aspects, taking a stable boy's unclean delight at rude witticisms over poor woman's physical differentiation from man; that could make her very body the inspiration of jokes—all evincing a cynical and vulgar contempt for woman as such; that could even have the vulgarity to lift the covers of the nuptial bed and disclose its sacred secrets to the gaze of others. Had any Catholic writer dared to utter a fraction of what Luther thus wrote and said, he would be an eternal and shameful reproach to the Church he so unworthily represented."

To give any idea, even the faintest, of this man's filthy and loathsome language would be impossible unless one is willing to descend into the gutter and wade in obscenity. The original sources are extant, and anyone who wishes to consult them may do so if he is prepared for the shock of his life. Then he will discover that even the Bullingers and Zwinglis of his own time were weak indeed in their description of Luther's language when they upbraided him for its "doggishness, dirtiness and lasciviousness." It is so downright disgusting and hopelessly obscene that no one can excuse or condone it. As his friend, the Protestant Köstlin, puts it, "his was a vehement, vulcanlike nature." Just so: but these vehement, vulcanlike natures are the very ones the Vice Purity Committees find in plenty in certain quarters of our modern cities.

Fr. Johnston says: "From a standpoint of morality, Luther's teachings and practical advice and example in conversation were infinitely below the moral standard hitherto held by the very Church he reviled and constantly below even the standard now generally accepted by the Protestants themselves. His claims, therefore, to 'reforming' the Church are pathetically weak. Instead of teaching a purer morality, he taught a lower. There is nothing in his teaching, by either pen or word of mouth, that is calculated to increase the love of purity, or of even conjugal fidelity, which in the Catholic Church has developed the fairest blossoms of maidenly chastity and conjugal love. A man or woman who is sexually weak will look to him in vain for advice wherewith to increase his or her strength in resisting the great passion—rather they will find in his word the opposite. This is no time to mince words. Therefore, I say deliberately that from his own words Martin Luther must be held responsible for bringing into the world the lowest standard of morality ever advocated by a leader amongst Christians—so low that I defy a Protestant to read him, though I would advise no Protestant *woman* to do so if she be not ready to read with moral safety. Both will feel considerably befouled by the reading."

Nietzsche correctly said of Luther that "he had the courage of his sensuality." We grant that much, but it is most painful and decidedly nauseous to deal with such "courage" and be compelled to descend into the cesspool of his immoralities, both of teaching and behavior. The task of dealing with the man who won for himself the reputation of being the most foulmouthed and coarsest of his age is far from being either agreeable or pleasant. Although we have not given a fraction of the indecencies that were habitually on his lips, we have furnished sufficient specimens of his ribaldry and obscene allusions to the unmentionable parts of the human body, its functions and sexual differentiations, to show that his language, character and example were not such as one expects to find in a professed reformer of Christianity. We would rather not expose to our readers the unspeakable vulgarity usually characterizing his utterances, and we would much prefer not to repeat for the public his own confession to the effect that he received his imaginary revelations in a privy, the imagery of which colored and tainted too many of his expositions of those revelations.

But Luther's partisans persist in forcing him upon public attention; and they have only themselves to blame if, under the limelight of actual quotations, his true words and doctrines and character are exposed to thinking minds, who by the thousands will come to see him in all his ugliness and deformity, and be forced to admit on grounds of modern historical research that he could not have been directly or indirectly called by God to reform His Church.

In our heart of hearts, we pity the man, regret his abuse of divine grace and deplore his lifelong antagonism to divine and human law; but when those who are ignorant of the facts resurrect and force this man on public notice in the role of a "reformer," "a liberator of humanity," "a model of domestic life" and "an instrument of God for the uplift of society," the interests of truth demand that such misrepresentation ought not to go unchallenged, and that the real portrait of the man as he actually was, ought to be given to the people.

The most scientific Lutheran historians now no longer make an attempt to deny his many and flagrant personal shortcomings. It is only those who are ignorant of the facts—that he proclaimed to the world that chastity is impossible and a delusion, that licentiousness is permissible, and that the gratification of the flesh is the aim of man—or those who, knowing them, deliberately close their eyes to his sinful teaching and abominable immoralities, who persist in believing that this moral leper and father of divorce and polygamy was a man of God chosen to "reform" the Church of Christ. Such men are not in a frame of mind to accept the verdict of Luther's contemporaries, nor are they willing to accept the results of the best historical research supplied by Lutheran authorities, which overwhelmingly testify to their hero's immorality of speech and teaching. In their ignoble course they are unfortunately not so intent on spreading the truth as they are in strengthening the Lutheran people in their errors.

The well-known rage and madness against the Papacy that gradually came upon Luther and consumed him to his last breath, making his contemporaries suspect they had to deal with one possessed by the devil, has descended to many of his advocates. Like their master, heedless of right or wrong or danger, they rave like maniacs against the truth as preached by Christ's Church, to keep their followers in ignorance and prevent their return to the faith of their fathers, in which alone can be found rest and peace and eternal happiness. Their efforts to injure religion, its clergy and institutions may be "much thought of by fools," as Melanchthon, Luther's friend, co-laborer, co-reformer, and co-hater of the Papacy once said of his master's writings, but they cannot and will not prevail against the Church which Christ founded and willed all men to accept under penalty of eternal damnation. Luther's imitators had better be wise in time and understand before it is too late that where their master failed, there is no hope of their escape other than by seeking refuge in the bosom of the Mother Church which he maligned, abused and opposed, but which still continues, as if he had never existed, to execute her heavenly mission and to invite all to be followers of Him who alone is "the Way, the Truth, and the Life."

In this little work we have had no desire to libel Luther's person, distort his doctrine or misrepresent his life work. We would willingly allow him to remain in his grave; but as his friends insist on resurrecting him, we have no alternative but to show the disciples of a system which is the child born of a great lie, and nursed and fostered in heresy and infamy, that Luther by his own works and teachings was a malicious falsifier of God's truth, a blasphemer, a libertine, a revolutionist, a hater of religious vows, a disgrace to the clerical calling, an enemy of domestic felicity, the father of divorce, the advocate of polygamy and the propagator of immorality and open licentiousness. These charges are serious, but we beg to remind you that we have not interpreted or edited Luther, as he took the liberty to do with the Scriptures, and as his friends did in the case of Melanchthon's letter to Luther and the modern issues of *The Table Talk*. We have merely quoted him from reliable sources and made him his own accuser and judge. The genuineness and authenticity of his statements on religious and moral questions can neither be doubted nor refuted. If any surprise or scandal in exposing his degrading and debasing sentiments results, the blame rests not with those who picture the man as he really was, but with Luther himself and his advocates, who have for the last four centuries deceived the world by representing him as a "Reformer" and a "God-inspired man."

Luther himself, be it remembered, felt keenly the vulnerability of his character, as is evident from the following significant words: "This is what you must say: whether Luther is a saint or a scamp does not matter to me; his doctrine is not his, but Christ's. Leave the man out of the question, but acknowledge the doctrine." No. We cannot do this. We cannot leave you out of the matter and accept your doctrine till you give proof that you are a "saint" and not a "scamp." Your Köstlins and other partisans may obey your orders, and hold that your "vehement and vulcanlike nature," as they describe you, was not incompatible with your role of a religious reformer. We cannot separate you from your utterances and actions. Your character must be taken into the count, and as you posed in the role of a reformer, we expect, in all decency, to find you a "saint," and not a "scamp." Which of these designations fits you the better? If you had been a man raised up by God to preach His doctrine and had led a life such as to prevent the finger of scorn from being raised against you, why did you complain so bitterly about the lamentable results of the teaching you wished acknowledged? As the life of a man is, so is his teaching and its results. Listen to your own confession. "God knows," you said, "how painful it is for us to acknowledge that before the advent of the gospel everything was peaceful and quietude. Now all things are in ferment, the whole world agitated and thrown upside down. When the worldling hears it, he is scandalized at the disobedience of subjects against the government, rebellion, war, pestilence, the destruction of kingdoms and countries, untold unhappiness as the result of the doctrine of the gospel." (Walch 7, 2556). Just so. You preached a gospel of your own manufacture and ignored that of Christ. What could you expect from your pride and rebellion but the spread of indifference to religion and an increase of immorality? Had you been loyal to the Church of your fathers and had you been actuated by her saving principles of reform, the results of your life work would not have been revolution, rebellion and war, but rather contentment, peace and true happiness such as ever follows in the wake of the saints of God.

Three hundred years go by. It is a long time. What Luther said of his work in his day, others, who were loyal to him and acquainted with the lamentable facts, confirmed and amplified. Hear this wail of distress from no less a man than the Lutheran theologian who, in the early part of the last century, compiled the Reformer's works in five large volumes. De Wette says: "The dissolution of the Protestant church is inevitable; her framework is so thoroughly rotten that no further patching will avail. The whole structure of evangelical religion is shattered, and few look with sympathy on its tottering fall. Within the compass of a square mile you hear four, five, six different gospels. The people, believe me, mark it well; they speak most contemptuously of their teachers, whom they regard either as blockheads or knaves, in teaching these opposite doctrines. . . growing immorality, a consequence of contempt for religion, concurs also as a cause to its deeper downfall. . . .Oh Protestantism! has it, then, at last come to this with thee, that thy disciples protest against all religion? Facts, which are before the eyes of the whole world, declare aloud that this signification of thy name is no idle play upon words."

Nearly a hundred years have rolled by since the preceding lines were penned, and from that time to the present, the De Wettes have been telling the world how Luther's work of reformation has waned and how it is gradually degenerating into humanitarianism. Should you want proof, take up some of the recent biographies of Luther written by his admirers, and learn the appalling indictment they frame against the whole religious system of which the Reformer is the father and defender. In one of these of recent date, "The author, without intending it, makes it evident that Protestantism is not a religion at all. It has no connection with God Almighty. It does not make for holiness of life. Its object is not the service of God. It does not concern itself with the salvation of souls. Its aim is simply to do good to one's fellowman; not spiritual good—that is out of its purview—but whatever will be conducive to his worldly comfort and advancement. Neither the service of God, nor sanctity of life, nor the salvation of souls is permitted to stand in the way of its achievements." Assuredly, if Professor McGiffert's Picture of Protestantism is correct, "the sooner," that excellent weekly *America* says, "thinking people leave it, the better."

In the days of Luther, one of his contemporaries cried out, "Do open your eyes and your hearts, you dear Germans, and use your reason, and do not allow yourselves to be led along by his [Luther's] coarse Turkish mind. Can the natural mind, say nothing of the spiritual mind, conceive that Luther had a drop of honor in him, to say nothing of the fear of God? God have mercy on such blindness." (*Anotamiae Luther* p. 1, p. 48 quoted by Jarke).

That advice is pertinent to our own times. Assuredly it is blindness not to recognize that Luther's Protestantism, "except in America, is mostly a part merely of the state machinery of the different countries in which it exists. Its various creeds are obsolete, effete, and not even the members of the sects which are supposed to hold them, pay the slightest attention to their declarations—indeed, in greater part, are profoundly ignorant of what their declarations are. Protestantism, in brief, has gone on disintegrating and dissolving until no one knows or can tell precisely what it is. Only one uniform, constant movement can be distinguished amidst its continual, whirling eddyings—and the direction of that movement plainly is towards rationalism. The dividing line between Protestantism and outspoken rationalism is invisible. There is none." (*Am. Cath. Quart.*, Vol. IX, 165).

Men of sense, which will you hear: the Church of Christ—One, Holy, Catholic, Apostolic—which calls you to sanctity and uprightness of life, or the hirelings who, as St. Paul says, "by pleasing speeches and good words" seduce the hearts of the innocent" and "make dissensions contrary to the doctrine" which the Master announced to free, vivify, and save the world?

To help all who are anxious to come to a knowledge of the truth as it is in Christ Jesus and His Church, it may be well to recall that Luther, before he formally separated himself from obedience to Rome, and when he seemed to abhor such a course, declared, "I never approved of a schism, nor will I approve of it for all eternity." In a letter written by him in 1519 to the then reigning Pontiff Leo X and quoted in the *History of the Reformation* by that partisan Merle D'Aubigne, he says, "That the Roman Church is more honored by God than all others is not to be doubted. St. Peter and St. Paul, forty-six Popes, some hundreds of thousands of martyrs, have laid down their lives in its communion, having overcome Hell and the world; so that the eyes of God rest on the Roman Church with special favor. Though nowadays everything is in a wretched state, it is no ground for separating from the Church. On the contrary, the worse things are going, the more should we hold close to her, for it is not by separating from the Church that we can make her better. We must not separate from God on account of any work of the devil, nor cease to have fellowship with the children of God who are still abiding in the pale of Rome on account of the multitude of the ungodly. There is no sin, no amount of evil, which should be permitted to dissolve the bond of charity or break the bond of unity of the body. For love can do all things, and nothing is difficult to those who are united." (See De Wette, I, 233 ff.).

These words have the true ring in them, and the pity is that Luther ever forgot their significance; for they not only contain a strong and unanswerable testimonial in favor of the Catholic Church, but they define the only position worthy of the true Christian and sincere reformer intent on the improvement of the unfaithful of Christ's Kingdom on earth. The Church is the only society upon earth where revolution is never necessary and reform is always possible. On the divine side, the Church is always perfect; on the human side, she is a mixture of good and evil. Reform is always in order, but separation never. When reform is needed, it must, in order to be blessed, begin within and not without the Church. Separation from the Church is not reform. To stand up in God's Church and to cry out for reform of real abuses and scandals, fired with genuine zeal and pure love for the beauty of Christ's Spouse, is a noble attitude. Such zeal, such love, and such interest is capable of doing all things. Had Martin Luther fought it out on this line, his name would have been handed down with benediction and praise, along with the great names of Hildebrand, Bernard of Clairvaux, Borromeo of Milan and Ignatius of Loyola, to all future generations. But undying loyalty to principle was not one of Luther's characteristics. His arrogance and self-sufficiency so dominated him that from a reformer he became a revolutionist. Although he declared that "no cause could become so great as to excuse separation from the Church," yet he allowed himself to be overcome by a radical spirit of free individualism against the divine authority of the Spouse of Christ, and under the mere plea of a resuscitated and purified Gospel, he substituted another foundation for that which the Master Himself had placed, and led a religious revolution which was both wrong in principle and wrong in procedure. The specific work he inaugurated abetted fresh divisions, created new sects, and bred interminable dissensions to the injury of the Kingdom of Christ. Humanity has paid bitterly during the last four hundred years for his rebellion against the Christian religion. The variations of his system of private judgment have left the more active intellect of Protestants everywhere today to question not so much this or that doctrine of Christianity, as the *why* they are Christians at all. Thus the foundations designed by Dr. Martin Luther for Christianity after four hundred long years of experience have crumbled away almost entirely, and nothing remains for intelligent Protestants but the alternative of either entering the fold of the Catholic Church to remain Christians, or becoming agnostics, which is a mild word for atheists.

Luther's work, as the plain historical facts conclusively show, has proven an unsuccessful experiment. It was the greatest of blunders. Like all similar movements in the past started in opposition to the One True Church of God, it was destined to fall to pieces and terminate in self-extinction. It had no internal consistency, or individuality, or soul, to give it any capacity for permanent propagation. Its teachings were an innovation and, according to their author, caused an increase of moral corruption such as was not known since pagan days. Triumph it could not.

Four hundred years have passed since Luther's Reformation scheme was given to the world, and in spite of all the attacks which the Church has had to sustain from heresy, she and her Supreme Head remain. The overruling arm which in its wondrous movements confounds the schemes of wicked men, interfered to preserve the religion of Jesus Christ which, though so mysterious in its doctrines and so opposed to corrupt nature in its morals, remains in open daylight in every quarter of the world to enlighten and guide and lift up and heal human nature. In spite of calumny, in spite of popular outbreaks, in spite of cruel torments, the Church lives on to unfold to a wicked world the purity of her morals, the sublimity of her mysteries, the truth of her doctrines, the majesty of her worship, and the hopes of eternal life with which she inspires her members. No other religion goes back to Christ; no other religion claims Him as Founder; no other dares to speak in His name and infallibly to address itself to His Divine authority to the nations and the peoples of the world. Why? Because no other religion is built, according to Our Lord's promise, upon a rock, on one and the same faith, on one and the same Church government, on the same complete unity, with the guarantee of His abiding presence and enduring protection till the end of time to safeguard the truths and means which He gave for the salvation of those who would believe and follow Him. "There is not," then, as the Protestant Macaulay says, "and there never was on this earth an institution so well deserving examinatioin as the Catholic Church."

Such an examination can only emphasize the fact that the world has no need of a new morality or a new religion. The ideal morality and the true religion exist. Our Lord Jesus Christ, who is the true Leader in the onward and upward march of humanity, gave the world His doctrines and His principles of morality as the standards and ideals of all true human progress and genuine reformation. These unchangeable and enduring standards and ideals He communicated and made over to His Church, which He empowered with His Divine authority to speak in His name and to convey to all mankind all things whatsoever He had commanded, till the end of time. In this divinely established religion, and in no other, men possess the grace and the force which are ever directed towards and needed for the reform, the uplift and the sanctification, not only of the individual, but of society at large. If humanity would be led aright, it must be led by men imbued with the spirit and the teaching of Christ's religion, men who will embody in their lives the perfection of virtue, purity and sanctity, and who will by word and example proclaim aloud the old, divine, immortal principle which has stood the test of the ages, that "righteousness exalteth individuals and nations."

There is no other way to meet the problems of our civilization, which are the problems of every other civilization that has gone before us or will come after us, and to determine man in his actions, in the family, in business, and in his civic relations to government. It is useless to perfect our institutions unless we seek first to perfect the members of society. Democracy will not save men, material prosperity will not save them, nor will intellectual or artistic progress save society; only the effort to "grow in all things like Him who is our head, Jesus Christ," will save the individual and save mankind. Without Him, who is "the Way, the Truth, and the Life," and without His religion, which upholds and preaches His standards and ideals, there can be no rejuvenation and perfection of either the individual or of society. We may organize, systematize, tabulate and use all the resources known to the boasted science of the period; but all will be useless to cope with the modern or the prevailing conception of human nature, the modern conception of man's origin and destiny, and all the other fallacies which constitute today the very essence of the spirit of worldly progress. Perfection based on this conception cannot be acquired.

Human nature was created by God and remains fixed. God is a necessity for us. Our hearts are made for God, and they will not be satisfied until they rest in the love and knowledge of Him. All due and proper perfection begins and ends in Him to whose image and likeness man is created. Only those peoples are truly cultured whose impelling motive is the perfection of the individual based on this conception; whereas that people is retrograde in whom there is wanting a proper understanding of the dignity of man. Before our days, people have turned their back on God and reverted to the decay and barbarism that followed the civilizations of Babylon and Rome. In an age like this, when everything is called in question, when the various relations of life are loose and undefined and when the very air is pregnant with hostility to religion, we cannot but look with alarm for the future of the nations if they go on unchecked in their course of pure naturalism and secularism, indifferent to the light of supernatural faith and engrossed in striving to rise above the natural by purely natural means.

Unrest, agitation, and widespread discontent, inherited from the religious upheaval of the sixteenth century, prevail throughout the world. The decadent, retrogressive and ruinous policies advanced by Martin Luther and upheld by his followers have distracted society, have divided Christianity and alienated thousands from the source of all true progress—only to lay the foundations of an atheism which is eating out the very vitals of all social and Christian life. The world is weary of all this. It needs social justice, it needs mental repose, it needs a reform of morals; in a word, it needs religion. There can be no real peace, unalloyed happiness, and genuine progress until it is brought back to the first principles proclaimed by Mother Church and held throughout the centuries; principles which subdued barbarism and tamed savagery; principles which renewed the face of the earth and spread knowledge, civilization and contentment among the nations of the universe; principles which gave foundation to human society and established peace and order by the wholesome doctrine of authority and respect for the rights of all.

Why not, then, labor to make the world Catholic, society Christian, and progress permanent by imbuing the people with the knowledge and the spirit of the Sermon on the Mount? The task is as noble as it is just; as great as it is full of reward for time and eternity. When there shall prevail the tender charity which Christ, the Founder of the Church, taught and exemplified in His life, and which obliges everyone to labor for the happiness of others with as much intrest as for his own, this earth will become a Paradise and the innumerable woes that now make it desolate—ambition, avarice, libertinism, war, fraud, pauperism and the other scourges, mainly the effect of our vices—will in a great measure disappear. "To restore all things in Christ," as the great Apostle Paul directs, to bring about the grand and sublime order of things so much desired on all sides and to promote the welfare of society and our salvation, it is necessary for all to be on guard against the false teacher and his destructive principles and, come what will, to remember that the watchword of all who would really and sincerely bring about reform must ever be the words of Christ, the true Leader of men: "Seek ye first the Kingdom of God and His justice."

May He who holds in His hand the hearts of all, and who alone knows the bounds He has assigned to the rebellious sects and to the afflictions of His Church, cause all His wanderers soon to return to His unity! Separation from His Church means, logically and practically, no Church [for them]. No Church means no Christianity. No Christianity, among intelligent men, means no religion at all, and no religion means ruin to the souls of men for time and eternity.

NOTE

1. A few facts will show to what an extent the loathsome leprosy of divorce has spread in our country alone. The total number of divorces granted in 1867 was 27 per 100,000 of the population. Forty years later, in 1906, there were 86 per 100,000; thus allowing for the increased population, divorce had increased 319%. In 1887 there was one divorce for every seventeen marriages; in 1906 one for every twelve marriages, and at the same rate we will have in 1946 the appalling number of one divorce for every five marriages.

During 1901 there were twice as many divorces granted among 74 million Americans in the United States as among the 400 million souls of Europe and other Christian communities. During the twenty years ended with 1906, Ireland had only nineteen divorces, or an average of less than one absolute divorce per year for her entire population of 4.5 million.

No loyal American and true Christian can view the divorce evil in our country with other than feelings of the gravest alarm.

—The Author.

APPENDIX

THE 33 CANONS OF THE COUNCIL OF TRENT CONCERNING JUSTIFICATION

Sixth Session—January 13, 1547

These canons are the classic statement of Catholic teaching on how man achieves salvation. Summing up the traditional Christian teaching, they address one by one both the errors of the "Reformers" and the idea that man can earn his own salvation. [It should be noted that the term "justification" refers to the presence of Sanctifying Grace in the soul.—Editor.]

CANON 1. If anyone says that man can be justified before God by his own works, whether done by his own natural powers or through the teaching of the law,[1] without divine grace through Jesus Christ, let him be anathema.

CANON 2. If anyone says that divine grace through Christ Jesus is given for this only, that man may be able more easily to live justly and to merit eternal life, as if by free will without grace he is able to do both, though with hardship and difficulty, let him be anathema.

CANON 3. If anyone says that without the predisposing inspiration of the Holy Ghost[2] and without His help, man can believe, hope, love or be repentant as he ought,[3] so that the grace of justification may be bestowed upon him, let him be anathema.

CANON 4. If anyone says that man's free will moved and aroused by God, by assenting to God's call and action, in no way cooperates toward disposing and preparing itself to obtain the grace of justification, that it cannot refuse its assent if it wishes, but that, as something inanimate, it does nothing whatever and is merely passive, let him be anathema.

CANON 5. If anyone says that after the sin of Adam man's free will was lost and destroyed, or that it is a thing only in name, indeed a name without a reality, a fiction introduced into the Church by Satan, let him be anathema.

CANON 6. If anyone says that it is not in man's power to make his ways evil, but that the works that are evil as well as those that are good God produces, not permissively only but also *proprie et per se,* so that the treason of Judas is no less His own proper work than the vocation of St. Paul, let him be anathema.

CANON 7. If anyone says that all works done before justification, in whatever manner they may be done, are truly sins, or merit the hatred of God; that the more earnestly one strives to dispose himself for grace, the more grievously he sins, let him be anathema.

CANON 8. If anyone says that the fear of hell,[4] whereby, by grieving for sins, we flee to the mercy of God or abstain from sinning, is a sin or makes sinners worse, let him be anathema.

CANON 9. If anyone says that the sinner is justified by faith alone,[5] meaning that nothing else is required to cooperate in order to obtain the grace of justification, and that it is not in any way necessary that he be prepared and disposed by the action of his own will, let him be anathema.

CANON 10. If anyone says that men are justified without the justice of Christ,[6] whereby He merited for us, or by that justice are formally just, let him be anathema.

CANON 11. If anyone says that men are justified either by the sole imputation of the justice of Christ or by the sole remission of sins, to the exclusion of the grace and *the charity which is poured forth in their hearts by the Holy Ghost,*[7] and remains in them, or also that the grace by which we are justified is only the good will of God, let him be anathema.

CANON 12. If anyone says that justifying faith is nothing else than confidence in divine mercy,[8] which remits sins for Christ's sake, or that it is this confidence alone that justifies us, let him be anathema.

CANON 13. If anyone says that in order to obtain the remission of sins it is necessary for every man to believe with certainty and without any hesitation arising from his own weakness and indisposition that his sins are forgiven him, let him be anathema.

CANON 14. If anyone says that man is absolved from his sins and justified because he firmly believes that he is absolved and justified,[9] or that no one is truly justified except him who believes himself justified, and that by this faith alone absolution and justification are effected, let him be anathema.

CANON 15. If anyone says that a man who is born again and justified is bound *ex fide* to believe that he is certainly in the number of the predestined,[10] let him be anathema.

CANON 16. If anyone says that he will for certain, with an absolute and infallible certainty, have that great gift of perseverance even to the end, unless he shall have learned this by a special revelation,[11] let him be anathema.

CANON 17. If anyone says that the grace of justification is shared by those only who are predestined to life, but that all others who are called are called indeed but receive not grace, as if they are by divine power predestined to evil, let him be anathema.

CANON 18. If anyone says that the commandments of God are, even for one that is justified and constituted in grace,[12] impossible to observe, let him be anathema.

CANON 19. If anyone says that nothing besides faith is commanded in the Gospel, that other things are indifferent, neither commanded nor forbidden, but free; or that the ten commandments in no way pertain to Christians, let him be anathema.

CANON 20. If anyone says that a man who is justified and however perfect is not bound to observe the commandments of God and the Church, but only to believe,[13] as if the Gospel were a bare and absolute promise of eternal life without the condition of observing the commandments, let him be anathema.

CANON 21. If anyone says that Christ Jesus was given by God to men as a redeemer in whom to trust, and not also as a legislator whom to obey, let him be anathema.

CANON 22. If anyone says that the one justified either can without the special help of God persevere in the justice received,[14] or that with that help he cannot, let him be anathema.

CANON 23. If anyone says that a man once justified can sin no more, nor lose grace,[15] and that therefore he that falls and sins was never truly justified; or on the contrary, that he can during his whole life avoid all sins, even those that are venial, except by a special privilege from God, as the Church holds in regard to the Blessed Virgin, let him be anathema.

CANON 24. If anyone says that the justice received is not preserved and also not increased before God through good works,[16] but that those works are merely the fruits and signs of justification obtained, but not the cause of its increase, let him be anathema.

CANON 25. If anyone says that in every good work the just man sins at least venially,[17] or, what is more intolerable, mortally, and hence merits eternal punishment, and that he is not damned for this reason only: because God does not impute these works unto damnation, let him be anathema.

CANON 26. If anyone says that the just ought not for the good works done in God[18] to expect and hope for an eternal reward from God through His mercy and the merit of Jesus Christ, if by doing well and by keeping the divine commandments they persevere to the end,[19] let him be anathema.

CANON 27. If anyone says that there is no mortal sin except that of unbelief,[20] or that grace once received is not lost through any other sin however grievous and enormous except by that of unbelief, let him be anathema.

CANON 28. If anyone says that with the loss of grace through sin, faith is also lost with it, or that the faith which remains is not a true faith, though it is not a living one, or that he who has faith without charity is not a Christian, let him be anathema.

CANON 29. If anyone says that he who has fallen after baptism cannot by the grace of God rise again,[21] or that he can indeed recover again the lost justice but by faith alone without the sacrament of penance, contrary to what the holy Roman and Universal Church, instructed by Christ the Lord and His Apostles, has hitherto professed, observed and taught, let him be anathema.

CANON 30. If anyone says that after the reception of the grace of justification the guilt is so remitted and the debt of eternal punishment so blotted out to every repentant sinner, that no debt of temporal punishment remains to be discharged either in this world[22] or in purgatory before the gates of heaven can be opened [to him],[23] let him be anathema.

CANON 31. If anyone says that the one justified sins when he performs good works with a view to an eternal reward,[24] let him be anathema.

CANON 32. If anyone says that the good works of the one justified are in such manner the gifts of God that they are not also the good merits of him justified; or that the one justified by the good works that he performs by the grace of God and the merit of Jesus Christ, whose living member he is, does not truly merit an increase of grace, eternal life, and in case he dies in grace, the attainment of eternal life itself and also an increase of glory, let him be anathema.

CANON 33. If anyone says that the Catholic doctrine of justification as set forth by the holy council in the present decree, derogates in some respect from the glory of God or the merits of our Lord Jesus Christ, and does not rather illustrate the truth of our faith and no less the glory of God and of Christ Jesus, let him be anathema.

NOTES

1. Cf. Sixth Session, chaps. 1, 3.
2. Cf. Sixth Session, chap. 5.
3. *Rom.* 5:5.
4. *Matt.* 10:28; *Luke* 12:5.
5. Cf. Sixth Session, chaps. 7, 8.
6. *Gal.* 2:16; cf. Council of Trent, Sixth Session, chap. 7.

7. *Rom.* 5:5.
8. Cf. Sixth Session, chap. 9.
9. Cf. Sixth Session, chap. 9.
10. Cf. Sixth Session, chap. 12.
11. Cf. Sixth Session, chap. 13.
12. Cf. Sixth Session, chap. 11.
13. Cf. chap. cit.
14. Cf. Sixth Session, chap. 13.
15. Cf. Sixth Session, chap. 14.
16. Cf. Sixth Session, chap. 10.
17. Cf. Sixth Session, chap. 11 at the end.
18. Cf. Sixth Session, chap. 16.
19. *Matt.* 24:13.
20. Cf. Sixth Session, chap. 15.
21. Cf. Sixth Session, chap. 14.
22. Cf. Fourteenth Session, chap 8.
23. Cf. Twenty-fifth Session, at the beginning.
24. Cf. Sixth Session, chap. 11, at the end.

TESTIMONIALS

This Book Elicits Praise in the Highest Key from Every Reader

Cardinal Gibbons:

"I thank you for your kindness in sending me *The Facts About Luther.* This work is most timely and will, no doubt, do service in many hands. Priests will likely be called upon to answer Lutheran laudations, and your work is just the thing for a busy man to read and be 'set wise.' I wish your book a wide diffusion."

Cardinal Farley:

"I send you my acknowledgment of the courtesy you show me in presenting me with a copy of your book. I bless your work and hope it will serve to put the facts about Luther before the reading public."

Cardinal Logue:

"I feel I can congratulate you on having produced a very instructing and useful book. For general readers who have neither the opportunity nor the time to study the more exhaustive works on Luther and his teaching, your book contains quite enough clear, solid information to give them a true idea of the so-called Reformation and the character of its founder. You not only give a graphic account of the progress of this rebellion against the Church and her authority; but I find that you give a full, solid refutation of the leading errors of Luther. I believe that any sincere, unprejudiced reader of your book shall find therein enough to correct any mistaken notions he may have had of this religious revolution and its tendencies."

BISHOP O'CONNOR, NEWARK:

"I congratulate you on the results of your historical studies and hope that our non-Catholic brethren will have their eyes opened to the facts about their hero. May your book have a wide circulation!"

BISHOP MCFAUL, TRENTON:

"I have looked through *The Facts About Luther* with a great deal of pleasure. No doubt it will do much good and have a large circulation."

BISHOP CUSACK, ALBANY:

"I have just finished reading your excellent book *The Facts About Luther*. Your wide reading of the latest historical discoveries condensed into so small a compass makes a most admirable polemic, just and adequate for the perusal of the multitude. I believe it will do much good."

BISHOP DOUGHERTY, BUFFALO:

"Please receive my sincere thanks for the present of your book entitled *The Facts About Luther*. I think it a splendid idea to give these facts in a popular, straightforward manner and within the covers of one volume, so as to demolish the idol set up by Protestantism. I have not the least doubt that your book will do an immense amount of good. Our people are hungering for such works."

BISHOP HAYES, NEW YORK:

"I congratulate you on your book entitled *The Facts About Luther*, which is an achievement from the point of literary work and especially of service to the Church. I wish the volume every possible success."

BISHOP MULHERN, IRELAND:

"Your volume, in spite of its modest pretentions, is a great and useful work. Many besides 'the man in the street' will receive from it enlightenment on a subject that has been to a great extent in the clouds as far as they were concerned."

THE ECCLESIASTICAL REVIEW:

Monsignor O'Hare's handy little volume states in clear, succinct form *The Facts About Luther.*

The author has utilized the works of the chief standard authorities on the subject in order to draw forth a genuine history of Luther's career, and a thoroughly reasoned-out summary of his doctrines on indulgences, justification, the Church and the Pope, the Bible, free will and conscience. The whole is a vivid presentation of Luther the man, the religious, the preacher, and writer. In it "the whole gamut of the apostate's life is described in a calm, impartial manner which permits no gainsaying." It is permeated by no "spirit of bitterness or bigotry," though of course it is not sweet or rose-scented. Moreover, the book, though clearly printed and agreeably legible, is issued at a price which makes it possible for it to attain a circulation equal to that given to *The Faith of Our Fathers* or *The Question Box*.

AMERICA:

Mons. O'Hare, stealing an hour here and there from the labors of a busy pastor, has popularized in his *Facts About Luther* what others have gleaned. All sincere readers of this book will own that the author has done his task well. After an introduction on modern Luther literature, he enters on a psychological study of the heresiarch's early years, which is followed by a close and readable investigation of Luther's attitude on indulgences, justification, the Church and the Pope, the Bible, rebellion, free will and liberty of conscience. A final chapter is entitled "Luther the Reformer." To write a book of this character is by no means easy, for the author has had in turn to play the role of an historian, a theologian and an apologist, and withal to present indelicate facts delicately, offensive facts inoffensively, subtle facts concretely. But in his *Facts About*

Luther Mons. O'Hare has admirably succeeded in doing this.

AVE MARIA:

A book that it was thoroughly worthwhile to write, and that has been written notably well, is *The Facts About Luther,* a brochure of 367 pages, by the Rt. Rev. Mons. P. F. O'Hare, LL. D. It has a good preface by the Rev. Peter Guilday, Ph.D. Insofar as scholars and students are concerned, authoritative books on Luther have not been wanting. Protestant Lives and studies of the unfaithful monk are multitudinous; and such Catholic authors as Janssen, Denifle, and Grisar have painted the protagonist of Protestantism in his true colors with a fidelity scarcely to be improved upon. The present work is differentiated from the volumes of such authors by its specific purpose: to reach the general public—a purpose all the more likely to be effected because of the popular style of the book and its inexpensiveness, twenty-five cents a copy.

CATHOLIC NEWS:

Despite the results of modern scholarship, Luther's admirers still attempt to rehabilitate their hero. Monsignor O'Hare's compact little book throws "a bridge over the chasm which now separates the Luther of 1917 from the Luther of 1883, and the contrast is so prominent that his conclusions cannot be ignored. The reader is brought in these pages into a close, intimate relation with Luther's friends and opponents, and every statement is based on the most reliable authorities in the Protestant school of historical science."

Monsignor O'Hare's work, despite his modest disavowal, could only have been done by a scholar. A library of Lutheran bibliography has been mined to supply the material of this informing volume. The author makes no unfair attack on the founder of Protestantism. He has not written in a spirit of bitterness or bigotry. As he expressed it, Monsignor O'Hare's aim and the method adopted by him throughout the book was "to write about Luther, not against him"; to quote the author's own words. Every Catholic should acquaint himself with the life story of the man whose followers can never explain away the anarchy of that immoral dogma: "Be a sinner, and sin boldly; but believe more boldly still."

THE CATHOLIC UNIVERSE:

Mons. O'Hare's book is a real addition to our popular controversial literature. It does not pretend to scholarship. Yet none but a scholar could have made the exhaustive study of Luther bibliography evident in its pages. It presents no fact not authenticated by competent authorities, Protestant as well as Catholic. It touches on nearly every point covered in the whole field of Luther controversy. Best of all, it lets Luther speak for himself, in words which the blindest eulogy can never explain away.

To read *The Facts About Luther* is to know as much as any intelligent man need know about the founder of Protestantism. Mons. O'Hare has succeeded in crowding into one compact volume not only a life of Luther, a study of his curious mental development, the story of the incidents leading up to the so-called Reformation and its consequences, but also a resumé of all his works, a review of the studies of the principal Luther authorities, and a sketch of the social and political conditions of his time. Add to this a clear exposition of the Catholic teaching on all the points assailed by Luther, such as indulgences, justification, the Bible, free will, the authority of the Pope, etc., and it is apparent that the Catholic layman has here an armory from which he can draw a weapon suited to any phase of the Luther controversy.

Mons. O'Hare has performed a great service to truth in providing a book at once so timely, so practical, so long-needed, so good-tempered, and—not least of its advantages—so cheap. It will probably take its place with

The Faith of Our Fathers, the *Question Box* and other widely circulated books of popular apologetics.

ST. ANTONY'S MESSENGER:

The picture Mons. O'Hare paints of Luther is so true to life that one can well forego larger and more elaborate portrayals of this historical character. Weaving the would-be reformer's own words into the story of his life and teachings and following them up with quotations from writers mostly non-Catholic, and favorable to Luther, the author has given the everyday man and woman the results of painstaking study and excellent resourcefulness in easy and understandable language.

The Luther of fiction and fancy is shorn of his halo, and the Luther of fact and history is seen in all his ugliness. The several chapters of the book are small masterpieces of condensation and clearness. Every objection that has done service these many years, and that in all probability will be called upon to do double service in this year of celebration, is met squarely and unflinchingly, and the decision is always on the side of truth. The Catholic doctrine is set forth in an unusually clear manner, and the false teachings of Luther are seen in their unscriptural and even blasphemous settings.

Mons. O'Hare displays the real Catholic sense of criticism. Along with his straightforwardness of attack, he carries the balm of charity and pity for the poor, misguided followers of Luther, "whose common sense and sense of decency saved them from their own faith."

We would most earnestly ask our readers, particularly those who come in frequent contact with Protestants, to purchase this book and to read it carefully and leisurely. They will find it the best intellectual weapon that is offered them in defense of their Faith and Church against the attacks of those who "as a class," are densely ignorant of the real Luther.

HOMILETIC MONTHLY, N.Y.:

This popularization of the latest researches into the life and teaching of Luther is intended to counteract the effect of current eulogies of the Reformation. The fourth centenary of that religious revolt has occasioned a campaign of publicity in praise of Luther and the movement which he started. Therein not the real Luther, but a Luther of fiction is set forth for public admiration. He is regarded "the foundation stone of modern civilization, the father of human liberty, the light of the world." Protestant scholars have long since learned better and no longer pretend to canonize the German heresiarch. But the results of their scholarship are not readily accessible to most men. Hence the value and timeliness of this work of Monsignor O'Hare.

This work is not a philippic against Martin Luther. Although the latter's personal character receives due notice, it occupies a relatively small space. Those Protestants—and their number is increasing—who admit the unsaintliness of their quondam hero, still maintain that the blessings of our day are the fruit of the Reformation, that the importance and justice of the movement which he inaugurated are independent of his personal character. It is, therefore, fortunate that the author discusses rather the teaching of Luther. Today in all branches of knowledge the historical method is the vogue; the study of origins is most highly prized as deeply significant. Now, if the origin of Protestantism in the doctrines of Martin Luther cannot bear the light of fair research, the boasted heritage of Protestant revolt is seen to be only an heirloom of human opportunism. Luther has lost his halo, the Reformation its divine sanction, the modern world its debt to both.

All this is convincingly set forth by Monsignor O'Hare, the better so since he quotes very largely from Protestant writers of scholarly repute. The author himself is too modest as to the value of his work; nor does the inexpensive, paper-covered book suggest the worth of its contents.

Every priest will find many new facts about Luther in

its pages. He would do well to distribute many copies of it in his parish, putting it in the hands of those who are probably picking up false notions of the Reformation from the secular press and Protestant neighbors.

THE WESTERN CATHOLIC:

The Facts About Luther is a splendid work. It is a treasure-house of Facts—only Facts, and Facts cannot be denied or contradicted. This work should be in every Catholic home to strengthen the faith and enlighten the minds of our people.

This work should be shown—given to your Protestant neighbors to open their eyes to the real character of Luther. We challenge any honest Protestant to read this work and then remain fooled any longer in regard to Luther or Luther's work.

MR. JOYCE KILMER, REVIEWER:

"I am delighted to have a copy of your work. It seems to me, after a careful reading, to be the most important historical work published for many a day. There is no doubt you have performed a great service to the Faith in collating and presenting the facts of the life and work of Martin Luther. Also you have performed a service to history in revealing a notable figure as it actually was, in stripping Luther of the halo and the robes of sanctity with which zealous partisans have invested him. Your limpid and forceful style and your admirable restraint add much to the book's value; controversial writers will do well to copy your methods. You leave the apologists of Luther absolutely no loophole of escape; you have written what must in all fairness be called an unanswerable book. Never again, it seems, can an intelligent Protestant speak of the founder of Protestantism except with shame. Of the human founder of Protestantism, that is, for the foul-mouthed renegade monk was after all only a weak weapon snatched up by the devil to use in his desperate effort to raze to the ground the

Church of God—an effort which most ignominiously failed.

"Your book will have a long and useful life and pass through many editions. It deserves a place in the library of every Catholic, whether that library consists of a thousand books or of ten. And even more surely, it deserves to be read by every Protestant who is willing to know the truth of history. But we pity the unfortunate people who have the task of reviewing it for Protestant publications."

THE REV. DR. GUILDAY, in a letter to the author, says:

"Every page of the proof has been filled with interest for me, and I feel that you have succeeded in accomplishing one of the hardest things in historical endeavor—to tell the story of all Luther's rottenness without polemic and without cloaking. Your book will be read with avidity by every Catholic worthy of the name, and your method of treatment precludes any attack from the opposite camp, except a bigoted one. That you naturally expect and just as naturally can ignore. I consider myself most fortunate to have my name linked with yours in this defense of the Faith."

The Facts About Luther is published with the Imprimatur of His Eminence Cardinal Farley, whose learned censor, Dr. Remy Lafort, wrote to the author as follows: "I have found your manuscript exceedingly interesting reading. I consider it well deserving of commendation, both for the style in which it is written and the manner in which the subject is handled."

If you have enjoyed this book, consider making your next selection from among the following . . .

Visits to the Blessed Sacrament. *St. Alphonsus* 5.00
Moments Divine—Before the Blessed Sacrament. *Reuter* 10.00
Miraculous Images of Our Lady. *Cruz* 21.50
Miraculous Images of Our Lord. *Cruz* 16.50
Raised from the Dead. *Fr. Hebert* 18.50
Love and Service of God, Infinite Love. *Mother Louise Margaret* 15.00
Life and Work of Mother Louise Margaret. *Fr. O'Connell* 15.00
Autobiography of St. Margaret Mary. 7.50
Thoughts and Sayings of St. Margaret Mary 6.00
The Voice of the Saints. *Comp. by Francis Johnston* 8.00
The 12 Steps to Holiness and Salvation. *St. Alphonsus* 9.00
The Rosary and the Crisis of Faith. *Cirrincione & Nelson* 2.00
Sin and Its Consequences. *Cardinal Manning* 9.00
St. Francis of Paola. *Simi & Segreti* 9.00
Dialogue of St. Catherine of Siena. *Transl. Algar Thorold* 12.50
Catholic Answer to Jehovah's Witnesses. *D'Angelo* 13.50
Twelve Promises of the Sacred Heart. (100 cards). 5.00
Life of St. Aloysius Gonzaga. *Fr. Meschler* 13.00
The Love of Mary. *D. Roberto* 9.00
Begone Satan. *Fr. Vogl* 4.00
The Prophets and Our Times. *Fr. R. G. Culleton* 15.00
St. Therese, The Little Flower. *John Beevers* 7.50
St. Joseph of Copertino. *Fr. Angelo Pastrovicchi* 8.00
Mary, The Second Eve. *Cardinal Newman* 4.00
Devotion to Infant Jesus of Prague. *Booklet* 1.50
Reign of Christ the King in Public & Private Life. *Davies* 2.00
The Wonder of Guadalupe. *Francis Johnston* 9.00
Apologetics. *Msgr. Paul Glenn* 12.50
Baltimore Catechism No. 1 . . . . 5.00
Baltimore Catechism No. 2 . . . . 7.00
Baltimore Catechism No. 3 . . . . 11.00
An Explanation of the Baltimore Catechism. *Fr. Kinkead* 18.00
Bethlehem. *Fr. Faber* 20.00
Bible History. *Schuster* 16.50
Blessed Eucharist. *Fr. Mueller* 10.00
Catholic Catechism. *Fr. Faerber* 9.00
The Devil. *Fr. Delaporte* 8.50
Dogmatic Theology for the Laity. *Fr. Premm* 21.50
Evidence of Satan in the Modern World. *Cristiani* 14.00
Fifteen Promises of Mary. (100 cards). 5.00
Life of Anne Catherine Emmerich. 2 vols. *Schmoeger* 48.00
Life of the Blessed Virgin Mary. *Emmerich* 18.00
Manual of Practical Devotion to St. Joseph. *Patrignani* 17.50
Prayer to St. Michael. (100 leaflets) 5.00
Prayerbook of Favorite Litanies. *Fr. Hebert* 12.50
Preparation for Death. (Abridged). *St. Alphonsus* 12.00
Purgatory Explained. *Schouppe* 16.50
Purgatory Explained. (pocket, unabr.). *Schouppe* 12.00
Fundamentals of Catholic Dogma. *Ludwig Ott* 27.50
Spiritual Conferences. *Faber* 18.00
Trustful Surrender to Divine Providence. *Bl. Claude* 7.00
Wife, Mother and Mystic. *Bessieres* 10.00
The Agony of Jesus. *Padre Pio* 3.00

Prices subject to change.

Seven Capital Sins. *Benedictine Sisters*	3.00
Confession—Its Fruitful Practice. *Ben. Srs.*	3.00
Sermons of the Curé of Ars. *Vianney*	15.00
St. Antony of the Desert. *St. Athanasius*	7.00
Is It a Saint's Name? *Fr. William Dunne*	3.00
St. Pius V—His Life, Times, Miracles. *Anderson*	7.00
Who Is Therese Neumann? *Fr. Charles Carty.*	3.50
Martyrs of the Coliseum. *Fr. O'Reilly.*	21.00
Way of the Cross. *St. Alphonsus Liguori*	1.50
Way of the Cross. *Franciscan version*	1.50
How Christ Said the First Mass. *Fr. Meagher*	21.00
Too Busy for God? Think Again! *D'Angelo*	7.00
St. Bernadette Soubirous. *Trochu*	21.00
Pope Pius VII. *Anderson*	16.50
Treatise on the Love of God. 1 Vol. *de Sales. Mackey, Trans.*	27.50
Confession Quizzes. *Radio Replies Press*	2.50
St. Philip Neri. *Fr. V. J. Matthews.*	7.50
St. Louise de Marillac. *Sr. Vincent Regnault*	7.50
The Old World and America. *Rev. Philip Furlong*	21.00
Prophecy for Today. *Edward Connor*	7.50
The Book of Infinite Love. *Mother de la Touche*	7.50
Chats with Converts. *Fr. M. D. Forrest.*	13.50
The Church Teaches. *Church Documents*	18.00
Conversation with Christ. *Peter T. Rohrbach*	12.50
Purgatory and Heaven. *J. P. Arendzen.*	6.00
Liberalism Is a Sin. *Sarda y Salvany*	9.00
Spiritual Legacy of Sr. Mary of the Trinity. *van den Broek*	13.00
The Creator and the Creature. *Fr. Frederick Faber*	17.50
Radio Replies. 3 Vols. *Frs. Rumble and Carty*	48.00
Convert's Catechism of Catholic Doctrine. *Fr. Geiermann*	5.00
Incarnation, Birth, Infancy of Jesus Christ. *St. Alphonsus*	13.50
Light and Peace. *Fr. R. P. Quadrupani*	8.00
Dogmatic Canons & Decrees of Trent, Vat. I. *Documents*	11.00
The Evolution Hoax Exposed. *A. N. Field*	9.00
The Primitive Church. *Fr. D. I. Lanslots.*	12.50
The Priest, the Man of God. *St. Joseph Cafasso*	16.00
Blessed Sacrament. *Fr. Frederick Faber*	20.00
Christ Denied. *Fr. Paul Wickens*	3.50
New Regulations on Indulgences. *Fr. Winfrid Herbst*	3.00
A Tour of the Summa. *Msgr. Paul Glenn*	22.50
Latin Grammar. *Scanlon and Scanlon*	18.00
A Brief Life of Christ. *Fr. Rumble*	3.50
Marriage Quizzes. *Radio Replies Press*	2.50
True Church Quizzes. *Radio Replies Press*	2.50
The Secret of the Rosary. *St. Louis De Montfort.*	5.00
Mary, Mother of the Church. *Church Documents*	5.00
The Sacred Heart and the Priesthood. *de la Touche*	10.00
Revelations of St. Bridget. *St. Bridget of Sweden*	4.50
Magnificent Prayers. *St. Bridget of Sweden*	2.00
The Happiness of Heaven. *Fr. J. Boudreau*	10.00
St. Catherine Labouré of the Miraculous Medal. *Dirvin*	16.50
The Glories of Mary. *St. Alphonsus Liguori*	21.00
The Three Ways of the Spiritual Life. *Garrigou-Lagrange, O.P.*	7.00

Prices subject to change.

St. Vincent Ferrer. *Fr. Pradel, O.P.*	9.00
The Life of Father De Smet. *Fr. Laveille, S.J.*	18.00
Glories of Divine Grace. *Fr. Matthias Scheeben*	18.00
Holy Eucharist—Our All. *Fr. Lukas Etlin*	3.00
Hail Holy Queen (from *Glories of Mary*). *St. Alphonsus*	9.00
Novena of Holy Communions. *Lovasik*	2.50
Brief Catechism for Adults. *Cogan*	12.50
The Cath. Religion—Illus./Expl. for Child, Adult, Convert. *Burbach*	12.50
Eucharistic Miracles. *Joan Carroll Cruz*	16.50
The Incorruptibles. *Joan Carroll Cruz*	16.50
Secular Saints: 250 Lay Men, Women & Children. PB. *Cruz*	35.00
Pope St. Pius X. *F. A. Forbes*	11.00
St. Alphonsus Liguori. *Frs. Miller and Aubin*	18.00
Self-Abandonment to Divine Providence. *Fr. de Caussade, S.J.*	22.50
The Song of Songs—A Mystical Exposition. *Fr. Arintero, O.P.*	21.50
Prophecy for Today. *Edward Connor*	7.50
Saint Michael and the Angels. *Approved Sources*	9.00
Dolorous Passion of Our Lord. *Anne C. Emmerich*	18.00
Modern Saints—Their Lives & Faces, Book I. *Ann Ball*	21.00
Modern Saints—Their Lives & Faces, Book II. *Ann Ball*	23.00
Our Lady of Fatima's Peace Plan from Heaven. *Booklet*	1.00
Divine Favors Granted to St. Joseph. *Père Binet*	7.50
St. Joseph Cafasso—Priest of the Gallows. *St. John Bosco*	6.00
Catechism of the Council of Trent. *McHugh/Callan*	27.50
The Foot of the Cross. *Fr. Faber*	18.00
The Rosary in Action. *John Johnson*	12.00
Padre Pio—The Stigmatist. *Fr. Charles Carty*	16.50
Why Squander Illness? *Frs. Rumble & Carty*	4.00
The Sacred Heart and the Priesthood. *de la Touche*	10.00
Fatima—The Great Sign. *Francis Johnston*	12.00
Heliotropium—Conformity of Human Will to Divine. *Drexelius*	15.00
Charity for the Suffering Souls. *Fr. John Nageleisen*	18.00
Devotion to the Sacred Heart of Jesus. *Verheylezoon*	16.50
Who Is Padre Pio? *Radio Replies Press*	3.00
The Stigmata and Modern Science. *Fr. Charles Carty*	2.50
St. Anthony—The Wonder Worker of Padua. *Stoddard*	7.00
The Precious Blood. *Fr. Faber*	16.50
The Holy Shroud & Four Visions. *Fr. O'Connell*	3.50
Clean Love in Courtship. *Fr. Lawrence Lovasik*	4.50
The Secret of the Rosary. *St. Louis De Montfort*	5.00
The History of Antichrist. *Rev. P. Huchede*	4.00
St. Catherine of Siena. *Alice Curtayne*	16.50
Where We Got the Bible. *Fr. Henry Graham*	8.00
Hidden Treasure—Holy Mass. *St. Leonard*	7.50
Imitation of the Sacred Heart of Jesus. *Fr. Arnoudt*	18.50
The Life & Glories of St. Joseph. *Edward Thompson*	16.50
Père Lamy. *Biver*	15.00
Humility of Heart. *Fr. Cajetan da Bergamo*	9.00
The Curé D'Ars. *Abbé Francis Trochu*	24.00
Love, Peace and Joy. (St. Gertrude). *Prévot*	8.00

At your Bookdealer or direct from the Publisher.

Toll-Free 1-800-437-5876 ***Fax 815-226-7770***

Prices subject to change.